LISTEN TO THE VOICES FROM THE SEA

(Kike Wadatsumi no Koe)

LISTEN TO THE VOICES FROM THE SEA

(Kike Wadatsumi no Koe)

— Writings of the Fallen Japanese Students —

Compiled by
Nihon Senbotsu Gakusei Kinen-Kai
(Japan Memorial Society for the Students
Killed in the War—Wadatsumi Society)

Translated by

Midori Yamanouchi
and Joseph L. Quinn, S.J.

Scranton: The University of Scranton Press

Shinpan Kike Wadatsumi no Koe
(Listen to the Voices from the Sea)

Edited by

©Nihon Senbotsu Gakusei Kinenkai
(The Japan Memorial Society for the Students Killed in the War — Wadatsumi Society)

Library of Congress Cataloging-in-Publication Data

Listen to the Voices from the Sea: writings of the fallen Japanese students. Edited by Nihon Senbotsu Gakusei Kinenkai; translated by Midori Yamanouchi and Joseph L. Quinn, S.J.

Scra nton: The University of Scranton Press © 2000
344 p.

Japanese original "Shinpan Kike Wadatsumi no Koe". Tokyo: Iwanami Shoten, © 1995. 8th Printing, 1999.
(Iwanami bunko # 33-157-1).

Includes index.

ISBN 0-940866-85-4 (pbk.)

1. World War, 1939-1945 – Personal narratives, Japanese. 2. College students – Japan – Correspondence. I. Title: Kike Wadatsumi no Koe. II. Yamanouchi, Midori. III. Quinn, Joseph L., S.J. IV. Title.

D811.A2 K513 2000
940.54'8252–dc21

00-037418

Distribution:
University of Toronto Press
250 Military Road
Tonawanda, NY   14150
1–800–565–9523

PRINTED IN THE UNITED STATES OF AMERICA

CONTENTS

ACKNOWLEDGMENTS

It was so long ago, but I remember so well how deeply I was moved by *Harukanaru Sanga ni* when it was first published. It not only moved me, but even deepened my sorrow over how those fine, able men from the University of Tokyo had to die in the war that they could not control and did not want. That was the book I really wanted to have people all over the world read, and perhaps I will have the honor of translating those writings one day. However, it has long been out of print, and therefore I took up the task of translating *Kike Wadatsumi no Koe,* its successor.

In the last stage of the war, many high school classmates of mine lost their older brothers in the same manner as did the authors of this book. My older brother's fate was the deepest concern of my parents, although they did their best to hide their fear from me and from my younger sister, who was then probably still too young to know the full scope of what was happening to the world—except for the fact that she often had to run to a bomb shelter with us, covered with a protective hood almost as large as her upper body. In those days we heard every evening on radio the farewell speeches of those young special attack forces' members, as they were preparing for their mission on the following day, including some whose names were personally familiar to us, as well as some from the same town whom we did not know. How we were able to handle such tragedies may only be explained in terms of the sense of national emergency and the sense that our lives were also uncertain and fragile under the threat of the bombing as were those of many other close friends of mine. Amazingly, as I look back at that time, hatred toward the enemy was not the primary emotion at all; in fact, it was almost absent—there was just the sense of fate, helplessness, and sorrow.

Throughout the past forty-five years of my academic life in the United States, it has always been a very hurtful experience whenever some Americans made a statement to the effect that those Japanese who were killed as special attack forces members, i.e., so-called "Kamikaze pilots," were mindless, robot-like figures, who simply followed orders and died. As I realized that *Kike Wadatsumi no Koe* has not been translated into English even though some fifty years have passed since its publication, I thought that, if no one else would take on the task, I should do so. As a person who lived through those painful days and months and shared their sorrows but survived, this is my modest effort—and perhaps a self-appointed duty—to give a human face to each of those fallen college/university students by making their writings available in English. I have absolutely no political agenda whatsoever. By reading this book the English-language readers, too, will perhaps recognize how much alike all of us are. The tragedy is not only that human life in general is precious but particularly that those young men, who could have contributed so much to the welfare of the world in the future, had to die. And they could not change their fate of having to fight and die in the war they disapproved of. After reading this, perhaps the peoples of the West may understand the Japanese a little better. I hope this modest contribution of mine will bring about that effect.

Because I wanted to have the best possible translation, I asked Rev. Joseph L. Quinn, S.J. (of the English Department at the University of Scranton, where I also am a faculty member), to be a collaborator. My reason for selecting Prof. Quinn was simply because, through reputation, I knew he was the best. I wanted to make certain that this translation would not suffer from any unintended feminine expression or an awkward phrase that might creep up in my draft, even in the slightest way. That is, out of my respect for the authors, I wanted the final version to be as perfect as possible. It is needless to say I was delighted that he accepted my proposal. We did our best to ensure that nothing would be taken away from the original writing. The process represents a true collaboration: I first translated as closely as possible to the meaning and emotion of the original, often with additional explanations. My draft was then re-written by Prof. Quinn, and then I compared his with the original. A problematic and time-consuming part of translating Japanese writing into English turned out to be the effort to find accurate and correct spelling for non-Japanese proper names which were written in Japanese *kana* syllables. All sorts of reference books were searched, but I also had the good fortune to be assisted by many knowledgeable people such as Mr. John Dean and Mr. Daniel Newman. I am also indebted to my older brother, Mr. Hiroshi Yamanouchi, without whose help I could not understand one particular selection, one which required the experience of someone who was the author's contemporary and who shared the intellectual experience of that time, i.e., the elite education of going through the higher school to the Tokyo Imperial University.

I am most grateful for my good fortune in having such a true friend, Mrs. Fumie Ogawa, who tirelessly took upon herself the liaison work between the Wadatsumi Society and me from the very beginning of this project; without her this book could not exist. I must express my gratitude to Mr. Taketomo Takahashi of the Wadatsumi Society, who played the major role in this entire enterprise, and also to Mr. Seiki Tago and Mr. Kō Yamamoto of the society, who read our manuscripts. Their suggestions are all greatly appreciated. And of course our gratitude goes to the Iwanami Shoten, Mr. Takao Hori in particular, for graciously granting me permission to translate the book. Certainly I cannot adequately thank Rev. Richard W. Rousseau, S.J., Director; John E. Sinclair, Assistant Director; and Patricia A. Mecadon, Production Manager of the University of Scranton Press, the publisher of this book; and of course I owe more than I can say in words to my collaborator, Rev. Joseph L. Quinn, S.J., Ph.D.

M. Y.

TO THE READER OF
Kike Wadatsumi No Koe
—NEW 1995 EDITION—

The *Kike Wadatsumi no Koe,* published in 1949, was not only enthusi-astically received by the reading public; it also became the psychological wellspring for the post-war peace movement. The work has also, and somewhat paradoxically, gained the status of a contemporary classic.

At this particular point in time, a half century since the end of the war, we are happy to present this new edition to the new readers.

Some revisions were found necessary for this edition, and a con-siderable amount of new material was added as well, all so that readers might better understand the psychological processes undergone by these young men who were about to give their lives. The idea was to link what was happening to the students personally during this last phase of their existence both with what was happening around them and with the war on a global basis.

Those who perished can live on, in the very truest sense, only if they are remembered. Regardless of changing times and circumstances, so long as their readers persevere in their sincere resolve to listen to the students' words, every single statement of those fallen ones will be deeply engraved on the heart of posterity.

The younger generations of readers were foremost in our minds as we readied this new edition for the presses, and our most sincere hope is that you young people respect our authors' collective plea that there be no more war. Indeed, "No more war and genuine peace" is their quintessential message, and may you make it your food for thought as you decide both how you wish to live your individual lives and how to form your views of society and of history itself.

Nihon Senbotsu Gakusei Kinen-kai
(Wadatsumi Society)
December 1, 1995

EXPLANATORY NOTES

1. The language (word usage, Chinese characters, etc.) of the original manuscripts has been retained except for obvious errors which have been corrected. Bracketed supplements have occasionally been employed by the editors. The use of parentheses follows the originals exactly.

2. A longer row of spaced periods (.................) indicates sections omitted by the editors. The standard ellipses (. . .) follow the original.

3. The Chinese characters and the use of *kana* syllables have been changed to the newer standardized forms, and in some cases words originally written in Chinese characters have been changed to *kana*. For those quotations, however, in which there are citations from literature, we have kept strictly to the original. For some of the more difficult Chinese characters *furigana* (how to read in *kana*) have been added.

4. Notes in the text have been placed within brackets, and double lines surround explanations of words that are no longer in current usage. [For this English translation, the translators' longer notations are footnoted when appropriate. Some terms which may require further explanations for the English-language readers are added in a closing Glossary.] The initial appearances of words and phrases that are of special importance are indicated by a * and explanations are provided at the end of the manuscript. [English translations of Japanese words are within parentheses.]

5. Brief biographical sketches have been provided by way of head-notes to the individual selections, and they are generally arranged in the following order: (1) date of birth and place of origin; (2) educational back-ground; (3) military history; and (4) the date and manner of death, as well as the author's military rank and age at the time of his death.

6. Indices are appended to the end of this volume, one tied to key words and terms and the other to the authors' names.

[7. Translators' note: All the dates of letters, when available, have been moved to the beginning in accordance with the usual English standard. The originals almost always follow the Japanese custom of placing the dates at the end.]

THOUGHTS

— INTRODUCTION TO
THE EARLIER EDITION —

by Kazuo Watanabe

This is a sequel to *Harukanaru Sanga ni (In the Mountains and Rivers Far Away)*. With regard to the policy for compilation, the first step involved the members of the Publication Department of the Tokyo University Co-op discussing it over and over; then, as their advisor I reviewed their decisions. Still later there was more discussion among the Publication Department people, a consensus was finally reached, and a definite point of view established. So far as I am concerned, I think the general direction turned out to be quite appropriate. In the beginning, I had leaned quite far in the direction of all-inclusiveness and insisted that it would be much more fair and just to include even rather fanatical Nipponism, or even a few short essays shading toward the glorification of war, but the members of the Publication Department did not show any sign of agreement with my position. The primary reason for their opposition was that the publication of this book must not at all affect negatively the current social conditions, and so on. I finally came to consider their position reasonable. Moreover, I thought, seeking for fairness and justice in a merely formal manner might in fact result in the contrary, i.e., a decided lack of fairness and justice. In addition, I thought about the fact that the very cruel condition that made a few of those fallen young university student-soldiers, even momentarily, write something that sounds like an outburst of ultra-nationalism, or even close to glorifying war, was that dark and extremely hideous national structure, the military, and its principal members. Therefore, such occasional *pitiful and painful* writings must actually be viewed as the voices, recorded in print, of the tormented spirits of young people who were driven to the utmost limits of sanity itself, and might be read more realistically as cries for help. Certainly we had to consider the possible ill effects of publishing those writings and also that their public exposition would be painful—even more than we could bear. I, therefore, agreed with the position of the Publication Department. Moreover, so many of the same people who had, in the first place, fanned the fires of propaganda before and during the war, spouting words that make those students' pitiful and painful

1

writings even more pathetic, have both lived through into an era of peace and prosperity and now behave as though the conflict had never occurred. It was in this way that I came to think it only fitting that the truly tragic voices of these students who are now bleached bones, who are the victims of such ranting—and victims also of their own youth and innocence—be paid the tribute of comparative silence, at least for the time being.

The above notwithstanding, on any and every page of this book you will find our authors anything but silent as they are progressively forced into a corner—as if to seek a death that was not natural death or suicide, but to be killed by others. Trained and at least partly educated to believe that the unnatural deaths toward which they were being herded were things of beauty—the metaphor was "falling cherry blossom petals"—the souls of these rational and indeed highly cultivated young scholars, young men so full of life and dreams, cried out in a kind of vengeful pain when they were strangled and forced to accept the irrational as rational, things they disliked as things they liked, and things unnatural as natural. These voices are penetratingly so sad that, to me, reading through them is all but unbearable. Even when the accounts are framed with such courage, grace, and acceptance, they are all so heartrending and hopelessly dark.

I think of the situation where human beings are pushed to the end and reduced to the level of beasts or machines. When I ponder the fact that, just before they are forced to be so reduced—and especially those young men of finer grain, who are gifted both with deep human emotions and a highly polished rationality—they are placed in such a position involuntarily, and can no longer have any hope of escaping, it is impossible to ignore their mournful voices. I want the absolute elimination from human society of anything that makes human beings, especially young people, suffer the fate of being pushed to such an end. War, any war, would necessarily involve just that. If I pointed a gun at someone, he would point a gun at me; if someone pointed a gun at me, I would point a gun at him as well. This may be the most simple example of what happens when a person is pushed into a corner; but, at any rate, we need to begin eliminating such situations. One is reminded of the words of Jean Jaurès [French Socialist leader who was assassinated on the eve of World War I, 1859–1914]: "I am not a fanatic for law and order, but I consider violence to be human beings' quintessential weakness." What war does is force this weakness, this shameful weakness, upon human beings, and it is a totally violent condition.

It is my hope that this book will be read by people from every layer of Japanese society, and especially by those who have completely forgotten about the recent war, who act as though it never existed. The carefree politicians who busy themselves in playing political games as if they have nothing else to do; those ladies and gentlemen whose lifestyles permit them to fully enjoy the benefits of high culture; the college professors who are so obsessed with the profundity of their theories; the policemen who follow orders unconditionally and wave white sticks or long poles; the mobs who attack courthouses with red flags in their hands and shout that "honorable people are coming through"; the businessmen who do not read anything except entertainment magazines; and the young students of today who once waved their tiny "maple leaf–like hands" while shouting "soldiers, Banzai!". . . The reason for my hope is that this volume contains a number of highly valuable human documents which are never seen in any of the popular war reportage produced by the mass media today. It is further to be hoped that, through their exposure to this book, readers may understand in some small way(s) why the peace which was finally and so painfully achieved must be protected at all costs.

When I placed on my desk the thick pile of manuscripts which the members of the Publication Department had compiled with such enormous and painstaking effort, and began to read through two or three pages of them, I saw a vision of white wooden crosses set up in an orderly fashion all along a dark field. As I continued to read, I saw blood seeping out from each one of these crosses. Such crosses should never be set up again, not even one of them.

If I may, I should at this point like to insert my translation of a short poem from a collection by Jean Tardieu [French contemporary poet, participated in a resistance movement, 1904–95]. The poem's title is "Glory of a Poet," published in France in 1943, in *Edition de Nuit*, and it offers a quiet and heartfelt prayer for those students who were forced to meet such violent and untimely deaths:

Since the dead are not returning,
What are the survivors to understand?

Since for the dead there is no way to lament,
About whom and what should the survivors lament?

Since those who died cannot but keep silent,
Should the survivors do the same?

August 31, 1949

Kike Wadatsumi no Koe
(Listen to the Voices from the Sea)

—Writings of the
Fallen Japanese Students—

Nagekeru-ka Ikareru-ka

Hata modaseru-ka

Kike Hateshinaki Wadatsumi no Koe

      Are these voices grief-filled or angry?

      But can they be silenced or ignored?

      Listen to the eternal voices of the boundless sea.

Ryōji Uehara,

Born September 27, 1922. From Nagano Prefecture. Entered Keiō-gijuku University, Faculty of Economics, from its Preparatory College, 1943. On December 1, 1943, he entered the 50th Regiment in Matsumoto City. He was killed in action May 11, 1945, as a member of the Army Special Attack Unit, striking an American Mechanized Division at Katena Bay, Okinawa. Army Captain. He was twenty-two years old.

My Thoughts

I am keenly aware of the tremendous personal honor involved in my having been chosen to be a member of the Army Special Attack Corps,* which is considered to be the most elite attack force in the service of our glorious fatherland.

My thoughts about all these things derive from a logical standpoint which is more or less the fruit of my long career as a student and, perhaps, what some others might call a liberal.* But I believe that the ultimate triumph of liberty is altogether obvious. As Croce [Italian philosopher Benedetto Croce 1866–1952] has proclaimed, "liberty is so quintessential to human nature that it is absolutely impossible to destroy it." I believe along with him that this is a simple fact, a fact so certain that liberty must of necessity continue its underground life even when it appears, on the surface, to be suppressed—it will *always* win through in the end.

It is equally inevitable that an authoritarian and totalitarian nation, however much it may flourish temporarily, will eventually be defeated. In the present war we can see how this latter truth is borne out in the Axis Powers [the alliance of Japan, Germany, and Italy] themselves. What more needs to be said about Fascist Italy? Nazi Germany too has already been defeated, and we see that all the authoritarian nations are now falling down one by one, exactly like buildings with faulty foundations. All these developments only serve to reveal all over again the universality of the truth that history has so often proven in the past: men's great love of liberty will live on into the future and into eternity itself.

Although there are aspects to all this which constitute something the fatherland has reason to feel apprehensive about, it is still a truly wonderful thing to feel that one's own personal beliefs have been validated. On every front, I believe that ideologies are at the bottom of all the fighting that is going on nowadays. Still further, I am firmly convinced that the outcome of each and every conflict is predictable on the bases of the ideologies held by the opposing sides.

My ambitious hope was to have lived to see my beloved fatherland—Japan—develop into a great empire like Great Britain in the past, but that hope has already been dashed. If those people who truly loved their country had been given a fair hearing, I do not believe that Japan would be in its present perilous position. This was my ideal and what I dreamt about: that the people of Japan might walk proudly anywhere in the world.

In a real sense it is certainly true that a pilot in our special aerial attack force is, as a friend of mine has said, nothing more than a piece of the machine. He is nothing more than that part of the machine which holds the plane's controls—endowed with no personal qualities, no emotions, certainly with no rationality—simply just an iron filament tucked inside a magnet itself designed to be sucked into an enemy air-craft carrier. The whole business would, within any context of rational behavior, appear to be unthinkable, and would seem to have no appeal whatsoever except to someone with a suicidal disposition. I suppose this entire range of phenomena is best seen as something peculiar to Japan, a nation of unique spirituality. So then we who are nothing more than pieces of machinery may have no right to say anything, but we only wish, ask, and hope for one thing: that all the Japanese people might combine to make our beloved country the greatest nation possible.

Were I to face the battles that lie ahead in this sort of emotional state, my death would be rendered meaningless. This is the reason then, as I have already stated, that I intend to concentrate on the honor involved in being designated a member of the Special Attack Corps.

When I am in a plane perhaps I am nothing more than just a piece of the machine, but as soon as I am on the ground again I find that I am a complete human being after all, complete with human emotions—and passions too. When the sweetheart whom I loved so much passed away, I experienced a kind of spiritual death myself. Death in itself is nothing when you look upon it, as I do, as merely a pass to the heaven where I will see her once again, the one who is waiting there for me.

Tomorrow we attack. It may be that my genuine feelings are extreme—and extremely private! But I have put them down as honestly as I can. Please forgive me for writing so loosely and without much logical order. Tomorrow one believer in liberty and liberalism will leave this world behind. His withdrawing figure may have a lonely look about it, but I assure you that his heart is filled with contentment.

I have said everything I wanted to say in the way I wanted to say it. Please accept my apologies for any breach of etiquette. Well, then.

—Written the night before the attack

Notes

*　　Special Attack Unit, Corps, Weapons, etc.: Towards the end of the war Japan's air strength had diminished to such a point that her leaders had come up with a desperate strategy, i.e., to freight down each plane with as lethal a load of explosives as it could carry, in the hope that the plane might make contact with an enemy ship. According to the Americans' own data, American casualties from such attacks amounted to 16 ships sunk and 185 ships damaged; the successful runs on target was said to be between 1 and 3 percent. The number of men killed in action during the course of these special attacks (all of whom were granted a special promotion of two ranks) was recorded as 2,527 Navy and 1,388 Army personnel.

　　Among other "special attack" weapons were the following: *Kaiten* (turning a fortune), a human torpedo; *Shin-yō* (shaking ocean), a motorboat equipped with explosives; *Ōka* (cherry blossom), human bombs; and *Fukuryū* (lying dragon), which attacked landing-boats from underneath with explosives from the ocean floor.

*　　Liberalism: Among the "wadatsumi fallen students" were some who were born between 1920 and 1922 and were therefore looked upon as part of a generation for whom liberalism was still at its glorious peak. Among these men were Ryōji Uehara and Genta Kamimura, who wrote very much along the lines that "liberty" and the "ideology of liberalism" were quintessential parts of "humanism." Such men considered the latter to be the truest of human conditions and the only legitimate ideal, but, after the Takigawa Incident at Kyoto University and the development of the "the emperor-as-an-organ theory" [by Prof. Takigawa], liberalism was no longer allowed to exist in Japan. The result of these things was that the political climate became such that to espouse liberalism was tantamount to being thought of as deficient in patriotism—even to the point of being considered an "enemy of the nation."

PART
I

—During the War Between Japan and China—

The Fifteen-Year War was initiated by the so-called Manchu Incident, when a plot to bomb the Southern Manchurian Railroad was executed near Lake Liutiao on September 18, 1931. Once the League of Nations adopted a resolution condemning Japan's action, she immediately withdrew from the League. Japan's aggression and the establishment of Manchukuo accelerated a rising and predominantly anti-Japanese national movement among the Chinese masses. Japan definitively entered into a total war, called "China Conflict," as a direct result of the Marco Polo Bridge Incident (or Lukouchiao Incident), a fracas between Japanese and Chinese troops which occurred on July 7, 1937—the skirmish provided both an excuse and an invitation for sterner anti-Japanese activity among the Chinese multitudes, and drew us into the quicksand of a long war.

Takaaki Ishigami

Born September 13, 1916. From Kagoshima Prefecture. After having graduated from the Seventh Higher School, he entered Tokyo Imperial University, Faculty of Letters, Department of Psychology, in 1936, and graduated in 1939. Conscripted and entered the barracks November 2, 1939. He was killed in action March 17, 1942, in Tienmên Hsien in Hupei-Shêng. Army lieutenant. He was twenty-five years old.

October 5, 1938

○ Late this afternoon I went to Hongō Post Office to ask about the postage for sending a letter to China. A poster stating that already "savings bonds are sold out" made an impression on me.

○ A lecture by professor Yasuma Takata [Professor at Kyoto University, sociology and economics scholar, 1883–1972] will soon be held at the University in classroom No. 38.

○ 10.7: I heard a rumor about the suicide of Blyukher [Soviet Commander General for the Far East. He was purged and put to death, but his honor was restored posthumously, 1890–1938].

○ On the other front, Germany and Czechoslovakia seem friendlier and there is even a rumor that they are about to forge a military alliance. On the other hand, we hear that the Slovaks are demanding autonomy. Look at this amusing comedy, or, rather, a tragic soap opera of nationalism! We can never afford to forget that behind it all is a titanic puppetmaster who is smiling in ironic glee.

○ The Soviet Union seems to be losing patience with even France. Nevertheless, a popular-front type of struggle should not be foregone.

○ 10.7: It appears to be decided that Dr. Kiyono [Professor Kenji Kiyono of Kyoto University, a scholar specialized in pathology and anthropology, 1885–1955] will undergo a psychiatric examination in Tokyo.

October 7

○ Four renowned works by Professor Kawai [Prof. Eijirō Kawai of Tokyo University, an economist, known also for his study on social ideologies, 1891–1944], such as *Shakai Seisaku Genri (Principles of Social Policies),* are now banned. Whether or not the professor should resign of his own volition has now become still another issue.

○ (Morning mental exercises) I was exposed to a reactionary lecture given by Navy Lt. General Ogasawara. The subject was the destruction of churches and the innumerable occasions on which Spanish priests and religious have been slaughtered. I wonder how they arrived at their figures on the number of religious who were killed. Would it not seem only natural, even necessary, that a new society has to be built by a new generation? ("Anti-Communism and My Religion").

    ○ I firmly believe that even studying is almost impossible without having some goal or target in sight.

    ○ Make atheism an acute weapon.

    ○ Some Imperial Universities' students are extremely cold-blooded and cold-hearted, and they are truly to be hated. They are nothing but a disorderly crowd of pure opportunists. How anxious they are to become instruments of the capitalist class, and how comfortable they are about accepting its favors! So thoroughly self-preserving! The healthy spirit of the Shinjin-kai [Newmen's Club, the student organization, founded at Tokyo University in 1918, which had a bias in favor of Socialism and was dissolved in 1929] of the past is nowhere to be seen today. Those students are nothing but the slaves of reactionary ideologies!

    ○ All right, let us move out to tackle "society."—Together!

    ○ I am legally allowed to be in touch with the general conditions of society, at least through a certain substratum thereof. Methods and ideology must first be firmly established; then, at least to begin with, we must go about uniting ourselves and—in any and every form it might take—become engaged in the "struggle."

I have finally come to recognize the clear difference which exists between individualism and totalitarianism (which is nothing more than an extension of the former) on the one hand, and socialism on the other. To obscure the distinction between the two is nothing but a strategy of the opposition's.

    ○ We cannot afford to close our eyes just because a given position seems to put a particular stress on "society." And we cannot allow ourselves to be confused by emotional *agitation* (propaganda). In fact, we are on the point of discovering that an emotion is in fact the product of a given situation; or, rather, the disguise that covers a changing situation even as it changes. At this point we are trying to get rid of both myth and any reactionary disposition.

    ○ Sentimentalism is something mankind cannot avoid. It represents the last place where the essential element of religion can escape to. To advocate this, no matter how strongly, would be just fine.

October 8

    ○ As Dr. Yasuma Takata has said, "Any rational scientific theory has at the very least to be something that could be developed at the level of international cooperation. Any insistence on the essential privacy of a project is nothing more than an admission that the development of one's theory is incomplete, that it has not reached the international standard. Or, all of this may of course be due to the perennial confusion about the distinction between theory and application." I would say that these remarks are truly and deeply insightful, that they amount to what we might call "revelations."

October 22

○ I must celebrate today because it is the day I first read a notable piece by Wataru Kaji [who organized the Japanese People's Anti-War League in China], "Zen-ei no Chichi (Father of the Avant-Garde)" [in *Senki 36–nin Shū (A Collection of Battle-flags: Short Stories by 36 Authors)*, a volume compiled by Eguchi and Kishi and published by Tokyo Kaizō-Sha, 1931, pp. 377–394]! Even as I reflect on the current situation, the fact that Kaizo-Sha is the publisher reminded me today—and with a deep emotion— of something that a friend told me a long time ago. When I was in high school, and Mr. Sanehiko [Yamamoto] was running in a general election in my hometown, an opposition party held an open-air rally on the corner of a state road near the Monopoly Agency and they were harshly critical of Kaizō-Sha, claiming that it was a hotbed of Socialism.

○ They say that Red [Communist] literature is unhealthy, but surely that is a red-hot lie!

○ Over a period of less than ten years, this "era" seems to have undergone significant development. But the truth is that fundamental conditions have hardly changed at all!

November 9

○ The fact is that in the so-called "miserable and downtrodden" slum areas the inhabitants "lead happy and vigorous lives, without a care in the world." A typical cross section of these people would be the school-children who serve as the protagonists in *Tsuzurikata Kyōshitsu (Composition Classroom)* [written by Masako Toyoda and published in 1937].

○ It should also be noted that the "cheerfulness" exhibited by grade-school children in a building placed squarely in the middle of a slum was specially mentioned in a report by Ms. [Ineko] Kubokawa, *"Tsuzurikata Kyōshitsu no Gakkō o Miru"* (*Observing a Tsuzurikata Kyōshitsu Type School*), in *Bungei*, 11, 1938.

○ I still think that the more primitive you make an environment and the places where people must live, you also make the quality of the lives that must be lived there more primitive. Similarly, I think it follows that the role of grade schools as an environmental barometer is a crucially important one.

The reason behind people's cheerfulness has nothing to do with whether their social standing or the environment is controlling them or not; it simply means that their environment has not as yet reached that stage wherein its influence over them is fully extended. ....

November 10

  o Concerning Jewish financial groups and the Comintern. I compare and connect the two of them in this way: we can never tolerate the existence of secret goings-on. Simply speaking, to be betrayed means being made a fool of.

December 30

  o *Yōnen-jidai (Childhood)* [1913–14] by Gorky [Maxim Gorky, the greatest Russian Proletariat writer, 1868–1936]

  —Learn well so that you can work by yourself. Do not bow your head to others. Live quietly and calmly. But keep your eye straight ahead. Listen to what everyone says, but decide on your own as to which is the best course to follow. . . .

  o [Some people are] blindly obedient just because exploitation by the state is compulsive.

Tomoo Yoshimura

Born March 1, 1922. From Gifu Prefecture. Entered Waseda University, Faculty of Letters, Department of Japanese Literature, in October 1942, from the Second Higher School of the university. Entered the barracks December 1, 1943. Killed in action at sea somewhere west of the Philippines on October 18, 1944. Army sergeant. He was twenty–two years old.

Reflections after having read Gorō Hani's *Kurōche* [on Benedetto Croce, 1866–1952, published in 1939]

1

I believe that Croce's true greatness lies in the fact that his all but absolute devotion to *gakumon* (intellectual inquiry and search for truth) is only qualified by his desire to serve other people. There is a phrase *gakumon no dokuritsu* (the autonomy and independence of intellectual pursuits): to say it is one thing, but continually living up to it is another, and an extremely difficult thing to do. Croce was certainly one person who really believed it and was successful at living up to it. During peacetime the phrase itself was quite popular, largely because during such a period there is plenty of time to discuss theory merely for theory's sake; but in today's world there is little opportunity for idle debating and, naturally, discussions of that sort have slackened off. Perhaps this is to be expected because they were not seriously debating it in the first place, but, all the same, it is regrettable.

The greatness of Croce lies not in his discussion itself but in the fact that his conviction remains unshaken. Peacetime or wartime, it is the same.

2

In harsh times, such as the present, scholars, in my opinion, divide themselves into two categories. The first is comprised of those who believe in their own scientific inquiry and who use it as a tool in making judgments concerning current events. The second group has chosen to forget about the pursuit of knowledge and voluntarily allowed themselves to be engulfed and swept away by what they believe to be the river of reality. Croce most certainly belongs in the first category, as we can see very clearly from the way in which he confronted the First World War. What happened then to those who argued that the reality was everything and let their passion alone dictate their conduct at that time? We can see it clearly. While Croce truly believed in scientific inquiry, I don't think he ever disregarded reality even slightly. This is clearly evident from the fact that he emphasized the importance of critical analysis, and kept on writing critiques of new situations in the [bimonthly] review, *La Critica*. His broad range of activity clearly separates Croce from pseudo-scholars who blindly believe in scientific inquiry alone and completely disregard reality.

Those who prefer to surrender themselves to the swirl of events would say that reality is so complex that a simple theory cannot deal with it; I would rather think it most certain that reality can scarcely be dealt with in terms of any *false* theory. Croce's theory was much deeper and stronger— his ideas had been generated out of such a correct analysis of history that accurate assessments could be made of any situation whatsoever, and without any surprises.

3

Croce placed the very highest value on critical evaluation.
He believed that the best use of historical analysis would be to put it

at the service of contemporary reality. Such a process would enable any people to make substantial progress in their pursuit of happiness. I would say that the same is just as true in our own lives as it is on the planes of history and science. By heeding Croce's insistence on the importance of "self-examination" we ourselves can acquire greatness. Conversely, the neglect of such critical evaluation merely because it is sometimes inconvenient would result in the loss of true happiness. I think that is what we would call our *kyōyō* (true learning and refinement). With respect either to an individual nation or mankind itself, that would be *gakumon* or intellectual inquiry. It is doubtful that a nation without *kyōyō* could attain either happiness or greatness. And that *gakumon* has to be critical analysis—I think that is what Croce contended, and it would be as fatal to a nation as it would be to any individual within it were self-refinement sacrificed to greed.

4

Croce also had a genuine interest in making a contribution toward the fulfillment of many of his fellow human beings. Just as sincere as his hope for general happiness was his conviction that one person's happiness would not cause unhappiness for another. Therefore, Croce remained humble, never became part of any power elite, and always maintained the purity of his precious scientific inquiry. The purity of scientific and intellectual inquiry did not mean separation from everyday life, but I believe that what it did mean was not to be defeated by a variety of strong outside influences. Despite the fact that it is probable a surprisingly large number of scholars believe that our scientific inquiry exists someplace apart from life and reality, the independence of scientific and intellectual inquiry from life makes no sense at all.

Croce was a man who maintained the purity of *gakumon* in the true sense of the term. It is only natural that a person with such a pure and strong conviction would not concern himself with the happiness of just a few other people.

5

When Jesus Christ said that he was king of the Country of Truth, Pilate [Roman procurator of Judaea and Samaria from A.D. 26 to 36—it was under his overseership that Jesus suffered and died] asked what the truth was. This was because Pilate was a man who had been washed away, who had washed himself away, by reality, and by the pressure of events.

I would think that for Christ, who saw through all that and far beyond, and had to believe absolutely in the truth, Pilate's question made no sense at all.

It is not blasphemous to believe that Croce shared somewhat in the same sort of wisdom exhibited by Christ on that occasion.

[Translators' note: Under the very strict and oppressive thought control exercised at that time, Croce was perhaps the most liberal author whose publication barely escaped being banned.]

Hidemitsu Ōi

Born October 2, 1914. From Tokyo Metropolis. Through Toyama Higher School, entered Tokyo Imperial University, Faculty of Natural Science, Department of Mathematics, in 1934. Graduated in 1937. While studying in the Graduate School, he was conscripted and entered the barracks, September 1, 1938. Killed in action on June, 14, 1941, in Shihshuyüan, Shantung Province, in northern China. Army sublieutenant. He was twenty-six years old.

—From *Ai to Shinkō no Tegami (Letters of Love and Faith)*, published by Fukuko Ōi, May 1943—

April 17, 1940

My Dear Mother:

The day of departure has finally arrived.

But I am going away in high spirits and good health; so, please take really good care of yourself and I pray that, when I return home after all the hardships that probably lie ahead, I'll be able to see you in even better health than now.

I am trying to act as though I haven't a care in the world and am perfectly balanced emotionally, but the truth is that I leave for battle amid many unsettled matters. That is, there are these feelings of emptiness and loneliness which accompany those of sadness at having to leave loved ones behind. I believe that I have prepared myself and am ready to head in the direction of serious danger, as I am fully confident in God's invisible but providential control of the situation. This is why I wanted all of you—Mother, Yoshimitsu, and Mieko—to understand my frame of mind and, because you understood, to send me off with at least a smile; but apparently the love between a parent and a child is far too deep and poignant for that. I do not mind your tears, Mother, but I beg you please to spend each day from now on in a cheerful mood, at least as much as you can, and in anticipation of the letters I will be writing. If I were to leave home with only tears for a farewell, I might feel that I was headed less surely for battle than for death. So, I really wish you would think of my going as though I were only leaving home with fishing gear and a sketch book. Please promise me that you are determined never to shed any more tears.

The beauty of the cherry blossoms and of the genial spring sun helped to put me in a tranquil mood and, as I reexamined what is in my heart, a variety of new emotions rose up. In the past we used to talk about the joys and pains of life and other complex subjects with a great confidence, assuming that we understood one another so well—or indeed I thought that I fully comprehended: but, now it seems clear that almost all of that was nothing but matters in the process of passing. I feel that salvation through Christ, and through Christ alone, is the only bridge of hope left for us linking [our indifferent world] to the unchanging world. What I suppose I am saying is that, even though my faith is itself not unshakable, it is by comparison far stronger than anything else in this world.

It must seem truly astonishing that a person such as myself, who in the past so truly hated and feared anything connected with war, can now concentrate so fully—to the absolute exclusion of all other thoughts, emotions, etc.—on learning everything there is to learn about preparing for war. But however startling a phenomenon this might seem to, say, a member of my family, to the person who is right in the middle of all this— i.e., to me—the situation seems more than natural. It is possible that someone, and sadly, might pose a question: "Are you then getting to be a soldier so completely?" The only possible answer I could give, in the in-terests of accuracy, would be a qualifying one: "Not really, but I am placed in the role of a soldier and going through a special training to function as a soldier." That is, I have "not become a soldier through and through."

What so far is the most painful and depressing aspect of my life in the military involves certain misgivings about the state of my emotions —gnawing doubts about what I have always considered very fine and keen emotions. What I am worried about is whether or not they may be deteriorating to such a point that I may no longer be able either to be afraid of anything or to react to anything. I have even felt the urge to assume a fighting stance more or less automatically, while remaining as a person with permanently keen emotions, instead of being reduced gradually to a beast. Still and all, I am certain that I would not commit an unreasonable act. It is possible that I might be taken off guard momentarily but I am confident that, given time, I'll move toward the final victory in the best way I can possibly manage. At this point of course I have no idea as to whether or not that final victory will cost me my life, but I can still set off in reasonably good cheer. I commend the efforts I am about to make to those of you who remain at home, and beg you to lead peaceful and pleasant lives while I am making them. Just as my death would be the Lord's will and therefore no cause for tears, so too even my survival should not be cause for any premature celebration—because it would not necessarily mean final victory.

Looking back over what I have written, it seems a rather long, gloomy report—but please read only my smile. From now on I intend to write you about much more interesting things, and lots of humorous and pleasant ones too.

I haven't written all that much lately, and for a while there I thought that my head might have turned to stone; but I realize now that I am still able to write, able in fact to write a good deal, and also, as something of a bonus, that human feelings are gushing out of me just as they do from ordinary people. So I'll be writing you now and then about what I am thinking and feeling, and I hope that, on the receiving end, the letter will provide food for pleasant conversation. With this I close my first letter.

Hidemitsu

[A letter to a minister]

Dear Minister:

Having landed at _____, and spent one night each at Peking and Tientsin, I am now in _____. Finally, either tomorrow or the day after tomorrow, we shall move toward _____. As an *emigré* from the so-called human world to the deepest part of China, I can taste the pain this country feels. What I heard of "yellow dust, thousands of feet thick," is literally true here, but, more than that, here a people who can be counted in the multi-millions are living in the dirt without ever knowing either hope or disappointment. It makes me wonder about the coming of the day when they will receive the glory of Christ.

With the Lord,

Hidemitsu

[A letter to a minister]

Dear Minister:

With prayers for God's blessings.

Please be assured that, thanks to God's grace, I am well. I feel very fortunate that, even in this war zone, I can quietly praise God with a hymn in the quiet of the evening. I can say that my present situation is filled with

God's grace. I cannot do anything about the constant threat to my very existence, because after all this *is* a war zone, but my peace of mind allows me to put up with things much more easily.

I entered a Chinese church for the first time this evening. It looked as though a prayer meeting was going on, so I stopped in on my way back from an inspection tour of the town. Middle-aged men and women and some older people were gathering. When I told them that I was a Japanese Christian they seemed very pleased; and with happy faces, they told me that they had a Japanese bible and went out of their way to produce it. I think they did so because I was looking at a Chinese bible with curiosity. I did not stay very long but was greatly pleased when, just before I took my departure, an old man tried to present me with a book, *Shutsu Ejiputo Ki (The Exodus)*. I thought it was so nice. Walking back through the town, although this village was burned to the ground, I realized in my heart that the village was so filled with the joy of believers.

I am full of thoughts for the church and praying for God's grace. Regards to everyone.

With the Lord,

Hidemitsu

"On *Karen*"[1]

We often hear of the sentiment called "*karen*," and I have often experienced that feeling myself. To feel empathy over someone who is tiny, small, or weak, is indeed one of the most desirable of the numerous natural sentiments we feel as human beings. Weakness in itself—if someone, e.g., is weak and has no one to rely upon but is lacking in substance himself—would not, I would think, cause us to feel any sense of *karen*. It seems that this sentiment is only roused within us at the sight of someone who is not strong and who still manages to maintain a sense of him/ herself, who somehow, and despite obvious short-comings, continues to give his/her best effort. When the weak expect the strong to protect them, then all it amounts to in the end is a lack of moral courage, and no sentiment of "*karen*" would be involved.

As a commander I am quite often powerfully moved whenever I see a soldier who, lacking in natural ability but supported by the sheer emotion of being sent off with Japanese Hinomaru flags, tries his very hardest to

---

[1] A term meaning pretty, lovely, cute, sweet, pitiful, and carrying a tender sentiment, complete with sympathy and affection, toward the person to whom it is applied.

come through even though the outcome might not be the best possible. The feeling sparked by such a situation is the emotion we call "*karen*."

I feel the same way when I see soldiers, with hands that are caked with dirt because of the long stretch of time between opportunities to take baths, trying as best they can to clean their weapons. They carry on with hands terribly swollen by frigid temperatures, and with rough-knuckled fingers that seem to be difficult for them even to bend. But still they carry on.

I get that same sense of *karen* and am also deeply moved when I see a soldier single-mindedly trying his hardest even though his efforts might be in vain, and despite the fact that he has already been put down as no good by his superior officer. These men have to have a world of their own, a place where they can show themselves off with pride. At the very least, they must have a loving father, mother, or siblings. No matter how sincere and genuine they are, they may receive a poor evaluation just because of their low talent level; they may even be nagged about unsatisfactory performance in various exercises. Even though they possess precious and jewel-like hearts, and even though their fathers, mothers, and siblings are hoping for the best for them and expecting so much from them, in the long run the Army treats them as feeble and powerless. Every time I come upon such a case, I experience the strongest possible emotion—*karen*—and feel so much for each of these soldiers.

....

Another occasion when I was deeply filled with the emotion of *karen* was one time when I saw a Chinese man and his child. The man was about forty years of age, tall and heavy-bodied, oval-faced and with full cheeks. He did not look particularly affluent, but neither did he appear to be as poor and dirty as those on the lowest rung of the ladder. He was standing still by the side of the road and watching the triumphant Imperial Japanese Army as they marched through. He was holding a small child of about four in his arms. Both of them, man and child, were after all citizens of a defeated nation, and I wondered how the strutting soldiers appeared to them and what their thoughts were. There was no sign of servility in their faces, and in fact, I thought that I saw China's future possibilities hidden in them—especially in the face of the child who was being protected by the defeated grownup. In spite of all that, they were not being given any sympathy now, or even glanced at; rather, they were being left behind in that cold village so far distant from civilization. While I went on marching, my heart felt as though it had been torn out by the sight of those *karen* people.

....   November 27, 1940

Akira Meguro

Born November 10, 1916. From Miyagi Prefecture. Through the Second Higher School, entered Tokyo Imperial University, Faculty of Letters, Department of Sociology, in 1937. Entered the barracks March 1941. Died on October 10, 1941, in a military field hospital in Yüehchou, central China, of an illness contracted on the battlefield. He was twenty-four years old.

[A letter to his father]

September 16, 1941

Dear Father:

Autumn is here. I was startled by the cool autumn wind after suffering from the well over one-hundred-degree temperatures we've been experiencing until now. The skies are beautiful too and are filled with stars. Insects are singing around us. In this alien land of China any insects—whether they are kōrogi (crickets) or matsumushi (Madasumma marmorata, a kind of cricket), or just about any type of autumn insect that we used to hear in Japan—make us soldiers feel nostalgic about home. So, whenever we get together and talk, our conversations are always limited to the mountains and rivers of home, and also to the food we enjoyed at home.

Father, our Yamamori Squad is now in Hankow [major city in Hupeh Province]. Our several months' training in that severe summer heat will now be tested, we hope successfully, during this autumn season. On September 9th, the day of the Chrysanthemum Festival, our unit completed preparations for moving out to what was announced as our next station. That is the town of Tangyang, which is some 350 kilometers beyond Hankou. It was 10 o'clock in the morning when our automobiles left in the quiet autumn rain, headed for a place which was to be my very first battlefield. Our automobile detachment unit of a few dozen vehicles moved forward over gentle, undulating hills, one following another. At times we could not move because tires became mired in incredibly muddy places; or at other times, all together and with enormous effort, we pulled vehicles up hills they could not have climbed otherwise. Other vehicles broke down completely. But after four days of traveling and innumerable hardships, our unit finally arrived here at Hankou at 10 o'clock in the evening on the 12th. It turns out that we are now about to embark on a ship, and with no idea of our destination. In any event, we really have no other choice than that of continuing to follow the imperial orders.*

....

Honestly, dear father, there have been so many occasions when I wanted to appeal to you and confide in you and mother as intimately as I did in the days of childhood. Perhaps these feelings were like those of a young bully who goes home to his parents to confess what he has done. . . . There were so many times when I wished so very much I could have you hear me out about so many things—times when I felt so alone and lonely that at night I just went out quietly to look at the starry skies.

Sometimes I even felt jaundiced and sorry for myself, thinking that the only place where I could possibly live would be in a kind and gentle place and amid the company of the tranquil souls whom I longed for. But I believe that even this sort of bad dream will be blown away once I face my first battle. More importantly, I have learned thoroughly that soldiers fight not so much by tolerating hardships as by utterly disregarding whatever hardships and pain they must endure. It makes me feel good to think that I too will not be defeated by any foreseeable hardships. Under no circumstances, father, shall I ever act in a cowardly manner; so long as I live I shall continue to move forward. The amulet that you so kindly sent me the other day is not meant for clinging to life, but it would make even a weak soldier a courageous one. The more I reflect upon the kindest thoughts and deepest love of you, father and mother, with which this amulet is filled, the more determined am I than ever to be strong.

....

I cannot find words to express anything close to adequate appreciation for what you, my parents, have done for me. Father, the house and home, which by your own hard work you built from nothing, will always be a beloved memory. I find it truly hard to believe that such a beautiful home, a little world so filled with perfect harmony, could ever exist on this earth. That was a piece of fine art that you created. In it we children were brought up so lovingly. There was never anything lacking or wanting—I remember the warm steam that surrounded us at dinnertime. Ever since I arrived here what I have thought and meditated constantly about is the object of art that you created, father. The fact that through you I was given the opportunity to see that beautiful harmony is enough to have made my life worth living. Father, your love has been so deep and I have received so much from you for such a long time. Your heart was such a deep loving heart. At this moment of time, please do not worry, and just think of me as doing the best job I possibly can. Now, I must go. The autumn wind is freshening a bit now, and it's wrinkling the moving water of the creek beneath the railroad embankment. I can imagine what a beautiful autumn must have arrived at home, Sendai, by now. This brings back those days in the much cherished past, which I could write about endlessly if I ever once started. So you must excuse me if I end this letter right now for today. Please think of me as I shall always be talking with you.

....

September 17

.... I am writing you, Father, because I have so many things, more than it is possible to write, I want to tell you. .... We arrived at Nanking on xx day of xx month. And we spent about a week at xx Battalion's barracks here. It was located at the bottom of Lion Mountain, where some stubborn remains of gun-emplacements showed through. Hawks were wheeling around the sky as though they were dancing. I was seeing the Chinese people for the first time personally, and what really left a strong impression were the masses of coolies. When we were ready to disembark from the ship, there were hundreds of them squirming around on the landing pier. They were all wearing rags so tattered that they defy description. There were old ones and young ones alike, all barefooted and walking this way and that way. They left an even stronger impression on me than had the numerous burned houses that I caught glimpses of on our way to the barracks. Things that will not be easy to forget are the scenes at Hsing-chung Mien. In the very early morning, masses of coolies go into the castle there with empty tin cans on their hips, and then in the evenings they come out again through the gate.

....

Note

*   *Ōkimi–Tennō* (Emperor): Following the *Imperial Prescript for Soldiers*, which reads as follows: "To receive an order from a superior is in fact to be considered the same as receiving a command from me." In the Japanese military, absolute adherence to a superior's order was expected of any and every soldier.

Kōichi Takemura

He was born March 14, 1914. From Akita Prefecture. Through Ibaragi Nihon Kokumin High School, he entered Tokyo Imperial University, Faculty of Agriculture, Department of Applied Agriculture, in 1933. Graduated in 1936. Conscripted and entered the barracks October 5, 1937. Sent overseas in September 1938. Killed in action on February 23, 1939, in central China. He was twenty-four years old.

A Bivouac on the Battlefield[1]

Once again, another star fell, and
  Humid evening dew began to chill the hands
    that hold a gun

The sun went down, and now stars are twinkling. . . .
  The gust of wind rages over the river, and a body is not
    yet recovered from its waves.

It was my battlefield friend who had been writing a will
  this morning. . . . Tears wet my eyes.

Tadahide Hamada

Born January 18, 1921. His native place is unknown. Entered Nihon Taiiku Senmon Gakko (Nihon Athletic College) in April 1939. Conscripted and entered the barracks December 6, 1941. Killed in action, November 23, 1944, in Changsha, Hunan Province, China. Army Lieutenant. He was twenty-three years old.

July 28, 1942
  Whenever I am absolutely exhausted, feeling so weary about everything, or tormented with high malarial fever, I am tempted to shout out my true feelings: "I am so sick and tired of all this maneuvering! . . . With grass as a pillow [translator's note: an ancient and poetic Japanese way of referring to travel or life on the road], our destination seems so far away—several thousand miles! Also, the words that want to come out when I think of the horrible roads ahead and the long way to Kengchou are: "Somehow I just don't care anymore. . . . I just want to die right here and now." This too is my naked true feeling!

---

[1] [Translators' note: These three verses were originally composed according to a much admired and frequently imitated Japanese metrical arrangement alternatively designated as the *"tanka"* (lit. means short poems) or *"waka"* (literally Japanese poems, including both *tanka* and *chōka*, long poems, which were rather popular in the earlier period, e.g., Heian Period). *Tanka* follows the form of 5–7–5, 7–7 syllables. Our aim was simply to translate the piece's meaning.]

When I picked up a pen for the first time in several weeks, I found that I had forgotten how to write some characters, and that made me angry. What in the world am I doing, for what?

The same hands which were once accustomed to hold mountain-climbing tools now carry a gun. I drag my utterly exhausted body to a mountain pass that resembles Karisaka [a ridge between Yamanashi and Saitama Prefectures]. As we advanced more and more deeply into these remote Chinese provinces I observed how all the surrounding mountains are covered with bamboo growth—nothing but bamboo. The shining sun lacquered the light green shade and the scene could have served as the very purest symbol of peace itself: in the middle of it, there was a small, beautiful village. I felt as though we were entering Shangri-la itself.

If no war existed, I seriously thought, these village people, located as deeply in the mountains as they are, would be perfectly content and thoroughly enjoying their simple way of life. There was a stream with clear and cold water running. But we soldiers had no time to rest and kept on moving forward. One time I caught myself thinking: "Why do I have to endure these hardships for the benefit of those who have stayed at home and enjoy a life of leisure [in Japan]?" Then I got hold of myself and shouted out loud: "No, I don't hate you! It's just that these hysterical emotions are making me think this way!" One day, in a drenching rain and knee-deep in mud, and as we kept to a forced march on a horrible road, I thought the only alternative I had left was simply "just to keep on walking until I dropped." Many times we marched in jet-black darkness, walking one step at a time and guided only by the faint silhouettes of our comrades ahead of us. Occasionally I could not keep my eyes open while still walking, only to be suddenly awakened by stepping into a puddle; then I would open my eyes and keep moving forward to try and catch up with those in front. Once I almost fell off a bridge, avoiding the fall by only a few steps.

August 31

On the third day, the 16th, I developed fever due to the combination of beriberi and extreme exhaustion brought on by the forced march; on the next day, the 17th, I could barely manage a walk of a few kilometers [to our embarkation point] to join a boat. I got some rest at first but, by the third or fourth day, I had to move around just like everyone else. I did not get much sleep for the next several days. I was finally relieved to find that I felt like eating something. For the first time in my life I had passed bloody excrement. It was the color of strong red tea and really ghastly. I was completely exhausted. When a human being reaches that stage of fatigue he simply can't stand up, even for a moment. The pain in my heart, or lung, my chest anyway, was so great that I wanted to tear it off; I also felt as though I were losing my mind, and my rate of breathing went up dramatically. Of course I had a soaring temperature and headaches that seemed about to split my skull in two. This condition is exactly the same as Minegishi's was just before he died of exhaustion some time ago. On the ship, even in the chill of early morning, we wore only a "fundoshi" (a loincloth), so naturally I caught a cold. We arrived in Lishui on the 22nd. After an examination on the following day, I was ordered to be hospitalized for a swollen case of beriberi and, probably, malaria. I was to be shipped back, immediately and by plane; so, without taking along any of my personal belongings, I was to be hospitalized in a field hospital for the very first time. For some reason both my strength and my spirits sank. I spent a night being fed rice porridge, and then headed to Kengchou on an airplane, my first flight in a long time. The hospital was absolutely packed. I was left alone and without care. I even thought that I was going to be left to become gradually exhausted without receiving any attention. There was nothing to do except to sleep, and nothing to look forward to except three daily meals that were unbelievably bad. Soldiers were continually being shipped back from the front, many of them only to be transferred again to Shanghai, Nangching, or some other place. Beginning on the afternoon of the day following my arrival, I suffered for four days through dangerously high temperatures of 39.7° centigrade, but since yesterday the fever has lessened. I am losing weight quite visibly, and my hands have become ghostly thin. There is no morning call and no "lights out" order at night, just one roll call in the evening—outside of that, the three meals are the main happenings of every day. I am sick of sleeping but can't stand staying awake either, and am preoccupied with the simple problem of where to put my body each day. I wish that a decision either way would come soon, either to send me back or simply to discharge me from the hospital, as soon as possible and definitely. Five days passed without any medicine at all, and on the sixth day they gave me something that looked like powdered medicine Wakamoto (a popular digestive). I suppose that I'm being treated as a person now, but nothing at all was done for my malaria and the fever was simply left to run its course. If what they want is to ship me away, I wish they'd do it quickly. What I really want is to begin a regimen of fighting this illness seriously. I don't miss my infantry company, but what I really do miss is eating those hand-rolled sushi in Tienchin [a major city in Hêpei Province in China].

Takehiko Fukushima

Born September 24, 1921. From Tokyo Metropolis. Entered Nihon Taiiku
Senmon Gakko (Nihon Physical Education College) in 1939, and graduated
in 1941.* Entered the barracks November 20, 1941. Killed in action in
Kueilin of Kuanghai, China, on January 8, 1944. Army lieutenant. He was
twenty-two years old.

I first came to know "Ichirō" at a mountain pass bordering two prefectures (Chiang and Meihsien) of Hunan province. The squad that I led
was resting after having completed a reconnaissance when, in the middle of
the Commanding Squad who were advancing, who should come along but
Sawada, and with him a cute boy, dressed in a plain but quite clean outfit
and leading an ox. The child had clear eyes and a nice straight nose, was
fair-skinned and appeared to be very gentle—in short, a handsome and re-
fined-looking youngster. "Hey, Jun-kō [a diminutive for Sawada's first
name], what a cute kid! Where'd you get him?" "Ah, ha. Isn't he though?"
"It was at Tachêping." "But hey, wait a minute, this is a *girl-child!* So
gentle and so darn classy!" "That's it, she *is* a girl." "Really! Oh, how pitiful
. . . , but she must be quite a walker! What a nice kid. A nice kid!"

Ichiro turned out to be very refined indeed, and added to her refinement was a truly beautiful smile which contained a very nice, innocent
shyness. Whenever she smiled her face took on a definite quality of quiet,
sadness. She was eleven years of age [note: in a Western country, it would
be ten: according to the Japanese style of counting age of a child, Ichirō was
in her 11th year], and cute as a "little boy" could be. Another thing that
made Ichirō very special was the fact that she understands a little Japanese;
so it was easy for her to be friendly and charming. Wearing casually a
"botchan hat" [a hat worn by young Japanese schoolboys] I traded for, and
moving along quite daintily, Ichiro mixes right in with the roughnecks.
During our ten days' stay in Meihsien, Ichirō was very happy playing with
our Wang Tung-chê, but she stopped visiting us for a while after some
friend persuaded Wang to run off.

Ichirō and I renewed our friendship during a period when I had to
spend every day inside the dormitory in Liuyang after I had seriously
injured my left foot during the course of a particularly grueling march, and
the pain was so unbearable that I actually wanted to die! In the meantime,
Sawada is as busy as a shoe-merchant with our young followers. Tarō is a
boy who has been with us ever since Honan and so, naturally, he lords it
over Ichirō. Sawada was also feeling terrible about two other guys, Ui and
Arai, who were teasing our little girl and sometimes made her cry. It was

understandable then that, because I was excused from drills and had plenty of time on my hands, she came to play with me.

I don't know how it got there, but I'd been playing an organ in the dormitory. On one occasion I got tired of playing and, in hope of finding a distraction, I dragged my feet to visit the Commanding Squad's office. Just behind one of the walls, I came upon Ichirō, sobbing and looking sad. When I asked what had happened, she said something about "Mr. Sawada . . . ," or "Mr. Ui. . . ." She was completely disconsolate and her face took on a look that was at once reproachful and far away—perhaps far enough away to see beyond the mountains. For a child of eleven the feeling of homesickness must be, by far, even stronger than our own.

"Hanchō" [note: here Ichirō is addressing the author by his military title, a squad chief]. My home is Tachên. It is far away, very far! But I want so much to go home. I really want to go home." As she sobbed out those words and clung to my knees, I realized how alone, forlorn, and helpless she must have been feeling, worrying about anything and everything. This was after all the case of a child, and such a little child at that —in Japan she would barely have passed for nine or ten!—being led around by a bunch of tough foreigners, and journeying to unknown and faraway places that stretched farther from home every day. Of course there was no hope of her getting home alone; so even if she were to run away, what could she do? And how far were these foreign soldiers going? She missed both a mother who had passed away and her father, said to be living in Hankow [major city in Hopeh Province]. Her childhood could not have been a very happy one, brought up as she had been by a grandmother and aunt and surrounded by cousins—but as for the house in Tachêping, the mountains there, and a pond where fish jumped, how she must have longed to see them again. Small wonder that she was desperate to get back there and to her past as soon as possible! Ichirō started crying again and kept repeating "Tachêping! Tachêping!" "All right, all right," I said. "Our group will be finishing up here soon, and after we do we'll all return to Tachêping together. We'll go home soon, and take pretty dresses and shoes and a lot of money with us. O.K.? So don't cry, don't cry. Go to sleep—that's what I'm going to do. O.K.?" I gently stroked her back and before long, tired from crying, she fell asleep on my lap. What a child! So sweet and pitiful, and at the same time the sad and unfortunate product of a defeated nation.—All this was Ichirō around that time.

It was about four or five days later she came to me as an adopted child. It was the evening of the day when we were hit with our first air raid: we had departed Liuyang and it was the first day of the Liling offensive, which we had been led to understand would be our toughest campaign yet. I was sitting half-naked and rolling a cigarette with Sawada when Ichirō happened along, looking as sad and lonely as always. "Hanchō!" she asked helplessly, "Where are you *'hsienshêng'* headed?" "Well, um. . . . *Hsienshêng?* We, *hsienshêng* are going on a punitive expedition, but we'll be back soon." Even though this was a lie, what else could I have said? I couldn't possibly have shared with her something that even we were so uncomfortable and apprehensive about ourselves, such as: "We're going to Kuangtung, but have no idea how many years we'll be on the march." I felt that the only thing I could do would be to try and make her feel a little bit better, even though the feeling would only last for a little while.

Ichirō wound up saying that "I go where Hancho goes," and Sawada too said that it was a good idea to have me adopt her. Naturally, however, just the idea of parting from Sawada must have made Ichirō feel a little lonely and fearful; she asked "Can I get to see Hsienshê Sawada every day?" So she was anxious to be assured that she'd be able to see him every day. In fact, just about everything on this journey of ours to nowhere was new to her eyes, since during Ichirō's life with us up to now there had been no one but Sawada on whom she could rely—both physically and emotionally. So, even though recently he had made her cry now and then, or even spoken harsh words such as, "O.K., then, go home by yourself!," she must have felt it difficult to say good-bye and to follow a new person whom she had only known for several days. We both assured her that she needn't worry and told her "Everything would be all right, we'd be together every day." So it was that Ichirō came to my squadron as an adopted child.

We began our march on the following day. Ichirō toddled along in front of me with my steel helmet and carrying a Chinese mosquito net barely large enough to cover the both of us, a little silk outfit and a leather Western shoe, all of which are something that Sawada somehow managed to requisition with a great effort as gifts to her, and a dangling canteen. Half-asleep in the dark, she walked right in front of me with her little steps, as we marched on one night after another.

Concentrating solely on putting one foot in front of the other, we traversed both dark roads that ran alongside paddies and long, winding hilly ones as well. We never stopped to make camp until it was almost dawn. Then, in the large central kitchen with its shelf provided for the household goods, we made do for beds either by laying down shutters or spreading mats. We all would go right to sleep without giving any thought to food or drink; but one can only imagine what effect this continual night-marching must have had on the morale and endurance of a tiny child.

When we finally stopped, Ichirō could hardly wait for us to take the knapsacks off our shoulders, and then she would cling to me and say: "Hancho, I am sleepy. So sleepy." I never felt so sad and pitiful about her as I did at this time. Without a moment's delay I'd take a shutter off its frame and place it on the floor for her as I soothed and comforted her, spreading out her mosquito net that she carried, and I put her to bed—most of the lower half of Ichirō's body was wet with the evening dew.

When I consider how a child of such tender years as eleven has marched with us some eighty or ninety miles, it's clear to me that I have never before fully realized what the human heart and the love within it are capable of and how beautiful they are. I said [silently to her]: "I truly am deeply sorry for you, but this is a war and now that we are in it together you must walk with us as far as we go. Whenever the war is over, and if we should win, . . . I don't know when, but, . . . I'll make sure that you get to go to Tokyo with us hsienshêng. Is that all right? Then we'll arrange for whatever help is necessary to send you to college, that's right—just for now, though, I'll put in a requisition for a nice pair of shoes for you. O.K.?"

Note:
*   Moving up the date for graduation: To bolster both the military and the labor force, the required length of study for all universities, higher schools, and colleges was shortened by three months in accordance with an Imperial Order of October 1941. Graduation for the next academic year, 1942, was also moved up six months. For the year 1943, a variety of laws proper to the different schools were altered and higher schools (including the universities' preparatory division) were cut down from three years to two. Additionally, five-year middle schools became four-year. In the brief histories of the authors on the following pages this explanation will be taken for granted.

Toshihiro Tanabe

Born May 19, 1915. From Okayama Prefecture. Entered Nihon University, Department of English, in 1934, and graduated in 1938. Conscripted and entered the barracks in Matsue, December 1, 1939. Killed in action, August 24, 1941, in Changsu Province, China. Army corporal. He was twenty-six years old.

December 11, 1939   Cloudy

....

In the morning, we anchored in a location where we could see the city of Moji on the left and Shimonoseki far away on the right. There we loaded coal, food, and other things. Although the sun was shining, the wind was cold. Perhaps one of these towns that I am seeing now will be the very last Japanese town that we shall be able to see for a long time to come.................

Even as we suffered from the seasickness and cramped living conditions, we now realized for the first time just how important this whole "process" is, i.e., being prepared for the opportunity of being killed in action in China. To put it simply, to be killed in action may be nothing in itself. However, we can understand how significant the process is by way of which a soldier reaches that point.

December 25   Clear
................Willow trees, in a rather unassuming manner, are raising their wintry arms toward the skies, and Chinese crows, each one with its long tail of black and white, occasionally come to sit on the branches, and then fly away in the direction of the castle wall—all the while making a strange noise that we are not familiar with. Now and then a few Chinese people in blue outfits pass along the road outside the castle wall, some riding on a ricksha, some carrying loads on their shoulders, others just pushing a cart. All of this is framed, as it were, against a background that is the far-stretching castle wall of Suchou [the southern part of Chiangsu Province]. The wall extends a long way, and stands there almost as though it is tired of history itself. Even if we came across the Hsüanhai Ocean, as indeed we have, into this present situation, and even if we could, e.g., win a temporary victory by subjugating some bandits, I doubt that the facial expression of this wall would change any. In the forefront of the vast panorama of these continental blue skies and a history that somehow seems almost too long, perhaps we too will be making a small broken chip of history. Our military rules, almost always too strict and often too narrow, may amount to nothing more than a sort of caricature in front of such an outrageously grand expression. Any scene in history, however, always must be dignified and somber.

While taking our ease on withered grass, and soaking up the warm sunshine, we listened to our Hanchō's [squad leader's] very interesting story of the battle of Hangkow. On our return trip we were singing military marching songs, taking our turn with other squads, and we finally arrived home. We ran into several Chinese civilians along the way. I thought that perhaps, since we were singing military marching songs, we might see smiles on some of their faces, but my expectation was not met: every single one of them turned away with a bitter and expressionless face, carrying their baskets along a path on the other side of the river. It was sort of a lonely moment. It could be that such things are only part of the sad profile of a defeated nation.   When I caught a glimpse of the old battlefield at Chapei [north of Shanghai International Settlement], and also whenever I see a single Chinese civilian, I reflect on how important it is for us to win this war. Whatever the situation may be, we must not lose the war.

I went to a canteen in the afternoon and had zenzai [a traditional Japanese red-bean sweet soup]. Some one was playing the song "Yoimachi-gusa" [a very popular sentimental song about a person waiting in vain for a loved one] on a piano. On a table there were *Eiga no Tomo (Companion to the Movies)*, *Ōsaka Mainichi* [a daily paper], and other reading materials. All of these things attract us and capture our hearts with a strangely powerful sense of nostalgia; I opened the pages at once and read on eagerly. We hardly ever have access to Japanese newspapers. Come to think of it, this very fact may be due to our feelings of security about Japan. In the newspaper there was a very large advertisement pushing the January issue of a magazine. But somehow it smells only of yesterday. It is hard to believe that it has been only twenty-five days since we entered the barracks ....

December 26 Clear
        ....

For the first time ever we had a nighttime exercise, and the daytime scene was almost completely reversed. As the night air drew on, there came the sound of dogs barking, one after the other. The same moon as shone over Japan climbed up in the skies' frosty air. The crows, those huge glossy and beautiful crows, have gone off home somewhere.

During the rest period in the afternoon military exercise, I composed a poem for the first time since I became a soldier. I have occasionally seen some war poems in magazines, etc., but lately I think that I have come to appreciate fully the straitened circumstances in which they were put together—within such short time limits and under great stress. When I want to write a poem at night, my own brain has stiffened as the result of what had happened during the day. Add to this the fact that activities such as the composition of poetry are frowned upon in the military. The only re-quirement, the one order, is to take the straightest possible path toward becoming a good fighting soldier. In times such as the present, making time to write a poem about something outside ordinary people's experience—war—is an extraordinary testimony to one's willpower. Even if a poem written under circumstances such as these turned out to be inferior in quality, it would represent a strong proof that such a firm poetic spirit could still be born. At any rate, the sense of that spirit as it was expressed by Rimbaud [a French poet, 1854–91]—"A misery as though the body itself were being torn"—is still much too remote for me.

I shall write about what happened last night. We have become so intimidated that we somehow find, each and every day, that we never have any occasion to enjoy ourselves: there is only the constant worry about being scolded after the evening roll call. So it naturally follows that, at least here lately, one never witnesses the gushing out of anyone else's humanity. It is as though everything were all packed tight within a hard shell. Be that as it may, our comrade Kohata has injured his foot and, just after lights out, he started to groan. Then Shimohara got up immediately and started to take care of him. Earlier in the evening Shimohara had been made to stand in a corner of the barracks [as a punishment] with a gun in the saluting position [i.e., holding it, with both hands, straight up in front of his body], and, at long last, had just been allowed to get into bed. His quick action on Kohata's behalf made me feel so wonderful at that moment; it was as though frozen water had suddenly began to run. Then the soldier assigned to night watch moved in to help, followed by the squad leader and even the instructor—they came one after another, all of them concerned about our comrade. I was under the bed covers, and really happy for the first time since becoming a soldier. Discipline alone would not do the trick: the only thing that really moves us is an appeal to our humanity. I don't think that it is all right to forget, even for a moment, that even a soldier is a human being too.

December 29

After a classroom session in the morning, I walked toward the Consulate building for the first time. The Consulate is an elegant, dark brown building. We conducted a close-order drill [hand-to-hand combat training on a company-wide basis) nearby. There is also a Japanese silk mill in the neighborhood, and I even saw two or three Japanese ladies for the first time in a long time. The scenery around here resembles that of Musashino Plain [around Tokyo]. I was looking at the spring scenery before me, while thinking of the Chinese characters for the word, "Musashi-no": it all brought some fond memories back for me.

It is an especially warm day today, almost warm enough to make us perspire a little. I can see some cherry trees around here, and I thought about how beautifully they will blossom in Spring.

When it is now and then brought to my attention during drills, I realize how totally lacking I am in any feel for sports. Whenever that happens, the anger that I used to feel long ago at a phantom target suddenly bubbles up again—and then disappears just as quickly. This anger is something I fondly remember; I feel as though the very center of my heart found a home in that anger.

January 5, 1940   Clear
................I pray that both my life and body might grow powerfully.
My desire for eternity.
Soldiers are human beings at the very end of the earth.
Soldiers are nothing but a world of glorified inmates.

—Snowy Nights—

Even after he has lost all hope
        a man continues to live.
Somewhere on an invisible map,
Or, perhaps even beyond the temporal dimensions of
        months and years so far away,
He dreams of a soft, red bud.
He holds out his hand to the freezing wind.
Even though the hand is covered with mud,
Although his brain only continues to live days in oblivion,

He relies on the faint warmth of the blood
        running inside his body
And continues to live on as a winter weed.
A hope like a glimpse of a remnant of snow from far off,
        please keep on shining.
No matter what light it may be,
It will be strong enough to guide the hopeless.
For those who, from the same spot on earth,
        look up at different stars,
Desolation and freedom of mind are intertwined.
It all helps me to remember that,
        at least once upon a time, I was a human being.

—Muddy Road—

It is a cold, muddy road.
A muddy road winds over the wild and endless plain.
The road climbs hills, bisects stretches of woods,
And is every bit as long and depressing as our deep,
        dark thoughts.
The road sucks the shoes from our feet
And coils itself around weariness just like a snake.
Sniffling along with dirty hands,

We slip and fall and get even dirtier.
Picture the line of soldiers—more like a straggle of animals—
Filing from field to hill, and from one hill to another.
A pain-filled procession of men
    moves forward silently
In the dust of an early Winter.
In their search for the enemy,
They make progress over the map of the unknown.
Forsaken by both love and beauty,
This army on the march disappears along the muddy road
Single-mindedly in the general direction of the end of the earth.
Very much like a long nightmare,
    the huge procession disappears into the night
    and is forgotten by everyone.

—Spring Thunderstorm in the Night—

It is a severe spring thunderstorm.
In the blue-white light of lightening stinging a steel board,
I stand alone like a stone sculpture.

The long battle is over
And now we are going back down Chang River
    [correct name for Yangtze River] in March;
But not before we had finished burying more than ten comrades
In winter's desolate Yünan Plain [another name for
    Honan Province].
Each of them fought well,
Shouted "Emperor, Banzai," and fell.
Also, those of us who carried them to their graves
In the midst of the raging wind and the cold swirling
    of yellow dirt,
Almost died of total exhaustion.
Our last salute to them was so sorrowful,
Given as it was while we stood on the freshly dug dirt.
Together we had eaten rice grains
    that were laced with pellets of ice,
Had crossed rivers dotted with ice floes,
And, in the very midst of ice storms, had fought our way
    across the mountain ranges
Against the most stubborn of foes.

They had been our friends and our companions on
    the march until today,
And now we have ended up burying them
    —and in soil inside enemy territory!
The spring thunder booms with particular harshness
    throughout tonight's storm,
And in its loud rumblings
I can hear our late comrades' voices.
During these days of rough weather
I often reflect on the dirt we turned in digging those graves.
And remember those whom we left behind in such
    an alien situation.
How many times already—through the empty space
    that now separates them from ourselves—
Have I heard those words that I cannot think of
    as human words!
The sounds are more like gasps, bubbling with blood
    and suggestive of the shedding of blood.
Sad guardian spirits protecting the nation!
As the spring thunder rolls through the night,
Could it be that you are taking up your bayonets again
And calling to us who are moving even farther away?
Some of you had your brains blown away,
While others were shot through the chest.
Just now the memory of your gasping—thick, heavy, and sticky—
    as you were staggering about and trying to shout,
Penetrates my own heart,
And something cold rattles through my forehead.
On a cargo ship and in the wild dark of this night,
A sorrowful history falls from the sky.
Go to your faraway home, spring thunder,
Before the bright daybreak of March arrives.
Carry my friends away—
    and go home, far away.

—Drawing Water—

A girl in bare feet
And with a wild, red rose in her hair
Comes down a hill in the sunset

To draw water for the evening meal.
On the stone pavement,
The girl's feet are pale and soft.
She pads her way to a stream outside the castle,
    to get water for the evening meal.
She scoops up still but sparkling water,
And gazes for a while at the sun set in the horizon.
Over the endless green ocean,
Wondering whether or not her own happiness will disappear.
Earlier today that huge red sun
Had also given her a glimpse of the beauty of May—
A wild pigeon singing on a small willow branch.
She doesn't feel sad when the sun goes down
Because, even as it leaves,
It has promised her tomorrow.
The young girl plants her feet firmly on the ground,
She is going home to the town inside the castle,
Where all business is now in the fading light of sunset,
With her load of beautiful water.

Kiyoshi Katai

Born December 7, 1915. From Nagano Prefecture. Graduated from Tokyo Teachers' College, Department of Literature, in 1940. Conscripted and entered barracks on December 15, 1940. Killed in action on January 17, 1945, on the bank of the Irrawaddy River in Myanmar (Burma). Army sergeant major. He was twenty-nine years old.

[A letter from Central China to his younger sister Sumie and younger brothers, Yasuhiro, Takehiro, and Shigeru]

It is after Higan (the Spring Equinox). A mighty thunderstorm has marked the passing of spring. I trust that you all prayed with utmost respect before our late mother's beloved spirit during Higan (Paramita [note: the designation for Buddhist services performed during the week of the Spring equinox]). My hope is that you will all help each other out and all grow up to be fine people. My own memories of mother are almost unbearable, here in this land of rain. I am glad to hear that our father is doing fine too, but I ask you all to please try your very best not to cause him any worries. As for me, I am very well.

I have passed the Spring Equinox[1]
Listening to the roll of thunders.

Hisao Yamagishi

Born October 26, 1913. From Kanagawa Prefecture. Through Shizuoka Higher School he entered Tokyo Imperial University, Faculty of Engineering, Department of Architecture, in 1937. Conscripted and entered Akabane Engineering Corps, December 1941. Assigned to fight in Manchuria, China, and the Philippines. Died from a combat-related illness, July 28, 1946, at the Second Army Hospital in Soshigaya, Tokyo. Army sub-lieutenant. He was thirty-two years old.

[from the author's diary]

January 11, 1942 Saturday Clear
    We are absolutely not either dogs or cats. We are not animals that only act in response to being beaten. I believe in myself.

July 28, Tuesday Clear
    Old order—new order.
    Am I a man who, fundamentally, belongs to the old order? No, that is not true. Am I a man who is really comfortable living in the new world order? Another negative. Am I a man who lives in the middle of both the old order and the new order by standing with one foot on each?—No again.
    The stars of the sleepless night have disappeared and the glorious morning sun shines and fills every corner. My heart was shaken by a mysterious something—whatever the dream held had somehow wandered away. Last night, I thought back with great fondness over things of long ago. It was good. I really miss my books and want so very much to read

---

[1] [Translators' note: This last is an example of *haiku* (in Japanese, a poem of seventeen syllables arranged in a 5–7–5 syllabic pattern), which aims to convey a flash of understanding through images, and all *haiku* must contain a word that indicates a season.—The structure of the original follows: Ka-mi-na-ri o // ki-ki-te hi-ga-n o // su-go-shi-ke-ri.

again. True. Also I would like to be able to go to the movies again. True.
I have such strong desire for peace. True. It is not a false statement of my
deepest feelings: I am a person with the greatest desire for peace.

—In Northern Manchuria[1]—

The horsetails I picked make me feel nostalgic,
    for it was at just about the same season when
        my sister used to pick them at home

I feel affection and pity for the soldier who is
    being punished and digging dirt,
    because it is his picture while still living on this earth
        [before his imminent death]

Yōichi Yanagida

Born March 5, 1919. From Okayama Prefecture. Through Taihoku Higher
School, he entered Kyoto Imperial University, Faculty of Letters, Department of Asian History, in 1939. Graduated in December 1941. Conscripted
and entered the barracks February 1, 1942, and entered Chiba Army Air
Defense School in May. He was killed in an accident during a tour of duty,
on October 1, 1942, in Kisarazu, Chiba Prefecture. He was twenty-three
years old.

[from *Gakudō-ki (A Record of the Way of Studying),* compiled and
published by Kenjūrō Yanagida, October 1943]

July 12, 1941

    Draftings into the service [*cf.* p. 137] have been very heavy lately.

    And, more than ever, I sense that this is a time of national emergency.
Every second we seem to be on the brink of falling into an abyss. When
will that fatal second arrive? It could be right now. A huge and invisible
storm is brewing, and runs. It runs. And an indeterminate something is
surrounding my body like a whirlpool. It pushes me up to the world of the
unknown. What sort of time are we living in? What on earth is humanity,

---

[1] [Translators' note: These two poems are written in a Japanese verse-form, the *tanka*,
5–7–5, 7–7 syllables.]

history, even the world itself? And who is keeping history in motion? It is like being tossed about in an angry sea. I can hear the wheels of a wagon drawn by phantom horses. I ask again: What is history? What is humanity? And what in the world are they going to do with me?

July 31

July has gone. In the midst of this huge storm that keeps driving away, it is already the third day since the Japanese Army has entered French Indochina. I cannot do anything about the fact that everything is being washed away by a powerful current.

October 16

A physical examination for conscription is scheduled for December, and we are due to enter barracks in February.

It is only to be expected that my heart will become more and more agitated as those dates approach.

I am thinking about going out tomorrow to dig potatoes with Mr. Matsumoto and some others. Perhaps it will change my mood. I would not like it to look as though I am indulging in the pleasures of life, but neither do I wish to be defeated by it. I do not wish to be defeated by anything and everything. I do not wish to be defeated either in life itself or by the invisible temptations of life. To the very end, until death itself, I want to keep and protect my individual human identity. I am also feeling peevish about going out now because it may seem to indicate a sort of defeat. This is the reason for my hesitation. I don't want to be defeated. I don't want to be perceived as being defeated. I want to continue to live my life with strength and integrity, whatever happens. I don't want to be defeated by anyone. I want to continue to live my own life. Regardless of what happens—I do not want to give in to that inner self who, regretfully, would betray me. I do not wish to give in. I want to conquer myself. I want to be victorious in life. I do not want people to say that I gave up on life when faced with certain death. My life has not been a life of compromise, and I do not intend to make it so now. I want to make my life a victorious one as my own life. I want to be victorious over whatever enemy. I don't want to think or be thought of as being defeated by an invisible enemy. To be victorious: this is my whole desire now. And I do not intend to lose. Even when I go to dig potatoes it is not because I am defeated—I am just giving my brain a rest from working on my thesis.

January 29, 1942

I had a picture taken at a Daimaru Department Store and bought some stationery, a service-bag [a bag to carry a seal, a military notebook, and other things essential for life in the service], and some other military items. I also bought a hat.

Professor Miyagi came to visit in the evening. We talked a lot about the military life, and the reconnoitering patrol on the Malaysian front. What is fate? What is death? All these questions were of course nestled close to my heart. I said nothing. I just listened. I do not even think about whether I want to live or die. What significance does it all have anyway? I do not know. All I want to do is to keep looking at the currents of fate —and the currents of history—and, finally, at the true nature of these things.

I was more than ever made to realize just how weak human beings are when they find themselves face to face with fate. All sorts of emotions are boiling up like a sea of fire. Perplexity, sorrows, desires—all sorts of emotions powerfully assail my heart. What am I really? Which one is not me? No, that is not right. All of them are me, the way I am. Something that rises up from an invisible and deep abyss—that is who I am. Only the surface can be seen, just the surface. Then just what is on it?

There is nothing left for me to write. Both my pen and my emotions are swallowed up within the self. Even though love's burning emotion, with the quiet surface, surrounds the house, my emotions do not care to communicate with it. Were that communication to take place my heart would be washed away. I cannot feel anything. But perhaps it is better not to feel anything. Oil must not be added to fire.

What is an emotion? What lies at the bottom of one's emotion? What am I supposed to feel? The only emotion I have is a sense of non-feeling. But what else could there be with which to wrap up an emotion? And what exactly is this non-feeling? It all turns around and back into the self.

Tonight is the last evening. I am not thinking anything. That is my question. My ideal state of mind would be not to expect anything and not to want anything.

Of course there is one last question: What is history?

Tatsuo Watanabe

Born January 4, 1916. From Shizuoka Prefecture. Through Shizuoka Higher School, entered Tokyo Imperial University, Faculty of Jurisprudence, in 1935. Graduated in March 1939. Conscripted and entered the barracks on April 10, 1940, and entered Army Accounting School. Killed in action in

Kyondo, Myanmar (Burma) on April 5, 1945. Army finance officer with the
rank of captain. He was twenty-nine years old.

[First-year draftees' training period]

The variety of rules, laws, procedures, etc., within the Army is based
on so-called *Gunji Tenpan Rei** (Military Affairs Standard Law), and its
main items are as follows: *Guntai Naimu-sho (On Military Internal Affairs);
Sōten (Drill Regulations); Gunjin Chokuyu** (Imperial Instructions on
Soldiers); Rikugun Reishiki Rei (Army Code of Etiquette and Protocol);
Sakusen Yōmu Rei (Code on Primary Strategic Matters); Shageki Kyōhan
(Firing Instructional Examples)*, and so on. Among them those that
invariably follow every stage [of military life] are *Gunjin Chokuyu, Guntai
Naimusho*, and *Rikugun Reishiki Rei*. No matter what particular examination it might be, whether the one given to first-year soldiers at their very
first step into the barracks or the one administered nearly at the end of the
military cadet* training program—soldiers were always tested on those
same three. Therefore, at least some general knowledge of all this material
had to be fairly well absorbed by those entering barracks. It was regrettable
that so many failed to recognize the serious importance of acquiring this
knowledge prior to entering barracks, and, therefore, neglected to study
adequately. Whether or not one had such prior knowledge was of the utmost
importance, such importance that it could in fact control the whole course
of the rest of a man's life. I myself was unaware of how necessary it was to
know all these laws and regulations before coming in, and even though I
had heard about their existence from Mr. Masuda, I still failed to get into
studying the stuff. However, I did at least have *Gunjin Chokuyu* memorized, and this one thing actually decided my fate at the crossroad of my life.
I shall try to give a description of all this in what follows.

The first achievement test was given on the day after I entered
barracks. The very first question was: "Respectfully copy the paragraph on
loyalty in the Imperial Instruction." Examinations on Imperial Instructions
are, in general, extremely difficult, but this particular instruction given to
soldiers is very long—requiring about twenty minutes just to read it
properly. As for the writing style of the text itself, it is so difficult that one
needs to depend on *kana* syllables [as a phonetic reading guide] for the
correct pronunciation; and in a strict examination you have to copy the
original spelling exactly, including the anomalous Japanese cursive style
kana (syllabary), if used in the original; or, to distinguish clearly and
correctly between "koto" in *kana* and "koto" in *kanji* character, or "mono"

in *kana* and "mono" in *kanji* character. It takes an unimaginably great effort to learn all this perfectly. At any rate, in ordinary examinations it is imperative for one to at least memorize the correct phrase. For the first test I would have thought that a minor error—such as an error in character-writing—would be overlooked.

Well, on this exam I was certainly not perfect in character-writing, and I probably made some other minor errors in wording, but somehow I was able to complete the whole thing fairly well. This was the reason for my later being given a passing qualification to be accepted as a military cadet. A close friend of mine and a classmate since my very earliest days of schooling, Mr. Tomimasa, a graduate of Waseda University, failed to qualify for the cadetship despite the fact that he is a very competent person —simply because he could not begin to recite the Imperial Instructions. At the end of June, he was shipped away to the front with the rest of the first-year draftees.

The second question of that examination was: "What is *Gunki* (The Military Drill-Book)?" I treated this as something that should be answered spontaneously and wrote: "Military discipline is comprised of the whole range of military rules and regulations and, along with these, a whole range of other matters in which the same discipline is maintained." This answer was almost completely unacceptable. The correct answer was to have been drawn from General Principle No. 4 of the Artillery (foot soldiers') Code: "*Gunki* is what enables everyone in the entire Army— everywhere on the battlefield, under whatever different circumstances and in the performance of whatever different variety of duties, from generals at the top to the lowest-ranking soldiers below—to follow a specific direction and to act in unison; in fact *Gunki's* strictness dictates the fate of the whole Army."—That is what I should have written. All the examinations which followed were the same: any commonsensical answer that one came up with from out of his own head (which is called *Shibutsu Sōten [Personal Rules]* in the military) was totally unacceptable. The sole requirement was the memorization of each and every word and phrase of the *Sōten (Drill Books),* without mixing *Shibutsu Sōten,* i.e., personal interpretation. This is a long way from the traditional [university] education that stresses the importance of how one is to think but, in a way, if and when you can manage to look at the wording of the drill books as simply the most accurate expression possible of a given ideology, then the demand for and expectation of such exact memorization might not seem unreasonable.

....

Field-artillery men have a very special relationship with their horses, to such an extent that our squad leader explicitly stated that to his way of thinking horses were more important than men. So it should come as no surprise that the most common sources of tears for first-year soldiers have something to do with horses. Twelve cart-horses are required to pull a field gun. At any given time the number of horses allotted to a single company is no less than fifty, since there are four field guns to each company. Our own squad was responsible for the care and feeding of ten horses.

There are a total of six stables, one of which is set aside for sick horses. Then there is a mixed stable, and a stable each for the 1st, 2nd, 3rd, and 4th company—each stable housing nearly a hundred horses. Inside each stable the horses' stalls line both sides of a center corridor, and within those spaces the horses are tied with ropes called *"nehari."*

The pole in each stall carries a wooden tag with the name of the horse and the name of its *"ketsuke"* (the man assigned to take care of that particular horse), along with a tag, "increase" or "decrease," which is the instruction for feeding the horse properly. First-year soldiers are initially taken either by a higher-ranking soldier or their squad leader to familiarize themselves with the stable, and to remember his *ketsuke* horse—the one each man is personally responsible for. Those with slow or dull memories are either threatened or beaten, and in this way their memories are freshened. Once he remembers his horse's name, the new man is forced to memorize the names of every horse in the entire squad: *"Shinjō"* (Deep Emotion), *"Tōdan"* (Eastern Bullet), *"Raiō"* (Thunder Yellow), *'Higaki"* (Sun Persimmon), *'Hazakura'* (Feather Cherry Blossom), *"Taisō"* (Great Frost), and so on. It takes heroic effort to remember them all. Next, a single horse would be selected and brought out into a place where he could be tied up. At this point the draftees are taught to approach the animal, are shown how to lift up a horse's hoof, and how to take care of and groom the horse's body, etc. Horses are very intelligent animals, and they are rather submissive when a person who knows something about them comes close, but when an inexperienced person approaches a horse the animal may become fractious.

We are taught to say "Oora, Oora" soothingly when approaching a horse and, while moving toward him gradually from the front side, to first touch his head, then the neck, and move down to his torso bit by bit. More out of fear of being hooted at by the older soldiers than from any fear of the animal itself, we suck up all our courage and come closer to the horse.

The tools with which we care for them are: a brush, a metal comb, a wooden comb, an iron spatula, a tub for washing hooves, a can of hoof oil, and a few other things. The brush, metal comb, and spatula are kept inside a bag called *"teire bukuro"* (a grooming bag). The method of caring for a horse is as follows: first, you use your hands and knees to prop up the animal's leg and you turn a hoof upward; next the spatula is used to clean the hoof by removing all soil, horse dung, etc.; then the washing tub is filled with water and the hoof rubbed clean with a piece of cloth. When the hoof is almost dry the hoof oil is applied in order to prevent the hooves from becoming too dry and possibly cracking. The sides of hooves must also be cleaned of any dirt and soil and then properly rubbed with the oil. Doing this rubbing the right way is so difficult that I cannot recall how many times I was yelled at by seniors for not applying the oil satisfactorily. Once care of the hooves is accomplished, the legs must be attended to with the brush. Next we wipe the horse's face, comb him shoulders to hips with a metal comb to remove all grime, and then brush that area. The tail and mane must be combed with a wooden comb. All the while senior soldiers are standing by and offering criticisms, saying such things as, "How long does it take you people to wash a horse?" or "You are just hanging onto that horse, not rubbing him!"—This goes on throughout the entire process, with the result that we concentrate completely on every phase of it.

This is the way in which the care and grooming of a horse is accomplished, but before even beginning this routine we must first lead the horse out of his stall and take him to drink water. There is an old saying to the effect that the best gauge of a horse's health is the amount of water he drinks. In other words, water plays such an important part in a horse's health that when he does not drink much it means that something is wrong with him physically. Moreover, if a horse is fed without a sufficient *mizukai* (giving water before food) he develops indigestion and becomes ill with something called colic—and dies suddenly. When one leads one of the horses out to the place designated for them to drink water, the horse's mouth must be made free by his attendant's removing *suiroku*, the bit. After hesitating for a moment, the horse will dip his nose into the water and begin drinking it, making noises like "kyuu, kyuu." While his charge is drinking, the attendant must put his hand to the horse's throat and not forget to count the number of times the gulping sound is made as water passes through. Each of these sounds represents about one *gō* [=0.381 U.S. pint] of water passing through the throat. If more than twenty "gulps" cannot be detected there is something wrong with that horse, and feeding needs to be adjusted accordingly. This water-drinking score is recorded on a chart called, appropriately enough, "the water-feeding chart," and it has to be constantly monitored.

The amount of water an individual horse drinks at a given time varies from more than 2-shō [a shō = 0.477 U.S. gallon] to more than five times that. The more water a horse drinks, the better the horse's health. So long as a horse is drinking healthily the soldier in charge of that horse can relax, but when the horse refuses to drink—signaling his refusal by shaking his head—his attendant has to use every means possible to make him drink again. A favorite trick when dealing with such cases is to float wheat bran on the water. Wheat bran is something horses are really fond of, and in this way many a horse has been fooled into getting back to his normal intake of water.

Once the task of getting the horse to drink water is accomplished, we make the horse secure at another designated place and proceed with the care mentioned above. But even as we go about securing the horses, as if they were waiting for the opportunity, they evacuate their bowels and the amount of manure is literally mountainous. We have to remove it immediately or else the recently—and painstakingly—cleaned hooves would be filled with horse dung, for they move back and forth, stepping on it. While one man leads a horse out of its stall others take the horse's litter or straw bed to the place where it is to be dried out. There is one piece of a stretcher-like thing called *"newara-zuri"* available for two men to use, but others cannot just stand by idly: they have to help by gathering up ropes, and use them to tie the *"newara"* (straw bed) and pull it outside. Such an enormous amount of horse dung and urine is stuck to these straw beds that we are repelled by the filth, even just to touch it, but we are so intimidated by the senior soldiers' iron fists that we do not even pay attention to the fact that our white working-clothes gradually become a yellowish brown from the mess; we even take it out by hand. But it is an enormous job just to carry a straw bed as far as the corridor, because each bed, stamped down and packed on the floor of every stall, is about 50cm (20") thick, and it is warm due to the fact that dung and urine on it have already begun to ferment. The straw beds, which are first moved from the stalls to the corridors, and then from the corridors to the drying area, are lined up in orderly fashion into something like ridges. When all the straw beds of a single squad are spread out, the whole space amounts to about thirty meters square. It is during the grooming period just before lunch, that we move the beds upside down. (This is called *"newara-gaeshi"* [turning the straw beds over]). During the most intense heat of summer the broken pieces of straw and the dung and urine are dried up and distilled into something like dust, and the whole mess flies like sand into every conceivable direction. In no time at all our eyes, noses, and mouth, as well as our work-clothes, become blackened with this baptism of dust. The perspiration runs down in a stream that traces out several streaks over our dirty faces. Without any rest from the heavy labor, our dead-tired bodies sag like pieces of rug, our mouths feel sandy, and we get sick. Each of these tasks—whether it be carrying the straw beds out or turning them over—is accomplished by having one squad compete against another, and the members of the slower squad must expect blows from the senior soldiers' iron fists.

When we have finished with all the outside work on the horses, the special private who has been put in charge for the week shouts the command to "Stop grooming!" No sooner is this command heard by the soldiers than the horses respond with a loud, collective neigh—"Hee heen"—and begin pawing with their front hooves. It seems almost certain that these animals understand our human language. Once the command has been given, we untie the horses from the place where they are secured and bring them inside the stalls. Before they are brought in the food bins which we call *"shokusō"* have already been filled with oats, chopped straw, and a mixture of table salt and water. Fresh hay stocks are placed in the stalls at a higher level. As soon as a horse is brought into his own space, and even though he is still wearing his bridle, he sticks his head into the food bin and starts eating hungrily. At this point we remove the *"suiroku"* (bridle) while verbally scolding the horse, we attach a "nehari" rope to him, and very quickly slip by his side to get out of the stall. Horses do not like any person to get close to them while they are eating, and they may kick or bite anyone who does. You have to be extremely careful when you walk by a horse while he is feeding. Once the horse is in his stall all that is left to do is to hang the bridle and grooming bag on the post provided, and then clean the corridor outside. This completes the caring and grooming process; then we all group up into an orderly line in front of the stable, and return to the company while singing military marches.

The stable staff is comprised of the special private who is assigned to the duty for that particular week, the regular day-staff men, those assigned to the nighttime duty, and others. The entire staff pays close attention to the cleanliness of the stalls, the horses' health, and so on—but a high percentage of them are genuinely rough men (frequently enough drawn from the ranks of those special privates of the drivers' squad whom I have mentioned earlier). The first-year soldiers are terrified, almost literally scared to death all the time because they never know when a raw bamboo stick or a whip might come flying their way. They would gladly do almost anything, would welcome helping out with just about any other job, if they did not have to go to the stables. There are three main jobs available which can free the men from stable-duty: the person assigned during any given week to look after the squad leader; those sent out to help out with the officers in training; and the group delegated to work in the kitchen. All of these jobs are also very grueling, but the men who get them are all very grateful for having been saved from the stables. In addition to these more or less regular substitution assignments there are a few others, such as: temporary assignment at headquarters, threshing wheat, storing ammunition, assisting the veterinarians—all of these alternative jobs are very warmly welcomed.

As the squad leader warned us in his opening talk when we first arrived, our training was to have been completed within such a short time —just two months—that we would have to work at full tilt the whole way. Indeed, it is such a busy life that there is no free time whatsoever—not a single moment—between getting-up in the morning and the going-to-bed time at night.

Two or three days after entering the barracks we were assigned to a *"sen-yū"* (literally, a "war- or battlefield friend") [this is a variation on the Americans' so-called "buddy system"]. This is a system whereby one or two first-year soldiers are assigned to look after a veteran: This relationship between the older soldier and the new man or men is called *"sen-yū."* The *raison d'être* for establishing this system was the opportunity it provided for veteran soldiers to teach and generally supervise new ones; conversely, the first-year soldiers would attend to their senior colleagues by doing different kinds of work for them. For this system to work ideally, those men who were in a position to exert a degree of real leadership through their training programs would do so, and with some sympathetic understanding, occasionally even to the point of offering *real* help to the less experienced men. The end result of all this, again from an ideal standpoint, would be that something like a military family would be formed; but in reality the fact is that it was not working out very well at all. Among the veterans there are, to be sure, some kind men who, whether physically present or not, would do their utmost to protect the junior in the best tradition of *sen-yū*, and would not allow any of the other older soldiers to lay a hand on them; unfortunately, however, not everyone was like that. On the contrary, there are many more than a few veterans who would perpetuate the abuse, particularly of their own junior *sen-yū*.

Again, ideally, it would be extremely advantageous for one of these new men to enjoy a *sen-yū*-relationship with an older colleague; but if a recent recruit is unlucky enough to get someone, for example, who has just become a first-class private, it would result in nothing at all positive —would indeed result in nothing but a great deal of discomfort. The *sen-yū* to whom I was assigned in the beginning was a physically small private first-class, a barber from Nakaizumi named Yutaka Mitsuoka. He was a kind man, but he could not be of much help at critical times simply because he was a first-class private.

Immediately following completion of the evening meal the first-year soldiers' daily schedule called for attending to weapons and uniforms. First of all, one's bayonet as well as that of his *sen-yū* has to be cleaned thoroughly. Once every particle of dust is removed from the bayonets we go on to the next task, performed just as thoroughly, of cleaning model-38 machine guns [single-loader, created for the Army in the 38th year of Meiji, 1905] and then treating them with a special oil called spindle oil, and when all that is finished, it is time to take care of both the long dress boots and the combat boots as well; then follows the polishing of spurs, bridles, chains, etc., etc. It usually takes about one hour to complete these tasks.

After a roll call the equipment and weapons which we have worked so hard over—even to the point of cutting into time we could have used to take a bath and/or pay a visit to the canteen—are inspected. We are told each and every time that our work is unsatisfactory, and then we receive all sorts of excruciatingly painful punishment.

....

On April 20th, I experienced the inspection of horses for the first time. These inspections are a constant part of the field-artillery squad's routine. Senior soldiers, squad leaders, and first-year soldiers all work incredibly hard in order to achieve a high score. From a certain point a week or so before the day of the inspection, the length of time devoted to caring for the horses and grooming them becomes longer—and it is demanded that we put our backs into the work. The focus of any inspection, and something that is taken quite seriously, has to do with the condition of the animals' hooves; of special concern is an area inside the surface of a hoof which can easily become infected or even decompose if it is not kept absolutely clean. This condition of infection/ decomposition must constantly be guarded against; or, if once a horse gets it, no pains can be spared in curing it before the time of inspection. Any squad which is found to have a horse that is afflicted with this problem is seriously dishonored; as a result, the squad leader and the other veterans become so nervous that they erupt into shouting at and condemning the *"ketsuke"* soldiers assigned to that particular animal. Nourishment is one of the items slated for the inspection but, since a deficiency in this area is one of those things that cannot be covered over in a hurry, the squad leader cannot complain much about it even if a grade of B or C is handed down. The grade for grooming is decided upon by the inspectors' dividing and checking the hair in a horse's mane or tail. There must not be any dirt or grime in these areas; to make certain that there is not we wash all the horses with laundry soap, even though this would normally be considered a violation of the rules. The squad with the most horses found to be excellent in all three categories—nourishment, good grooming, and the proper maintenance of hooves—receives the greatest honor. And this is why, in order to keep the horses in absolutely tip-top condition, the physical labor undertaken by the first-year soldiers and the pain they must endure are far beyond what one would ever imagine.

The procedure for the inspection of horses is as follows: we bring out the horses whose grooming is completed and line them up in the order in which they appear in the registration book; put a leather *suiroku* (halter) on the horse and take him to a white-ash square chalked onto the ground in front of the inspection officer. At this point the horse's *ketsuke* soldier, legs spread wide apart, takes up a position in front of his charge, and while holding the two halter-straps extending from either side of the horse's head, he calls out the horse's name in a loud voice and then he just as loudly lists the horse's habits.—For example: "Higaki, has a tendency to bite, to kick, and to rear backward."

At the first inspection station, the hooves are examined by having an assistant raise one of the horse's legs and show the hoof. Nourishment and grooming are checked at the second station and, at the third, the horse's performance capability is exhibited by having his handler pull him along at a canter. An order may be given to stop the horse suddenly in mid-canter and, in case this should in fact occur, an assistant is made available to the handler. But this assistant is often kicked, and sometimes seriously injured, so those who are eligible to become assistants live in dread of the assignment.

The color of a horse's coat may be dear-fur (bay), flue-fur (gray), or horse-chestnut fur (chestnut): I have learned that the more purely white horses—whose coats are called moon-fur—are not desirable for military service because they provide such good targets for the enemy.

Notes

*   *Gunjin Tenpan Rei:* In the Army, there is a specific set of *Sōten* (Drill Regulations) for each branch of the Army, e.g., *Hohei Sōten* (for infantry), and *Kihei Sōten* (for cavalry). These manuals described both the methods of fighting and the principles behind them, as well as the military's training system in general. There were also *Kyōhan* (Instructional Illustrations) for each and every subject area, such as *Kenjutsu Kyōhan* for Japanese fencing training, and *Taisō Kyōhan* for physical training. In addition there are *Sakusen Yōmu Rei* (Code on Primary Affairs of Strategy) for the entire Army, and *Guntai Naimu Rei* (Code on Military Internal Affairs).—All of these are collectively called *Tenpan Rei.*

*   *Gunjin Chokuyu* (Imperial Instructions on Soldiers): It was issued in 1882 (15th year of Meiji), and became the most important of all the *Sōten* for the Japanese Imperial Army. It began with "Our nation's Army is always under the Emperor, . . ." and it describes the history and the function of the Imperial Military under the Emperor as Supreme Commander. Then it goes on to out-line the history of the Army. The following sentence was the foundation for the absolute obedience required in the Army:

"When a lower ranking soldier receives an order from one of a higher rank, the former must consider the order as in fact received directly from myself, the Emperor."

Then there were the five articles which begin with: "1. The loyalty to the Emperor is the leading principle of all military men."—Loyalty, courtesy, courage, fidelity, and commitment to a simple life were to be respectfully repledged at each and every morning and evening's roll-call time. There was also one particular sentence which directly related the emperor and every individual member of his army: "I am the supreme commander of all of you soldiers. I therefore rely upon you as my trusted retainers, and you should look up to me as your head."—This was later thought to be the basis for the independent authority of the commander-in-chief. Regarding the spirit of loyalty, moreover, it was stated in the *Gunjin Chokuyu* that "One must be prepared for *gi* (duties) heavier than mountains, and death should be thought of as a lighter thing than a duck's feather.—Do not violate that honor and make any mistake that would incur disgrace."

When taken together with the *Gunjin Chokuyu*, the teachings included in the *Senjin-kun* (The Field Service Code, issued in January 1941) actually forced people to commit suicide rather than to be captured, and were therefore the cause of such tragedies as the Okinawa civilians' group suicide, that of "Banzai cliff" on Saipan, and many others.—This code contained the lines: "Never bring upon yourselves the dishonor of being captured alive, and never leave behind any disgraceful name after death."

*   *Kanbu Kōho-sei* (the rank of officer cadet) and the means to avoiding it: In the Army, special privileges were available to those young men who had already graduated from institutions of higher learning. They could volunteer to go through the cadet officer process and become either officers (A-category) or sub-officers (B-category). As the theater of war broadened, however, what had been a voluntary system virtually became an obligatory one. Nevertheless, a small number of student-soldiers purposely managed, either by refusing to take the examination for the cadet program or by deliberately choosing to fail it, to avoid this "special privilege," and by so doing they remained in the position of lower-ranking soldiers. There were actually two different sources of motivation behind individuals' refusals to become cadets. In the first place were the cases of those young men who had serious questions about the war itself and who consciously concentrated on avoiding any active role as leaders in its prosecution. Then there were others. Because the privilege of becoming cadets was coordinately linked to a longer period of military service, and also to the probability of being killed in action (which was much higher for the lower-ranking officers than soldiers), they simply made their own futures—their lives—the first priority. Without necessarily having any clear ideas about war, such men of course did not respond spontaneously to what others seemed to regard as the nation-at-large's more or less natural call to arms. Insofar as the Navy was concerned, those who had graduated from institutions of higher learning, i.e., higher schools, colleges, and *daigaku yoka* (preparatory divisions of universities), could volunteer to become *yobi-gakusei* (Reserve Students). In this program they were given "special privileges" whereby they could be commissioned as Naval Reserve Ensigns without having to pass through the intermediate stages of being sailors or petty officers.

Gorō Fukunaka

Born May 20, 1916. From Chiba Prefecture. Through the Waseda University's Second Higher School, he advanced to Waseda University, Faculty of Political Science and Economics, 1939. Conscripted and entered the barracks, January 10, 1941. Killed in action on Bougainville, the largest of the Solomon Islands, on February 10, 1945. He was twenty-eight years old.

February 1, 1941

Dear Mr. Ōkanda:

I am so deeply touched by your many letters. Now at last, twenty days after entering the service, I have my first chance to write to you.

Perhaps, since you have had no military experience, you might find this hard to believe, but we first-year draftees have absolutely no time to ourselves—not a single second from the time we get up in the morning until "Lights out" at 9:30 p.m. Of course there is no time whatever for study.

For someone who hated the military training classes as much as I did, even though it was only two hours a week, in just one week things got so bad in general and the training was so absolutely harsh that I was about to die right there, but, I feel more like a human being under such training nowadays. What does this tell you? The military is many, many more times a terrible [the author's original usage] place than I ever expected. Ultimately, one year of military life will suck the humanity out of anyone and everyone. The second-year soldiers treat us draftees like slaves—no, more as though we were machines—and their sole aim in life seems to consist in subjecting us to various forms of pain and abuse. I was forced to participate in various forms of barracks "games," such as the train-game, and the heavy bomber game [see note on Naimu-han, p. 117] that I had previously only heard about through rumor, and every night the groaning sounds of leather footwear can be heard. One of the draftees was cut so badly with a sword-sheath that he had to take four stitches and be hospitalized as well. Those with rank as low as corporal bear themselves almost like gods.

The *"Ra"*[1]-Company, to which I belong, is a horse company and, because our work also involves handling anti-aircraft machine guns, taking care of the horses is quite a job. The current second-year soldiers entered the service on February 1st of last year, but for a full year they were never allowed to go out; finally, the first Sunday after we came in, they were

---

[1] *Ra* is the forty-first of the Japanese *kana* alphabet.

allowed to enjoy the fresh air of the outside world. Among the fifty-three first-year draftees in our company, as many as twenty-one of us hold the qualification for military cadet. In fact 250 of us, about half of our entire battalion of five hundred first-year men, have that qualification. I would say that all this is certainly due to the fact that we are a technical corps. Even before they entered barracks, about ten of the twenty-one qualified men in our company had already been studying the required texts. One especially keen one, as soon as he learned that he was going to be in Suzuki Company, learned all that he could about anti-aircraft machine guns and had memorized more than some three hundred technical terms. They often get us cadet candidates off to ourselves and give us training tests, but I always suffer a miserable defeat.

I found out that all twenty-one of them except four of us had already thoroughly studied the books that I saw at the bookstore with you before entering the barracks. These four (I am one of them) have had the books sent to us and we are now trying as hard as we possibly can and are determined to pass the test for becoming military cadets. I get up quietly in the middle of the night and study in the toilet, so I can only sleep for about four hours every night. But, despite all this, I am afraid that it is impossible to compete with those who came already prepared. Because of the horses, our company has a heavy handicap compared to the others, because caring for these horses requires so much time; therefore, out of the dozen of our men who were qualified to take the test last year, only two passed. Mr. Ōkanda, now I have to start again writing to you from a toilet. We were chased out of the auditorium at 10:30 p.m. and sent to bed. Actually it was just starting today that we were allowed to stay up until 10:30 p.m. to study in the auditorium. That is why I started to write to you from there, but 10:30 came right in the middle of this letter—so then I began to continue writing in the toilet. I feel rather hopeless about passing the military cadet test. I do not think that I can compete with those who have completely mastered the book, and the collection of questions. I heard that the examination will be administered in early April.

Even a *sen-yū* [*cf.* p. 54, or "military friend"] who I thought was O.K. has begun to show his true nature. We are being beaten, on the average, twice a day. There is not a single soul in the barracks who is like a human being. I even feel that I myself am getting away from being a human being. As to letters, except for the three I wrote to my uncle the night I entered barracks, I wrote one apiece to Mr. Shimizu, my mother, and to my older brother. I am very much concerned about my younger brother in connection with the higher school, but there is absolutely no time to write him. I wrote to my older brother that I would enjoy a visit from him. Since they are not all that strict about visiting times, if it were a Sunday we could talk with each other for about three hours. On the Sunday, four days ago, my elder brother came to see me. When I wrote to my mother, also from the toilet the previous Sunday, I could not stop my tears from falling. I wrote to her that I was doing fine and working hard, but the fact is that my feelings are as miserable as those of a dead person. If a second-year soldier ever finds out that I wrote this kind of a letter, I will probably be killed. As for all the letters from outsiders, their names are duly recorded.

Sorry for writing all about myself but, at any rate, and please, Mr. Ōkanda, stay well and strong. Please tell Taizō also to stick it out. I have received letters from some fourteen or fifteen friends, but there was no time for writing replies. If you should see Mr. Ishii, please say hello. I received a letter from him also.

Well, then, I am going to excuse myself.

Last, but not least, please extend my best to my uncle and aunt [i.e., your parents].

Gorō

To Big Brother[2] Keijirō

Tadashi Kawashima

Born January 17, 1916. From Saitama Prefecture. Through the Preparatory Division, he entered Tokyo University of Agriculture, Department of Agriculture, in 1937. Graduated in 1940. Conscripted and entered the barracks, December 1, 1940, and transferred to the Northern China Garrison, China. Suffered injuries in action, January 30, 1945, in Chianghsi Province, China. Died on February 3, 1945. Army lieutenant. He was twenty-nine years old.

January 31, 1943   Clear

At 1:30 in the middle of the night, headquarters called to send us on a punitive expedition at 5:30 a.m.—A hike in the cold and dark on what remains of the snow.

One soldier from Nakazawa Company hit a Chinese civilian with a rock. Full of blood and with his skull smashed, the man fell to the ground.

---

[2] The writing indicates that the uncle and aunt in this case are one of the author's parent's older siblings and his/her spouse. That makes Keijirō an older cousin of the author, hence he addressed him with an honorific of *taikei* ("big brother"), though this form of honorific may also be used among close friends to indicate respect, with either a first name or a surname.

The soldier kicked him as he lay there, and then used another stone. I could not stand watching that. But the officers of Nakazawa company were there too, taking it all in coldly and without emotion. Apparently it had all been done by order of Sublieutenant Takagi. A particularly heartless man! When I think about what happened to that innocent man I ask myself why I did not try to come to his aid, even though it would have been too late and a useless effort. When I think like that, a wave of self-reproach hits me. A woman who must have been his wife was weeping as she held on tightly to the bleeding man. But he didn't die! In fact, as soon as the troop moved off, he got up and, supported by his wife, plodded away very slowly.

I would never, ever, allow any child of mine to be a soldier—anything but a soldier! . . . Peace! World peace is the very highest priority.

If we, Japan, should lose this war, we will be meeting the same fate at the hands of our enemies. So, absolutely and if nothing else, we must never lose the war.

February 10, Clear

An instruction has come down from Division Headquarters "On winning the hearts of the local population." Absolutely. This is something long overdue, since it is impossible to control the local residents by arrogance and scare-tactics alone. It is in fact a wonder that as yet no revolt has taken place as a result of the atrocities which the garrison has perpetrated in the past.

Perhaps this is no more than what was to have been expected because, after all, the whole China Incident [*cf.* p. 10] is a war started in order to fuel the Army's self-serving ambition.

One incident occurred where some twenty members of two regiments, officers included, were murdered by village people. It seems that at last what one was wondering about not happening *has* happened.

July 19, Clear

The differences between reserve officers and officers on active duty remind me of the child protagonist in *Shuju no Kotoba (Words of a Man of No Insight)*, by Ryūnosuke Akutagawa. The work of Mr. Active Duty is characterized by extreme deficiencies on his part in planning and preparation.

Their simplistic guilelessness is indeed like that of children.

I really feel for the pains those [reserve] officers assigned to serve under such a commander must endure.

Jirō Shinozaki

Born March 2, 1910. From Nara Prefecture. Through the Preparatory
Division, advanced to Dōshisha University, Faculty of Letters, Department
of English Literature, in 1931. Graduated in 1935. Conscripted in April 1938
as a replacement soldier, and sent to the battlefield in central China.
Discharged in May 1940, only to be reconscripted in August 1941. Killed
in action, in Eastern New Guinea, which was a territory of Great Britain at
that time, on January 18, 1944. Army corporal. He was thirty-three years old.

September 25, 1938
   From all the letters I've received from my wife so far it seems clear
that an end has come at last to the matter I have hopefully awaited with a
warm glow in my heart. The fact is that my wife is not pregnant. And, on
the very brink of being hurled into war, I find myself without the hope of
a child who would enable this body and soul of mine to live on forever. The
cold weather has arrived here on the continent much earlier than it would
have in Japan, and it is already full-fledged autumn in China. With merely
a rush-mat to sleep on it is chilly enough; I spent a lonely and sleepless
night thinking sentimentally about all these sorts of things.

[A letter addressed to his wife, Hisako, dated March 15, 1939]

   Conditions are apparently worsening here in occupied city N, as a
terrorist fifth column continues to be very active. They must be working in
consort with the terrorist elements in Shanghai.
   The trouble is not confined to the city itself, for even in the outlying
areas our people are being forced to carry out large-scale punitive expe-
ditions. I have some bad news to relate today. My old company, Takemura
Company (the company that I belonged to when I first disembarked), is
located in a mountain village some fifteen miles east of the city, but it
suddenly ran into the whole main force of the enemy. Takemura Company
immediately went into action but, after two days and three nights of
pursuing the enemy, there were said to have been many, too many, either
dead or missing in action. Headquarters has confirmed that there were
twenty casualties just from my old company alone. Without giving much
thought to what I was doing, I couldn't help putting my head down to pray
in silence. Other companies have also suffered considerably, and the entire
battalion is now in an irreparably damaged condition. Please pray night and
day before the Buddhist tablet of the deceased [note: a reference to the
household Buddhist altar which most Japanese families maintain in order

to pay respect to their departed ancestors] for the souls of those killed in battle. They had been conscripted into the war just as I was, and I spent an entire day—my heart filled with a million mixed thoughts of sadness and mourning—asking myself whether or not it was all right for me to be here at headquarters, and safe—I feel so sorry and guilty. So vivid and extreme were my painful feelings as I experienced this grief over lost battlefield friends and the tragedy of war, that I had to express my sorrow and beg for forgiveness. However, now I can only think quietly of my heavy responsibilities as a member of the headquarters staff. Clenching my teeth all the while, I will do my very best single-mindedly to carry on with the intelligence work. Tonight we are blessed with a beautiful moon. For one who has been drafted into this war so far away from home, . . . the comrades' misfortune. . . . And what is to become of me? If . . . ! . . . and of my wife . . . ? I really would like her to be mine for life, and forever. I wonder if I am being selfish to want that? I'm sorry. I was just talking to the moon.

[A letter to his father, dated October 1, 1939]

The torrid heat of summer has left us and the coolness of autumn is now returning to the continent. Fortunately I am blessed with good health and doing my very best at my job. Just now I am feeling rather emotional—sentimental, and also deeply touched—as I look out the window at Mt. XX, and at what is left of the site of the several severe battles that were fought at the time of the capture of XXX Gate. Now that I have joined the Sacred War against Chiang Kai-shek, who has been gnawing away at China's long tradition of some three thousand years, I imagine that my seniors who have now passed on would be smiling as they watch the growth of the New Japan.

It is remarkable how security has been restored to this city. The difference between now and a year ago, when I first landed here, is as that between light and darkness. My heart is full of deep emotion. Even our civilian compatriots who reside here are practically swaggering, and just the other day they were conducting an anti-British demonstration march inside the city. Here at headquarters, along with policing and punitive actions, I am working very hard at public relations and pacification, trying to win the people over by taking advantage of this period when the enemy seem to have lost their fighting spirit: I am very busy but enjoying my special task of collecting and distributing propaganda leaflets and other materials. In fact, I have just finished proofreading a leaflet that we plan to spread around an area where guerilla activities have been observed, and packed it ready for shipment. I am also in charge of all the newspaper business.

Although I may not be fully up to the task, I am serving the country as best I can, and am betting my own life on that service.

According to the information that I have received, the war news seems to be quite positive, and the task of pacification and maintenance of this Chiangnan [an area on the south bank of Chang River] battle line will be completed in the near future. In contrast to the return of public peace, I constantly feel sad about the ordinary good citizens of China. They are really suffering from the huge drop in the value of *fapi* notes (the paper money of Jewish lineage commonly used by the local people) [note: the paper money, which was China's legal tender—issued in 1935 as part of the Chiang Kai-shek Government's currency reform, a reform carried out with the support of Great Britain], which brought down the value of their money and caused them terrible hardships. This whole situation was obviously the result of a terribly wrong foreign policy on Great Britain's part to colonize China and its currency system, a policy which was put in place concurrently with the Chiang government's wrong-headed policy of exporting silver. So far as the masses are concerned, it would only be natural for them to do their best to retain the value of their legal tender *fapi* notes, and trust the Chiang Government in order to protect their own lives as well as the economy. In this regard, their plight is a direct result of the foreign policies of Chiang's Nationalist Party, the policy that appeared to be wise at first but, as it turned out, had a seriously wrong side, that is, the side which once the pro-Communist policy was adapted at the Hsian Incident [the reference is to an incident which took place in December 1936, when what was then the Northeastern Army under Chiang Hsüeh-liang, quartered at the time in Hsian, detained Chiang Kai-shek, and resulted in the formation of a joint war front against the Japanese on the parts of the Communist Party and Chiang's Nationalist Party] considerably helped the Comintern [the Communist Third International] to spread Communism. In this sense, the Nationalists' attempt to use the Communist Party was converted into themselves being used by the guerrillas. And the end result was today's condition, one in which they are unable to control the situation and have become victims of their own poor planning. This is what has created the current situation, and this is what I confronted when I arrived in China. I am more surprised than ever at the strength and the deep-rootedness of anti-Japanese sentiment, and also by how powerful the economic assistance and the ambition of so-called "outside" nations are. I think that furnishing the basic groundwork for forming an organization which could facilitate cooperation between China and Japan would nowadays be the most crucial issue. Since Germany and the Soviet Union have recently concluded a non-aggression pact, Japan, more than ever, will be more or less on her own.

[A letter to his wife, Hisako, dated March 31, 1942]

Spring has come to northern Korea. Now that I am blessed with a child, the most precious fruit of our beautiful love, I feel entirely different from when I was sent to the battlefield in central China for the first time. Even though we are so far apart, with mountains and the ocean between us, I have never before experienced such heartwarming feelings. While I am talking to you about how you might go about cultivating this little joint creation of heaven and earth, just remember how I have always told you that it is a life's work and that it requires self-cultivation on both our parts. I am also thinking how truly blessed I am about my good fortune in being able to feel so much beauty and pleasure about you back home.

I recently read an article in the paper which told of how the Ministry of Education is dropping English-language courses from middle schools' curricula, and this led me to feel a strong animosity toward the national government. I am quite certain that in America the study of things Japanese has increased tremendously since the outbreak of war between the two countries. I would think that anyone hoping to win out over an enemy would want to get to know that enemy very well. I would like to raise my voice and to say very loudly that now is precisely the time when the study of English should become more widespread—let the general population become better acquainted than ever with the enemy nation!

Back at the time when I was working actively in the press corps in central China, I used to underline and translate whatever articles in the English-language papers I considered particularly important. Every day I would present that material to the Chief of Staff, and even then I used to wish that those responsible for the conduct of the war had been able to absorb this sort of knowledge all by themselves. But now, as I face this same sort of thing all over again, I am feeling more keenly than ever about it—I feel absolutely sad and alone.

[A letter to his wife, Hisako, dated Shiwasu (end of the year) 1942]

I am ready to leave for the war zone in the south, where things are going worse for us every day. Perhaps it is only to be expected of someone who has been awaiting these orders for some time now, but as I face the present reality I realize more than ever that I am nothing more than an ordinary draftee. No, I may be even less than that. I close my eyes . . . what comes to my mind is my lovely child, wife, father, mother, younger sisters, and others. I cannot ever forget your face—and your eyes—the night before I left home for war when you said "Please don't make me a widow!" As a human being, as Jirō, I have the zeal and the determination to build up our family and to reach the goals we originally set; but now I find myself in the middle of this predicament of wearing a military uniform. But you and everything about you are deeply engraved in my heart. Whenever I have a chance, what always comes to my mind is "everything" of you. I want to do this and that, I must do this and that, I want to do at least that, I want to do much more that sort of thing, and so on—and there are so many hopes to realize and such high ideals to live up to, and perhaps I'm even more avaricious than you are when it comes to living and life. My life would have no meaning if I could not contribute to our society fully, to my heart's content, in a way or ways that are appropriate with whatever scholarly learning I have managed to acquire over these many years—however shallow that learning might still be—and with whatever personal character I have been able to build up over the same period. It pains me deeply that I am unable to put my desires to work, so very deeply that at times I am barely able to hold still.

However, now under the seriousness of the war situation, all of that has to be shelved for the present in favor of a military uniform filled with only the purest of thoughts of the nation.—With the fate of life and death.

Now that it has fought down normal human emotions and been purified by patriotism, my heart has seemingly been elevated to a certain height. Or, is it that by fighting with so many pains in my heart, I am fooling my heart in the end? No, I don't want to think that way. I simply want to think that I have won over all the struggles of the heart, and that it is a genuinely patriotic heart.

The one and only thing that I request of you is that, transcending the matter of my life and death, you will always live, and live in the beauty of both body and intelligent mind and amid the swirl of the same deep emotions we shared at the time of our wedding. By cultivating all our sweet memories in our hearts, if and when the day comes when I return home alive, then those new deep emotions will be the greatest of our lives. They will be even much deeper than what we experienced the last time of the China Incident. For me to pray for the safety of the home I left behind is the same thing as praying for the safety of you and our child, and is also a restatement of my love and attachment to you and Katsuko—aside from my endless gratitude, of course, for the parents who brought me up to be the way I am.

My greatest happiness in all this wide world is to have you as my wonderful companion and Katsuko as my beloved child. I have always said that you are a woman of great common sense, and possessed of perfect beauty and health besides, but it is not nearly that simple. Your willingness to share so completely in my way of looking at things and your graceful yielding toward my ideals makes you nothing less than my heart's sun. Every day in every way everything about you—that is, your looks, nature, and personality and all the rest, that are continuously being shaped, make you more beautiful than anything else that exists, and the object of my worship. I cannot help thinking that nothing in the world is comparable to you. Although this military business has kept us so far apart against our wills, at least you have Katsuko at your side. There are bound to be some difficult matters and some pain, but please stay strong and you will enjoy most of the things about her growing up.

I am leaving for the south with full confidence in my survival. Please stay the way you are. I wish that your spirit and your health remain the way they are now. I want you to live with passion in quietness, and also to allow the quality of quiet to pervade passion. I can see your face before me now. Your dark and passionate eyes, your tightly closed lips at once so lovely and so dignified, your beautiful breasts—this image of you never leaves my mind.

But I must set aside what some would consider such unmanly thoughts.

No more anxiety about the family back home, not at all! Also, I am in fine physical shape. Having thrown myself into the pre-operations training, I can say that I am ready to leave for the land where coconut trees grow. This is truly a matter of deep satisfaction to a man and I am determined to do honor to my emperor's wishes. A painful determination. . . .

I am going into battle trusting my fate to passing time. "*Nin-un mu-sa!* (Trust everything to fate, and not upon human action!)" These were the words my father used to say so often.

Without a doubt about our nation's strength, I leave for the battle-field as one of the many men who are going to win this great war for the Emperor.

PART
II

—The Period of the Asia-Pacific War—

Japan, already stuck and gasping in the Chinese quagmire, and relying on Germany and Italy's better positioning—although there was no hope of ultimate victory—on the European front, jumped into the Pacific War on December 8 [i.e., December 7, U.S. time], 1941, with a surprise landing in Kota Bharu on the Malay Peninsula, and the surprise attack on Pearl Harbor one hour later.

All this took place under the rubric of advocating the "Greater Asia Co-Prosperity Sphere," and the war was called the "Great Asia War." As the front expanded, Japan's war situation worsened, and during the last phase of the war this deterioration was the reason for many young people being killed in vain under such policies as "student mobilization" and the deployment of special attack forces.

Setsuzō Hirai

Born January 2, 1918. From Mie Prefecture. Through Himeji Higher School, entered Tokyo Imperial University, Faculty of Jurisprudence. Graduated in March 1941, and he was appointed as a judicial officer on probation [or probationary judge], Ministry of Justice. Entered the Navy Accounting School April 15, 1941. Killed in action near Buna, New Guinea, September 5, 1942. Navy finance officer with the rank of lieutenant. He was twenty-four years old.

[From his diary during the period when he was on
board the light cruiser *Yura*]

February 28, 1942

It is already the last day of the month. Very boring days—not only today but every day lately. We have nothing to do but to gaze at the sea, the skies, and the ship-charts.

It seems that I have learned lately the art of passing hours gazing at clouds and spending whole days watching the sea. When I chat with simple-minded people, they don't seem to have anything to talk about except getting drunk. I tried to discuss the future of East Asia with the chief engineer. Apparently they have no interest in anything except conquering. They only think of painting all in red [i.e., to make a territory of Japan]. How could we ever call this war a "sacred war"?

I have a headache today. Perhaps I caught a cold. At any rate, how wonderful it will be if I could deny everything and attain the philosophy of life which posits absolute nothingness. So far as mankind in general is concerned, are the social groups which we refer to as nations really inevitable developments, or are they not rather the haphazard products of history?

March 1

Although we completed the process of entering the anchorage at 1:30 a.m., I could sleep only an hour or so last night on a deck without a roof, because the enemy's air attacks, starting the night before, became so severe. Since very early in the morning, the enemy airplanes frequently came to attack us again throughout the morning. I would think that the landing parties must also have suffered considerable damage. The blood of our precious compatriots is being shed here too. The sacrifice of individuals is viewed with a surprisingly cold eye in light of the fact that it is being made for the survival of a nation, or rather, the survival of several million Japanese people. But among them, there must be many wives and children who are already on the street with no place to go, because their husbands, fathers, and brothers were conscripted and sent to the war front. Should the nation be so completely blind and unconcerned about those personal sacrifices? Is the current social policy sufficient the way it is?

In the early evening, we were subjected to a torpedo attack for the second time. The first one was February 11th. Fortunately, it passed through in front of the ship, barely missing, and caused no damage. We dropped depth bombs [a bomb that explodes at a certain depth in water, designed for use against a submarine], and the destroyers, *Nagatsuki* and *Minazuki*, assisted us. ....

Tokutarō Tazaka

Born April 29, 1917. From Hiroshima Prefecture. He entered Nihon University, Medical College, in 1937. Graduated in December 1941. Conscripted and entered the barracks January 26, 1942. Killed in action at Bangka Straight, southeast of Sumatra, as his ship went down, June 8, 1945. Army medical officer, lieutenant. He was twenty-eight years old.

[A letter to Miss Chizuko Okamoto,
— sent from the 67th Unit, Eastern Section]

April 9, 1942

I apologize for communicating with you most recently only by postcard, but it is extremely difficult for those of us who live in the barracks to mail a letter like this unless we get an opportunity to go out.

The one thought that never leaves my mind, day or night, concerns you. My feelings toward you have become even stronger since I entered the service. My desire to be with you and to talk with you is so painfully strong that perhaps it even exceeds your own. My concern for your physical well-being is as deep as the way I feel about my own, and it is especially so when we have to be apart like this.

For a man, his sense of responsibility for his family, and also partly something like his male ego and ambition, all combine and assert themselves in the public phases of his life. That is the arena where a violent battle, though without sparks, is waged constantly. This thought of mine that I have to be placed in that predicament from now on is felt with a special keenness when I think of my responsibility toward you.

It would be the happiest of all possible lives, a dream life, if I could lead a righteous and humble existence as a small-town doctor, a friend to the sick and the poor and screened from the public-at-large, while protecting my little family—you and myself—and our immediate families, but . . .

In the midst of this Great East Asia War [*cf.* p.63], which calls for the entire nation to direct every effort toward the one goal, I may be the only officer who writes and reflects on this sort of thing; but it must be the relationship between the two of us that makes my blood, which should be boiling along like a raging torrent, to run like a softly flowing river. That does make me strong as well as weak. However, I firmly believe that I can carry out my duties here thoroughly even if I do not give up thinking about you. If I compared myself as I am today with the man I would have been had I come here without ever knowing you, I would realize that the actual me is a much more stable person. For this reason, I am most grateful not only for knowing you but for being able to expect so much in the future. As you can see, therefore, I want very much for you to take good care of yourself.

Truly believing that your name and your body are so closely and so tightly linked with my own and also by thinking that to place such great value upon you and to value myself are actually one and the same, I am maintaining my self-respect nowadays. You do understand, don't you?
. . . .

Kinji Ōshima

Born February 12, 1917. From Hyogo Prefecture. Through the First Higher School, he entered Tokyo Imperial University, Faculty of Medicine, 1938. Graduated in December 1941. Entered the barracks as a navy short-term active medical officer in January 1942. Killed in action on July 29, 1944, at Tinian Island, Mariana Islands. Navy Surgeon Lieutenant. He was twenty-seven years old.

[A letter to Professor Tomio Ogata, Professor, Tokyo Imperial University Medical School, from the battleship *Yamashiro*, September 6, 1942]

Dear Professor Ogata:

It has been a long time, Professor. When I am on board ship I lose all desire to write any letters. The life of a navy doctor is not at all so busy as "no Saturdays and no Sundays" like that song "Work on a Battleship"[1] in the navy that I used to listen to. Mondays still run through into Fridays, but in actuality the days just go by without any sort of differentiation. I used to worry, especially when I first boarded the ship, over feeling rather vague about things. This feeling that things are moving along busily enough, while I have no energy to work on anything, may be a symptom of the loss of the frontal lobe. Someone likened it to a midbrain condition in mesence-phalic animals, but it is not quite that bad.

The reason that I had an urge to write to you after so long a time is that I found your book, *Sokoku-ai to Kagaku-ai (Love for Fatherland and Love for Science),* at a small bookstore near the docking facility at one of our ports of call. Just like everything else that is printed nowadays, the book does not have a particularly attractive cover, but it caught my eye immediately because it was stacked right in the middle of a row of old, dirty books.

At best, the books found at any port are usually nothing more than volumes of light stories. Culturally speaking, life on board ship is nothing more than an extension of that sort of thing. In this noisy steel box where I cannot hear either percussion sound or stethoscopy, the kind of record music that I am able to hear is just jazz and popular songs. Among our high-spirited young officers Eiji Yoshikawa's *Miyamoto Musashi* is most popular. And I even heard that someone who criticized it was penalized for doing so. I have never read the book, but I wonder to myself just exactly why I should be impressed by any fiction authored by Yoshikawa, even if Miyamoto Musashi was a great man.

There is no way I can avoid getting to know these young and sincere officers. As they came through the education process which is at the absolutely opposite end to that of the Higher Schools, they know exactly where responsibility for the war lies. They also know their etiquette. However, I do not wish to adjust myself to fit "toward the lower" direction.

I heard that there are essential secrets for succeeding in the navy. They fall under the following five items: (1) mark; (2) salutation; (3) documents; (4) fool; and (5) theorizing.

"Mark" means graduates of the Naval Staff College or those special courses on gunnery. This sort of training might well lead to acute observation, but should life in general be like this? They say that, although

---

[1] There is a phrase, "Monday, Monday, Tuesday, Wednesday, Thursday, Friday, and Friday," i.e., Saturdays and Sundays are given up in the navy, and training goes on every day.

arguing theoretically is a reliable route to success, it is never as good as just being a fool.

I have written two or three long reports since I arrived here. The documents that find their way to us are either "absolutely classified" or at least "classified," and, all of them are written in the literary style [not in vernacular style]. The classification of the documents has nothing to do with the quality of their content—what we have here is exactly like the story you told us about Instructor M back when I was a student. Aside from and in addition to the difficulty that reading any report written in the literary style presents, writing in that style is even worse—by far. The reason for a report's clarity when it is written in the literary form is simply that, when a report is written in that form, it is virtually impossible to express any variety of tone, any nuance, etc. One has to stick to the form even though its content may be slightly different from one's exact thought. I do not know whether or not Pasteur [Louis Pasteur, 1822–95, a French chemist and the father of modern bacteriology] wrote his numerous theses in a vernacular that everyone could understand, or whether they were written in a pretentious and high-sounding literary style. One thing I am certain of, however, is that he would not have used such long "pillow-words" or conventional epithets.

The expression "Waste-paper Navy" has grown out of the vast heap of documentation that exists in the navy. The exasperation connected with not being able to have a book when I want to read one—whereas in Tokyo the only problem would be a matter of choice between, say, Iwanmi-Bunko books or others—makes me feel the pain of loss here even more deeply.

When I first came on board I wanted so much to do something that would be a cornerstone of the future civilization. I thought I wanted to do the kind of work that would contribute to the navy's future health and hygiene. But I have since come to realize that I must pay the greatest attention to the present. That is, I must put to their best possible use the traditional ways of maintaining and improving our forces' combat capabilities. We must keep every individual man in top health. It is utterly regrettable when we have to send sailors home, youngsters who are as cute and innocent as children, for something like pleurisy. But, at the same time, I am determined not to lose my desire and drive for research. My desire to study to my heart's content is unchanged, even though it may have to be at such a place as a military medical school. On the other hand, added to it is an urge to transfer from this huge ship to a little destroyer where, while traversing the rough seas together, I would get to know every individual sailor's face and family background.

I have been able to get hold of many books that I used to regret not owning, and I am now able to read such journals as *Igaku to Seibutsu-gaku (Medicine and Biology),* something I have been behind in until now. Now I must do everything that I can possibly do to take advantage of this given situation. I believe that when I am able to return to the research office, the whole future—whether I continue to enjoy high productivity or will be let go because "You cannot do your job anymore"—will depend solely on the strength of my willpower at the present time. Just now I am ready to begin your *Sokoku-ai to Kagaku-ai (Love for Fatherland and Love for Science).*

Respectfully,

Yūichi Asami

Born January 1, 1918. From Saitama Prefecture. Through Chiba Horticultural College, entered Kyushu Imperial University, Faculty of Agriculture, Department of Agricultural Chemistry, in 1939. Graduated in December 1941. Entered the barracks February 1, 1942, assigned to the Eastern 77th Unit as an air defense soldier. Killed in action during the course of an air raid in Chiba at Chiba Army Anti-Aircraft School at Konakadai. Army lieutenant. He was twenty-seven years old.

[From his diary]

September 27, 1942

She came to see me. Now I have mixed feelings about wanting to see her at this point in time; and, at the same time, also not wanting to see her. . . .

*

A soldier of twenty-five who has been comforted like a child by a visit from a younger sister—

When I eat so ravenously I find myself reflecting upon the fact that I am a university graduate [so why am I eating like this?].

*

The chestnut that I steamed last night has the fragrance of my grandmother.

My dear sister. It has the fragrance of my mother.

*

The desire to eat is an instinct in its concrete form, the instinctive saving of a bag that has been thrown onto a patch of grass.

*

Sent my younger sister home. Walked with her for about thirty feet. Such a rare occasion!

*

Such love and affection that I wanted to turn around for just one more glimpse! But she had already gone.

*

The moon has not yet risen. The night with only a few stars somehow conjures up the feeling of waiting for someone.

September 28

To . . . "Good morning." I cannot help but notice the oil stain on my uniform.

I still have sufficient emotion to blush.

September 30

The significance of letters for the military life: it highlights expressions that are nothing less than crazy.

*

Dear Mother. What a busy night it was tonight—human beings are so self-serving, aren't they?

*

In a world where there are people everywhere who possess some sort of special knowledge which goes beyond common sense, is it a paradox not to want to consider such knowledge legitimate?

October 7

Good is encircled by sorrow and pain. How about the color of black?

*

My position—there are times when I lose sight of my position, and I am not referring to the mere occupation of space.

*

"This is the time. This life is the life." Such is my judgment in the shifting midst of all the confused masses.

*

—But I should reflect even more deeply.

*

Though not exactly the words by Renard [Jules Renard, a French novelist, 1864–1910], this is close: "Greta, don't you think it would be more pleasant if we did not think that much? Don't you think so?"

October 11 (Sunday)
   Some people act outrageously.
                              *
   The air outside the hedge smells of cosmetics.
                              *
   A dog looks hungry.

October 13
   "The crowd of people who are oppressed."—Dostoyevsky
                              *
   At high noon one can almost hear the sound of chains.
                              *
   Heavy feet, big shoes, a philosophy without laughter.

October 19
   The letter I received last night from my father suddenly made me realize how graciously he was treating me—as a full-fledged, grown-up person.
                              *
   Today is the festival day of my hometown village shrine. My father wrote: "By this time—for you too—all this must already have become a memory of a long time ago."
                              *
   Tears fill my eyes. He is so kind in trying to insert the happy time of my youth into the brutal life I must lead today.
                              *
   The warmth I felt on a cool Autumn day eating the red rice [ceremonial rice cooked with small beans]; the way the *nishime* [vegetables cooked in a traditional way] felt on my tongue; my sisters in brand-new dresses; and the sound of those [festival] vendors' whistles.
                              *
   Enticed by the sound of whistles and drums,
   I came to a mountain festival; but
   I am not fond of mountains, for I miss towns.
   When the wind blows there is only the
   sound of leaves.
                              —Hakushū [Kitahara, renowned poet]

                              *

   A young boy does not know much about self-criticism. I miss the time of my youth so much my eyes are filled with tears.

January 13, 1943
> Rain and wind outside
> Dear Father—the sorrow is the rain
> —the evening brings the cold rain:
> My father is no longer home—
>   [This winter his father passed away.]

January 28
> A moment of loneliness touched me in the midst of a mass of strangers.
> It's a flood, a flood! One key location-point has been washed away.
>   *
> When I look intently at the Chinese character of "father,"
> When I find the Chinese character of "mother."

February 28
> —I want to call that way. Facing the moon, I whistle. . . .
> It is an evening quite close to the coming of spring.
>   *
> Goodnight. It is the end of a day with nothing to do but to sleep.

April 13
> I do not wish to say that it is something which is due either to my age or to the environment.
> —Only one wish . . .
>   *
> As expected, poetry has left me.

May 30
> Returning home. Have I ever done anything in the way of filial piety?
>   *
> My death is inevitable. Everything ends with death.
>   *
> Old age puts a brake on a person's determination.
>   *
> Tears fall. In the middle of a train, I see myself as a member of the audience at a tragic drama.
>   *
> What do I propose to become? I must not give up on myself.

August 6

"I have no space in which to rest. There is not even a place to hang
my hat. . . ."   —Mansfield [Katherine Mansfield,
                                   New Zealand short-story writer, 1888–1923]

August 22

What a pitiful person I am! I am like a hair that is created to protect
a precious head and gets cut off just because it is ugly. Darn it! It cannot
even become fertilizer.

*

My life is being held hostage.
Day and night, it is becoming emaciated in a dark and humid pawn-
shop storage area.

*

It seems to me as though life in this world is like playing endless
music. Death dances all over the place, and all the movements are bloody.
A rest in the musical score—I take a breath, but the sound of a drum
keeps on.
Dissonance—pizzicato, something dreamt up by these ghosts of
human beings, spins its way throughout an idiotic intoxication.
Death again begins to dance across the scores.
Well, shall I start dancing too before the conductor's baton breaks?

November 18

Went to Shibaura to learn something about ocean shipping.

*

All day long a cold rain wet the quay. A poem flows out of my
completely chilled body.

*

A single ship is weighing anchor and heading for a decisive battle
zone in the south. Its name—Shibazono-maru—was freshly painted over
in the color of clear ocean. [Translators' note: All Japanese commercial
vessels had names ending with "maru," while military ships did not. This
particular ship has obviously been mobilized for military use, and its
original name was covered in paint.]
A crane is pulling military supplies up into the gray skies.
"Chikushō! (Darn it!)" "They don't look as unhappy as we are,"
mumbles a non-commissioned officer who stands alongside the supplies
which are about to be hoisted on board.
Those soldiers in summer uniform in the cold rain.
I suppose they must be in sorrowful preparation for the farewells and
for the homesickness which will follow them, but . . .

Genta Uemura

Born January 1, 1921. From Mie Prefecture. Entered Chuo University, Faculty of Economics, in October 1942, through its College Division, Department of Jurisprudence. Conscripted and entered the Central 38th Unit on January 10, 1943. Killed in action on April 21, 1945, on the main island of Okinawa, during the course of a battle in the Ginowan (Gino Bay) area. He was twenty-four years old.

June 19, 1943   Saturday

Weight: over 17-kan (i.e., about 64 kilograms, or roughly 140 lbs.)

Oral exam for cadet status.

For the first time in a long time I got things off my chest and straightforwardly gave voice to my thoughts.

With regard to America: I said that, from what I understand, America is a country that absolutely applauds the democratic form of government, and this forced a smile from Intendant Tsuchiya. Then I added that Americans have the same strong sense of patriotism that we Japanese have, and that, I believed, it would prove most difficult for us to be finally able to win this war decisively. At that point a major questioned me sharply as to whether or not Americans have any shortcomings at all. I replied: "They have no history, but that alone will have no bearing on the outcome of the war." When I started to say that the enjoyment of their personal lives was most Americans' goal in life, I was sharply questioned: "Wait a minute. Are you using the language of the enemy, 'enjoy', so casually?" I ended up arguing about the senseless prohibition against using everyday English terms such as "news" and replacing them with Japanese equivalents, *hōdō*.

After that, the discussion turned to the issue of hostile feelings toward the enemy, and things heated up considerably when an examining officer told me that "You seem to want to approach everything from a materialistic standpoint," etc.

I also discussed the issue of total national mobilization. My chest certainly felt altogether clear and refreshed.

To have such an intensely incise and pleasurable discussion with military officers!

June 21   Monday

Written exam.

My score should be almost zero, and somehow I must fail [the exam]. It would simply be terrible if I ever end up with the B-rank of cadets [*cf.*

p. 52] only because there are not enough candidates. Now all I can do is chase the dream of being discharged.

I have just passed through numerous dilemmas, but now, somehow, I just want to feel the fresh air of freedom.

Can I be in the world outside the military, even if it will only be a month until I am called upon to fight in the next campaign?

I want to practice filial piety toward my parents, filial piety in the true sense of the term; then do some traveling; then, quietly feeling lonely and sad—and shedding pure tears—about myself for having been born in this most unfortunate time; after that I shall die.

Based on my experience of the harshness of military life for half a year, I felt as if I understood for certain how those of us who happened to have been born in this generation must live. The reality of war, regardless of whether that war is just or not, connects all of us to a sort of nihilism.

Military sects, the world of politicians, ideologies, laws, politics, the economy, society, culture, etc.,—all of these things are nothing but little petals of the flowers that were blossoming over the peaceful life of the past.

I am slowly getting close to developing the mental attitude with which one must face death, i.e., being killed in war, but I will never be fully prepared unless I can return home and see my mother and breathe the air of our house once more.

In that regard, I feel so sorry for those new recruits in Shizuoka. I heard that they are about to be shipped away to the Solomons. They are in full uniform, and just waiting to be on their way to the battlefield. At their farewell show last night those of the recruits who can sing well were putting their very hearts into the singing of sad songs, one after another. I can sympathize more than ever with the position of men on active duty compared to that of the reserves.*

July 1   Thursday

Athlete's foot is giving me the hardest time. Starting this morning, someone will exchange with me and take on my kitchen duty.

I wonder whether or not I will get over athlete's foot before I go to Chigusa [a military training field in Mie Prefecture].

In the meantime, how about a dream? Will my dream of being discharged end, and will I be shedding tears again? I wonder whether or not it was true.

It is difficult to believe how strongly a human being can long for freedom.

I wonder whether it was true in the past that liberalism [cf. p. 9], as a social ideology, spread a certain poison through society. Since I came to the barracks, I have really come to appreciate, for the first time, the fact that our longing for freedom is truly part of a human being's very nature. I will never lose this beautiful and innermost feeling—forever and ever.

July 2   Friday   Cloudy

What is the matter with this year's cool weather? As of yesterday we are allowed to go semi-nude, and yet a jacket still feels just about right.

Since I am scheduled for a medical checkup today, I talked with the sub-officer in charge [see note on *shūban kashikan*, p.93] and arranged to have Superior Private Nakanishi of the Armory Service's 4th Squad replace me.

Because of this, I was struck by a Superior Private. It was a really beautiful uppercut. I have been beaten many times, but have never seen a man with such a splendid arm. I felt that my body had slid over lightly, then realized that I was lying on a bed as though I were in a dream—but my ear remained benumbed and still rang and kept on buzzing a while longer. On the same occasion I was also struck by Ichirō Yasuda, but this second blow did not hurt my cheek as much—it had grown accustomed to it.

In normal society, were a man struck, the blow would have a definite psychological impact on anyone who took pride in being a contributing member of that society. For those of us in the military, however, who have been enduring severe uppercuts innumerable times, the resultant pain has gotten to seem something on more or less the same level as the absolute misery of having to get up every morning at reveille.

"The philosophy of striking other people."

"The philosophy of being struck."

I should like the time to reflect on these things.

July 3   Saturday   Rain

The heavy downpour that began last evening has not let up at all.

I dreamt a dream last night. It was strange from whatever angle, and you might wish to consider it. Right after I came into the service, at least for ten days or so, I used to dream regularly and tirelessly. But those dreams were all about things like being out of breath after making some escape, or still being scared to death after having run back home. They were all rather childish and totally foolish, but, last night and for the first time, a woman appeared in my dream. It was Yasuko Hayashi. Why did she appear in my dream? Until then I had completely forgotten about her. More to the point, she is not the one I knew well, and we have never been intimate. . . . There was also a round-faced man with a fair complexion who appeared in a casual kimono, and, all to himself, he was volubly arguing about political matters. I stood alongside him, humbled and yet listening intently to his most disagreeable argument. The content [of his ranting] has now melted away into the dream, but I remember being simultaneously disgusted over what he had to say and totally fascinated by his appearance.

Also [in the dream was] the time I went to a theater with a grandmother of Ōmiya. But, why has it come up in a dream now? It was the day of the Celebration of the 2,600th year [of Japan's history]* when the grandmother passed away. In those days, not yet, . . . not quite yet.

The three dreams were interconnected with a single chain.

But what a strange dream, and especially dreaming about people whom I have never thought of before, even in dreams!

Dreaming.—It is a useless procedure and in the army we should be getting the soundest sleep possible. Yet I dream so often.

"Soldiers and dreams."

July 5   Monday   Cloudy and then rain

It is raining and raining every day.

For nearly half a month I did not wash my undershirts and underpants.
. . . .

Oh, how could my heart have been so torn to pieces, day after day, by a dream of being excused from military service? To be in a serene state of mind. . . . But even if I went home—even when I think of going home something heavy seems to dangle before my eyes.

Perhaps I should now have a heart-to-heart talk with the dream. Whether to be killed in action, to die of disease, or to return home alive—it has to be just one of these three options.

The pleasant thing about death is that, once experienced, it is over. It would be more than I could hope for if only I could walk into that comfort of death, but . . .

The pain of facing death, especially when I so desperately "want to live," is so terrifying that even just to think of death makes me wish to turn my face away.

"Returning home alive"—There would be so much of life—as large as a mountain—living things. How is it that everything, having grown up in the midst of death, has to walk into the real death?

"A living corpse" is an affected and showy term, but I suppose that in its disregard both for the future and for hope itself it contains some real truth.

Is it such an absolutely foolish thing for me to still be afraid of death and also to think so much about a fulfilling life after receiving the red slip, the conscription notice?

Is this the same case as that in which a man who was already buried under a tombstone would find himself in: to wish to have one more nice warm meal? Darn! Why do I have to think like that?

"War!" Goethe's Faust is quoted as having said, "Oh, another *war*? It is the one word the intelligentsia dislikes to hear." But for us too this is not only the one word we dislike to hear; not only does it take our bodies free of charge, but it also snatches from us something even more crucial—our humanity itself. Moreover, I do not believe that this war will come to an end while we are still alive.

A long time ago, it was possible to avoid getting involved in a war simply by disappearing into the mountains as a Buddhist priest. No more. If it were still possible to do so, all of Japan's mountain temples would be overflowing and the natural order of things would be reversed.

—Life and death

—Individual human beings and living.

—We and war.

At the present time most of these all but mutually opposing things are hopelessly intertwined. Yet I still want to live.

July 7

Got up at 4:30 this morning. Now I am on a train.

Both my heart and my eyes are comforted by the green rice paddies [we pass].

To Chigusa. It is my understanding that the entire trip back will be on foot, and this is a source of concern. And yes, today is the sixth anniversary of the China Incident.

It really does not matter how long we wait; there is no longer anyone who hopes that the war will end soon—just because there is no chance of the war's ending.

At a certain time on a certain day the time will have arrived for our children and grandchildren to weep over the Han race's [Chinese people's] revenge.

What if I should have been a Chinese youth?

The reality is that, as an individual Japanese soldier, I am the smallest unit in the hateful Japanese military organization.

July 11   Clear

How great! How pleasant! And how splendid [the scene of the plain is]!

There are mountains, plains, and a river in the Chigusa Plain. However, the training is extremely tough. How many times have I thought of my body as being only a hair's breadth from death! Each and every day I thought that I would fall down on the job, but as of yesterday, I have finally been appointed a horse-handler. The irony turned out to be that the horse given into my charge, Seiyū, is a mean horse, indeed the worst in the company. I cannot cry even if I wanted to cry. [i.e., Nothing could be worse than this situation]: a Ganta [variation on the author's first name] for a *ganta* (mean) horse! Is this what we call the military? Among the January draftees still remaining here, I am the only soldier who is being worked to death in this barn. I feel like complaining, like saying "I get upset just to think of the comparatively easy jobs my comrades are assigned to." But, once I reflect on the fact that I am quite literally living the life of a common soldier on the lowest possible level, then I feel better.

I tried riding on Seiyū. This is the first time I have ridden a horse.

[Today is] the 11th. There was inspection today.

July 14 Clear

Yesterday, I returned from Chigusa, and at last . . .

All day yesterday and continuing into today, I was tempted by the thought of committing suicide. But there is my mother to think of, a mother who waits so anxiously for my return home—if indeed I can return home. What an irony of fate, and of life, that I should have passed the cadetship exam! I cried, and from the bottom of my heart. When I am alone I cannot stop crying even now. Four more years in a military which I have always hated ever since I was a little child? Why should I want to spend four or even five more years?

Darn it! I want to be dead. If it were not for the fact that my mother is still alive I, most probably, would have decided to kill myself yesterday.

Four or five more years of being a living corpse! I shall be almost thirty years of age by the time I get to return to society. Irony of ironies! The fact is that I only barely passed the test. Just a tiny bit off my score, perhaps a point or so, would have changed my fate so greatly.

July 15 Clear

I received a letter from Midori last night. She writes that she posted it from the school. Well, anyway, I did write a postcard to my mother, but [I wonder if it reached her].

All right—so long as I am alive, I am going to try so hard at this training that it will ruin my health! Heck with it!

July 16

As of last evening, my assignment is that of horse-barn maintenance—the same situation as Shigehiko Mori. Those who are heading for invasion-beach training have left for Nishiki-hama beach [at the tip of Kii Peninsula].

Four or five more years of this life of death.

I have to make a firm resolution to consider myself as having really been dead ever since June 12th.

A young man with a beautiful heart who loved his mother and completely believed in his ideals died on June 12, 1943.

I cried. I cried today from the bottom of my heart.

That same young man who, once upon a time, walked to the point of exhaustion in search of some books on legal philosophy, was fair-complexioned, slender, and tall. . . . Of course there were some happy times.

Death must be absolutely beautiful.

One must end his life quietly and with serenity.

It has to be like the death in the play, *My Town*—[performed] by Bungaku-za group in the Tsukiji Little Theater—that I saw with Ōsawa some time ago.

Otherwise, the only wish I have left is to spend a day with my mother—just a day out together, crying together, even just one day.

Dear mother, please forgive me for *fukō* [a shortcoming in filial piety], which I did not wish for.

"A human is born, suffers, and dies."

July 26 Sunday

Yesterday I returned from a leave of three nights and four days. This might be the very last visit [with my mother] for me. Mother says it might be three more years or so [before I can come home]. I said perhaps four or five more years. The fact is that the situation is such that I may have to give up the hope of *ever* coming home.

Nothing is gained by brooding over the past, but I wonder why I ever passed the military cadet exam.

It must be that during the oral section of the exam I impressed the examining officers as quite a straightforward young man. I know that I am far superior to my petty peers when it comes both to ideology and guts, but how can it be that the temporary exhilaration of a few passing moments should ever turn around to produce this terrible result!

How many more years will it be over the course of which I will have to cling to life? Ever since I grew in intelligence and began to study political science, economics, and the law—though perhaps not deeply enough—I came to realize that the military is the worst and the lowest enemy of every ideology. And I used to think that the term "time passes" was an expression descriptive of how one's fate flows, carrying with it a tone of rather conscience-related regret over having wasted time; but now I shed a tear of sorrow and say "time, go away"—even if this means the sacrifice of my youth, love, passion, and all of that.

Agony and sorrow: if these abstractions only existed on the highest possible ideological plane, experiencing them would involve a certain kind of self-satisfaction—just because they would only exist within one's own mind. But [the actual experiencing of agony and sorrow which is now my lot puts things] on the lowest plane [—the bottom—that will ever be possible].

September 27   Monday   Cloudy

The examination was given today to divide us into A-class and B-class.

I figured that I would wind up in the B-class cadet group, and that would be fine, but as it turned out I did not do well because I had not studied enough.

One of the typical annoyances about the military examinations is having too much time. There are always too many people on hand, and too much time. I would like, just once, to demonstrate this wastefulness of the military for the benefit of civilians.*

I have just heard that, at the universities, the study of all literary disciplines [i.e., departments outside the natural sciences] is to be terminated. [See *gakuto shutsujin*—student mobilization, p. 137]. The situation has finally come to this: just one more step before student mobilization.

When I come to think of it, my brother died at the right time. It has been almost six years since. He was a brilliant man and, right down to the marrow of his bones, a thorough believer in Liberalism. Were he living today, he would no doubt have created a tragic situation by committing suicide.

Even six years ago, however, I thought that there was something suicidal about his death. It was a clear case of suffering "the separation of ideology from reality," and I think that it would have been much more appropriate had his death actually been a suicide. He certainly succeeded in disguising it so splendidly that it could indeed have been a suicide.

I—the less intelligent one—am still alive. I am living for my mother. During this confusing period of time, which could appropriately be called "the end of the world," I imagine that my mother must be hanging onto life no matter what, with her teeth tightly compressed—by treasuring her precious and happy memories of the past—until the day when I return home.

Dear Mother: Please persevere. I may not have been much of a son from the standpoint of filial piety, but at no time have I ever forgotten you—ever.

Notes

* *Kokka Sōdōin* (National Total Mobilization): The system which, under laws such as the National Total Mobilization Act of 1938, enabled the state—after the all-out war between Japan and China—to control and utilize any and all human and material resources.

* Active duty and reserve duty: The physical examination for the conscripts, which were based primarily on an individual's physique [more so than his actual physical condition], classified men into A-class and B-class (later subdivided into B-1, B-2, and B-3) and C-class, as passing. Depending on the number of men needed for any particular year's conscription (and, when there were more A-class personnel available than were necessary, by means of a drawing), those who passed were conscripted into active duty. For several years the others were made reservists (e.g., regular reserves, second reserves, militia soldiers, etc.). Toward the end of the fifteen years of war, however, and in preparation for the anticipated battles on the Japanese mainland, even the men who did not originally qualify for active duty were conscripted.

* Festival in Celebration of the 2,600th Year of the Imperial Calendar: 1940 was considered to be the "2,600th year of the Imperial Calendar" and many celebrations were held throughout for the twin purposes of elevating Japan's fighting spirit and to promote the national spiritual mobilization. The restrictions on singing, dancing, and making musical sounds were lifted, and all activities of this sort peaked with a ceremonial festivity commemorating the date of Emperor Shōwa's enthronement. A crowd of 54,000 people gathered in front of the Imperial Palace.

* *Chihōjin, shaba* (civilians, non-military world): The world outside the military was referred to as *shaba* or *chihō* [the literary meaning is "local" or "indigenous," but these words were used by the military in a peculiar way]. So far as the Japanese Military were concerned, these words were applicable to every human being except for military personnel themselves and those administrative officers and other civilians who were given the title of *gunzoku* (civilians in military service). Once an individual entered military service, he would change from a *chihō-fuku* (civilian's clothing) to a military uniform. They were also forbidden to use *chihō-go*, the standard civilian language, and were forced to learn the military style of communicating.

Daihō Sanada

Born March 19, 1917. From Fukuoka Prefecture. Through Yamaguchi Higher School, he entered Tokyo Imperial University, Faculty of Literature, Department of Chinese Philosophy, in 1939. Graduated in December, 1941. Was conscripted and entered the barracks on February 1, 1942. Killed in action off the Philippine coast, September 30, 1943. Army lieutenant. He was twenty-six years old.

My dear Mother:

Exactly as you predicted, right now I really have nothing to say. The only thing is that tears, which I have not experienced in many, many years,—such an unceasing shedding of tears—came upon me. I have never felt so deeply about my sinfulness as I have today. How could I cry like that? I wonder about the outpouring of tears you must have shed for me from the moment I was born up to now. I will never be able to measure it. Now I am going to write down my memories of you, Mother. I remember that I was very often taken to see a doctor. Even though it was a life of poverty after father passed away, you told me that "You are not just a child of mine: you are an honorable child of the Buddha—and a treasure to the nation"; and you paid special attention to our physical well-being. After my father passed away you were the mother who, beyond your means, took care to pay such careful attention to us that we would not grow up with inferiority complexes. This was especially true for me when I entered middle school. I remember one evening when you took me to town and told me that I was getting a brand new outfit, and I thought I was going to be taken to the busy downtown. As the beautiful lights of the city first appeared and we at last reached the entranceway to the main street, you suddenly and for some reason walked toward a dark alley. I wondered what was going on, and followed you. I remember that so very clearly. You entered a store which sold both new and old clothes, and tried different jackets on me, then finally bought a *kokura*-jacket [i.e., one made of Japanese duck cloth, the usual navy-blue outfit for students] that seemed a little too big for me. Moreover, before we left the store, you repeatedly told the proprietor that you would pay for the jacket later. On the way back home you turned to me and said with a smile: "The lining of this outfit is flannel. Right now you might think that it is a little too big, but you will soon grow big." As I remember all this now, I get choked up.

I remember something else connected with when I was in about the third year of my middle-school period [equivalent of American 9th grade]. My older brother was in his 5th year [equivalent of 11th grade]. It was the end of the year, there was no money and no *otoshidama* [gift of cash to a child to celebrate the New Year] such as our friends had; nor anything joyful for our family at the end of the year. Everything felt empty and chilly. At this point my older brother turned his dissatisfaction toward you, mother. He said our father had dedicated his entire life to religious causes, and left six children behind without any visible means of support. Without any financial reserve, he called us brothers to his deathbed and said: "You don't have to become an important person. You don't have to become a wealthy person. You don't have to become a scholar. But please, each one of you, become a man who can chant a prayer to Amitabha. When you need money, I shall send you some from the Pure Land (Buddhist heaven)," and died with a nice smile: that was all such self-centered nonsense, my brother said. My brother said that it was all our father's fault for leaving mother and the rest of us brothers in such a painful situation. In great sorrow and with tears in your eyes, you then said to my brother: "It does not matter how much you blame me, but please do not blame your late father." I realize now how badly money was needed to make all sorts of payments, particularly at the end of a year.[1] I cannot help but imagine the pain you must have been in. You stood there in front of a dresser with the right arm in "futokoro" [i.e., tucked inside a collar in the chest area of a kimono], and, with tears in your eyes, staring at some fixed point. Then, as if you had made up your mind about something, you suddenly got ready to go out and left the house. All six of us children had sad expressions on our faces and were keeping our heads down. I was feeling a strong anger toward my older brother, and waited at a foot warmer for you to come back. That same evening all six of us stuffed ourselves with all varieties of food, including the traditional noodles for the New Year's eve, and plenty of fruits and cookies. You ate almost nothing yourself, but you were smiling as you watched all of us being so happy. We also received generous "otoshidama" and spending money on the New Year. I still wonder how much you cried, and how much pain you must have gone through. All in all, this is a very painful set of memories for me.

After my father passed away you became someone who completely bypassed what might be called the everyday pleasures of life in this world. My youngest sister Seiko was only a year old when he left us. You even went to sit alongside teenage girls and learn how to sew professionally— just to earn some money to pay for our tuition. There is no end to my memories of those days. And I am choked by painful but sweet tears. You went through hardship after hardship, mother. Instead of giving you reason to be proud of me, it was I who made your already narrow shoulders even narrower and your thin chest even thinner. And, this time, although per-

---

[1] In Japan it is a traditional expectation that all debts are to be cleared away before the arrival of the New Year.

haps it was a natural assertion of the male ego, I had done something quite foolish. You told me "Daihō-san, to receive money from others for purposes of education is something to be grateful about, but to accept money, as you did this time, for something unworthy, is something that a mother's heart does not permit. I shall most certainly repay it." In shame, I felt myself to be such an utterly sinful soul. The only thing I could do was to break down and cry. In addition, you said, "Use this mistake, Daihō-san, as an opportunity to move forward, and then to move forward again, and eventually to become someone who can even be thankful for it by turning it around. I believe in you, Daihō-san. You will do it. And you are the type of person who can do it. I believe in you." Oh, what a huge and bottomless love and benevolence! What thoughtfulness far beyond what I could ever deserve! Oh the mother's love and trust that were and are shining over me! How could I ever dream of living without making things better? A mother, who accepts all of her children's pleasure and happiness as if it were her own, and what a terrible act of impiety it is to betray this parental love! From now on, for sure, I am resolved to put an end to this shallow life, and to be reborn into a stronger existence. Mother—the only one in the whole world for me—I hope that you will take good care of yourself.

> *Gasshō* (a gesture: joining the flats of the hands in veneration, i.e., respectfully)

Atsushi Tsutsui (former surname: Nose)

Born August 21, 1918. From Chiba Prefecture. Through Shizuoka Higher School, entered Tokyo Imperial University, Faculty of Jurisprudence, in 1939. Graduated in December, 1941. Entered the barracks February 1, 1942, and entered Army Intendance School. Missing in action in eastern New Guinea, territory of Great Britain, in February, 1943. Army intendant lieutenant. He was twenty-five years old.

[A letter to his wife, Taiko, 1943]

February 5, 10:30 p.m.

My Dear Taiko:

I am writing this letter under a dim light in a humble inn. Our originally planned date of departure, the 5th, has been postponed to the 6th, tomorrow, at noon. This time there is no doubt about it. During the three days of our stay here I found the town of Hiroshima rather uninteresting.

Everyone was in a rather strange psychological state, and some of our men even stayed away overnight. Wherever I walked in town, I received salutes. I have acquired a copy of *Ryoshū (Loneliness on a Journey)* [by Riichi Yokomitsu], volume 2. Sachiko recommended this novel highly, and I wonder about what sort of emotional condition I shall be in reading the book on board ship. And I have finished *Haha wa Sakebi-Naku (Mother Screams and Cries)*. I am undecided as to whether or not this fiction is a masterpiece, but in my present predicament I found it very interesting. I feel I can understand well the mother's combined joy and sorrow in bringing up a child. In the end, I want to call out to you in my heart: "Please take care of everything for me."

.... This place is still cold, and especially this thin futon bedding. Perhaps I want a little too much luxury, but I really miss a good warm futon.

I suppose that Keiko must be in bed by now. I take out a picture to have a look at her. She is so adorable! I can almost see her face as she looks at me and talks to me in a baby talk that is almost ready to become words. I hope she will grow fast. Please try to prevent her from catching a cold. I keep talking about these things too much, but you can easily catch a cold too and so please take care of yourself. I forgot to tell you something that might help—when you go to bed why don't you use a shoulder cover? Your sister in Yōkaichiba [in Chiba Prefecture] was saying that she keeps drafts out by placing a towel between her baby and herself. Well, I am about to go to bed myself and will put myself to sleep reading a fiction or something.—I say "Good night."

Atsushi

March 31

My dear Taiko:

I mailed a postcard from here, but I am not sure whether or not it reached you. I was fortunate enough to find someone who is flying back to mainland Japan, so I am entrusting him with this letter.

As soon as we arrived at our destination, Rabaul, we found out that we were heading for New Guinea. Right now it is the most important area in the war and where the hardest fighting is going on. Additionally, and before they even get there, our forces are decimated by the horrendous combined might of the enemy submarine fleet and their air power. The enemy makes bombing runs here too all the time.

We will be leaving shortly. I feel certain that my life will not be spared much longer, and I have readied myself psychologically for that eventuality. I hope that you will prepare yourself for it too, just so you will be able to conduct yourself in the best possible way at that worst possible time, just in case—there is a one-in-a-million chance.

Everyone here, with tragic and heroic hearts, seems to be glaring in the direction of the faraway skies over America and Britain. Now that the situation has reached this point I have, as I said, summoned up a certain resolution and readiness for the worst, but still, when I think of it, I feel as though there were many things that I should have taken better care of. Perhaps this is all just the last pitiful gibberish of an imperfect human being.

I assume that you all are well. At least at the moment, I too am well enough. Two men have already come down with dengue fever, however. I regret that I cannot contact my brother, who is now in south China, or Sanae in Manchuria. I can imagine how cute and adorable Keiko must have grown to be by now. I have to say good bye to the image of Keiko now. I say farewell from far away to your bother in Yōkaichiba and all others, as well as to everyone in Tōgane. I have also written it on the postcard, but in any case you would probably laugh at a modest poem that I happened to compose:

> What can we do about
> happiness and sorrow—?
> One must know that this moment itself is happiness
> Adieu (Good-bye).

Atsushi

Jūji Ichii

Born December 13, 1919. From Niigata Prefecture. Entered Azabu Veterinarian College in 1939, and graduated in December 1941. Entered the barracks on February 1, 1942. Died in [an Army hospital], Niigata Clinic, August 24, 1944. He was twenty-four years old.

April 1, 1942

....

—Outline of my medical condition leading to hospitalization—

On Army Commemoration Day last month I ate too much red rice (rice cooked with red beans, and served on a day of celebration) for lunch, and probably because of that—and probably too because of the usual and extremely harsh training which we had to undergo on that day—I began suffering diarrhea. Even though I have been very careful ever since, the Army barley-rice (rice mixed with barley), unfortunately, does not agree with my system; in addition, I have gotten so exhausted over the past several days from studying for the military cadet exams (*cf.* p. 52) that the diarrhea keeps hanging on.

October 9

I was so happy about your letter of the other day, because I felt that you had really gotten in touch with your true feelings. The only thing a person in a sickbed can count on is someone else's kind heart. One yearns to lean on everything, and when I actually do lean on someone who supports me, I feel that that person is very kindhearted.

Although it is something that I paid virtually no attention to when I was strong and healthy, I now feel that everything and everybody are separated into two distinct categories: the well-intentioned and the evil-intentioned. The middle group between the two, those I might label the unconcerned, seems to have disappeared.

They seem to treat me with the attitude that they are kind to those weaker than themselves while they deal malevolently with those who are stronger than themselves. Perhaps I just feel this way because of the bias I have because I happened to be sick. ....

As of the moment, I am petrified at the thought of meeting any or all of the men who know me. These people would by now have moved ahead farther and farther, walking right over me. Even those who started out at the same starting line with me less than half a year ago have now gone so far ahead that I doubt I can ever catch up.

I wonder whether or not, with this body of mine, I could ever make up for this handicap even if I spent my whole life trying to.

Will I ever get well?

Will I again be healthy enough to be able to work just like anyone else? Even if I should recover, I am afraid that it may be just well enough to stay home idly, without doing much, and perhaps I might never be well enough to work. And I am even beginning to have internal doubts. At the same time, I also feel like asking some questions: about just how far medical science has advanced; about why we have to fight a war; and about how much of a contribution my having served in the army for two months amounted to. Is the Empire of Japan in such a state that it has to mobilize a person such as myself, who throughout his life has constantly been in poor health? And how much have they done for me since I became really ill?

I do not believe I would have fallen this sick had I not become a soldier. Perhaps I would be comfortably sitting right now in a swivel chair at the Ministry of Agriculture and Forestry. Such a scenario would be beneficial for all concerned—for my parents, my country, and for myself as well. I wonder how many of us, right here in this clinic, are thinking the same way. Maybe I am the only one.

The others would be lucky if they did not think this way. And, indeed, whether or not they are aware of matters similar to those behind my own personal considerations, they *must* not think this way. [—If they can keep their minds clear of such things] I suppose that they might be able to recuperate in tranquillity.

July 31, 1943

My temperature is 37.5°. My pulse is about 90, weight 38.5 kg, and I am extremely weak.

Death is simple. However, there is a reason why I cannot and should not die. Once a man is given a life, he must continue to stay alive until the last possible moment, and just suppose it has been ordained that my life is to last another month or two? I do not think that my body can survive this summer heat.

Ever since about the 20th of July the breath that issues from my chest has been foul, and the night sweats are awful. My body feels so languid that I cannot even stretch out my legs and lie still quietly. I even have to hang on to a wall on my way back from a toilet that is less than forty feet away.

I am currently spitting out phlegm that is just like pus but, if only because of elderly parents who are anxiously waiting for my full recovery, I simply cannot die. Now that I am sick, they love me more than ever.

Until my brother returns home from the battlefield my parents' well-being is my responsibility entirely.

—Popular songs on the military [from his notes]—

"Song of Four Seasons"
Spring is a joyful time, as I stand guard
    alone and looking lonely,
Failing to salute because I am too busy
    watching the female students on their way home
        from viewing the cherry blossoms.
    Lightly, a ten-day heavy imprisonment.
    Hear, hear.

Summer is likewise joyful, the entire regiment
    practicing water-horse as a unit.
Taking a nap in the afternoon and awakened by a bugle call.

Lightly, it is time to go and take care of
the horses. Hear, hear.

Fall is joyful too, the whole division conducts
an autumn exercise in unison.
Among them, the most notable was a
transport soldier admired by a cute girl, and:
Lightly, a sweet potato was presented. Hear, hear.

Even winter is joyful, all second-year privates
huddled together in front of a Manchurian stove,
Roasting rice-cakes and speaking of women,
Hearing the footsteps of the officer of the week,
Lightly, salute and hide the rice-cakes. Hear, hear.

"A Counting Song"[1]
(1) Even though it is done in the service of the nation
I feel so sorry for myself, sorry for one who came to join
this army which people hate—
and who had to take a tearful farewell from the girl I adore

(2) I have to live like this for three more years,[2]
everything is regulated by a bugle call,
—including the hours assigned for sleeping and for getting up—
Each and every day is so long, as I cry all day long,
being shouted at by the second-year privates I hate.

(3) Even the Sundays, every seventh day,
and the holidays, which should be times of joy

---

[1] [Translators' note: these two poems follow the traditional Japanese *Kazoe-uta* (counting songs), in form, i.e., the first syllable of the verse matches the first syllable of the number; although the first section does not follow the form, it may well have been a draft for the second section, and it is usually composed in 5, 7–5, 7–5, 7–5 syllables. In this section the author omits the 5 syllables in the beginning, but for the second "counting song," he correctly follows the form.]

[2] The typical duration of conscription used to be for three years until the Washington Armament Limitation Treaty, which forced the Japanese military to cut down its size. As a consequence, following the newly created law on conscription, effective as of April 1927, the length of service was shortened to two years for the army and three years for the navy.

I spend doing laundry for that same second-year private
    whom I hate, and each day is a day of tears.

(4) The sun went down early, and the moon is up.
    In the moonlit glow
I feel so sorry for myself for having to shine
    the second-year private's dirty muddy shoes.

(5) There are no nice things such as family visits,
    separated as we are by mountains and the sea.
Oh, but the joy of receiving a letter when one finally comes!
    The writing of my dear Mitchan![3]

(6) Immediately following roll call
    iron-fisted punishment comes down like rain and hail.
I crawl into bed, crying miserably,
    and dream of my mother's face back home.

(7) Without even leaving enough time to bite into a roll filled
    with red beans,
    a bugle call is sounded for lights out.—
A five-foot bed with a straw mat thrown over it
    —this is our dreamland!

(8) I awaken in the midst of a deep sleep to stand the
    night-watch duty I deplore,
and which involves heavy imprisonment
    should I ever fall back to sleep.

(9) Inspection for the first term, second term, and third term—
    The fall exercise has already ended;
and when, soon, those hateful second-year privates
    Will leave the company
then we will become god-like figures. [See *Naimu*, p. 117n]

(10) In just one more day we shall be second-year privates,
    and the springtime of blossoming flowers will be here;
    I sure want to show my Mitchan as soon as I can

---

[3] "Chan" is a diminutive form of a suffix "sama" (Miss, Mr., Mrs., etc.) to be added to a person's name. This may be equivalent to "My Dear Little Michiko" or "My Dear Mitsuko."

the reward for diligence
and the number of stars on my uniform.

"Counting Song"

For One:

Although justifying themselves by saying that it is all done
for the sake of the country,
There are certain men who are so foolish as to volunteer
for the army which the people actively dislike.

For Two:

Because I came here, deserting my dear parents
And giving up my personal life,
even though it is given for the Emperor.

For Three:

In order to maintain the Army's rules and morality
Everyone knows that, for soldiers,
wine and women are forbidden.

For Four:

Soldiers standing guard duty at night go without sleep
When morning comes they stay on their feet
throughout the day,
Indifferent to the extremes of either heat or cold.

For Five:

You never know when a surprise roll call might be scheduled
—Awakened in the midst of the very deepest sleep,
and having to count off numbers and report.

For Six:

And then there are the impossible and totally
unreasonable orders from senior officers
that one must obey.

For Seven:

Every Saturday, every seventh day,
we must endure sanitary inspections,
weapon inspections, we suffer so much by
inspections of every possible kind.

For Eight:

> Left the barracks' gate in desperation to have some fun.
> > —Was away five minutes too long,
> > > and heavy imprisonment followed immediately
> > > > upon my return.

For Nine:

> This rule is quite clever.
> > Everything is regulated by a bugle call: whether to go to sleep
> > > or to get up, or of course to take part in exercises
> > > > —and even for the three daily meals.

For Ten:

> Payday every tenth day:
> > It is only 1 yen and 50 sen [i.e., 1.5 yen];
> > > not even enough for a sea biscuit.

For Eleven.

> The commanding officer has the best job—
> > always on a horse, whether going or coming, and
> > > guard soldiers stand in line presenting arms [to salute].

Notes (A short glossary of words and technical term used in the above selection)

* *Jū-eisō* (heavy imprisonment): Under the Army Punitive Law, there were prisons —divided into heavy and light—provided for those who violated the rules of barracks life.

* *Suima:* The prescribed method for crossing a body of water on horseback.

* *Shichō-hei* (transportation soldiers): Those assigned to carry and transport all the things that an army needs, such as food, arms, and ammunition. It was the least prestigious assignment.

* *Shikan* (officers), *shūban-shikan* (an officer of the week), *shūban ka-shikan* (a non-commissioned officer of the week): Those officers who are on duty for a week's duration (officers and those with equivalent ranks) and non-commissioned officers. In the army, these latter are: *sōchō* (sergeant major), *gunsō* (sergeant), and *gochō* (corporal); in the navy, *jōtō heisō* (higher warrant officer), *ittō heisō* (first-class warrant officer), and *nitō-heisō* (second-class warrant officer). Officers who normally resided out-side the barracks also had to move into them for the duration of their dutyweek, and attended to matters such as roll calls (checking attendance, etc.) and patrolling the barracks, accompanied by the non-commissioned officers of the week. While on patrol officers wore a red-and-white shoulderstrap.

* *Tekken* (iron-fist) *seisai* (discipline): A form of discipline which involves striking the violator very hard with one's fist.

*   *Ikki* (the first period): The first six months of training after recruits entered the barracks.

*   *Sasage-tsutsu* (presenting arms): A form of saluting—the soldier holds the gun straight up and out in front of him with both hands, and fixes his eyes on the receiver of the salute.

—Officers' Ranks—

	ARMY		NAVY
Gensui	(marshal)		(admiral)
Shō-kan	(officers with *shō* suffix, i.e., generals):		
Taishō	(general of the highest rank)		
Chūjō	(general of the middle rank)		
Shōshō	(lower-rank general)		
Sa-kan	(officers with *sa* suffix, below generals):		
Taisa	(colonel)	or	(captain)
Chūsa	(lieutenant colonel)	or	(commander)
Shōsa	(major)	or	(lieutenant commander)
I-kan	(officers with *I* suffix):		
Tai-I	(captain)	or	(first lieutenant)
Chū-I	(lieutenant)	or	(sub-lieutenant)
Shō-I	(sub-lieutenant)	or	(second sub-lieutenant)

ARMY	NAVY

—Ranking of non-commissioned officers—

Jun-shikan	(lit. sub-officer, i.e., non-commissioned officer)		
jun-I	(sub-officer)	or	*heisōchō* (chief warrant officer)

Isamu Nakamura

Born September 2, 1922. From Tokyo Metropolis. Through the Preparatory Division, Tokyo College of Physics, advanced to its Faculty of Mathematics in 1941. Entered the barracks in December 1942 as an air soldier. Killed in action, April 22, 1944, in Hollandia, Western New Guinea, a territory of the Netherlands at that time. A lance corporal. He was twenty-one years old.

April 16, 1943

What the military life has given me:

1. The individual and the whole. The thoroughness that must be involved in working toward a specific goal.
2. The uncertainty of death and life.
3. The impersonality with which mass killings must be faced.

☐ With regard to the fact of how deeply rooted my heart's desire is—although I used to snip it off whenever it sprouted even the slightest bit—I would now say, in unison with the teaching of Shinran [Buddhist priest, 1173–1262, who founded the Jōdo Shin-Shū sect], that:

1. There is no genuine uncertainty, or even a convenient uncertainty; and
2. There is no true agape or eros.
    —What does exist is the violent, alternating current that
        pulsates between these two!

☐ What is the military life that engenders this sort of desire?

    —A totalitarian dictatorship—(nation)

From here,
        —learn also the dictatorship of individualism—(society)
            Both place too much importance on just one side of
            genuine human experience!!
            Make rational what is absolutely irrational!
            Turn into irrationality!!
    I think of the life of the proletariat in which there is no culture and no
pain.
    And, here, almost all human beings live that life!

May 29
☐ Look, do you see . . .
An airplane
Flying away leisurely
in the mild blue skies of the morning
(The sunlight warmly makes a diagonal pattern on the barrack's
garden)
This is the children's picture book of the Showa Era.
They say that children's tales exist even in an era such as the present,
so messy and bent out of shape.
But . . .

August 11

☐ Was my heart still stiffened?

My heart is shut tight even when I look at a cloudless blue sky. Perhaps the opposite is true: it is this stunning blue itself that is making it that way.

I must become a person who can smile gently at anything and on any occasion, regardless of where or when. I would really like, with a big smile, to close the curtain down on a story just as the angel-like children in Melhen's fairy tales do.

September 26

☐ You, a madman!
Rather, the real truth is in you.
Those who call you foolish or stupid
are nothing but crazy themselves.

October 8

☐ I love my fatherland without reservation.
But
I have no fatherland to love—
    for the soul that peeked into an abyss. . . .

November 5

☐ Hay, Mr. Tamaru! I have to recognize the fact that I am just a green-horn with burning hope.

I have such a strong attachment to and love for mathematics!

Oh, Tamaru!

When I can get hold of a book on mathematics, I turn into a simple little pragmatic child.

After having completed the night duty last night, and carried my tired body to a study room, what do you think I worked on until past 11 o'clock? It was a book on concurrence, which I brought from Takasagoya[1] when I was permitted to go out for a break two days ago.

(At the same time I am fully aware that my mind has become less sharp in the area of mathematics.)

Oh, Tamaru! I was so happy, just like a kid.

Starting today, I will always have an inner consolation. I am reminded of Newton's words, to the effect that ". . . [the happy one] is a child picking up sea shells on a beach"!!

November 7

☐   I have such a strong attraction toward the systematic.

Perhaps I will never be satisfied with merely *sentiment pensée* [the author's usage] (sentimental thinking).

November 11

☐   What a quiet joy my life has become since I began to read a book on mathematics!

(My heart has been surging continually. My heart has been carrying nightly conversations with sage philosophers and poets.)

But, lately, I do not visit Pascal [French scientist/philosopher, 1623–62] or Prof. Nishida's [philosopher, Kitarō Nishida, 1870–1945] secret home; neither have I had a discussion with Baudelaire or Kenji Miyazawa [a poet and an author of children's tales, 1896–1933] at some café. . . .

I just so desire, from a distance, to look at things as do Kant and Abel [Niels Henrik Abel, Norwegian mathematician, 1802–29]. It is simply that I am so immersed in them and adore their great and yet childlike search for the truth.

December 5

☐   On a day of leave, I got together with my older sister, Katsuko, and my younger brother, Yutaka. A whole swarm of emotions choked me up as we talked about many things.

Over the course of ten days, and without knowing what to do, I fought the pains of my body and soul. I want to recapture the past two weeks of my life, as if to drive a wedge very deeply . . .

☐   The problems of life:

The problems of culture:

—And what sort of attitude should I take about such issues in this military life?

What a pity that my life today is such that I have to grit my teeth in order to control my impulses, my wanting to wade into the study of philosophy—no, rather, my desire to confront all sorts of the problems in life. . . .

Do I have to find my soul's consolation by looking at a page of advertising which features the Iwanami Complete Works Series?* (9 p.m. in the evening)

December 8
□   I am running away.
      My heart is running away from this military life. Is that all right?
      Look at reality head-on and without falsification! (At night)

—[A letter to Mr. Yoshio Tamaru]—

April 29, 1943

Greetings.
      Today (the 29th), once again, we were quite unexpectedly allowed to leave the barracks for an "extended break" (i.e., until 8 p.m.); and I have just enjoyed a leisurely nap here at Takasagoya. Now, in the study, in the gathering darkness of dusk shortly past 5 o'clock, I have been indulging in a whole variety of thoughts without really concentrating.
      Faith—nature, mathematics—a proletariat society and the military—*poésie* (poetry), and *pensée* (ideology). . . . How has the military life affected me with respect to all these things?
      I wonder whether just thinking things over, without any real concentration, could be an excuse for the fact that all the things I mentioned above have been squashed by military life. A poem, with only a word here and there and part of a phrase, comes to mind; and a breath of the old passion for mathematics rushes through my heart. I wonder whether everything has been lost!?
      (Perhaps you are upset about this letter, thinking that this is rather weak-minded and unlike myself. But I must honestly tell you that I am in no way defeated. Everything is about to explode violently inside my chest. Regrettably, however, there is really no time in which to act freely.
      But perhaps even this is just another excuse, so I better stop. At any rate, and whatever happens, what I cannot stop is my writing!) . . .
      What has the military life done for me?
      What have I gotten out of those fleeting thoughts in the middle of the night?
      That is the idea of the four *hōin* [ascetics or mudra] of Buddhism! They are the following: religious austerities are all painful; religious austerities are in a constant state of flux; certain religious austerities are selfless; and *nirvana* [Buddha's passage to spiritual existence] is lonely and quiet. (Do you not think that I am being taken in? Quite the opposite: I am not restricting myself to the merely obvious and convenient meanings of these four ascetics.)
      The military life is something that feeds off the one great central issue of life and death.—
      A path to *agape* [god's love] as a collective entity.—

But this is the deepest of my reflections, one that pops up even when I do not wish to think. Right, it has to be only one of the potentially unlimited number of paths my life could have taken up to this point! . . .

But what, then, have I really gained from it all!?

While I grit my teeth—and when I face up to the harshness and trials of the military life and see the ugliness behind it, my heart can always turn toward nature—and to my passion for mathematics, to advance steadily and surely, step by step in the harsh, cold air. It has been one of my personality traits since before I arrived here—to retain a certain purity even for a brief period. This way of looking at things moves me powerfully. Every night I think about how I want to live life like Pascal when I get out of the military—live a life where I can spend every day quietly and calmly with mathematics and Buddhist prayer.

But just then another one of my traits asserts itself and, yes, gives rise to a confident smile—just like a strong-bodied man's who stands erect on a corner in some city, pounding his chest and looking around at the people . . . from the standpoint of one living amid the extremes of this military life, I cannot help but think of the inherent contradictions within a stratified society. I cannot help but feel compassionate toward those poor people who struggle on from day to day. And I would like to imitate Lamb [Charles Lamb, English essayist, 1775–1834] by throwing a bunch of flowers into the middle of the confusion of a big, greedy city.—Each night, stepping over my aspirations like Pascal, I shall go to bed wearing a smile. (And be relieved to know that this is no lie). . . .

What, finally, I most wonder about is why these two alternating currents of emotion hit my heart so much harder than they did before I got into this life. . . .

It is because of this very restrictive life, and, correspondingly, of the much greater awareness of the ego inside me, that I cannot avoid discovering the ugliness within myself.

. . . This is all about me for now.

—And when all is said and done, in the end I will not change!!

My having said that, however, perhaps you would not believe that this sort of letter could come from me. You might say that, instead of receiving a conceptual letter of this sort, you would either have me write a one-word poem or else send you the results of some mathematical research. I have no answer for that. But please trust me.—I shall hand deliver them to you soon, and with a great big smile thrown in.

(It is already past six o'clock) and I have been writing this letter for over an hour now—stop and then write and stop and then write again! —But is it all just meaningless empty chatting? I wrote simply because I wanted to free you from worry and, too, because of my deepest friendship with you and because I feel so close to you.

Please wait in the anticipation that my letters will become more and more substantial. Well, then, stay well.

I am making an oath that you and I will walk the path together to the supreme Buddhist way.

Yours,

Isamu

[December 19]

Dear Tamaru!

Greetings. Sorry that I have taken so long to reply to your letter. It is probably because I am such a poor correspondent. But, right from the start, I want you to believe that I am living as I always have been, without even the slightest alteration.

As always, I am reading books on mathematics today, knowing that the mobilization order is coming up tomorrow. Almost all of my fellow soldiers are seriously shaken emotionally, almost to the point of frenzy. When facing this sort of situation I could not avoid recognizing my own stubborn strength—a strength probably derived from my basically introverted disposition. Only I am anxiously waiting for the books you are sending me. And, one thing that I regret is that I cannot send you something about the *"α hyōgen-tai"* ["alpha expression form"] [an expression used by Niels Henrik Abel in his theories on groups in mathematics]. But, at this particular point in time, is there anything that I should be speaking out about!

Having said all that, however, please do not consider this as an arrogant and presumptuous rebellion on my part. Lately I have been thinking, and from the very deepest level, about where, without the ab-solutist's mind-set, life itself really exists. I tore up many letters that I wrote to you, but it was simply because I listened to the absolutist's silent suggestion. It does not matter how sincerely we talk with one another; even if it be about religion and god(s), it is nothing more than mere noise unless the words are in accord with absolutist thought. It does not matter how purely we tried to study philosophy, make poetry, or do mathematics, —it would all be nothing but garbage if we did not heed the god(s)' silent suggestion. The sun has already set on modern culture. O.K.? Even if you do not hear from me again in the future, please continue to walk the path to the supreme way of Buddhism, because I shall be waiting there alone, with smiles. As I said, the sun has already set on modern culture.

However, should we hide away in a medieval hermitage and spend a night just talking with God alone?—No. There is only one path for us: as creative elements of a creative world, we must find God's words in every step of poetic composition. Historical reality is a world filled with dreams, biased views, and self-assertion. This is its true nature. The only way to think properly about a historical world is to become one yourself, and to act like one—to think of a number by becoming the number itself. This last has become everything to me lately. It is not for me to become a rebel within the world of mathematics like Galois [Évariste Galois, a French mathematician, 1811–32], or to become a worldly person like Gauss [Carl Friedrich Gauss, a German mathematician, 1777–1855], but it is Abel—who knelt down in the middle of numbers themselves—whom I love infinitely.

My dear friend! I shall keep walking on as always regardless of how harsh my future predicament really turns out to be. Steadily and firmly, I shall be walking along my way a step at a time; so why should there be anything to be ashamed of even if my hopes should end up as just that?

Everything is *heijōtei* [to accept with a normal/usual heart]; so, what should I object against? I hope that you too will continue to walk your own way without being false to yourself.

December 19, midnight

When I open books each night and get into my mathematics, the sorrow of life disappears into somewhere far away on a night train,

Along the side of mathematics—
Yours,

Isamu

Note

*   College students and books: One of the most painful things for student soldiers to endure was the fact that they were not free to read in the barracks. In the army, most often there was a complete ban on books, and even in the navy it was only permitted to keep books of a certain definite kind (such as those dealing with the way of samurai—*hagakure*).

[The reader will find] such cases as Tokurō Nakamura and others who continued their reading even after entering the military. All of this activity took place under very exceptional circumstances whereby soldiers were allowed to return home during their time off on Sundays. Under such circumstances, there were student-soldiers who, until just moments before their deaths, continued to strive—even through the most extreme difficulties—to form an ideology for themselves. A good example of the extent of the difficulties which they were willing to undergo can be found in Yoshio Hayashi's *Waga Inochi Getsumei ni Moyu (My Life Burns in the Moonlight)*, though he is not one of the authors in this book. In the army only two months before the end of the war, there were even some who read books that were especially forbidden, such as the German edition of Lenin's *State and Revolution*. They managed to do this by tearing the sheets right out of the book and reading them, sheet by sheet, in the barracks' toilet. Then they would tear the sheets into pieces and throw them away. In some cases they even had to eat them.

Osamu Takei (former surname, Hanaoka)

Born June 9, 1917. From Tokushima Prefecture. From Wakayama Higher Commerce School, entered Kyushu Imperial University, Faculty of Jurisprudence and Letters, Department of Economics, in 1939. Graduated from the above in December 1941. Conscripted and entered the barracks in February 1942. Missing in action, May 26, 1945, near Myingyan, Myanmar (Burma). Army lieutenant. He was twenty-seven years old.

[From a memo written prior to entering the barracks]

A strong attachment to life cannot be elevated to the height of a powerful affirmation of life; moreover, the affirmation itself was the road of "now," leading directly to the place of execution.

[From a memo written after entering the barracks]

At last the die has been cast.

My one prayer will be that the new life might serve as a nurturing food for my true nature. With only abstract ideas, there is nothing I can do.

There has always been a winter, but, for this year at least, spring-time came many times. Deep in my heart is a sharp feeling that I can only call *akugare* [translators' note: an ancient poetic word which refers to the anxiety caused by being away from where one is supposed to be].

What a void these so-called superior officers are! A perfect one-word description of their behavior is *"kyōtai"* (disgraceful conduct or crazy behavior)—a word that I should like to pass along to them.

The man named Prime Minister Tōjō has a face like a short-necked clam with a mustache. A rainbow of history is being woven inside this empty shell. Would that mean that Tōjō is a poet? Oh, good grief!

Stretching arms just like a spider. . . . Soldiers!

. . . Just as our ancestors called them "ground-spiders or trapdoor spiders," those [soldiers] would, probably, call them "ground spiders" with a strange and grotesque pronunciation.

There is no history in the barracks, but there is a myth.

The master of the myth talks about a religious sect, Seichō-no-Ie (lit. House of Growth), and preaches the great spirit that breathes through all creatures.

As Baudelaire [Charles Pierre Baudelaire, French poet, 1821–67] stated, is not the death involved in the loss of spirit a true death? I feel that there are two kinds of death: the death that is endured as life itself drips away, and the kind of spiritual death that can be squeezed out of a living person.

A train is passing by in the darkness, with lights like a chain of memory.—My hair that was chopped off is floating down. [Translators' note: Every member of the Japanese Armed Forces had his hair closely cropped.]

Dear hair, dear hometown, the smell of a foreign land—

I want to let my hair grow, even in a dream.

Clothes and skies, all pure blue.

All sorts of winds are blowing through.

With demonic voices. . . .

I wonder what the center of a human being is, where it is located. Mr. Hakkō Ōshima [a poet] will be wandering about the streets of Tokyo; my friend Taguchi will be skipping lectures at the university and going frequently to a hospital; and Shinnuma will be chatting with his wife behind a huge wine barrel about France or something like that.

Nakao is in a *tochka* [i.e., an underground pillbox]. I bet he is no longer reading books on Nishida's [Kitarō Nishida's] philosophy.

As for me—I am standing here, open-mouthed, watching a horse inspection.

What a splendid set of legs there are on a horse!

I want to feed the horses but, if I did, that would put them on their mettle and that would make them troublesome for us.

The horse that dances with red hooves.

Oh, a man who is being pulled by a horse . . . !

Darn it! A man cannot even control horses. Incompetent consciousness and a sparkling instinct. . . . Moreover, a fact does not necessarily mean a truth.

The ultimately valuable truth has to be that the man controls the horse.

Oh, a crowd of people! Those quarreling barrels!

The dirty water in the barrels!—And the falsehood that is being created! (There is not a thing to be created/made.)

Of course there have to be some ups and downs.—In order to be created.—Everything.

The stars are tranquil tonight.

I think of the life led by the nuns at our Catholic convent, who stood near a window with wounded hearts; with their withdrawing hearts they lived and then finally died, and [I think of] their lives that must be, just like those stars, absorbed at a discreet distance from our real world.

(May 25, evening)

We must live, even if it means wearing a mask.

Those who are working, and yet not working, are saying "Hoi no, hoi no ho (Yo-heave-ho)" in unison.

My time is crying, but my watch is laughing.

Simply because I am able to think, I would not think.

While I am writing this, a lecture is still continuing on the interpretation of certain of the essential points to foot-soldiering.

"Trust is power," says the lecturer. Two timeframes seem to be oddly juxtaposed, and, in the midst of this confusion, I heard expressions such as "*inujini* (to die in vain like a dog)," which I had long forgotten.

Those happy, idle people who become upset over a window, yet not upset with a double window.—Real anguish exists inside idleness; real anguish, moreover, melts into the window itself.

Give Us the Liberty, a film by the French director René Clair, is being shown for the last time, at least in our country, at xxx Theater.

—Everything is ending! [dying out?]

I am still alive.

Even though I am being treated like a complete fool.

Even the one who looks down on those who treat others as fools, is himself looking down. However, how do we ever become fools? Perhaps we can become fools.

Hey you, you with those drunken legs at that exit door in Crimea [at the Crimean War], and with a face like a shell that was dropped from a container, you are following orders! Right! Left!—Biting your lips, just like a jaguar.

Make a mad dash! Defeat them!

The essence of governing consists of being pulled rather than pulling, being forced rather than forcing, and being seen rather than seeing.

—This is political science both of the spirit and of the social structure. Ironically, a decision-maker cannot be a decision-maker: the rules begin from the spirit of those being ruled.

All the structures which exist are, somehow, compounds of barbarism and democracy; certain specific systems which managed to survive were simple absolutism, aristocracy, and an entangled structure.—Like a rope.

I shall not speak of monarchism.

A thing one cannot speak of: the god of politics.

—I am writing this in a toilet.

Ah, but I am also awaiting a journey southward. The freighter, I am told, has a very low ceiling and you can hit your head even when sitting. There is no light in the evening—only hot temperature [to suffer]. So long as I am in such a heavenly place, I shall write poems with all my might, and neither shall I write short poems. I shall write long, long poems; poems of full strength, poems as piercing as nails. Call wind where there is no wind, and I shall write red songs on the pages that flutter and turn themselves. I shall write songs of a country of fire, songs of a port on fire about the corpses of the continent, and of emaciated nature itself. Oh, I shall include it all—all snakes, all candles, all frills—and all fruits too will be over-ripe.

A human race, having built itself up with its own hands, and defended itself with its own blood, then goes about using its hands again to destroy itself! A name!

Kōichi Itao

Born October 2, 1923. From the Tokyo Metropolis. Entered the Tokyo University of Commerce in October 1943 from its Preparatory Division. Entered the Takeyama Naval Training Corps in Yokosuka, on December 10, 1943. Killed in action as a member of a reconnaissance boat unit, in the sea east of the mainland, Japan, February 18, 1945. Navy sub-lieutenant. He was twenty-one years old.

September 22, 1943

The graduation commencement of the Preparatory Division* of Tokyo University of Commerce [current Hitotsubashi University] is held at the Kanematsu Auditorium of the main university. For all of us today will be a day to be especially remembered, and forever. We gathered at the university at 9 a.m. It was the first beautiful autumn day with clear skies since September had begun. It seemed as though the day itself was celebrating our leaving the Preparatory Division and advancing to the University Division. ....

The ceremony was rather formal and conventional and not at all exciting. There was a talk by President Takase—I fell asleep for about ten minutes—which finally drew to a close. For me the whole thing was a blank sheet of paper, and the speaker more or less a mannikin.

I was in time for Prime Minister Tōjō's lecture. This must be a foretaste of what is to come; something that is going to have a decisive impact upon the various phases of our fate. The end of the extension for student conscription [cf. p. 82] is at hand, as is the end of all education in the colleges and universities in the fields of law, liberal arts, and economics —as well as their restructuring.

So one day in the very near future a dramatic turnaround in our fate will occur. At this particular point in time, there is neither optimism nor pessimism. Rather, instead of becoming all stirred up emotionally, we must simply make the best of things insofar as we are capable of determining for ourselves what that best is. And all this has to take place within the realm of the behavioral constraints placed upon us here, and has to be based on our recognition of the actual reality we are facing. Those of us students, who are pursuing the truth, must not be engulfed by the new situation in which we find ourselves, at least not to such an extent that we stumble when the time comes to make rational judgments and take firm action. ....

[A letter to a friend, dated September 5, 1944]
In response. Thank you very much for your postcard, which I have read with pleasure. There is no *"jūgo"* [literally, "behind the guns"— refers to folks back home, or those who are left at home, behind the front lines] or anything right now. You too are doing your work under the supreme command of the nation, just like us soldiers who are fighting in the war itself. The Ministry of Education has never been a very intelligent outfit, but lately the situation seems to have become worse than ever. At the present moment Japanese education is about to plunge into massive confusion. Perhaps they would never be able to understand that propagandizing by way of such mottoes as "working is education"* is nothing but a game, just playing with ideas. Look at the fact that all the broadcasting by Mr. Nagata, Chief of the Bureau of the Ministry, was immediately and severely challenged by the students in letters to the newspapers. I suppose that those who have no grasp of reality will die without suffering heartache or any regrets.

Perhaps you know a friend of mine, Kikuo Satō. He too will have to enter the barracks without having first attended his commencement exercises. He has been reading Fichte's [Johann Gottlieb Fichte, 1762–1814] *Doitsu Kokumin ni Tsugu (Reden an die Deutsche Nation).*

The lack of thoroughness of educational ideologies is causing no end of disorganization in today's Japan. We hope that you who are still remaining behind will build a new educational system for our nation; I hope also that, by doing so, you will be pleased to smash the false ideas that have penetrated deep within our leadership's skulls.

....

Notes

* Preparatory Division: Under the old Japanese educational system, "*Yoka*" or a three-year preparatory division at the same educational level as colleges or higher schools, was the next step for students after they had graduated from a high school. Preparatory divisions were established at some of the old system's university-level institutions, such as Tokyo University of Commerce, Hokkaido Imperial University, and most private universities.

* "Work is education, and education is work": The partial mobilization of students in the workplace [such as ammunition factories] which began in 1938 was expanded to the very destructive full-time students' mobilization of 1944. It was in its attempt to justify such policy that the Ministry of Education came up with its "Work is Education" idea.

Takashi Satō

Born October 29, 1933. From Shizuoka Prefecture. Entered the Tokyo Art Academy, Department of Oil-Painting, in 1943. Conscripted and entered the barracks as a communications soldier on December 1, 1943. Killed in action on Luzon, an island in the Philippine chain, July 25, 1945. Army sub-lieutenant. He was twenty-one years old.

Rain and more rain! This continuous downpour started yesterday and has not let up since. I am finally recovered from my exhaustion and have some time for serious thinking today. "Oh, the rain!" I sigh as I try to look outside through a steam-clouded window. The labor service [i.e., students who were mobilized to work for the war effort in factories and such. See the note above—"work is education"] is off today. I went to the school, had something to eat, and then went by myself to a museum, taking the time to look at every one of the old paintings and writings. No one, however, would ever know how much time I spend just sitting alone in this quiet room and how I hurt inside, or how desperate is my search for something. I finally felt relief, and found hope, in the magnificent and powerful line drawn by Chikuden [Chikuden Tanomura, a prominent literary man and artist of the late Edo period]. I am not certain about just how many hours I spent in front of that painting. Finally, and feeling that all other paintings did not matter, I simply slipped away and left the museum. Outside there was only the drizzle of the rain, and two or three people who were braving it to walk the paved street. I wanted to hold on to the inspiration which I had felt so deeply and clearly just now, so, as I walked I looked at nothing but the surface of the street about three meters in front of me, and walked back to the school. I wanted to write down that strong impression in my mind as clearly and as accurately as I possibly could.

.... I pictured my mother's forehead and her eyes—and believed that it was possible to ignore myself completely so long as I think of my mother. I thoughtfully resolved to draw a portrait of her if and when I am able to return home again.

In the evening, I thought again of my mother. It somehow seems to me that the pronunciation of the word *"haha"* [a term used among adults in reference to one's own mother] sounds too discordant.

—I go to bed in search of a dream [of my mother].

Somehow, more than usual, I feel like painting something creative, or whatever—I wanted to do something; but I am troubled by the fact that I am unable to make any smooth progress. This same problem has plagued me all day. Today, I ended up destroying the size-#25 painting which, last evening, I put so much effort into improving. It was just as unpleasant to look at as it is painful to go to bed with it in the condition it is now; on the other hand, I simply cannot paint anymore. Oh, well, I shall wait until tomorrow and let the oil dry a little; then I want to put on some new colors, fresh and clear ones. All the same, what a regrettable situation! Indeed, even as I write in this diary, it makes me feel uncomfortable to see the painting leaning in a corner of the room. It looks as though the man in the picture is laughing at me. If I could have faith in my own abilities—and, or better yet, know where my strength lies, there would be no pain. But I am just an unfortunate fool who does not even know what kind of a painting he is capable of today. Still, paintings are not the sort of thing that one can plan out with exactitude ahead of time. There is no way to go about it except with firm persistence and patience, no matter how many hundreds of hours it may take. In this sort of business any discussing or arguing is useless; the important thing is the end result, not a theory.

I actually feel helpless when I look at the old, clean design of a poster that I have on the wall. It is 1 a.m. already and I am not even the least bit sleepy. I need to continue my effort, single-mindedly and with all my energy, to produce the very best of the kind of work I am capable of.

For a few moments there it occurred to me that, in little more than a month, I would be entering the army barracks; but I prefer to think of the time that is left me before then—a period of what should be pure joy. I have not given up on life, far from it, but neither have I made any special preparation for the fate that I know is coming my way in one month's time. Between then and the present, I should think it would be enough for me to live each day of my life as fully as I possibly can.

Once again I have opened and read *Chieko Shō (Selections from Chieko),* a collection of poems by Kōtarō Takamura (a poet and sculptor, 1883–1956). I have always yearned to feel the heart of this poet, even a little, and throughout the collection I have achieved at least partial understanding; but my unpoetic and, to this point, totally unfulfilled life seems to be utterly remote from getting to the heart of poetry of this quality.

I wonder what my mother is doing. I regret that I wrote to my father the other day telling him not to go to too much trouble to come to see me [with her], if it is too difficult. The truth—and my earnest prayer—is that I want her to visit me no matter how difficult it might turn out to be. At this point I am not ready to set my feeling down in writing. For me now, I just really, really want to see my mother. Hurry, the sooner the better!

I do not feel as though it would do me much good right now even if I went home. What I really need right now is another human being's love for me. The natural beauty surrounding my hometown is great, but it holds no attraction for me just now—everything would be perfectly fine if only I could see my mother. I cannot see the remote skies over Manchuria [the three northeastern provinces of China wherein Japan established the "state" of Manchukuo]. I suppose that by now the night lights of Talien [the gateway port city of northeast China] are few and far between, and that by this time the train whistles at the port are making their lonesome, hooting sounds.

I suppose that, in a not so remote future, we too will be in a similar situation. I wonder where and in which direction I shall be heading. No matter where it turns out to be it will doubtless be pleasant, during off-duty hours, to think of the things of long ago. I am convinced that, by hanging onto my many dreams and thinking through the numerous changes my life has undergone in the past, I will be able to maintain my artistic sense/ sensitivity no matter where I may be stationed, or under what circumstances.

I wonder about what my friends might be doing while I am away. Perhaps they will be making at least some progress, and my guess is that they will be working away busily on a great many paintings.

The young girls whom I liked very much will be getting married off —to men I do not even know.

I suppose that people who never expected to die are dying and leaving this world.

My life too may very well be a thing of the past soon. However, and regardless of what happens, the only things that would never, ever change would be the paintings which I have produced up to this point, along with all the pains—and sometimes the agonies—that went into the making of them. Those paintings of mine will remain mine forever. Not one of them is what I would call a masterpiece. There are ten or so that I think are quite good. I would like to give the rest of them away. ....

It now seems to be definite that I must enter the barracks [*cf.* p. 137 for the note on "student mobilization"] on December 1. All my memories of the past leading up to the present now seem to be in the category of dreams. From this time forward, the only thing to do is to meet reality head on. I want to avoid this endless introspection involving my personal life and past. However, my life bears the scars of many wounds. My wounded heart as well as my disappointed hopes are my past and will remain my past even if some great events lie in wait in my future. However, I have the feeling that I shall most likely be destroyed and disappear without ever having the chance to find my own way, something I could accomplish by reflecting on and comparing the many years of my life as a student with my military experience. What an evil thing this is for humanity in general and what a betrayal of the individual!—But, when all is said and done, fate rules everything.

Shin-ichi Katō

Born February 21, 1923. From the Tokyo Metropolis. Graduated from Hirosaki Higher School, and in 1942, entered Kyoto Imperial University, Faculty of Economics. Entered the barracks in Korea on December 1, 1943. Killed in action in Myitkyina, northern Myanmar (Burma), on March 19, 1945. Army superior-private. He was twenty-two years old.

November 10, 1943

On the day I arrived there had been a light rain ever since morning, and both the mountains and the town all looked so nice and clean! For Kyoto to have been so cleansed on the day of my return after a long absence must, I thought, be a divine favor—and I felt so very grateful.

While I was still in Tokyo I thought that this would be my last visit to Kyoto before entering the barracks; so, I made plans to visit a whole variety of places—once arrived I wanted to be here, there, and everywhere. But now that I am in Kyoto I am unable to get started on anything that I had planned, primarily because there are so many things that I have to take care of, such as making preparations for entering the barracks. In this regard a special problem has been created due to the peculiar emptiness that a friend of mine left behind. He has entered the barracks one step ahead of me. Just for today, however, I wanted to live out the twenty-four hours as a full-time college student; so I attended classes, spent a lot of time reading books I had always wanted to read but never had the opportunity to get to before, and did whatever I could to take care of some leftover chores. Busy as I was it seems that I spent a lot of time just sitting in front of my desk thinking of nothing in particular—I kept reminding myself that the most important thing of all is to maintain one's intellectual life.

Both the mass media and the general public are in quite an uproar over the college students' conscription; but, so far as we ourselves are concerned, the situation is much more than merely unwelcome—we are secretly enraged. When I consider the fact that, now that we are about to go into battle, those sympathizing with us are the very same people who, several years ago, spoke out in favor of the general roundup of students, it makes me more keenly aware than ever that most people are only interested in externals. Their sole concern is over the fact that we have to enter the barracks in the middle of our university careers, and they are in total disregard of what is going on inside each of us—in our hearts. It is true that there are some students who are manipulated by the media and dance to its tune, but both press and public completely fail to understand that we who were students at the time of the roundup are the same human beings now as we were then. It is so sad that they have failed to recognize our common and enduring humanity, whether we be pure students or student-soldiers—they can only see us in these different, and quite separate, roles. I just wish they would leave us alone, provide us with a little more quiet.

These past two months comprise the one time in my life when I could be most serious, and also the one time when it was most necessary to be so. Frankly speaking, we are all simultaneously feeling a bit fearful about the future and less than confident about what we have accomplished in the past—and not only intellectually. Whatever the case, we are the type of people who, when we get up in the morning, cannot even think of going ahead to the next duty unless the conclusion we reached based on what we did yesterday is fixed and filed away in our minds.—This is no more than fundamental logic.

All of the above notwithstanding, I can and do deeply feel the thoughtful kindness of the boardinghouse people, and that of the neighbors as well.

Note
*   *"Gakusei-gari"* refers to the hunting or rounding up of college students: In February 1938, the National Police Bureau conducted searches for "idle" students, i.e.,

those who were skipping classes. Some 3,486 young men were arrested over a three-day period and were made to sign a written contract or repentance. They were released after being forced to pay their respects at the Imperial Palace. In August 1940, "A notice regarding students' self-discipline" was issued, and it prohibited both college and high school students from entering any movie theater on weekdays. There was also a total prohibition and/or restrictions against entering any café, bar, or other recreational establishment. Raids on delinquent youth among the working youth, i.e., non-student, were conducted too, and over 20,000 were arrested within a half-month period after it took effect in late August.

Kiyoshi Hirai

Born April 20, 1924. From Miyagi Prefecture. From the Second Higher School, he entered Tokyo Imperial University, Faculty of Law and Letters, October 1, 1944. October 10, 1944, entered Toyohashi Reserve Officers' Cadet School. Killed in Sendai during a bombardment, July 9, 1945. Army sublieutenant. He was twenty years old.

September 25, 1943

I returned home Sunday morning after being hosted most courteously by the Shibautas at their home in Fukushima City. Mother is urging me to change my major to one of the natural science disciplines.* I am fully aware and deeply appreciative of this parental concern for me—to choose the best possible path as a student who has been working as hard as I can at being a student all these many years; but I am not enthusiastic about switching my field of study to a medical or an agricultural department, and so I was very upset by the suggestion. The life of a student of literature is after all the life I have chosen, and I have worked very hard both in initiating it and in following through on it.

November 30

Once again my mother's insistence has intensified; she urges that I change my field of study to natural science so that I shall be able, at least for the moment, to avoid conscription. She speaks of her only son and of the mother, herself, who prayed and hoped only for his growing up safe and strong. The very thought that it is possible for that son to be killed on a battlefield while she stands by powerlessly is something that she would find it unbearable to entertain. Her appeals to me have been so serious and sorrowful—almost tearful—that her worries and concerns must be painful enough to be mind-threatening. In attempting with every ounce of her being to persuade me, mother was alternately demanding and cajoling, and she came up with arguments from every conceivable angle. In the beginning, her suggestion that I switch my field of study to natural science was not much more than a calculated desire to have me "graduate from the university with an assured future," but now her mother's instinct is, so to speak, smelling her child's blood! It is almost as though she is, and with uncanny accuracy, predicting my death. Of course there will be no hope of survival if I should become a pilot, just as there will be scant chance of it if and when I should become a fighting officer in the Sendai Aoba Division. It is against this background that mother speaks so sadly and thoughtfully: ". . . I am afraid that, considering your personality, you are going to dash forward recklessly and will eventually be killed."—I too had been thinking that my personality is indeed an invitation for disaster; so I was stunned that she had scored a hit so directly on target. I find myself deeply regretful over the fact of my stubborn nature!

Moreover, to die so young, even as a flower's petal falls, is what I truly want. Yet I cannot say that the way my parents think and feel is just an emotional leftover from some liberal ideology.

I wept in my heart and joined my hands in veneration, but I had to wear a smile on the outside when dealing with my loving mother's appeals and entreaties. What a contradiction and what a dilemma to be in! I wept with pain in my heart because of this struggle between two souls in conflict, and ended up crying out loud. . . . Mother, I really do understand how you feel, dear mother, but the times we live in and the education that I have received do not allow me to go along with your wishes. Please, please forgive me for the great impiety of dying before your own time has come. . . .

Note

* On the subject of changing one's major to a scientific field: Those students who were sent to the front because of the end of their deferments in December 1943 were those in law and the liberal arts, plus some from agricultural science. The students in the various fields of natural science, in engineering, medical science, and those in national teachers' training programs, were permitted to continue their studies. As a result, there were many, many students who attempted to transfer into science. There was, for example, the case of the six "anti-war, anti-military" students of Seikei Higher School, of Mitsubishi Zaibatsu lineage, who took medical colleges' examinations in three different medical schools so as not to overload the same college [which would increase the probability of all failing together], and five of them were able to escape being among "the students departing for the front."

Hiroo Kikuyama

Born September 6, 1921. From Mie Prefecture. From the Third Higher School, he entered Tokyo Imperial University, Faculty of Jurisprudence, October 1941. Entered Hisai Infantry Corps, December 1, 1943. Killed in action at Ipeal Village on the Island of Luzon, in the northern Philippines, April 29, 1945. Army lieutenant. He was twenty-three years old.

October 11, 1943

Why in the world am I taking up arms for the Emperor? Am I doing it for ideological reasons connected with the motherland, or because of the love which I unquestionably bear toward my parents, or even for the pure natural beauty of the mountains and rivers of Japan that was always my *furusato* (hometown)? Am I about to fight for all of these things, or just a part of them?—Anyway, I have not, at least just at present, gotten around to answering the question of why I should have to risk my life. If things could only be as they were two years ago, when I was so terrified at the thought of death that I kept getting up in the middle of the night to check my face in the mirror for a death shadow. Then again, when I had happily chosen the path of martyrdom as my only means of escape, I would have been glad to board a plane or climb into a submarine just to throw my life away. Now, however, I share the feeling of that elderly author [Tōson Shimazaki, 1872–1943], who recently passed away, saying that "even though I am in my present condition, I still wish somehow to keep on living." So how can I arm myself and go off to fight a war on some distant battlefield? As I turn off the light I peer out from a window of this room at a clear 13th-day moon. Watching the white snow-like cloud of the night, my psychological readiness during an earlier period to hop into a fighter plane seems dreamlike indeed.

I firmly believe that the basic rule of morality is to be honest with one's own heart. It has to be a case of "pretending to be bad," if not one of downright hypocrisy, for a person who really wishes to survive to man a warplane at the very same time—particularly a plane that carries a high casualty rate with it. The obligation to go into battle is excusable whenever having to do so is a question of one's fate (of course this fact itself is the problem and also most important . . .), but to choose to join the army or navy or to fly a warplane is something that requires an individual's own conscious and cold-blooded decision. Any such determination is not to be imposed upon another human being, or made even for oneself on the basis of temporary excitement.

How could I, who have witnessed such foolish and even contemptible behavior among my many friends and acquaintances—and even in myself as well—throw my life away just for the benefit of a few of those friends who are still around whom I respect, as well as for one professor whom I hold in high esteem? This is especially the case since they too are in no way desirous of my death. The best and most understandable reason has to be—is—I myself. As I take pen in my hand to review the situation, this way of thinking which I have settled on seems inevitable. If this is indeed the case, however, then death itself does not seem to have a clear definition. Sometimes I think that it is all just a matter of fate.

....

Oh, somehow, now I must face myself as frankly as possible. I have been putting off having to think things completely through, but now the time has finally arrived. I feel impatient! However, I want to try and think calmly.

October 20

I want to write about what happened yesterday. I paid a visit in the afternoon to the grave of my friend, Taguchi, at Tama cemetery. I arrived there at 4:30 p.m. But, no matter how hard I tried, I could not find his grave. I looked everywhere, inspecting tombstones one by one, until finally I even lost track of where I was and even wound up once at the edge of a highway. I became so desperate that I even called his name out loud—"Taguchi!" Still I could not find his tombstone. I felt as though I would be letting him down if I could not pay my respects at his gravesite, especially on the last day before my departure from Tokyo, so I kept on searching for his grave even though it was getting darker all the time and there was no one else around. I picked up a book and some flowers that I had left at a well, and had just about decided on giving up and leaving the place—and, possibly, on returning some other time. Then I found that I still could not give up, and once again walked around in an unsuccessful search for his grave. Finally, and just as I was about to abandon my project once and for all, I happened to glance at the tombstone just behind me—it was Taguchi's grave. I was delirious. I talked to him out loud. I even had the illusion that his tombstone moved. By the time I got some fresh water and put flowers and incense sticks by the gravesite, it had become so dark that I could barely read the letters on tombstones. What happened was not just good luck. I cannot explain it in any way except that Taguchi called me. To a certain extent I do believe in the existence of spirits. And I told Taguchi that even though I was going off to war I would not be killed in action. I told him that of course I would have to risk my life, but would live to get over his death and to carry on. Perhaps I am slightly exaggerating, but it just might be that the thought of death has not yet taken a realistic shape in my mind. The only really important truth may be the very thought of not wanting to die. As Rilke [Rainer Maria Rilke, an Austrian poet, 1886–1926] wrote, a loved one who has passed away will live on in the memory of a living person. Taguchi is alive in my heart, in Masahiko's, and probably in Iwamiya's heart as well. When I think about my own death I wonder who, outside of my parents, would take a similar attitude—and I feel a bit lonesome. However, even if there were only someone who would just believe that in me there had existed an earnest dedication to life, I think that would be more precious than anything else. To live as earnestly as one can—there is nothing else that really matters.

April 25, 1944 [After entering the barracks]
....

I shall try to write down what has gone on since December 1, the day when you and I, though in different places, first put on a military uniform. I do not know about you, but lately I have begun to wonder how it came to be that I arrived here so light-heartedly, because that was really a strange attitude to take. Of course you could simply say that it was all due to the fact that we came here in such a serene state of mind, but I still think that on that first day there should have been some very serious considerations to mull over—on that day when my fate had already become so definite. But whatever may be the truth about the gravity of the situation on that day, I have the feeling that, even if we should have to face a graver one we would be able to handle the challenge without any problems, and, so long as we were given the proper orders, without losing our poise.

We were the only recruits, so it was only natural that we had to work hard, but an unduly harsh round of duties within the barracks began almost immediately. From the moment when I kicked off the covers and got up in the morning until the lights were turned off at night—there was nothing in the barracks that could not be used as an excuse for being reprimanded except during military training outside in the bitter cold. At times we were forced to remain standing in a corner of our squad room even after the lights had been turned off. As a result of all this we even welcome the outside military training—no matter how cold and difficult it is—where at least we can smoke cigarettes openly, and there are not so many occasions for being knocked around physically.

While on the matter of physical punishment, it might be noted that by the end of December and in early January we were regularly beaten with *"jōka"* [the leather slippers that are worn inside the barracks] and with leather belts. There were some who were made to stand up for two hours and then brutally beaten and kicked senseless because, our seniors said, the serving of rice was too slow. As you know so well, I am not clever and neither am I quick with regard to physical activity; so, obviously, I was not excepted from the sort of treatment I have just described.

They say that the buglecall which signals lights out carries this message: "Oh, you poor recruits!—You will be going to bed in tears again." And as a matter of fact, I often did have to cry myself to sleep in an "envelope" [i.e., bed] after having been beaten a number of times and shoved into bed. I wept not because of the pain but, rather, because of those feelings of outrage and indignity which I had to endure. It seems that my morale was completely undermined. It is called "five-month training," but I kept computing how many more days still remained out of those five months, and I continued counting down just about every single day. I would look at a cold moon on my way to the toilet at night and keep thinking about how many more full moons I would be seeing from there. I claimed that I wanted to go to the front, because soon it was more a case of "nakigoto" [lit. words with tears, i.e., whining a gripe] than anything else. I recall having written you about this "nakigoto" of mine around that time and, if I remember correctly, getting a rather stern letter from you in reply. You told me in your letter to "trust in the healing power of time and be strong," and that was very close to the same advice I had been giving myself.—But under the circumstances which prevailed at that particular time, nothing but "nakigoto" was really possible.

I could not really feel anything even when I learned of the "gyokusai" [lit. meaning is the shattering of a precious stone, and the literal reference is to death with honor, but in practice the term was used in connection with battles in which everyone was killed] of Makin and Tarawa [the Japanese garrisons on both these islands were completely annihilated in November of 1943] or sending off regiment after regiment of soldiers to the battlefront. I naturally wondered how I could go on with this kind of life. Even though I understood how it had come about, I could not fully accept it, and therefore, at least subconsciously, I went about criticizing the war, the nation itself, and other important things. I am all but certain that my general attitude was detectable in your letters too. ....

Note

*   *Naimuhan, Naimu*: Everyday life in the barracks was known as *"naimu"* [inside duty], and each company was divided into *"naimu"* squads. The soldiers lived in a large room that was at once sleeping quarters, dining room, a room to take care of their equipment, and a recreation room. The idea was to create group living family-style. Officers lived outside the barracks as a matter of principle, and separate quarters were also provided for non-commissioned officers. The result was that within each squad soldiers with seniority, such as lance corporals and superior privates, rose to something approaching godlike status. The new recruits found themselves assigned to take care of everything for the older men. They laundered for them, handled their meals for them, and, except for the time spent on their own military training outside, even took care of the seniors' military equipment and shoes. The real hell for the recruits began once the roll calls after the evening meal were completed. The torments inflicted by the older soldiers were varied and included weird and abnormal private punishments such as the "train game" and the "heavy-bomber game." Some recruits committed suicide because they could not endure such treatment any longer. The grotesque and oppressive nature of these human relationships and of everyday life in the barracks has been described in Hiroshi Noma's *Shinkū Chitai (Vacuum Zone)*.

Hachirō Sasaki

Born July 7, 1922. From the Tokyo Metropolis. Having graduated from the First Higher School, he entered Tokyo Imperial University, Faculty of Economics, in April 1942. Entered the Takeyama Naval Training Corps in Yokosuka, December 9, 1943. He was killed in action, April 14, 1945, in the skies over the Okinawa Sea as a member of the Shōwa Special Attack Unit [one of the groups which later came to be called "kamikaze pilots"]. He was twenty-two years old.

February 18, 1941 Tuesday

Prof. Abe's [Yoshishige Abe, renowned philosopher and educator, 1884–1966] lecture on *"Shūshin"* (lit., personal conduct, or moral education) covered a variety of topics, starting with friendship and continuing on to the relationship between the social structure and individuals. There are always so many themes strung throughout his talks but, even though I cannot recall them all in any detail, the story of his friendship with Kageo Uozumi left a particularly strong impression on me.

I also attended a presentation given by John Morris [a lecturer at the First Higher School]. Some of the subjects he covered were: the weather in the Himalayas; high-pressure winds over the Tibetan Plateau; an oxygen engineer; meteorology; the Tibetan people; and people's working lives at high elevations. Everything was completely absorbing, and there was much to learn from Morris' lecture, because he brought out the fact that these people's passion for the mountains is not meaninglessly metaphysical or abstract, but superbly scientific.

February 9, 1943 Tuesday

Made very slow progress on *Das Capital* [by Karl Marx] once I got into the second volume. It is certainly a rambling and ambiguous work. There were also many interruptions, and my own impatience certainly did not help matters.

Got into *Rekkyō Genseishi Roshia (Modern History of Russia as a World Power)* [by Noboru Ōrui, published by Fuzanbō in its Hyakka Library], and was amazed by the high-handedness of Lenin and Stalin. I would like to see their like in Japan too. According to today's news, it seems that our forces have withdrawn from the South Pacific. German-held Stalingrad has now fallen to the Soviet Army, and Rostov [the southern part of the Russian Republic] also seems to be threatened. It seems that Hirasawa's message is now applicable: the time has come to harden ourselves against pity. I feel terrible when I reflect on my personality. If I were somehow able to retreat to a safe haven, I would be better off making my field of specialization natural science or something like it, where I could put all my energy into the single-minded exploration of natural scientific theories, and would thereby be guaranteed immunity [from the military]. But the dice have already been thrown, and now there is nothing I can do now except to deal wholeheartedly and sincerely with whatever I have to face. A path will open up somehow. There is none right now in front of me, but a path will appear after me [for others to follow].

February 11 Thursday

I have re-read several selections by Kenji Miyazawa [a poet and the author of stories for juveniles, 1896–1933]. I was more impressed than ever by passages such as "It is impossible to experience individual happiness within an unhappy society," and "Indicating some new development that is right and beautiful in itself, not just a reflection of the falsehood and affectivity of conventional religion and morality."

This type of thinking certainly applies to Utopias such as the one described [by Miyazawa] in *Gusukōbu-dori no Denki (Biography of Gusukōbu-Bird)*. In these imagined societies the contradictions of private production, as well as those of wars, etc., are presented as self-evident. The crucial thing is how to go about making such a society a reality. That is the only problem. The situation in Russia provides at least one hint. The world is walking along the right path. What we need is the creation of a society wherein the selfless service of one's country is made to be a reality, and of a world in which every person does his or her best according to his or her ability—and has the guarantee of being rewarded accordingly. It is only in such a world that human beings can walk a straight path.

People must not concern themselves with trivial matters: the ideology that will guide society in the future is that true joy must come through one's personal work and love.

May 14   Friday

In the past, capitalism has kept on expanding and expanding even while revealing a whole set of contradictions. At every stage of its expansion the study of economics has likewise advanced, and bit by bit it has pushed ever closer to a satisfactory analysis. By the time Karl Marx [a German revolutionary philosopher and economist, 1818–83] made his contribution, it might have been said that the structure of capitalism had been scientifically analyzed with something approaching completeness. It must be borne in mind, however, that the society Marx saw and studied was one in which the opposition between management and labor was at its very height. And ever since then Marxism is most often advocated whenever the opposition between management and labor turned extremely harsh, in situations usually brought on by sudden and serious shifts in the economy. Capitalism of course came about through the ever-shifting waves of a turbulent economy and achieved an ever greater rate of expansion until now; when it is finally facing the threat of total extinction. Once imperialism switched over to state capitalism we would have to say that, not only quantitatively but qualitatively, capitalism had completed its evolutionary round. State capitalism is not a higher level of capitalism. I think that state capitalism is a denial of the whole system—and we are squarely in the middle of this conversion period. The study of economics itself is such a confused affair that those of us who live in the confused world dominated by it have to be willing to change our *ethos* [set of guiding principles, i.e., our general outlook about the race, basic social norms, and cultural values and attitudes], whether we want to or not. As we confront this conversion period we have to say farewell to the *ethos* that invited the rise of capitalism and, guided by a new *ethos*, carry on with shaping the outline of the society we are obliged to construct.
....

Individualism is the ethos of capitalism: the new ethos needs to be some form of totalitarianism, appropriate either to a nation or the world itself. The world's new *ethos* will be found at that point of connection where the safety of the people who work for society as a whole needs to be guaranteed by society as a whole. The discovery will not be made just now simply because we are in a time of transition, but singing to the tune of "totalitarianism" would not accomplish anything unless those objective conditions existed within which such genuine social justice could flourish.

To this end, I feel that concerns such as the insurance business should be the first to be nationalized. Once the others go that same route, what a beautiful place this world will be! In such [an ideal] world there would not be a single person who would in a narrow way think only of himself. Just suppose that everyone's every action were based on a desire for the welfare of others and indeed of the world. . . . Although up to the present only vaguely, I have given all this a lot of thought, and have concluded that such a principle, i.e., a pure love for other human beings, would most certainly lead us into a new world. I sometimes wonder when this world of love will ever be realized but, until it is, our duty is to lay the ground-work for a society in which no one will have to feel any needless anxiety.
. . . .

Even today, when something approaching the *ethos*, guiding principles, of a new era can at least be glimpsed, and while the material foundation for it is actually under construction, we cannot afford to overlook the fact that some relics of the old capitalist system are still lying about here and there. If that deeply rooted power, which possesses the most intricate of all survival techniques, could quickly be smashed by way of our country's losing the war, maybe then the defeat might ironically be considered a blessing. Such a result would be like something new that rises from the ashes, like the phoenix, and that is exactly what we are all looking for.

It would not really matter if we were defeated once, or even twice; so long as at least some Japanese people survive, Japan will not be destroyed.

Already we seem to be the "carp on a butcher block." I am not being pessimistic but one must simply recognize what the facts are. We have to get through this period of hardship and move forward.

June 11   Friday

I received a letter from Mr. [Tsutomu] Ōuchi the other day. I can imagine what hardships a man of such talent must endure, striving mightily as he is to build a new life in the midst of farmers. I cannot accept his view of history, however. Even if Mr. Ōuchi is correct in assuming that history moves on apart from the individual, and even if the individual is a mere atom in an electric train, I would say our duty would be to learn how to live as such and, as atoms, to live lives of sacrifice. Anything else would be living a lie. Economics is more than just making a prediction that a socialistic world will eventually be brought about in one form or another. The point is actually to bring such a world into existence. We should never lose sight of the fact that these days a new *ethos*, a new way of looking at things, is gradually being established. Everything would be fine if only we could cultivate the right things!

Mr. Ōuchi also says that I should never give any thought to being killed in action. He says that to die under any circumstances outside of those dictated by one's own responsibility is either mere heroism or a temporary emotional high, both of which are foolish. He says too that he does not wish to be killed in the service of a reactionary cause, and that neither would he be impressed by anyone who dies in such a way. He tells me that he is not impressed by the story of Byakko-tai [the "White Tiger Troops," Aizu Band's young boys' suicide-attack squad in the Boshin War of 1868] or by Shinsen-gumi [the "Newly Chosen Group," an assassination team organized by the Tokugawa Shogunate in 1863 under the famed Isamu Kondō]. In my opinion, however, my going to fight in a war can also be considered an honorable duty. I think that, for a young man living in Japan at this point in history, the opportunity to participate in the actual making of history is an extraordinary honor. I approached the study of economics as though my life depended on mastering it, simply because I had chosen that discipline of my own free will and considered it my duty. In addition to pursuing my studies, I was fortunate enough to be blessed with superior physical strength and perhaps a greater capacity than most for putting it to practical use; as a result, this means that I also have the honorable obligation to dedicate myself to the nation. I look upon both of these duties as sublime in nature. I am not certain as to whether the whole tone of our war effort is reactionary or otherwise. I can only say that such and such duties and responsibilities are assigned to us and that our only goal is to live up to them. Whether or not the cause is reactionary, my wish is to do my very best. I wish to die most beautifully as a person in the midst of a supreme effort. Perhaps Byakko-tai was reactionary, but their death was truly sublime—ultimate beauty in itself. As for me, I am not overly concerned with matters of form and style, and neither do I wish to be known by future historians as a great man. As an unknown member of society, my only option is to live and die while remaining faithful to my duties and responsibilities.

July 29   Thursday

I am back in Tokyo after winding up a camping trip in Karuizawa. On the day of departure [on July 23], we were scheduled to meet at Ueno [station] at 5:30 a.m., but I thought there was no way I would be able to get there on time. Fortunately, I happened to run into Hirasawa, who was also at the meeting of 22nd, and he too was going on the trip; and so by staying overnight at his house I was able to make my connections.

On this camping expedition I saw university students for the first time as they really are, an experience I never had with my colleagues in economics. Perhaps I should say, rather, that I was able to reach out to the real human being behind the exterior of "a university student." I found that I could touch their genuine selves, their raw humanity, with no pretension, something I could not find among the students of economics, who camouflage their ugly, opportunistic, and selfish meanness and often get themselves involved in unreasonable arguments, and are conceited and vain as well. I think that the camping trip was just fantastic, and the additional fact that Hirasawa was with me made each and every day immeasurably meaningful.

Upon returning to Tokyo I read the newspaper reporting that the Axis situation was perilous indeed—things are going badly along the eastern front and in both the Mediterranean and the South Pacific. Moreover, with regard to Italy, it has been reported both that the Fascist Party has fallen apart and that Mussolini has resigned (See the note concerning the Badoglio Regime on p. 196). It came to me that we were caught in a truly sad state of affairs, and even in the bewilderment of it all I had to think very seriously about what I must do. We are not professional soldiers and neither are we technicians and engineers assigned to work under them. At least theoretically, we are supposed to be their leaders, and are not allowed to be so naïve as to be impressed by such sayings as, "in our profession, hearts are won over by other hearts—discussing pros and cons would be beside the point." I suppose that whatever happens would happen no matter what, and that I must follow my own path as far as it leads. My stomach turns over when I see the lifestyle of the very rich, as I did in Karuizawa, or the conduct of soldiers—as if they owned the world!—which I have recently witnessed, and even the way in which bureaucrats and capitalists carry out their existence. In the long run, however, I guess that things will take their own course.

December 8

Today is the third anniversary of the Great East Asian War, and it is also the day before I enter the barracks; that is the reason I am writing a diary of my very last free day in *shaba* [the world outside the military].

Last night, to begin with, and thanks to Mr. Kurihara and Tazawa and everybody else, I was given a truly splendid "good-bye" party; today I went to say good-bye to Mrs. Koyanagi, Mrs. Hotta, and Mrs. Katō, and received from each of them very kind elderly-woman-like words—and each word very uniquely their own. Mrs. Koyanagi said, "Since I am a military man's mother, I am not going to say *'Itte irasshai'* [the standard formula for seeing off people who are expected to return]. I say to you, rather, *'Ikinasai'* [an imperative: 'Go']. Whenever I get to see you, I assume it is for the last time. While you are gone, even though I cannot be of much material help, I will give as much emotional support as it is possible for a military mother to give. So go—and without having to worry about anything at home." Mrs. Katō said, "No matter what you have to do, make sure and return home safely." I appreciated and was most grateful for these very kindest thoughts of theirs.

Also, in the evening, the members of Yukimushi ["Snow Bug"—the name for the alumni branch of the Traveling Society of the First Higher School] were thoughtful enough to come around, and, talking away to my heart's content, I was able to spend my very last night home with them. I was deeply appreciative. Each member of the group wrote well-thought-out words and phrases on a Japanese flag,* each expression reflective of their true personalities. On the eve of my departure, I was really touched deeply by my good fortune in becoming acquainted with their genuine feelings—true feelings delivered without any pretense. I was especially surprised to have Hirasawa give me a haircut! It was such a joy and so far beyond any expectation on my part.

If I were to write in detail about a whole variety of things, there would be no end to it. However, memories are things that are more precious than anything one can put down on paper, and they should be kept in one's own heart. So I think I shall not be foolish enough to try and confined limitless thoughts to the limited space of a piece of paper.

After they left, my younger brother and I talked about family matters, and I also shared with him as many of my thoughts as I could. Because I have a younger brother, Taizō, I can depart without leaving my heart entirely behind. I have complete confidence that he will not only follow my wishes but will even supplement what I lacked. Taizō will build up the Sasaki family into a great house.

I shall give evidence of my very deepest self by trusting it to the flow of the current of eternal history. As far as our emotions with regard to our personal relationship with others, there are always many tiny waves—likes and dislikes, love and hate, and so on; but despite all the variables everything is ultimately resolved by the power of something greater than ourselves.

Lastly, about my will.

When this matter of ceasing to be a student and becoming a soldier was first decided upon, it was my intention to write a will to each one of those associates of mine and also to those I am indebted to for their kindness. I started off with a very long letter to Hirasawa. But, as time passed, the original excitement, or should I say the first feeling that I was facing a gravely serious crisis, that certain sort of heavy feeling about having to go to war, all gradually died down. So too, as I came closer to settling into my resolution, I finally realized that such letters to all those people would be rather meaningless, and gained the insight that all too often the motive behind writing letters like that is based either on simple sentimentalism or a false sense of tragedy. I realized, in other words, that in writing a very long letter one tends to become overly intellectual and that, when this tendency is exaggerated by sentimentalism, some idle falsehood will inevitably implant itself in that same letter. The first letter I wrote, the one to Hirasawa, was just like that. I found it very difficult to avoid beautifying the past, or, for that matter, to prevent self-justification from creeping in. Therefore, I absolutely decided never to write my will.

So I shall not write a will. I simply hope that those who were so kind to me in the past may walk along straight paths and live out each of their natural lives to the fullest. Everything must be left to the great heaven to resolve: my only hope is that each of my friends will face the judgment of world history without fear. My prayer is that all of them might walk their paths in happiness and good health. And I hope and pray that, in their forward progress, each one of those people I care for will keep in their hearts—to whatever degree and in each one's own way—any impression that I, the human being named Hachirō Sasaki, have left upon them.

With this, I am closing my diary. December 9, 1943, 2:40 a.m.

"Love," "War," and "Death"
—A reflection on Kenji Miyazawa's *Karasu no Hokuto Shichisei (Crows' Seven Northern Stars or: The Great Dipper])*[1]—

Kenji Miyazawa is one of the poets I most adore and respect because of his upbringing, his character, and the personal flair he has acquired. His ideology, something that runs straight through the core of all his works, is most important and touches my heart powerfully. The idea that is summarized in his verse, "unless the entire world becomes happy, there can be no individual happiness," is so right, pure, and sound—a human being's love, as a human being, for beauty—that it is inexpressible in a single sentence. This same ideology, moreover, deep and filled with an

---

[1] [On the occasion of the university students' being sent off to war, a class reunion of the First Higher School's Literature II Section was held on November 10. Hachirō Sasaki read this essay on that occasion, and it may be considered as his will, with the theorizing on Kenji Miyazawa as something of a pretext.]

oriental fragrance, exactly corresponds to those ideal conceptions of people and of society that have been developing inside myself for some time now. Concerning Miyazawa's views on war, I would say that his portrayal of them in the children's story which I have already mentioned, entitled *Karasu no Hokuto Shichisei,* exactly expresses my feelings on the matter. This is the reason for my citing references here to the entire text. I was once given the nickname "Crow." And now I am applying to be a navy flier. Perhaps there is a certain symmetry even in such silly details; but, at any rate, I shall attempt to write down exactly how my thoughts are running by explicating Miyazawa's views as they are found in the text itself.

Although it is something of a secondary element to the points under present discussion, I cannot say either that at the present time the part involving the Captain and his love, Gunboat, has no connection with myself—but I shall let that go for now. What touches my heart the most is the scene where the Captain, even while anticipating that he will be killed in an action against the enemy the next day, prays, "I do not know whether or not it is better for me to win this war or for the Copper Pheasant to win. It is all according to your wish. I am going to fight as well as I can because fate has decided that so it must be. Everything, absolutely everything, is as you wish."

And another thing about Miyazawa that touches my heart is his deeply human and most beautiful way of thinking with regard to "love," "war," and "death"—a way of thinking that comes across clearly in the passage where, as he was burying the Copper Pheasant, he prays: "Oh, Lord Majel [a made-up name of a god he is praying to], please make this world to soon become a place where we do not have to kill an enemy whom we cannot hate. If such a thing were to come about, I would not complain even if my body were torn to pieces many times over." When we face up to issues such as these in our own deepest selves, is there any more human, beautiful, and even sublime way of doing so? And in this whole world is there any other setting wherein one's courage and strength as a human being, in the very truest sense of that term, are so beautifully expressed? So let us not toss this story off lightly by saying "It is only a tale for children."

The images of "love," "war," and "death," both reflected upon by and reflecting on those who possess genuinely right, pure, and sound hearts, must be exactly so.

Of course, I would never say anything like: "I do not know which is better, to win the war or to lose it." I believe that the advancement of human history can only be achieved when every race and every nation makes its best effort to work for the good and the benefit of the people and for the nation's greater prosperity. I also believe that every nation which finds itself in a war has the obligation of fighting through it with a positive attitude. On the issue of whether we are going to win or lose the war, however, I cannot afford to have an opinion. On the contrary, we theorists who happen to be students of economics have studied about what the source of the advancement of world history is, about why wars have to happen, what the end results of them might be, and what would be the keys to winning or losing them. By seriously studying problems such as those just described, we came to understand what real productivity is—not just inside a factory or with a single production process, or indeed any productivity that we can see—but the productivity which is involved in that whole entity we call the national economy. Although we should consider this last as a concrete expression of the nation's total strength, we also learned that, at the same time, it is a fateful and inevitable power which transcends all the efforts of our individual idealism. We can no longer be conceited over the power of our individual strength, and neither can we believe that our personal effort is linked to the hope for our nation's victory and for the liberation of all Asian peoples. The only thing we can look forward to is that, from the view-point of world history and transcending the position of the individual citizen, our private effort might be conjoined to the nation's in fostering the advancement of that history. I do not want all this to be confused with the philosophy of Hajime Tanabe [a philosopher and professor at the Kyoto Imperial University, 1885–1962], but in these matters we can really and truly—and at one and the same time—be both citizens of the nation and citizens of the world. If we insist on being only Japanese and on maintaining only Japanese positions, then we shall really have to hate our enemies, Great Britain and America. My own attitude, however, is much more humanistic, and something like that of Miyazawa's Crow. This way of looking at things does not require me to hate people whom I do not have to hate. That is my thinking. In all honesty, those slogans that our military leaders spread around strike me as phrases that may sound good but are basically empty, and which are spread for the sole purpose of inflaming the masses. Also, I always want to be on the side of those people who are in the right, just as I wish to be on the opposite side from those who are essentially either wrong or arrogant—regardless of whether they are the enemy or so-called allies. To us, likes and dislikes, and love and hate as well, are all purely human concerns, and I cannot love or hate someone just because of that person's nationality. Of course it would be quite different in a situation where one is confronted by an antagonist and when neither is able to understand the other because of differences in nationality or ethnic differences. I would not wish, however, just because of differences in nationality, to fail to respect something that is in fact noble and beautiful—or to fail to recognize as such things that are ugly and contemptible.

Then why am I volunteering to be *"Umi no washi"* (sea eagle), a naval flier? Right now my feeling about this is that, even though I am Japanese, I am quite detached from any narrow *chauvinism* [narrow-minded and phobic ethnocentrism]; therefore, the stance that I must adopt at present is purely that of a human being, just a man, without any reference to nationality. Even though I am not like Carlyle [Thomas Carlyle, 1795–881], who found himself to be a human being who had been brought into this world without any knowledge of either a father or a mother, I was still more or less accidentally placed in the land of Japan and given into the charge of my father and mother; so I simply wish to fulfill my fate as a student who accepts the responsibilities that have been placed upon him. After careful consideration, my present wish is, with all my might, to live out what is left of my life in accordance with that fate, and with the twin benefits of the academic training I have received and a body that I have disciplined and built up. The way I feel now is that all of us should accept the fates that we were born with, do our best in each's own predetermined way, and fight as hard as we can. It is only being a coward to use foolish excuses in attempts to escape and hide from what our fate has decreed. Let us move forward together along the path that has been laid out for us, and leave it to heaven to decide whether the final outcome will be victory or defeat. I believe that the advancement of world history depends on each one, in his own privately ordained way, doing his very best. Although I am merely a single human being, I wish to live to the end as a human being, through and through, without ever being a coward.

In order to make this world right and better, we are making a pile of stones—one stone at a time. We want to pile the largest and the most stable stones available on the tower that our predecessors built. If we set an unstable stone, it would cause the tower to tumble down, taking with it all those stones piled by others—I would not want to be that sort of stone. I hope that, if possible, our fatherland will play a major role in the new world history; and we have to do our very best to make it possible.

With respect to our nation's domestic situation, far too many antiquated customs have not been shaken off and still exist. This situation concerns me a good deal, and it makes me feel that, in themselves, our will to win the war and our determination to persevere until the end are not enough. I would also think it imperative that we take the responsibility upon ourselves both for the structure of society and for productive relations within it, things that must be carried out along rational and scientific lines. In the final analysis, the only thing we can do is to work as hard as we can at whatever assignments are handed to us. I would say that to hope for anything beyond that would be disrespectful toward the divine.

Note

* Flags, seeing off, and *"sen-nin-bari"* [a thousand people's stitches]: When the conscription notices for military service were received, many of those so designated went to a shrine to pray for good and lasting fortune during their time of service, and they also sought protection by visiting their ancestors' graves. It was believed too that wearing a *"sen-nin-bari"* [a white cloth with a thousand red-threaded knots, with a different woman making each knot] around one's waist brought good luck and protection from enemy bullets.—It was another custom for friends and family members to write farewell messages or words of encouragement on the white portions of a Japanese flag. Afterward, each of the departing young men would wear such a flag over a shoulder, and would be sent off at the railway station by his family members, neighbors, friends, acquaintances, and others. All such "send-off" gatherings were usually organized by neighborhood associations and/or the Patriotic Women's Society.

Kinpei Matsuoka

Born August 10, 1923. From Toyama Prefecture. From Shizuoka Higher School, entered Tokyo Imperial University, Faculty of Economics, October 1943. Entered the Eastern 48th Unit, Toyama City, December 1, 1943. Killed in action outside Moulmein, Myanmar (Burma), May 27, 1945. Sublieutenant. He was twenty-two years old.

September 27, 1943

What is Fascism, I mean really? Is it a reactionary movement in opposition to that era which, beginning with the Renaissance, seemed to signal the triumph of rationality and science? Are authority, pure experience, instinct, and the power of creative imagination, as Morris Cohen [an American philosopher, 1880–1947] wrote in *Reason and Nature,*[1] all phenomena that were brought about by anti-rationalism? As I see it, the definition can be given in one brief line: Fascism is the escapism of our time. As a consequence of that dead end of the awakened consciousness which followed the Renaissance, I suppose that Fascism is something that was pushed forward in an attempt to make some sort of a logical advance.

---

[1] Cohen, Morris R., *Reason and Nature: An Essay on the Meaning of Scientific Method.* 1931.

To deal with this contemporary society of ours, which has reached the ultimate in confusion, the easiest way would be to make an appeal to divine inspiration. As a rational society becomes more and more complex, it is only natural for its government to take pains to build unity. However, a solution to a given society's state of confusion, a confusion which stemmed from that same society's rationality, needs to be looked for in a strictly rational direction. Alfred Rosenberg [in 1930 he expounded a race-theory in his *The Myth of the Twentieth Century*; 1893–1946], a pet of the Nazi leaders, stated that, in Nazism, Germany had found an ideal political form for the twentieth century. A Nazi nation was created by arousing the masses through the creation of a temporary emotional high, and then dragging them around in total blindness. . . . But an emotional high is just a temporary thing, and what would the blinded ones find themselves in the middle of when they are once awakened from it? All sorts of liberty are stolen away via government control, and the only thing left would be the government itself—a government that demands complete submission from its people. A very powerful constitutional state would indeed remain, but that same nation would soon fall victim to a logical contradiction. Under the pressure of any rational criticism it would be forced to face the reality that its self-destruction is imminent. So do not allow yourselves to be drowned in Fascism. Fascism is a temporary excitement which the young are likely to get into. We should be cool and calm and straighten up the disorganized situation: we should not leave behind a source of trouble for a hundred years to come. Right now, Japan is caught up in this sort of excitement. To be so excited would be all right for the masses, but those who are to be bulwarks of the nation should never allow themselves to be distracted by harsh and temporary emotion. Be calm, take up the sword of rationality, and untie the confusion.

Finally, I too have to move off to the battlefield. The privilege of academic deferment* has been abolished, and the time for us students to help fight the war* has actually arrived. I cannot explain my feelings right now except that everything seems so complex and weird. After working hard and getting through the national educational system, which is known as the Ginza-dōri [i.e., then the equivalent of New York's Fifth Avenue or Park Avenue, as they were then] of learning, and even succeeding at entering this Tokyo Imperial University, I have at last been able to reach this point. I, who in three years (or, rather, in two-and-a-half years) would be in a position to take my place in society as a full-fledged scholar, am now leaving the university and departing for the front because of the nation's demand.

Am I unwilling to give up my life? Perhaps that may be the case. For a human person, it does not even matter whether we are speaking of totalitarianism, or of the relationship between the whole and individuals, or of any such thing—as if we understood them in the first place. In the final analysis, the one clear-cut point of view is that, when all is said and done, what one has left is oneself. To push my logic a bit more, I would have to think that there is no such thing as a completely selfless person in the whole world. Any person who thinks in terms of the nation and of the whole picture is one who is trying to see beyond that point where the whole and the individual are in harmony, that is, they are the people who were in search of locating the point where the whole and the individual connect. A soldier is supposed to show selfless devotion to his country, but can they all say for certain that they have given up self? Soldiers may be seen as noble just because their occupation, what they are moving toward and directly facing, is war and death, and in the nation's defense. .... Ah, but what on earth is the reality? What would be the limits to a human being's ability to control his thoughts? What are human beings supposed to do? What am I supposed to think? What could be proven to be the solution to it all? .... Even though I realize that it is not everything, I certainly do not wish to give up my life. My seniors, and now I myself and even those younger than I, are all dying off as they get into action. Death. Death.—What is death, really?

I shall leave that question unanswered. Older soldiers, and my own generation as well, are all getting killed or injured in the effort to build up Greater Asia[2] and to ensure our own nation's peace and tranquillity. Let us leave aside those who are merely injured and think of those who are being killed. They are dying, hoping for and believing in the construction of Greater Asia and the maintenance of a prosperous Japan. The same is also true with me. Those who are killed can rest in peace if and when the establishment of Greater Asia and Japan's prosperity have been achieved. But what happens if those goals are not achieved?—In the latter case, the dead will have to carry the burden of their regrets beyond the grave.

Someone has said that a war is easy when you are winning, but becomes very difficult once it turns into a defensive struggle.

Speaking out straightforwardly, I should ask the government whether or not this war, in which Japan is now engaged, is being fought with any

---

[2] An expression that was used to justify the war of aggression, pushing the idea that, with Japan in the lead, all Asian nations would prosper.

probability of winning? Cannot it be that the government is forever fighting on with only an empty dream of victory? Can they tell us citizens with any degree of certainty that Japan will definitely win? Are there not always some nearly impossible conditions attached to any such positive assertion? Oh! But my argument eventually came to founder on the rocks. Only the students majoring in natural science are allowed to stay on at universities, and the rest of us have to move on to the battlefield [see. p. 113 for the note on changing majors to the natural sciences]. I can no longer find a solution for this uncomfortable feeling I have about my personal predicament of having to face death. I am almost about to fall into an anti-war ideology; perhaps I already have. It just might be that, once I enter the barracks, there will be an end to it. Then, perhaps, I shall not think about anything, and it is possible that would be the happiest path of all; for the more I think, the more contradictions I find myself involved in. Man, however, must be a *"roseau pensant"* [from *L'homme n'est qu'un roseau faible, . . . mai d'est un roseau pensant*] i.e., a thinking apparatus. Even though human beings do have the ability to think, they do not possess the ability to solve all problems. In the final analysis, human beings are also meek and lack courage, but to have no ability at all must mean that there has been no effort. I certainly studied so hard, and made my very best effort to try and solve anything and everything; but it was just a one-scene dream. It was a dream of a dream. ....One consolation is that the academic world is still very vast. There is still no limit to the number of unknowns, even though world-class researches have been carried out. Indeed, *"gakumon"* [i.e., intellectual pursuits and learning] is forever. In the opinions of those of us who are searching for eternal truth, there is nothing more meaningful or worthwhile for a man to do. Compared to this search, something like a war is no more than merely a one-scene comedy. I would think that, facing absolute truth, military expansion might perhaps be seen as less important than the making of a spider's web. Human beings are weak, however, and for this minute phenomenon [i.e., war], I have to sacrifice my researches into eternity.
....

My short life seems to be coming close to curtain time [i.e., the end]. Once I actually go to fight the war, it will mean that my life has ended. On the one in a million chance I should return home alive, then a curtain for my new life would be raised. Then I shall build a new life with a new design. When I reflect on the short life I have lived, I would like to write something down, just as it comes to my mind. This may all be similar to the rush and confusion that rakes place at the end of a century. With the thought that I have forty or fifty more days left in my life, my hope is to study eternal truth from the standpoint of a cool rationality. In spare moments, I should like to go over this life of mine that is a little over twenty years in length, and which I am almost embarrassed to call "my life." Perhaps the people of a later generation may use what I write down as a reference, as a piece of an ordinary person's private life in the 20th century. If so, perhaps they would laugh at how pitiful and weak the human beings of the 20th century are.

....

October 4

....

Now that I have calmed down, or, rather, come to feel quietly desperate over the fact that I can no longer continue my academic pursuits, I suddenly have an overwhelming urge to read novels. I pulled [Dmitri Sergeyevich Merezhkovski's] *Kamigami no Fukkatsu (The Death of the Gods)* [the first part of a famous historical trilogy with the collective title of *Christ and Antichrist*] from a bookshelf to read. .... Oh, how I wish that in the past I had read so many, many more books. And there are still so many more books that I have a great interest in. There is no limit. This state of mind is more or less captured in the motto: "The sun is going down, but I still have a long way to go."—Calm and composed, I am going to spend the rest of my life reading books.

I learned that a famous phrase coined by Shingen Takeda has been adopted as an official people's motto: "Man is a castle, man is a stone wall, man is a moat that surrounds the castle." This phrase leaves itself wide open to hostile criticism, but, even aside from that, "Man is a castle, man is a stone wall, man is a moat that surrounds the castle, empathy is a friend, and revenge an enemy."—This was the motto, the basic principles, and the philosophy of Shingen, the man who never built a castle. As we take a close look at the leading figures of the Sengoku Era [the age of civil wars], we can see that they paid a great deal of attention to civil administration. Shingen himself was one of them. .... [What he said was that in] "the state [or province] of Kai, though it is small, all the people are castles and moats. If this were translated into arms, a ten-thousand-man army would not be anything to be afraid of." Shingen's magnificent political ability is clearly evident [from that statement]. In such a confusing time in history, therefore, a small mountain state, located between powerful states, could achieve such a great victory that it would carry over to the capital itself. Indeed at the present time, the hard fighting of the Soviets makes us think that Shingen has been reborn. When the Germans launched their human avalanche against Moscow and Stalingrad, those who defended [the cities] by becoming "castles and moats" were in fact those same Slavic farmers who had been called and treated as ignorant and unintelligent. ....

What today's human being is hoping for the most is "peace." What does the word really mean? If we were into a discussion of true peace, we would have to realize that any such thing will never come until mankind is no more—there will always be other wars over such things as natural resources, the state of the economy, etc., even when the military conflict is over. The subject of the morality of war has occasionally been discussed in recent books, but can there be such a thing as the morality of war? Anyone who kills a man will most certainly be sentenced to capital punishment, simply because he killed a man. It is obvious that people are killed in any war, so how can we morally accept it? Does this mean we have adopted a morality that accepts people being killed? There is repeated emphasis on the broader view, on the general good. But if we are to look at a war from a broader view and with the general good in mind, why can they not set things up in such a way that it is not necessary to kill anyone? And how, even while killing people, could they possibly make a distinction between a broader view in favor of the general welfare and a narrower view? All killing is evil. To give life to a dead person—any such proposition is nothing more than an example of the contemporary philosophy's kissing up to an unpleasant reality. Philosophy should be something that leads people. To attribute either life or morality to those who are gone would be an insult to our civilization itself, as well as a man's self-deception concerning his own actions.

....

November   (A certain day)

I left Ueno [Tokyo] on a night train on October 25, and traveled here and there before arriving home on the afternoon of November 9. That was about a two-week period, and during that time I visited a lot of places and did some sightseeing; I also took the all-important physical examination for conscription* and passed into the Second-B category. I was surprised because I had been quite sure that it would be the First-B category. My habitual way of thinking ran into many roadblocks over those two weeks. As a result, I was privately surprised more than once, and even had to change my thinking to a certain extent; at other times, my original ideas were reinforced. At any rate, I learned that there was considerable room left within which my thinking might continue to develop.

The very first thing that occurred on the train was my meeting with a couple of students from Waseda University; and since the three of us were all going to be sent off to war, we shared the long ride to our family's hometown without ever becoming bored with one another. We were so into our talking and discussions that we did not even realize how far into the evening hours we were getting. They seemed to have been quite impressed by the send-off the Ministry of Education sponsored on the 21st at the Outer Garden of the Meiji Shrine. I regret the mistake of not having attended that event. I had meant to go and indeed was even at the front door, but decided against it at the last minute with an excuse that my foot was hurting due to an overly tight shoe. I wish I had attended though. The Keio University student's send-off speech, by the way, was not very good. I did listen to speeches throughout the event over the radio, but that speech was inappropriate and very poorly done. [On the contrary] the departing address by Ebashi (of our university, Faculty of Letters) [Shinshiro Ebashi, who read an address of farewell in response to the send-off address, entitled "We Certainly Do Not Expect to Return Alive"] was excellent. Perhaps everything turned out all right in the end. It may well have been that the send-off speech had been poorly done deliberately in order to make Ebashi look better. Prime Minister [and also Minister of the Army] Tōjō's speech followed the usual pattern: what he wanted to tell us was what we more or less expected. As I talked on with my fellow passengers, I found out that both Mr. Tōjō and Minister of Education Okabe [Chōkei Okabe, a member of Tōjō's Cabinet] were quite unpopular—so I felt sorry for them. .... Approximately one-third of the train's passengers were university students returning home [to their families' hometown where they are officially registered] for the physical examinations related to conscription. Somehow the feeling of sharing the same fate—a feeling that follows a question like "You too?"—filled the air inside the whole length of the train. Cigarette smoke filled the same air. .... In search of tranquillity, and also attracted by the quietness, I visited Seki hot-spring [in Niigata Prefecture, near Akakura hot-spring], about three miles from Sekiyama. It is truly a superlative place for solitude, and I will probably never again come upon a place like it. I tried very hard to think very deeply, and then even more deeply; but my mind has not yet settled down. Occasionally emotion pulls at me, and I lose my mental poise and become a fool; again, and when the quietness returns, a muddy cloud comes down low and hangs over me.

I contemplated at Bessho hot-spring with Mr. Kikuchi. I contemplated lonely and alone at Seki hot-spring. I also talked things over and exchanged thoughts with Mr. Hiroshi Shimizu of Waseda University. In a room at the Wakaba Inn, I had the same sort of discussions with my friend Mr. Fujimoto, and, later, with Mr. Miki as well. I contemplated continually, in any and every place where I happened to be. Not all of the thoughts that resulted from all that are suitable for publication: for human beings in general, there are always secrets that cannot be shared with anyone else. Such a secret, indeed, is a demon in one's heart, and a person is extremely afraid to touch it. I did try several times to open up, but the demon arrogantly remains seated—and grinning—in the deepest part of my heart.

I would like to face death in contentment, and I want to die feeling proud of my death. The only solution to death is to die satisfied with what one believes in. In my case, that belief is the construction both of a new Japan and of a new Greater Asia. To construct something new, creating a better and greater thing—for me this would be sufficient cause to commit my life. I can happily go on to die if I believe that my humble life will live on in a new great Japan and a new Greater Asia. If that were to turn out to be the case, then death would really mean life. That would be "to live by dying for the great duty."

I saw a movie, *Muhō-Matsu no Isshō (The Life of Lawless Matsu)* [a movie by Mansaku Itami, directed by Hiroshi Inagaki, played by the famed Tsumasaburō Bandō and Keiko Sonoi, who was killed later by the atomic bomb]. Perhaps due to the state of mind I was in just before entering the barracks, or, possibly because of Tsumasaburō Bandō's superb performance, the film left a particularly strong impression on me. I was able to enjoy it as one of the best shows in recent years, and seeing it will remain in my mind as a most memorable event. .... There were so many "cuts" [i.e., portions removed by the censors] in the movie! While portraying the life of Matsugorō, the part where he falls in love with Madame Yoshioka was completely removed, as was the scene of Matsugorō's death. It occurred to me that the power of censorship was fully demonstrated in this film, and I thought it really regrettable.

Memories of things in my past such as field days at school, lantern marches, the sound of [festival] drums, etc., all run through my mind as though it were a revolving lantern itself. Everything has disappeared into the past as if it was all a faint dream. I wonder when I will ever get to see a lantern march again, and when I ever will be able to soak myself in the pleasure of a field day. I am about to lose my mind! I want to beat a drum. I want to be part of a lantern march. And I yearn to see the long-sleeved kimono [translators' note: the fancy type of kimono worn only by a young maiden at very special occasions]. War, war, war: This is all much too strongly a fatal matter for me right now. This world is absolutely dark. What morality can be found in any war? A war for fulfilling one's greater duty? What is one's greater duty anyway? All that is nothing but a fool's sleep-talk.

So long as I feel that it is to be my fate, I would not give even the slightest thought to having to go to the battlefield. However, is this really the answer to the question of my fate, and will this world ever be able to return to peace once again?

Let them call it liberalism, militarism, or totalitarianism: they are all means to an end. Japan must walk, and is walking, her own road alone. If the war's goal had not been the achievement of a peace, then what else could it have been? Perhaps it is uncertain whether or not the years around the 3rd of Showa [1928] and after was a period of true liberalism, but I know what Japan was like then and I miss those years. I miss the past. I want to keep on chasing the dreams of the past.

I do not know how to cope with today's reality, and feeble-heartedly pursue faint dreams of the past. I dream a shallow dream of victory in the future—like a castle in the air.

Be far more strong. I want to become much stronger. That's all.

Notes

* Temporary exemption from conscription: The government measure offered temporary exemptions from army service to young men who were either enrolled in school or were living overseas. Certain limits to the extension of these exemptions were set by revision of the Military Service Law after 1939. Step by step, the exemption was lowered from the original twenty-seven years of age to twenty-six, and then to twenty-five.

* College student mobilization for war: The government's policies were made known through the publication, on September 22, 1943, of the "Measures to Strengthen the Internal Situation":

(1) The temporary exemption from conscription for college and university students was terminated (See the preceding note). (2) All university classes in the fields of law, belles lettres, etc., shut down, and the colleges were to be consolidated. (3) Expansion and consolidation of the schools for natural science and the engineering fields was instituted, as well as a system for extending the time before the students in those disciplines were to enter military service. A further development took the form of an emergency imperial order of October 2, 1943, "Temporary Special Law on Extension of Conscription of Students Enrolled in Colleges and Universities," which abolished the very system of extending conscription. Once this order was issued, those who reached the age of twenty were to take the physical examination for conscription immediately; they were ordered to enter the barracks on December 1st for the army, and for the navy on December 9th and 10th. However, because of the national requirement, the students in the fields of natural science, engineering, medicine, and four specific sections of agricultural science, plus the students in national teachers' training centers, were given extensions before entering military service; so, in the end, it turned out to be the students in jurisprudence and the liberal arts and a portion of those in agriculture who were mobilized for shipment off to the front.

*   The physical examination for conscription: With the "Conscription Law" of 1873, and the "Law for Military Service" of 1927, all males twenty years of age (in the last year of the war, which by that time was all but lost, the age was lowered to eighteen) served in the military pending the results of this physical examination. At the examination, depending on their physical condition, the men were separated into grades of A, B (with 1st, 2nd, and 3rd categories), C, D, and E. Of those, A, B, and C were passing (the men in A group entered the barracks on the active-duty roster. B group and C, which originally were excluded from the military, entered the service when needed, and as reservists). D signified the physically handicapped and failure of the examination, and E referred to those cases which were to be carried over to the following year. As a special privilege for the benefit of those with higher education, there were such provisions as an extension for conscription as long as they were in a university, the status of a special cadet, and a shortened active military service for teachers' college graduates.

*   Send-off party: On October 21, 1943, at the Meiji Shrine Gaien (outer garden) Stadium, a farewell ceremony was held, sponsored by the Ministry of Education and the School Patriotic Corps Headquarters. About thirty-five thousand "student-soldiers" (those students who became soldiers through advanced graduation and student mobilization) attended, representing seventy-seven colleges and universities from Tokyo and nearby prefectures. They were sent off with a message from a student of the Medical College of Keiō University, and they silently marched off in the cold rain toward the end of Wadatsumi [the fate of death in the battlefields in and over the oceans]. A great many of them shared the same thought as the one expressed in Shinshirō Ebashi's "Response" speech: "We Certainly Do Not Expect to Return Alive."—The event concluded with everyone joining in to sing *"Umi Yukaba"* ("If and When I Went to Sea [to Fight for the Emperor]"), a quasi-national song of the period, and then with three cheers of "Long Live the Emperor."

Takashi Watanabe

Born December 2, 1922. From Kanagawa Prefecture. Entered Sugamo College of Commerce, Tokyo, in April 1941. Entered Takeyama Naval Training Corps in Yokosuka, in October 1943. Killed in action, October 27, 1944, off Leyte Island, the Philippines. Navy sub-lieutenant. He was twenty-one years old.

When I wonder if and when I will ever be able to see you again, my primary emotion of sorrow turns to pain; with my heart so lonely and desperate, I cannot help but feel deeply depressed.

It was you, you who were so abundantly full of life and were everything to me at times; it was you who gave me hope and joy throughout my very difficult life of commuting to college.

Before I leave for the war, I want to thank you from the bottom of my heart.

I want to leave for the war in a manly manner by quietly putting all the pain and the sad emptiness in a tiny silver box. But, of course, I shall always be feeling those pure and beautiful eyes of yours on me. That is the only remembrance of mine that I can hold dear, and I cannot trick myself into forgetting it all at once.

Only God will ever know anything about you and me, and I am glad it is that way! It is only because things are such that my remembrance can be at once so beautiful and so sad.

You who have loved me so and spoiled me so—

You were just like a dear mother to me, though I remember the one time when I was surprised to meet your serious and stern eyes.

A variety of your expressions—the smiling face, the snobbish face with eyebrows sternly lowered, the time you passed me by with such a solemn look—now my heart is so filled, and simultaneously, with such pleasant longing and such sad thoughts.

Please do not scold me for being hopeless and faint-hearted. I was thinking about so many things that I wanted to write you about, but now that I have actually picked up a pen I find that I am no longer able to write anything—because now my heart is overflowing with only the most desperate and choking sort of sorrow.

However, I think that only God knows what I am writing you in my heart, and that He will be kind enough to convey it to your fair heart.

In the predicament in which I currently find myself, I cannot help thinking this way.

Good-bye, my Rose Marie. Ah! I do not think that I will ever be able to see you again—ever.

—Written the night before entering the Naval Training Corps.

Yasuji Suzuki

Born June 12, 1921. From Kanagawa Prefecture. Entered Meiji University, Department of Arts and Letters, in 1939, and graduated in December 1941. Entered the barracks in April 1942. He was killed in action, May 27, 1944, in Kohima, Assam state, India. Army second lieutenant. He was twenty-three years old.

—I parted from my younger sister at the ticket gate of
      Hayakawa [in Kanagawa Prefecture] train station—

There was no word to leave behind,
>   tears came to my eyes as I said, "Please stay well."

>   —At Nebukawa station [Kanagawa Prefecture]—
I could not bear to keep my eyes on my cousin
>   who kept running after the train, waving a hand,
>   knowing she could never keep up with the train.

>   —Inside the Minobu Line train—
The train is already running through Kai Gorge;
>   My heart has endured the immense sorrow of parting.

[The above poems are traditional *tanka*.]

Takenori Nakao

Born March 31, 1923. From Fukuoka Prefecture. From Fukuoka Higher
School, entered Tokyo Imperial University, Faculty of Jurisprudence, in
1942. Entered the Saseho Second Naval Training Corps, December 10, 1943.
Killed in action, May 4, 1945, in the sky over the sea southwest of Okinawa,
as a member of Kotohira Suishin Special Attack Unit. Navy first lieutenant.
He was twenty-two years old.

October 2, 1943
One walker spoke cheerlessly to another as they passed in the
morning: "A rainy day in early autumn is depressing, is it not?" It has been
raining continuously since yesterday. Ginkgo-tree leaves, turned slightly
yellow, lie scattered on the muddy ground, trampled by the shoes of
passersby.

I see so many young men wearing brand new [university] caps. We
have just had a ceremony yesterday celebrating the university's new students, but there must be many of them this morning who are rather
troubled by the news report about having to enter the barracks in December. It is only natural that they should feel unsettled in the face of this new
situation. Here they have just finished unpacking their luggage, and now
they have to ship it all back again. I met Kazunori for the first time: he
seemed a little uncomfortable because he was not familiar with the
surroundings. ....

[A letter to Mr. Fumio Yanagiura] Evening of the 9th [October 1943]
.... I am going to copy here what I wrote down the other
day—my reflections on life and death. It does not convey my idea quite

fully, but, since rewriting is at present impossible, I am copying the original:

The date is approaching for the physical examination for conscription. It is time for me to quit my life as a university student and to enter the military, but I still am unable to have a firm conviction. I had thought and hoped that, by graduation time, I would have reached a certain higher level of mind, but now the day to leave school is right in front of me and I am still like Chiu A-mê [Kyū-A-mō in Japanese, the big fool] of the Wu Dynasty—and I cannot stand it. I think that, once I enter military service, I have to be prepared for certain death.

What is death?

Montaigne [Michel Eyquem de Montaigne, 1533–92] said that death itself is nothing important. He added that it is the fear of death itself that makes death seem important. If one regards death from a material point of view, it is nothing but the extinction of a physical body. Even granting that a soul cannot exist without a physical body, any discussions dealing with the matter of life and death in terms of the simple coming into being and subsequent extinction of a physical body cannot coexist with a proper grasp on the matter of life and death as they really are. Is it an ultimate truth to think that when a physical body dies the soul also dies, or, rather, that the soul lives on even after the physical body dies? It can be said that our lives amount to nothing more than the outward manifestations of this or that individual, absolute person; but the content of life does not exist on anything like such a transcendental plane; rather, life cannot exist apart from the real world which is constantly changing. If what we have been saying is true, it follows that life and death are not the life and the extinction of a single physical body; also, neither would it be possible for us to seek a world after death apart from this world and beyond the universe. The deep secret of life and death can only be understood by grasping the meaning of this world's constant changes by way of entering deeply into them. Death, in other words, is not a separate entity from life, but it can only be known by searching for the meaning and significance of life. Death comes to all of us who are given life on this earth and to everything that exists in this real world—but rather than as the end of life we must think of it as just a point in life. To live well is to die well; therefore it can also be said that, by dying well, one can live well.

We can solve the whole question of life and death by searching out the way that will enable us to live well, and by participating in that natural law of this world which makes our lives meaningful. Both life and death exist in every hour and every second of our daily lives.

As one enters military service in readiness for the sacrifice of his own life on behalf of the Emperor, he once again has to stare death straight in the face. Moreover, once arrived at the battlefield itself, and when exposing oneself under the heavy smoke of big guns and amid showers of bullets, at each of these times I shall feel death's stern figure standing right beside me. In this way, one step at a time, I shall come closer to the real meaning of life and death, even as I tighten further the stiff cord of my determination. Death, though, does not only exist on the battlefield; each hour, and each second, is death. If we look at things that way, then no extraordinary determination is necessary in order to face death. It would simply be a matter of being willing to dash toward the best life has to offer by summoning, more than ever before, all one's courage of body and mind.

I simply intend to carry on with my *gakumon* (intellectual pursuits and searching for the truth)—by continuing to walk a step at a time and as a man, and by so doing solve this question of life and death. .... I am looking forward to the day of visiting with you.

[Another letter to Mr. Fumio Yanagiura]
December 7, 1943

Dear Mr. Yanagiura:

I picked up a pen with the intention of writing a letter as the last "visit" from the "shaba" (the land of the living, i.e., in this case, the world outside the military); but thousands of words overflow from my heart and I am lost as to what to write. After having returned to Kashii [in Fukuoka City] on the 4th, I read your letter(s) and telegraph(s). I feel terrible and apologetic as I think of you, on the evening of the 28th, trying to find me, searching for me in the gathering dusk of the Kashii train station.

You must have seen continuous and endless trails of footprints on the beautiful sandy shore of Mei-no-hama or Shingu Beach [beaches in Fukuoka City], have you not? I think there was a poem, by Tōson [Tōson Shimazaki, 1872–1943] or someone else, that described such a scene. I feel as though those several strings of footprints which intersected each other there were made by ourselves. We do not know where they begin and where they end, or where they might cross and where they might part again—there is something so impermanent and so sad about the footprints on a beach.

Even though the prints were to be erased by the action of the waves, we would still be able to sense the powerful and reassuring steps, taken one after the other, of the person who made those prints. When I recognize the powerful walk of the person who visited that heap of sand and then left, I feel encouraged. It is indeed true that we do not know either the past or the future; when I stand firmly in the present, however, I feel the power that fills my own legs. I also recall a letter from Katō in which he wrote that "We must walk forever: we must continue to walk forever."

Takenori Nakao

To Mr. Fumio Yanagiura

Tokurō Nakamura

Born October 2, 1918. From Yamanashi Prefecture. From the First Higher School, entered Tokyo Imperial University, Faculty of Science, Geography Department in October 1942. Entered the barracks in Narashino, Chiba Prefecture, October 1, 1942. Killed in action, October 21, 1944, in Dulag, Leyte Island, the Philippines. Army lance corporal. He was twenty-five years old.

February 20   Saturday   Clear

The *gakumon,* the pursuit of knowledge, should set the condition of life. That is my cherished contention. Yet, it seems that at the present time the exact opposite is the case: *gakumon* is being led about by the condition of life (Statement by instructing officer Asakawa).

That is absolutely the case, so what in the world is going on? It makes me fearful for the fate of my country.

March 14   Sunday   Clear

To live is to die, and to die is to live: such a situation may indeed exist.

Pick out an outline of ideas from natural phenomena. [*Shi to Yūjō (Poetry and Friendship)* by Toshihiko Katayama. Published in February 1943.]

Oh, I want to be more life-centered! ....

April 28   A fine clear day

In the afternoon, I went from Shibuya to my dormitory. I met Mr. Tamaki and heard some recent news: a telegram arrived from Germany about Karl Wils[1], a friend of mine—he had been killed in action in Stalin-

---

[1] Three years earlier, the author had rescued Karl Wils after the latter suffered a serious mountain-climbing accident on an *iwaba* [a rocky ledge] on Hodaka Mountain in the Northern Japan Alps. The author attended Karl Wils throughout the night and saved his life.

grad. I heard that Karl's rank had been that of a superior private. And, that happened in the winter time. I suppose that he too was among those whose death had been mourned in [Beethoven's] *Fifth Symphony*. Wils' life had already almost been lost on a rocky ledge of Hodaka mountain; as things turned out, he did not even last four full years afterward. I am reminded of many things about that evening.

I wonder whether, perhaps, he was one of those killed in a tank, his dead body buried in it. Whatever the situation, it was simultaneously so far away and yet so very seriously similar to my own life.

[No date given. Most probably April 29, or 30]
The lowering of one's intellectual ability. The diminution of intelligence. Against such things we should struggle with all our might. But, even that would only turn out to be wasted effort! ....

In a tank, I run westward through the field of Musashino. Musashino![1]
Zelkova trees [*Zelkova acuminata*] and cedar trees, bamboos and miscellaneous trees . . . and the smells of the field. I smell the aroma of the soybean soup being prepared for the evening meal, mixed with the fragrance of young plant shoots. What a joy that was to recognize those fragrances, however faintly, in the midst of the smoke generated by a light-weight tank. I kept manipulating the gear which operated the tank, hoping all the while that those fragrances and scenes and the sheer joy of being in it would continue endlessly.

I heard about the Order of Cultural Merits (or, Cultural Medal). Professor Yukawa finally received the honor, and the event comes like a cool breeze in this chaotic world of today. .... We will only be able to say that our nation's culture holds the premier position in the world if and when this Cultural Medal achieves global recognition.

May 9   Sunday   A fine clear day
The University's May Festival has rolled around, and I spent a full day reading books leisurely. One was *Kōjin-shō* [by Yoshishige Abe, a noted scholar] and another *Shisaku to Taiken (Cogitation and Experience)* [by Kitarō Nishida, a leading philosopher]. The latter was about Poincaré [Jules Henri Poincaré, French mathematician and scientist, 1854–1912].
....

---

[2] [Translators' note: name for the plain of the broader Tokyo area, some parts of which, until the closing stretches of World War II, had remained untouched from long ago.]

A commentary on literature by Junsuke Suita [a scholar on German literature] caught my eye. How poisonous and negative. . . . I cannot help but feel disgust and rage from the very bottom of my heart. We are not working to attract sympathy or to get attention from the people. We are standing up to bear arms, ever so quietly, and that is the way it ought to be.

May 15

We can so easily become a frog in a well. I cannot always say that there is never a time when we indulge ourselves in easy self-praise or self-satisfaction, or are so perfectly self-contented without really knowing ourselves. Praising Japan's beautiful points and positive qualities, and shedding tears and being generally impressed over our many heroic deeds, are natural things to do—but that should not be all we do. We have to situate ourselves within and pay more attention to the big picture. What are the things we can truly be proud of? What should we be proud of? And, again, what do we really mean by pride itself? We have to reflect upon ourselves thoroughly. And we have to reject cheap emotion and self-importance as we would tinware.

When I hear prolonged and excessive self-glorification, I want to throw up.

The Japanese people are supposed to be much more modest. Only if we can go quietly about making those great sorts of contributions which would be deeply felt in the hearts of all mankind throughout the world, only then will the greatness of the Japanese race brilliantly adorn universal history.

Empty posturing without real strength must be completely rejected. Real strength is not something that can be easily attained—or attained with just an ordinary amount of effort.

Solely because we are the nation which has never been defeated, should we rest on our laurels and do nothing? I am not saying, of course, that to be proud of our country is at all a bad thing. But the issue at point is that, regardless of how bad the defeat a nation suffers or how sad the situation it falls into as a consequence, all that matters is whether or not the people manage to maintain a lively and positive national spirit, and never allow themselves to stumble down the miserable path of defeat. They should be able to exhibit the real strength that rises from the very depths of defeat itself.

When I think along these lines, I feel like going back to reading history. We must search through history, widely and in depth. If we did so, we would never be content to indulge in meaningless self-glorification or self-satisfaction. There is nothing which would endanger a nation more than that sort of "dreaming," and there has never once been a conceited nation that has risen and prospered.

Regardless of how hard we try, we cannot escape from the limitations that history imposes upon us. ....

May 18

I heard that an organization called *"Bijutsu Hōkoku-kai"* (Serving the Nation Society for the Arts) was founded. It joins *"hōkoku-tai"* (Serving the Nation Troop), or *"hōkoku-dan"* (Serving the Nation Corps), or *"hōkoku kai"* (Serving the Nation Society), and so on.* People seem to think everything will be great if only the term *"hōkoku"* is used in the beginning of any name. Perhaps people may be thinking it is enough if they just add on "Serving the Nation Society for the Arts" too; people may be thinking it is enough if they just keep on painting pictures of war. We should say that they could not be more wrong. They talk out loud and in a grandiose manner without even thinking about what *"hōkoku"* really means. I am both concerned and hopeful that what they are doing will not turn out to be *"bōkoku"* (destroying the nation) rather than *"hōkoku"* (serving the nation).

No matter where I look, I see evidence of the same phenomenon, i.e., an abundance of ritualistic and superficial sycophancy toward us [i.e., the students mobilized for the war]. This is a contrived attitude, far from genuine, and it could even become a dangerous situation if we do not soon make a move of our own.

May 20   Thursday   Rain

I saw a friend today who has never lost the essential quality of his own humanity, even though, and with great courage, he had to fight his way through this extremely harsh life. [Translators' note: the metaphoric flavor of the original comes through more like "a life of autumn frost and severe sun."] The sight of him provided an immeasurably powerful inspiration for me: I must do my very best to train my mind to be stronger. ....

May 23   Sunday

With the sun shining upon me, I stood in an advanced post, carrying a rifle. I noticed that the green shade of the huge zelkova tree in front of the barracks had turned a much darker green. I mused over how, just the other day, the tree was barely beginning to show leaves, but . . . [At any rate, serving] as guards of the troops which remained is rather neat and pleasant.

"I sure wish that I could get some education, at least for my children." These words, vibrating through the midnight air of the post, and so sincere and thoughtful, touched my heart deeply. The long shadow of Sergeant M. passed in front of me, first going and then coming back.

July 28 Monday

.... "In order to be able to view my conduct with clarity, and to walk surely in this life, I have always maintained the strongest desire to learn how to distinguish the truth from the untruth." [*Hōhō josetsu (Discourse de la Méthode)* by René Descartes, a French philosopher, 1637.]

August 5 Sunday Clear

.... A copy of the memorial pamphlet honoring my friend Inada was sent to me, and I spent all day reading it. It touched me in a special way and my heart was filled with deep emotion. .... It felt as though our hearts had been deeply stabbed and gouged when I learned that, while he was at a sanatorium in Ichikawa, knowing or not knowing that only a very little time was left in his life, he still kept on reading *Fukuso Kansū-ron (A Theory on the Functions of Complex Elements)* and *Furansu-go 4-shūkan (French in 4-Weeks),* and even wrote some Japanese poems. We must be loyal and true to ourselves until the very last moment of our lives. We must never discard our true duty before we have drawn our last breath. Is there any more regrettable way to live than just staying alive and, at the same time, being untrue to oneself?

September 9

On our way home from maneuvers, Instructor A and myself somehow got involved in a conversation about the current state of education. I was deeply impressed and touched beyond words when I recognized the sincerity of his strong longing toward and great respect for *gakumon* (the pursuit of knowledge), and also of his genuine and intense patriotic concern over the situation in which the nation today finds itself. ....

Italy's surrender has been reported. How is this going to affect us emotionally?

September 19

Recently, during *naimu-han* duty (Inside Duty) [see the note on p. 117] I came across *Hakutō (White Peach)* by Mokichi [Mokichi Saitō, 1882–1953] and a collection of poems by Kihachi [Kihachi Ozaki, 1892–1974]. The simple realization that someone here reads Kihachi's poetry brings me such great joy. ....

September 21

.... The *ken-etsu* (inspection)* of new conscripts was postponed because of the rainy weather. The night before the inspection—a time with many implications.

February 11, 1944

Fire was burning red in the fireplace. Through a clouded window-glass, the quiet shade of a lamp reflected the quietly dancing snow. A pineapple dish and red tea of the English variety were on the table; they pleased our tongue more than ever.—What a pleasant feeling of tiredness!

I remember, with utmost loving longing—like a golden dream—how dusk fell on a particular evening four years ago today. So very well do I remember that day, when the Sanbon-yari (Three Spears) Mountain climbing was completed, that I decided today was a good day to pick up a pen again. I pray that this ink will never dry out, and on my part will make every effort to ensure that the prayer is answered. I am also most certainly aware of how important it is to read; nevertheless, I feel it is even more important to write. I think too that the matter of just exactly where the essence of writing is is a very important issue. Someone has said that "To write is to be deeply rooted in the broad and vast love for human beings"—something like that. Well said, indeed.

Upon reflection, it seems to me that I must face and answer the question as to why I wanted to start writing again. Merely writing notes to show to others, or keeping a diary with the intention of showing it to others, are most certainly writings of no value; in fact, they are definitely of a low order and, in a way, merely a distorted sort of scribbling. Time after time I get this very strong urge to write—just a simple need to get things down on paper. It has also been my experience, however, that, again and again and for a variety of reasons, those same urges disappear like bubbles, and without becoming actual letters. Lately I have come to think of this as a regrettable situation, even though I do not really know the reasons for it.

As far as I am concerned, I think that, once my desire to write is lost, my life will lose its meaning as well. Fortunately, things have not yet reached that point. I concluded in the end, however, that to make that desire disappear like bubbles would be too cruel a thing to do. I am fully aware that it would be pointless—and, as well, a temptation that should be rejected out of hand—to put off writing until the very best working conditions might become available. At the same time, I also think I should try my hardest to achieve something as close to those conditions as is possible. This is all part of the reason why I made the decision to start writing on this paper.

I myself cannot predict what, if anything, will come of all this writing in the future. One thing I do know is that there must never be any self-falsification—this I can say with confidence.

This requires an extraordinary amount of effort on my part! And I must do all I can to keep my mind in good shape! I must learn to laugh as much as I can at the degree of my own weakness, but I must also work as hard as I can—and stay mindful of my own strength.

February 14

Once again I read *Doitsu Senbotsu Gakusei no Tegami (Letters of the Fallen German Students)* [Japanese translation of selected pieces from *Kriegsbriefe gefallener Studenten*, compiled after World War I by Prof. Philipp Witcop of Freiburg University, and published in Japanese by the Iwanami Publishers as an Iwanami New Library book]. The book continues to be rewarding no matter how many times you read it, and it is especially impressive to read here. These writers are sincerity itself, and happy were they who, in a trench and under the light of a candle, read the bible, read Goethe, cited Hölderlin's [Johann Christian Friedrich, 1770–1843] poetry, and longed to listen to Wagner's music. They were fortunate, because they did. . . .

One notation is particularly noteworthy: "Not a single insulting word about us was found in a letter recovered from the body of an enemy casualty."*

I envy the strength hidden within the German race that could have produced such serious, even great students. I have come to realize that the fine qualities of the Japanese military—such as their transcendent conquest of the fear of death itself, their courageous charges, etc.,—are not necessarily unique to Japan. I cannot help but to renew my belief and trust in the true strength of the really genuine and lofty type of rationality. As I reflected more and more over the fact that every last letter I read had been written by men who, only shortly thereafter, went on into heavy combat and were killed in action, my heart was more and more deeply touched. There were some writings among them that were written on the very day of the author's death after having been seriously wounded, or, certain fragmentary entries had been completed and sent in by friends from the battlefield, or there may even have been one written while its author was actually firing on the enemy.—I feel my head lowering in respect for these powerful pieces.

Generally speaking, the descriptions of Christmas are particularly beautiful. When we were young, too, Christmas was a world of *märchen* [German term for fairy-tale]. I feel so sorry for the Japanese children who do not have too much of *märchen* in the first place, and even more so in light of today's trend toward losing even more of it.

February 18

.... Completed my reading of *Bunka Chiri-gaku (Cultural Geography)* [by Tarō Tsujimura, and published by Iwanami]. I felt the vastness of his *"gakumon"* (the pursuit of knowledge), its degree of difficulty, and his limitless hopes for pursuing his subject further. I should like to gain strength by thinking of Mendel's [Gregor Johann Mendel, Austrian botanist, known for his Mendel's Law, 1822–84] words:

"Stay alert! Soon my time will come."

February 22

This is the day I learned about the death of Professor Mitani [Takamasa Mitani, a legal philosophy scholar and professor at the First Higher School, 1889–1944]. Such a sorrow for Japan! A giant star has fallen. As if looking at a shooting star. . . .

We were almost the very last students of Professor Mitani, and I was lucky to be one of them. My association with him began when I was in my first year, with his lecture on legal economy. I always chose a seat in the very first row, exactly below the lecture desk, for listening to his lectures. It was then I learned about Schweitzer [Albert Schweitzer, Alsatian medical missionary, noted theologian, organist, and philosopher, 1875–1965] and Stirner [Max Stirner, German anarchist, philosopher, 1806–56] for the first time. Prof. Mitani's lectures on "knowledge and faith," "On Prof. Iwa-moto," and his memorial address at the funeral service for Professor Iwa-moto were delivered with deep emotion; I can remember his powerful spirit.

On the 17th I learned of Professor Eijiro Kawai's passing.

An individual's great personal character is not something that comes about just because one wishes it to come about. Airplanes and ships can be manufactured, but the great personalities—both of the past and in our own time—are treasures not only for Japan but for all humanity. The more such treasures a nation has, the greater that nation is. The experience of internal pain helps to develop a great character; conversely, a nation that has not experienced real pain can never be called great.

February 29

It is a beautiful day just after a snowfall, and a strong wind has blown through. From the roof of a garage building something really like snow-smoke has blown up, and it reminded me of Yase-Yane (Yase Loft) on Nishiho Mountain in March. I felt sort of happy, yet I also felt somehow sad. My feet were cold. I wonder why such things as snow and ice, and clouds and wind, move my heart so much?

March 1

March has arrived. Again I miss the mountains in snow. Today I finished reading *Peter Camenzind* [1904, by Hermann Hesse, German-born Swiss novelist, 1877–1962] in one breath—and with extraordinary emotion. It was even more romantic than a similar impression made on me by *Jean-Christophe* [by Romain Rolland, a French author].

I too feel a desire to write an autobiography, and on the same emotional level. I cannot say that my life in the past has not been colorful, which is not necessarily the same as saying that everything has been all beautiful and shiny. In many senses I have not yet touched the core of life, and I must strive to be more genuine and much more single-minded. —And it would be all right to have more dreams! ....

March 5

.... One must be good and always stay good even when placed in the midst of others' viciousness and the cruelty of fate itself. In the middle of many painful disagreements, he should never lose his gentleness and kindness, and must undergo such experiences without allowing the opposition to touch the treasure of his inner heart. I wish to remain mild even in the most severe fights, remain good in the middle of evil people, and to be tranquil even in the middle of war.

To live undiscovered and without being taken notice of by others —how potent and powerful such a life is! In contrast, those people with evil qualities cover the earth and, soaking themselves in the sun, steal the social positions and happiness of others—those evil ones who might best be described as the living dead! There will be no prosperity for a nation if and when the longing for the truth is lost.

March 12

.... The tragic details of what happened to Scott's South Pole Expedition touched the hearts of the whole human race and left every soul in a state of unrest. The same had been true over the fate of Giordano Bruno [an Italian philosopher, considered a heretic, who was burnt at the stake; 1548–1600], and over that of Socrates as well.

Poland is a country whose history is full of ups and downs. It fell in the seventeenth century. But it revived after the First World War. Shortly thereafter, though, it was recently once again swallowed up by Germany. It is a nation with endless rises and falls. The same is true with Italy. Largely due to Garibaldi's exceptional ability, the modern unified Italy was first established after a long history of division. Recently, however, it seems to be splitting again.* Both are nations that undergo frequent transformation.

However, the glorious existence of those heroes and heroines whom Poland has given birth to—such names as Chopin, Madame Curie, and others come to mind—is a fact that people around the world cannot either ignore or erase from history. So too the forebears of modern Italy—Dante and Copernicus [a Pole actually], as well as Galileo and Da Vinci—they are all cultural treasures commonly shared by the whole of the human race. Just as no crime can ever be erased, so too the contributions one leaves behind cannot under any circumstances be denied. We could say that the greatness of a nation depends upon the production of people sufficiently talented to provide the impetus for enriching the foundation of human life. No matter what fate the future may hold for Japan, we were born with the fate to stand up and carry it. We must not restrict our striving to mere pleasure and ease, for, no matter which beautiful flower or delicious fruit we are concerned with, its root can only be cultivated through suffering and persevering.—I must not die.

March 27

.... Where or in what can the meaningfulness of life be found? Can it be found? Untidy brain! The springtime of life that is lost! One second runs into another and the flow of time does not rest for a moment. Do you know about *Urashima Tarō* [an old Japanese folk tale about a man who saved a sea turtle one day and as a reward the latter invited him to a sea palace]? Well, then, what should we do? ....

March 31

How can the sense of morality be raised? Once the sense of reason is lost, there will never be a manifestation of moral sense. The sense of reason, in fact, is based on a sharp sense for the truth. A will for reason cannot be born unless there exist an enlightened longing and reverence for what is true and genuine. It is easy to talk about moral sense. It is also so easy to shout about it out loud. To see it come into fruition without its foundation, however, would be even more difficult than trying to catch a fish out of a tree.

I have felt in recent days that I am not more than merely "alive." The I who is only "being alive" is of almost equal value, though not quite, as the I who is "being dead." Lately I have been pondering over many immoral acts that, in the past, I consciously or unconsciously committed. There are some which can be redeemed: there are some which cannot be redeemed.

When I think of these things I feel sad. But I cannot stop thinking about them just because.

April 3

I was standing at the front gate, and I did something bad. The fact is that I displayed a despicably bureaucratic attitude—[a sort of arrogance].

A certain boy urinated near the gate, and I chided him for that behavior. When I looked at the boy, pale-faced and runny-nosed, I myself, who was doing the chiding, felt very sad. Now and then this bureaucratic arrogance shows up in my personal attitude and, whenever it does, another side of me despises it. At those times I inevitably feel an increased sense of self-condemnation. I must set about doing something to eradicate this flaw. ....

May 12

Attended by an unusually deep emotion, I finished reading *Alt Heidelberg* [a German play by Meyer-Förster, dealing with young love and student life at Heidelberg University]. I am extremely happy that I was able to have my own Heidelberg.

May 13

Finished reading *Wakaki Veruteru no Nayami (Leiden des jungen Werthers)* [by Johann Wolfgang von Goethe, 1774]. The process that led to his death could not help but touch my heart so deeply. ....

I wonder whether or not I have been lying to myself lately. I wonder whether or not I am too satisfied with easy compromise. I wonder whether or not my sharp and uncompromising sense of justice has been numbed. It is frightening—truly frightening.

It counts for nothing just to be kept alive; the thing is to live! We must not be "kept" [like household pets]. Everything. . . . It is better that we wait, though.

June 5

To my dear father and mother:

I shall never forget your *on* (great favor) in bringing me up, over such a length of time, to where I am today—and through all sorts of pains and difficulties. Moreover, I have never done anything in return for that great favor. Please forgive me for my numerous *fukō* (lack of filial piety). The more I think about this, the more deeply do I feel my repentance. I wish I could close my life in the ice of the South Pole, or at the bottom of a Himalayan glacier, or atop an ice-wall, or, if none of these buried under the Turkistan desert. But the god of destiny did not thus favor me.

Everything has been a tragedy, but I also thought of how true it is, as Akutagawa [Ryūnosuke Akutagawa, 1892–1927] has also remarked, that when we become parents and have children, the tragedy of life has already begun. I pray for blessings upon my unfortunate father and mother.

June 20, 1944, 8 a.m.]
   To my dear Father, Mother, and younger brother:
   At Tatsumi Inn, Miyuki-cho, Ōsato, Moji City   Tokurō

Everything was so sudden, and, moreover, it all happened the way it did due to the very tiniest of fate's ironies. But I am not particularly surprised. At least I felt fortunate to be able to see Katsurō [his younger brother], even for an hour. Actually, by that time I was already supposed to have embarked, in which case I could not have seen anyone.

   For a variety of reasons, I had to spend more than ten days at an old inn with broken roof tiles, in a pitiful town of Moji that was all weathered by smoke and dirt. Probably you may have already read in the newspaper that I will be sailing off in a few days, leaving many and very special memories behind. Had I known your phone number, I might have been able to phone you and talk for a bit, might even have had an opportunity to visit [translators' note: at about this same time the author's parents were evacuated from Tokyo to Yamanashi for safety's sake], but I suppose that this too is a factor of fate. I certainly do not know where we are headed for next. Of course it is sure to be at one of those fronts on which the fighting is most intense. I assume that, at least most probably, I shall not be able to write you a letter for a while—(perhaps for a considerable length of time). Just by coincidence, my friend Takamura is going to be with me; and he is riding in the car adjoining mine. In whatever situation we may find ourselves, I think we will be able to console each other and make our hearts the richer for it.

   It is regrettable that I did not happen to have the books that I really wanted to keep with me, but nothing can be done about that. However, I did bring several other books with me.

   Upon my departure, up to the very moment I left from the barracks gate, those seniors and senyū (comrades-in-war), who for the time being are remaining behind, took care of my every need. Emotionally, as well as materially and financially of course, they sent me off with a farewell gift. I could not stop my tears from falling. All this was very much the same goodwill which my dormitory mates showed me when I entered the barracks. I am far from confident about how I could ever return their favors to those fine people. Unlike classmates at school, the only bond of unity that came to exist among these *senyū* friends of mine had been formed by a fleeting accident of fate, and I did not even know the home addresses of many of them—indeed, of most of them. Very probably I will never see most of them ever again. Nevertheless, the kindness they showed me, so beautiful even in its smallest manifestations, and so many other sincere expressions of their goodwill, will never leave my heart all the rest of my life. ....

I did write both to Professor Tsujimura [professor and head of the Geography Department, Tokyo Imperial Univ.] and Director Abe [Yoshishige Abe, a prominent scholar, who then headed the First Higher School]. I regret that I was unable to write to Mr. Aramata, who has been the professor in charge of my class since my first year as well as the moderator of the mountain-climbing club, and also to Mr. Tōyama of the First Middle School. So, please convey my warmest regards when you have a chance. I think that perhaps I shall have an opportunity to see Mr. Morris [former lecturer at the First Higher School] again, but if anything should happen to me (and of course that probability is strong), please tell him how it happened and also how I have been getting along since I last saw him; also, there is a letter from me to Mr. Morris (currently in Katsurō's keeping) that I would ask you to pass along to him. Should he not visit Japan, you will find his home address [in London] written down in the address section of my latest "Mountain Diary." Finally, as to the handling of the things I was keeping for him, Katsurō has instructions on what to do with them.

As for myself now, I have not quite regained tranquillity in my heart. That is simply because I cannot accept or understand everything. Is there anything more meaningless than for a "human being"—especially if he amounts to anything at all and has his own personality—to be ordered about at will, with total disregard for his thoughts and impulses, and without receiving due respect, by the whimsical brain cells of a certain unreasonable stranger, and to become a mere mathematical function? Whatever happens, I have no wish to dwindle into something like a piece in a chess game.

At any rate, I am keenly desirous of returning to the classroom as soon as possible and doing my best to accomplish my original mission. While in this current predicament, I cannot help but feel a strong regret over the fact that my youth is being stolen away little by little. The work that I was going to carry out is something of such significance that, I believe, it is reasonable to say, not even one other person in Japan would be willing to tackle it. Moreover, and considering the advantages I had, I do not believe that there are many people, even in the whole world, who could do the work. Although it is certainly not my aim, I firmly believe that the completion of my study would bring truly great honor and glory to Japan's position in the world, far more than would the winning of a war or the occupation of an island or cities.

Of course it is needless to say that, even for me to have advanced as far as I have, I owe so much to Prof. Tsujimura but, at the same time, Mr. Morris' influence cannot be disregarded. He taught me what a true human being, and the human race itself, has to do. I feel too that it was he who taught me what *gakumon* (the pursuit of knowledge) really is. I cannot forget the words he said to me, "Devote yourself to science!" was what he said on a certain evening, as I sat in front him, stirring red tea with a Tibetan silver spoon, in a room with a Tibetan fresco hanging. ....

Please allow Katsurō to study to his heart's content. I think you can trust him and let him do what he needs to do. I cannot help but think that I do not want him to experience the loneliness of having to worry so much about getting a book, or some such matter. In fact, the more I think about him, the more pity I feel for him. .... The current situation is too cruel and restricted for study. I think it is so unfortunate. The other day, when he came to see me for the last time, I talked to him, under the supervision of an officer, in a very businesslike manner in the officers' quarters: I thought he had tears in his eyes while he was looking down and painstakingly taking copious notes on what I was saying. I felt so sympathetic and sorry for him.

So long as the present situation prolongs itself, I am utterly concerned with the future of my homeland. Just saying that Japan is a very unique country does not exempt it from the usual rules of history. To think so would be as comical as someone who boasted that his body was specially made and therefore not subject to the rules of modern biology. Even assuming that we will win the war, it is most certain that we must give serious thought to what kind of a future condition, and for a long time to come, today's situation will usher in. History will decide as to who was really a true patriot, and who was not. As for myself, I don't care whether I receive meritorious medals or not; I shall be satisfied if the value placed upon me in the permanence of history is that of a truly patriotic person.

Should you hear that I have "died," please do not believe that death came from an enemy bullet, and against my will. For when the battle situation gets extremely harsh, and when it is time, I have accepted the idea of taking my own life, and indeed intend to do so.—But I would like to think, and somewhat to my surprise, that there may very well be only a faint ray of hope for me. ....

Already it is getting dark. Now I have to get ready and take care of a lot of details connected with the departure. I shall leave in good health. Please take really good care of yourselves, and do not worry about me. [Just in case of my death] I left my fingernails and hair for you at the regiment the very last minute before I left.

To Katsurō:

I have written down a variety of things in another place. When I went out on supervised leave today for my last haircut, unexpectedly I was able to get some books at a nearby bookstore. I am carrying them with me just for pleasure. These are titles:

1. *Gēte Shirureru Ōfuku Shokan-shū (Collection of Correspondence between Goethe and Schiller)*, vol. 1, translated by Eiichi Kikuchi. Published by Sakurai Shoten. ¥5.50

2. *Bungaku to Bunka (Literature and Culture)*, by Kenji Takahashi. Published by Ayu Shobō. ¥2.80

3. Duplicate. *Keisei-teki Jikaku (Self-Consciousness in Formation)*, by Motoe Kimura. Published by Kōbundō. ¥2.50

4. Duplicate. *Saikin Sekai-shi Nenpyō (Most Recent World History Chronological Table)*. Sanseidō Publishers. ¥1.50

As far as the things I asked you about the other day go, I know it is bothersome, but please take care of them steadily. I did inform the dormitory people about the general situation.

P.S. Because of the government limit placed on traveling, my friends in Dormitory North No. 27 will also have trouble getting to any place west of Kōfu (unless of course certified by the Ministry of Education). If so, I think that the only places they can climb will be Oku-Chichibu (interior of Chichibu), centering around Enzan, or the southern part of the Japanese Alps from Kōfu. Perhaps the former could be best utilized. When they stop by our home, would you please take care of them for me? Perhaps treat them to tea, or milk, or whatever, and to their hearts' content. I would sincerely appreciate your doing this favor for me.

Note

* *Hōkoku-kai, Hōkoku-dan, Hōkoku-tai* (Serving-the-Nation society, group, or corps): All of these refer to the government-sponsored nationalist movement organizations, such as *Dai-Nippon Sangyō Hōkoku-kai* (Great Japan Serving-the-Nation Society for Industry), and *Dai-Nippon Shōgyō Hōkoku-kai* (the same for Commerce) of 1940, *Dai-Nippon Genron Hōkoku-kai* (for speech making) of 1941, and groups called *Hōkoku-dan* or *Hōkoku-tai* organized in each school (translators' note: *tai* means corps, *dan* means group).

* *Ken-etsu* (Inspections): Higher-ranking officers conducted on-site inspection in such areas as living up to military rules, the state of academic military training, participation in field experiences, etc. An inspection required everyone to be at their best and at their most attentive. In the military training in the college/higher school setting, it was also called *saetsu*.

* "Not a single insulting word about us. . . .": In a letter of one Hugo Muller, contained in the *Kriegsbriefe gefallener Studenten (Letters of the Fallen German Students)*, translated by Kenji Takahashi, was the following: "I am enclosing a French soldier's postcard notebook. . . . What surprised me was that there was not a single insulting word about us (German soldiers). . . ." The author's use of the terms "enemy" and "our side" suggests awareness of the fact that Germany and Japan were allies during World War II.

* "Recently, however, it seems to be splitting again. . . .": Between July 1942 (when Mussolini lost power and the Fascist structure fell apart) and the Spring of 1945, there was bitter opposition between the Badoglio Regime in southern Italy under the Allied occupation and the new Fascist regime in the north.

Kenji Nishimura

Born March 25, 1922. From Gifu Prefecture. From Taihoku Higher School, entered Kyoto Imperial University, Faculty of Jurisprudence, April 1942. Entered the barracks on December 1, 1943. Sent to the war front in the South [i.e., Pacific] in May 1944. Killed in action on July 10, 1944, on Saipan Island. He was twenty-two years old.

[From a letter sent to his older brother, #1]

January 27, 1944

I received your letter dated January 20th the night before last, but I have just finished reading it through from the beginning to the end for the first time this evening. I was pleased to read about your life in Kyoto [translators' note: it could be "the life of my brother who lives in Kyoto]. It certainly has gotten cold the last two or three days, hasn't it? It would have been so nice if you could have met Mr. Suzuki. Please let me know the address when I see you on your next visit. I feel such very deep, heartfelt sorrow about Prof. Yanagida's younger brother.—Tissue papers arrived from Mother. I would think the fact that the package got here safely must be owing to her special, parental love. Brother, I am rather concerned about if you came to see me on the 23rd. Let's see one another at the meeting room on the 30th. I have not written much to our father and mother lately, so would you please tell them that the package has arrived safely via air mail? Incidentally, has anything for me arrived in Kyoto? I am anxious for it to come. And I am happy that my soul does not and cannot completely give up my adoration for things beautiful even in the midst of this global tragedy. I suppose that even to kill oneself means to insist on the self to the very end. Please pray for my health, I who am reminiscing about getting warmed up in a *kotatsu* [an old Japanese-style foot-warmer with a quilt on it] when actually I am warming my fingertips with the glow from a cigarette.—Dear older sister-in-law, Father and Mother, please write to me.

[From a letter to his older brother, #2]

April 4

The true significance of the phrase *gakuto shutsujin* (college/ university students departing for war) [see the note, p. 137], runs deeper than simply saying that students are temporarily giving up their pursuit of knowledge and taking up guns, but the real significance is that the students have taken up guns and swords. The fact is that students have already and altogether ceased to be students; they have even forgotten how to pursue knowledge. But I have my own way to follow. In my soul, there are also the souls of my father, who is prudent, loyal, and a very good person, and of my mother, who is so courageous and loves me with such a selfless heart. My actions are all regulated by those two loves. So, I keep thinking that, even when moving about among a large number of people, I am not merely a single individual but a person who contains all of the above.

Please let me hear from you about the books you have read lately. Today is the 4th, isn't it? Next Sunday will be the 9th, and then we shall be together. Please get well by that time. Dear older sister-in-law, thank you so much for the postcard.

[From a letter to older brother, #3]

April 14 or 15

I have to go away for the time being.

I hope that the both of you will take really good care of yourselves, and treasure the baby to come—and, please, never get sick, not even a tiny bit. I too shall be in good health. . . .

The cherry blossoms are showing off and competing with one another's beauty as though in pure celebration of their glory and honor; hiding the sorrow of their fall, which is to come soon. Well, then, I shall be looking forward to hearing from you.

From Ken

Akira Yamane

Born November 21, 1924. From Osaka Metropolitan Prefecture. From the
Third Higher School, entered Tokyo Imperial University, Faculty of Letters,
Sociology Department, October 1944. Entered the barracks December 17,
1944. Died at the Army Hospital in Changsha, Hunan Province, China, July
8, 1945. Army sergeant major. He was twenty years old.

[From a diary kept during the period when he worked at the Osaka
    Armory under the provisions of the students' mobilization]
August 26, 1944

A human being is a weak vessel: while healthy, he works high-
spiritedly because he knows that his country is counting upon him, but
once his body is worn out, he wants to think only of himself and to discard
everything else. He anxiously starts counting with his fingers for the next
holiday. Yet, he would not thrust even one more step forward to pull his
feet out of the huge current of this world. Perhaps he does not have that
much courage either; perhaps he has merely become a piece of machinery.

[From his memorandum book during the period of his studies in Tokyo]
October 20, 1944 Cloudy, occasional sun. Warm.

At one o'clock in the afternoon, I skipped my lunch and went to a
Kokumin Taikai (a citizens' meeting) at Hibiya Park Auditorium to hear
Prime Minister Koiso's speech. The auditorium was already filled to capacity, however, and those who could not get in were waiting in line, and
we would have to listen to the speech over a microphone. It seemed to me
that it would not be worthwhile to listen to the speech without being able
to see the speaker's face, so I turned back and attended the French class
by Professor xx . It was over before three o'clock. Then I went to Ueno
and visited the Science Museum. It is a fine institution for promoting the
interests of science in general. I returned to the dormitory at five o'clock,
and with the help of beans and water suppressed my hunger pangs.

—At the People's Meeting at Hibiya—
At Hibiya, there were people who
        had been gathering ever since the morning.
Spare time does exist even in this busy world.

November 5 Cloudy. The weather improved in the afternoon. Strong
wind in early evening. Quiet and tranquil at night.

I can sense that we have a full-fledged autumn already upon us. I had planned to visit the Nezu Art Museum and Professor Takagi [in the morning], and then to pay calls on Mr. Hijikata, Chie, and Mr. Ogata in the afternoon, but a single siren, sounded at 10 o'clock in the morning, caused the whole plan to fall through. About fifteen minutes after a preliminary air-raid warning siren, an air-raid emergency siren sounded; it would have been a typical siren, except for the fact that a single enemy plane had actually been sighted. The air-raid warning was cleared just before noon, but what a nuisance that one plane had proven to be! That one warning siren had served as a better alarm than ten thousand words of warning would have been to sober up the minds of those residents of Tokyo who had allowed themselves to become intoxicated by the positive aspects of the war's progress. Real tension has already been felt among Tokyoites, and after this there will be many more people who will not be able to sleep in peace. I think, however, that the enemy's intention has nothing to do with so passive a thing as a war of nerves; I feel sure that the carrying out of a gigantic air raid, and in the near future, is a major part of their plans. Given the fact that our defensive strategy is said to be in place, there should be no reason to be afraid, but how could we realistically prepare to defend ourselves [from the sort of large-scale raid which threatens]? How effective is our civil air defense? To keep our people from becoming so uneasy, we need to ask the government for appropriate instruction based on the experience of massive air-raids in other places. Of course, it would be foolish to think that an adequate defensive posture could be achieved merely by putting gaiters on legs, but perhaps something of the sort might be enough to have some effect, to cast a kind of spell which would calm people's anxiety. As an immediate measure, use a backpack as an emergency bag, and tuck in a set of underwear, heavy shirts, drawers (or long johns), a vest, woolen socks, *waraji* (Japanese-style farmer's footwear), towels, strings, a medicine box, and bank or postal savings-books. Even though we cannot do anything to forestall the event, it would be a forlorn fate and extremely depressing not to have the essential thing, *essen* [food—the author's original usage].

At 2:30 p.m., the preliminary warning was off. At 4 o'clock, Chie came. She brought *ohagi* (a traditional Japanese rice-ball with a sweet, red-bean covering) and *tempura* (deep-fried dish). I was delighted and most appreciative, for it has been a long time since I last had sweet things to eat.—I was so thankful and so deeply touched that I literally had tears in my eyes!

I read *Cyrano de Bergerac* [Cyrano, the protagonist, was a real-life figure, a liberal ideologist of the seventeenth century] by Edmond Rostand

[French playwright, 1868–1918]. The edition I read was a translation of the French play I had seen the day before yesterday. I was thinking of the time when it was written [and under the same circumstances that exist here presently], and of how the season was also about the same. In the last night-scene in the park [of the Sisters of the Cross], platane [*platanus orientalis*, chestnut in the original play] leaves have fallen during the night. Thinking of the scene, [I[1]] picked up platane leaves from a street with a tram-car line on East First Avenue, and spread them all over; and also dropped leaves ne by one from the second floor of Shintoku-kan [a boarding house].—[In the scene on the stage, I remember that] colored lanterns in yellow and blue, etc. were used to illuminate a scene so becoming to the sad "end of Cyrano's life"! Compared to the magnificence of Germany's Tell [William Tell, the protagonist] in an earlier period, in a play by Schiller [Johann Christoph Friedrich von Schiller, German dramatist and poet, 1759–1805], *Cyrano* has truly a delicate □□□□□□□ [7 letters undecipherable], an ultra-French atmosphere. Right now I am at a corner of Musashino Field, where leaves are falling from zelkova trees; while, in imagination, I am back in the time of and reading stories about Cyrano and Christian and Roxanne.—Especially right after an air-raid warning. . . .

I read Yūsuke Tsurumi's *Beikoku Kokumin-sei to Nichi-Bei Kankei no Shōrai (The American National Character and the Future of the Relationship Between Japan and America)*. A highly respected scholar, he brilliantly foresaw and, as early as 1922, warned about the uncertainty facing the future of the U.S.–Japan relationship. It is a fascinating book. I wonder how many Japanese today really understand America; indeed, in my opinion we could count only a very few among us who would even *want* to understand America. And how do things stand with respect to us students? It would be very difficult to win a war without getting to know ourselves through knowledge of the enemy. Ah.—

November 8 Cloudy.   A sprinkling in the afternoon which turned to a full-fledged rain in the evening. Midnight: windy, although clearing is expected.

---

[1] Translators' note: The subject of this sentence was omitted in the author's writing, and it would naturally follow that the subject is the protagonist of the play; but, since there is no such scene in the original play by Edmond Rostand, it is translated here as if the author is the subject. However, the translators were puzzled by the fact that, Higashi Ichijō (East First Avenue), with a tram-car line, was in Kyoto and not in Tokyo. Yet the author was obviously in Tokyo that day, for the Nezu Art Museum and friends he planned to visit were in Tokyo, and he was visited by a lady whom he was originally planning to see that afternoon. (m.y.)

In the morning, I was chilled to the very bone, and the weather makes it unpleasant to go out. I saw in the newspaper that a movie about Kamikaze Special Attack Forces and naval battles off the Philippines is to be shown at Hibiya Hall. So, I excused myself from xx [a class] and went to see it. I entered the hall a half-hour before the show. The line was very, very long—like a long snake. Inside, the auditorium was dirty. A cartoon of "Fukuchan" [a popular cartoon at that time, of a little boy named Fuku] and a submarine was shown [first]. The cartoon, by any standard, was just fatuous. It was followed by two touching newsreels.—Very touching indeed.

Later I stopped by a place for *zōsui* (a porridge of rice and vegetables) behind the Aoki-dō store, and found food as well as warmth in it. In this regard, *zōsui* is better than [the more regular meal of] rice. Returned to the dormitory at 3:30 p.m., but found that my *Vater*[2] had already come and then left for Meikei Hall. Later, around 4:30, we met up at the dormitory and had dinner together, and then he left for Kōfu at about nine o'clock in the evening.

Received a notice of *soldaten* [soldiers—author's usage in German] for conscription.

October 1944

To my dearest friend, As I face conscription;

Japan in April of 1942—it was not what you could call "a new dawn of the New Japan, full of energy, hope, and vigor"; rather, it had a sort of "ten-o'clock-in-the-morning" flavor. From that dark night until this morning, I carried out my existence as a living member of Japan, but the heart of me as an individual and the nation's heart were not necessarily in harmony. It is of course needless to say that the two are deeply intertwined; it was only just this morning that I felt myself and the nation come together. I suppose that the case of Japan at that time must have had much in common with that of a young boy climbing a hill—and full of hopes for a boundless future. When you add the concept of education to that of the nation and of the individual, then perhaps we could say that this too comprised part of the flow within the current of historical reality.

My life as a student at the Third Higher School came to blossom so brightly and brilliantly. My first task was to disrupt the old routine I had followed over my young boyhood. The anniversary festivals, the contests against the First Higher School—they all had this special meaning for me.

---

[2] [Translators' note the author's use of the German word for "father" which was quite common among the higher schools' graduates who had followed a German concentration track]

My various club activities also provided me with an important opportunity. I think I can say that the main current of this whole epoch [author's usage] played its part in the breakdown of my old self. I jumped into this destruction wholeheartedly, but neither could I be altogether satisfied with that destructive nature alone. In the bottom of my heart, there was something which could not be completely destroyed, even with this fanatical uprooting. Perhaps we might call it an intellectual conscience, or, more simply, a scholarly nature. But, in the final analysis, I felt that unless I could stand on some such foundation, there would most certainly follow an uneasiness not easily describable in words. Anniversary festivals, games against the First Higher School, our club life. . . . To me, all of these phenomena were full of the highest spirits. All these experiences not only comprise something I still sigh over but they were played out in a sort of Garden of Eden wherein life was lived out to its fullest possible intensity. As the *bild* [image, author's usage in German] of my eternal adoration, it became a place from which I could never again return to reality. Through the course of such a Dionysian [i.e., impulsive] life, I was able to perceive what I now consider to be my *grund* [foundation—author's usage in German]. Therefore, if it were now, it would have to be something special indeed that could shake this foundation. Of course, whatever the specific occasion was—whether it was the contest with the First Higher School in those days or something else—the primary reason for my finally leaving the club was that I was not successful in finding there what I was really looking for.[3] There is no question about the fact that I bear the primary responsibility for having left the club. I think, however, that although it did not reach the depth I desired to reach, there were some other things that were enough to shake such a foundation. First of all, the nation and the school became separated into two unrelated worlds; then there was the wishy-washy educational administration of the government itself; and finally, when the school administration attached the school to that side of the government, the very same school and the students who attended it separated into a division within a division. Since

---

[3] Translator's note: This section is rather ambiguous. One might be reminded that it was quite common among those elite higher school students at that time to write rather pretentiously, perhaps in an attempt to make their writings appear more mature and sophisticated. This writing seem to reflect also the intellectual trend of that time among them, i.e., the philosophy of German idealism, particularly Hegel's, and often referring to his concept of *Aufhabung* in their discussions. Thus, most probably, what the author wrote meant that "through those experiences, such as anniversary festivals, I was well on my way to transcend to a higher level, as in the concept of *Aufhabung*, but. . . ." (m.y.)

the union between government and school was a superficial one in the first place—achieved only after the school had wavered back and forth—I do not think that the students were the only ones who held onto old ideas. Not only did I personally feel that aforementioned gap between myself and my fellow-students, but, additionally, and in common with those very same students, I was aware of the huge separation that existed between ourselves and the school as an institution. I handled the first gap by taking up a position of solitude, and as for the latter gap I was more or less forced to adopt an attitude of acceptance—so the two of them were separated inside me. This is a point on which I feel that I owe a sincere apology to the Third Higher School. Somehow a link of reconciliation must be forged between myself and it—and between myself and the nation—and that link has to be based on the foundation I have discussed above. The time of beautiful harmony between my full-spirited activities, the school, and the nation is now gone. I am a student of the Third Higher School. In light of all this it is possible to anticipate new harmony, one in which I can thoroughly immerse myself in a blend of my foundation and the school of the future. But at least so far as I am concerned, the school as it exists today has become nothing more than a means to an end. The school has the simultaneous functions of being the means to the students' future and is in fact the goal in itself; so this is why I felt more lonely than ever about such a life. With regard to the link between individuals and the nation, I know that this is a matter which you too must have been distressed over so I shall refrain from talking about it here.

Having said all that, however, it might be asked whether or not my life was standing truly and solidly on that foundation. What I can say for sure is that I did live with that expectation. The separation of the three entities—my life, the school, and the nation—this was my serious mental concern throughout the period.

The war is getting more and more serious. The tie between my foundation and the nation seems to be getting weaker, while ideas such as "work is study" [*cf.* p. 107] and "student soldiers" add to the tangle. At any rate, the mobilization order of May 1944—(actually it was true with *arbeit* [work/ labor, author's usage] in January and March of 1944—though I did not then participate)—made me recapture the harmony between my life, school, and the nation. I was genuinely happy and went to work with energy and joy; it lasted for about a month. The physical exhaustion and the force of my habit of life, however, were no match for the heavy pressure of reality—and I screamed out. By way of taking advantage of the frailty of such high-handed ideas as "work is study," I escaped to the latter. The more real life demanded the former, the more would my desire for the latter continue to increase. The simple fact is that my body became more exhausted each day; mentally, each tense day was followed by another tense day.

With the end of the student mobilization in September, however, and in correspondence with the law of action and reaction, my mental life also went limp. All that remained were fear and hope linked with thorns. One voice says "entering the barracks," another "entering the university"; so, I became a person who took leave from reality and lived for a dream of the future. Yes, the entrance to Tokyo Imperial University was finally realized, but the powerful scholarly spirit that would and could have brought me back to the foundation did not seem to be available. Now that a dreamlike life in Tokyo has come down to earth, I am beginning to reflect upon it in all its variations. Now the desire to return to reality has awakened, and it is an extremely happy crisis to be in. (At a guest house in Kago-machi, Koishikawa, Tokyo, October 1994)

Tatsuo Miyazaki

Born July 1, 1919. From the Tokyo Metropolis. From the First Higher School, entered Tokyo Imperial University, Faculty of Science, Department of Anthropology, 1943. Entered the barracks in June 1944. Died of illness contracted on the battlefield, July 20, 1945, east of Manila, the Philippines. He was twenty-six years old.

June 2, 1944

Dedication to My Father and Mother

As I look back so far into the past, ever since that time so distant that I do not even remember it, it was you, Father and Mother, who nurtured and brought me up until today. What comes to my heart now is your most loving kindness as parents, and all the memories of those days, so long ago and far away, are so vividly in my heart.

What chokes me up now is my careless conduct, my so many and so thoughtless words and deeds in the past.

How many times did I swear that I would be a devoted child and live up to the duties of filial piety, and then, without anyone else knowing it, would shed tears over being such an unfilial child. Yet, because of my selfishness, how much pain, dear Father and Mother, did I cause you and how often did I push you close to desperate sorrow? I do not know how to apologize when I think of things like that, but can only bow down to the ground before you. Despite all the things I did, you were always so understanding, and you brought me up with your own true strength.

It was no one else but you, Father and Mother, who gave me the conviction and the strength to attain righteousness, and you also taught me to open my eyes to the beauty of being genuine and true.

Because of you, I was able to develop my own ideology and belief freely. I know the fact that I am now able to soak myself in the pure pleasure of having found someone whom I can call a true friend, and also to have the joy of being looked up to by younger people—all this is because I was brought up by you, Father and Mother, under your protection and influence. When I chose Anthropology and the study of Islam, the field no one wanted to pay any attention to, it was you who gave me so much encouragement with your warm understanding and empathy, more than anyone in the world could ever give me.

And so I was granted the pure happiness—probably as rare a thing as it is possible to find on this earth—of sharing with you the joy and the quiet pleasure that my modest work and small progress brought me.

Relying on your trust and understanding, I decided today on my companion for life. And, although modest, this is also meant to be a genuine modest gift to you from your impious child.

Dear Father and Mother, please stay in good health, and accept my deed of piety.

With my eternal gratitude, I make this dedication to you.

Tatsuo

June 12, 1944

Dear Tomoko:

For the first time I saw the person who is your true friend. And, more than ever, I felt very strongly about how beautiful a true friend could be either for a woman or for a man.

I cannot help but pray that, through the agency of your marriage to me, the friendship between the two of us will continue to grow even more strong and sound.

Unless our marriage advances our march toward the truth in every way, then, at least to a degree will our joy most certainly be overshadowed.

I always seek the light.

My hope is that you will seek it with me.

Be full of confidence that your growing up in good health is also a true joy to your friend, and continue to build yourself up cheerfully and richly without ever forgetting the path you were meant to take in life.

Tatsuo

[From the notes that were entrusted to a certain officer going home on leave for the purpose of liaison work]

To Tomoko: September 3, 1944

I wonder whether or not this note will ever be opened by your hand—without knowing whether it will or not, I shall continue writing it.

September 3, 1944   Afternoon

Last night, I departed from Tokyo just as the city was ready to fall quietly asleep under the moonlight. Indeed there were so many emotions that filled my heart! Everything has been settled by the national policy, however, and so my only choice is, and with as much courage as I can muster, to go to the assigned post. Something tranquil surrounded my heart's core. The train kept rumbling along, and the scene outside the windows was that of a peaceful, moonlit world. However, and as perhaps was to have been expected, my heart became uneasy at about the time we passed Fujisawa [Kanazawa Prefecture], and, I did not know what to do except close my eyes and continue to pray fervently for your health and that of my parents. ....

September 12   (morning)

Having ridden out the bad weather of yesterday and the day before yesterday at anchor, our ship is now quietly moving forward between the beautiful chains of islands in Korean waters.

Myself a mere sport of the strange finger of fate, I greeted the morning of the 12th—the day you so anxiously waited for by counting on your fingers—on a terribly uncomfortable ship, headed for the south seas, and comforted only slightly by the peaceful existence of these islands I have never seen before.

Throughout last night and the night before, and even when I would doze off for just a few moments—I continued to dream dreams of you and of my mother. When I would awaken and find myself on this ship, I would be overwhelmed by an emotion so sad that no words can describe it adequately.

I suffered from terrible diarrhea and high fever for about three days, but fortunately everything is all right now. The only things that I pray for are that my parents and everyone in Fujisawa may enjoy the very best of health, and that I might reach my destination safely.

As I gaze at the islands before me, what goes back and forth in my heart is the very hometown of my soul—the autumn scene at the lake. All the while that I look straight and quietly at the present situation, my thoughts fly back to my home and wander about in the southern skies. Thinking of what your thoughts must be today, I privately cry deep in my heart, and send you my fervent prayer that you will be well. I even feel as though I can guess the entry you are making in your diary today.

September 20

We have reached Takao [Kaohsiung, a port city in southern Taiwan]. I have not heard beautiful Japanese spoken for a long time, and I am now in a world that, in the past, I have never even thought about—I sense that I am a person in the middle of a severe "living struggle" [author's original in English]. As a humanist child on journey, I want to retain as much of the beauty of human nature as is possible, but I am silently spending each day witnessing the unpleasant reality of many hearts becoming less kind.

From now on, our ship will be heading toward ocean waters known to be extremely dangerous. I could not help but pray for the longevity of my military luck, and also for the health of my family and of my hometown.

A life without anything fine and delicate about it [in the original, the author used the English word "delicacy"], and a life without light, would make anyone weaker. I really feel like crying when I reflect on the fact that a heart without tenderness is the other side of this weakness.

My heart is finally ready for self-sacrifice on behalf of the motherland.

I simply keep praying. I pray that we might reach our destination safely, and that I shall be up to serving my fatherland well enough. I pray also for the safety of the entire convoy.

September 25

Our ship has not departed Takao because a new convoy has to be put together and the weather has been bad, plus the fact that the vessel itself is in extremely poor [combat] condition. This horrible shipboard life, a life far beyond any imagination, has lasted nearly three weeks now.

How many sleepless nights have I spent in the ship's hatch, so vividly remembering the night of *Wallpurgisnacht* [the female devils' mad party, well known from the description in Goethe's *Faust*—in this case, the festival at the University of Tokyo which takes place on the eve of the May Festival]. It is a life of extreme desolation and rudeness, carried on in the fear of uncertainty and amid foul odors. Several horses have already gone down, and, one by one, even human beings are beginning to fall ill and decline.

My effort to maintain an independent life of my own while continuing my search for *Schönheit* (beauty) and *Wahrheit* (truth) was in fact truly pathetic—was really a war in itself.

Some soldiers stagger around like wandering demon ghosts; others scream and roar like animals.

In the midst of conditions wherein man's finer characteristics and more tender sentiments are lost, I, the child on journey, am still seeking love, and with longing heart remember the mountains and rivers of home, and the faces of my parents and of my wife.

I truly wish you the very best of health.

Kōken Matsumoto

Born March 19, 1920. From Okayama Prefecture. From the Preparatory Division of Jōchi (Sophia) University, entered the University's Faculty of Letters, Department of German Literature, in 1940. Entered the barracks, May 1944. Killed in action, May 15, 1945, in Okinawa. Army superior private. He was twenty-five years old.

June 5, 1944
.... Here lately, at times such as sunset, I often look up at the skies with the palms of my hands pressed together. I do not think that I can continue to live alone.

I hope that each day represents some sort of progress. Progress? It has to be at least a step toward becoming a resident of heaven. I want to read the bible. In order to be loved by others, one must first dedicate one's love to [God]. Religion—is it opium? A church—is that where religion resides? Happiness is illuminated only when it is far way. Moonlit clouds, faint light from a star—is heaven filled with such scenes? I wonder whether or not heaven is truly so quiet and comfortable as that? In our world, at any rate, joy only comes after we exhaust all our strength. ....

June 7
.... Since we are without books, we should have stored up much more of *logos* [the author's usage] (an intellectual approach to things). To love—. How splendid and happy is the world we live in!

To enter from a narrow gate [note: an expression for passing the entrance examination to a top-ranked university] should not lead into an easy death.

"Open the door of fate with the flame of a precious life"—those are the words Professor K wrote for me. ....

June 29

....

I shall continue to live. I shall walk on.
The shadow of a forest which is my destiny to reach
    is becoming clear and clear
Reflections upon my eyes and heart.
    It seems to be a "death."
—But, that shadow of the forest must be bright,
    and quiet, and it must be healthy.

[A tanka poem sent to a younger sister while the author was en route to Okinawa]

My younger sister, because she has no mother,
    who is tying her wedding obi-sash and putting make-up
        on her today, as she is getting married

Tarō Tsukamoto

Born October 4, 1923. From the Tokyo Metropolis. Entered Keio Gijuku University in March 1943. Entered Takeyama Naval Training Corps in Yokohama, December 10, 1943. Killed in action as a human torpedo, January 21, 1945, in Ulithi Islands (atoll group), northwest Caroline Islands. Navy first lieutenant. He was twenty-one years old.

It was an innocent dream of long ago,
    In the shade of green leaves, thinking with a smile,
        of the person I played with.

Is my unlucky aunt going to build my shrine
    in the dead-end street where sparrows peck red berries?

[The above poems are *tanka*]

Takashi Ikoma

Born December 14, 1920. From Gifu Prefecture. Graduated from Gifu Prefectural Teachers' College, First Division, March 1941. Entered the barracks, January 10, 1942. Killed in action while in training at Karen Kōhoku Airport, Taiwan, July 15, 1944. An army lieutenant. He was twenty-three years old.

I wonder whether the white blossoms of the wild rose hedge
    that fragrantly bloomed on the backgate at home
      are still continuing to blossom now

                [a *tanka* poem]

Tsuneo Fukazawa

Born September 28, 1918. From the Tokyo Metropolis. From Urawa Higher School, entered the Tokyo Imperial University, Faculty of Natural Science, Department of Geology, in 1939, and graduated in December 1941. Entered Takeyama Naval Training Corps in Yokosuka, January 1942. Killed in action en route to Borneo from Manila, the Philippines, July 17, 1944. Navy first lieutenant. He was twenty-five years old.

On a dazzling and glaring sea, far away
    a coconut floated and distanced itself

I am glad indeed to be still alive, when I read
    the overflowing loving heart of a person
      in a beautifully written letter

Now that I cannot sleep with many thoughts in my heart
    only my tongue feels a cigarette

              [The above poems are *tanka*]

Jiroku Iwagaya

Born June 10, 1923. From Shizuoka Prefecture. Entered First Shizuoka Teachers' College, April 1941. Graduated in September 1943. Entered the barracks on March 10, 1944. On December 23, 1944, killed in action as his ship sunk off Luzon Island, the Philippines. Army lance corporal. He was twenty-one years old.

❀ ❀ ❀

November 6, 1943

I am scheduled to enter the barracks on March 10th, and the day gets closer every day. The news about the battles around Bougainville Island [the northernmost island in the Solomon chain, South Pacific] is reported in today's newspaper. It says something about a large transport ship suffering serious damage, a battle-cruiser sunk instantaneously during an enemy attack, and so forth. Why should anyone have to die by being swallowed up into that vast ocean? The death of a Japanese is grieved only by the Japanese: the death of a foreigner is grieved only by foreigners. Why does it have to be this way? Why can we human beings not develop to such a point that all human beings, simply as just fellow human beings, might grieve together in our sorrow and share our joys as well? A person who loves peace . . . for weak-spirited me, there is no way to avoid being keenly touched by words of this sort.

Just because a man is a foreigner, a Japanese views his death with derision. This is something I could never come to understand, regardless of how hard I thought about it. It is said that the Japanese people are proud of "being the Emperor's subjects, it is the symbol of being alive."—But, in that case, just exactly what happens to their personal pride?

How pitiful is the case of those who die of exhaustion after swimming in the sea for three or four days. . . .

Such a person thinks of nothing, and is desperately anxious and impatient because time is running out on him, and things finally reach a point where his heart just stops—

Death occurs for everyone. But this particular sort of death, although it has always existed, has, as it were, appeared in the world as something unconscious. . . . If I were to meet my death in the sea, I wonder whether or not it would be an unconscious death.

A certain day in March 1944

Third-grade children sang a song for me—"Tajima-mori" [a legendary figure who introduced mandarin oranges]. That made me happy, even though I did not know exactly why. Perhaps it was because there was something about the performance that made me feel a certain sadness as well as happiness. At any rate, I was happy.

Those lovely children sang "Tajima-mori" for me.

I think I shall always and forever remember that; it will deepen my reflections about having been a teacher. . . .

Another day in March
   Youth Corps members gave me a farewell party, and I was extremely pleased. I thought that the joy of just spending two or three hours surrounded by a lot of cheerful noise was very nice indeed.
   I am going to war but am going to leave war out of it. Perhaps no one would understand these words. Right now, however, I do not possess any fighting spirit sufficiently beast-like to take another person's life.—In this pitiful frame of mind, and feeling as though I am being sucked into a whirlpool, I take my departure for the war.

Tadanobu Yamanaka

Born March 5, 1922. From Nara Prefecture. From the Fifth Higher School, entered Tokyo Imperial University, Faculty of Letters, Department of Ethics, in April 1942. Entered the Ōtake Naval Training Corps in Kure on December 10, 1943, and later transferred to Takeyama Naval Training Corps in Yokosuka. On August 15, 1944, collapsed while in training at Yokosuka Navy Communication School, Fujisawa Branch (Fujisawa Electric Surveying School), and died at Yokohama Naval Hospital. Navy lieutenant commander. He was twenty-two years old.

June 22, 1944 [at Takeyama Naval Training Corps]
   After I leave here, I have to go through about four months of technological training, and be commissioned, then I will be sent to the front line, either to deal with more of life—or death. I am psychologically prepared for whatever I have to face, but I do not wish to think much about death. It will simply come when it is time for it to come. There is nothing for me to do but to follow the dictates of my fate. And I do not wish to make a big thing about arranging for a will, or other such things. The only treasure I am leaving behind when I die will be my *Tagebuch* [a diary in German]. Until the time comes, i.e., in the limited time I may still be allotted to live, my only hopes are that my own life might be fulfilled and that I can very carefully protect this *Tagebuch*. A record of a truly and a seriously lived life—is it not enough to have this? There is no need to be impetuous: one should calmly wait for one's time to come. I am inclined to feel like being alone. At the times when I am experiencing high personal feelings, I am reading *Begiff der Angst* [by the Danish Existentialist philosopher Sören Aabye Kierkegaard]. There is no high and no low in my *Tagebuch*; neither is there any superiority or inferiority. There, only the total self exists, and if I simply manage to express myself in it, that is enough.

August 1, 1944 [at Fujisawa Electric Surveying School]

Lately, I have somehow regained enough composure to be able to think. These days, I finish each day's work in a very bureaucratic fashion and then, in a manner of speaking, I keep looking at myself. I am not stepping—not even one step—outside of my personal affairs. Quietly, without a word, I am protecting myself. It may be *egoistisch* (egoistic) but this is the only way it can be. ....

If someone, via telescope, were watching this world from the world of stars, he would be witnessing a masterpiece of a drama in the process of unfolding. Even I have a *rolle* (role), perhaps a bit larger than a thousandth of this huge drama of history in the making.

I am not the type of person who can just stand around and watch as a bystander—I have to be right into things. How is it going to be? The wheel of fate has begun to turn, and it does not know when to stop. I hear that, within this year, we will have the end of the war in sight. I wonder what sort of an end it will be? At any rate, we are being toughened up for the confrontation. Further, the process follows a single, specific form; and in it the self is vanishing more and more into nothingness.

I have a sort of pitiful feeling. I feel as though I, the self, am vanishing away totally into the movement of history, a movement which is surpassingly vast and immeasurable.

Shin Hasegawa

Born April 12, 1922. From Fukushima Prefecture. Entered the College Division of Meiji Gakuin, 1942. Entered the barracks in December 1943. Army special pilot cadet. On April 12, 1945, he was killed in action on Okinawa as a member of the Special Attack Unit. Army sub-lieutenant. He was twenty-three years old.

April 20, 1944   At the Army Flying School

I have a sudden urge to read the works of Ryōsen [Ryōsen Tsunashima, a critic of ideology, 1873–1907].

The petition of Amida Buddha (Amitabha) has been a miraculous source of assistance and, stemming from my belief that the end is imminent, my heart desires to pray through a repetition of the sacred name of Amida:

Simple things are beautiful
Plain things are beautiful
Things naive and pure or ingenuous, are beautiful
Things grand and placid, are beautiful.

When being supplied with lace-up boots, when getting a meal, or while waiting for a meal when hungry, people's posture and expressions suddenly change. Starting tomorrow, when I go to the dining room and sit down at a table, I am going to pray with *nenbutsu* [i.e., repetition of the sacred name of Amida]. I am horrified when I think that I too must have that disgusting look in my eyes. So I am going to pray *nenbutsu*—and with my eyes closed.

April 26

In the morning, when all during the time of *kanpu masatsu* (rubbing oneself with a dry cloth), instead of using a towel, I was doing it with my shirt, a certain person said, "Why on earth did you fail to report that you forgot your towel? Besides, it is absolutely insolent to use an undershirt which is the Emperor's property! Rub with your hands." And then he slapped my face.

I feel a kind of despair about human beings, and especially about the humanity of our contemporary Japanese. I believe that never in history has there been a time when human beings were as far removed from the gods as they are now. And I wonder whether or not, from now on into the future, the day will ever come when religion can be treated with importance and respect.

Dostoyevsky's life in Siberia—

I wonder what kind of life he lived among those ferocious fellow-inmates of his. The only book he was given was the Bible. Think of him.

May 10

About the military cadet examination, and other examinations, while I was at the home unit. . . .

Truly ludicrous. It is so absurd to stick with such an inefficient and primitive system, more appropriate to a grade school, according to which not a single error of a letter or phrase can be tolerated. . . . It is a pity that such a thing still exists in our nation's military which, in all other respects, faces the war of today and tomorrow with the very finest and latest modern apparatus.

May 23

The books that my mother sent to me, *Ryōsen-shū (Collected Works of Ryōsen Tsunashima)*, and *Kirisuto-kyō no Honshitsu (The Principles of Christianity)*, by Harnack [Adolf von, 1851–1930], were confiscated by □□□□□.

In this kind of a place, what do they mean when they ask me to make a serious reflection, or by *shūyō* (self-cultivation)?

May 24

From now on, until the time for death comes, how desolate will my heart become?

As a matter of fact, will the Japanese race . . . ?

October 22

—A Doubt—

The children of today who do not know anything
They are fine the way they are.
The wretched ones are ourselves.
Those who came about ten years before us,
of my older brother Tasuku's time,
They are better off than we are—
because they were able to live like human beings
at least for a short while.

November 29

If only our pains and death would contribute, even the tiniest bit, to the happiness of our fathers and mothers, brothers and sisters, and those whom we love, then . . .

January 2

Born all alone,
to die, also all alone.

Yesterday, I loved,
Today, I anguish,
Tomorrow I die.

Kierkegaard [Sören Aabye Kierkegaard, 1813–55] (?)

The weak one, the pitiful one, your name is humanity.

January 18

I heard a talk given by an infantry officer who had spent a long time on the battlefields of our Central China operation.

He talked about how they killed prisoners and women soldiers—in a way that was so hideous such words as cruel and inhumane are inadequate.

I felt a little relief about having transferred into the Air Corps. Perhaps, in the final analysis, it may be the same thing, but at least I do not have to do any killing by using my own bare hands.

Whatever we might call it, the beastly nature—or whatever—in the human being. . . . I thought very seriously over the fact that it is so deeply rooted in our natures.

Ever since the creation of this world of ours, human beings have made absolutely no progress.

Any question of justice is no longer an issue in this war: the whole thing amounts to explosions of hatred between national groups.

Not one of these opposing groups would probably stop fighting short of their total self-destruction.

How dreadful! How shameful, indeed!

Ah, the human race—monkeys' relatives!

Kiyoshi Takeda

Born July 13, 1922. From the Tokyo Metropolis. From Tokyo Higher School, entered Tokyo Imperial University, Faculty of Letters, Department of Japanese Literature, in April 1942. Entered Takeyama Naval Training Corps in Yokosuka on December 9 1943. He was trained at Kurihama Navy Counter-Submarine School. He was killed in action on April 14, 1945, when his ship sunk off Cheju Island, Korea. Navy second sub-lieutenant. He was twenty-two years old.

—Missing my parents—
Skin of a persimmon is peeled off so smoothly—
and I long for my mother

[Translators' note: The author was struck by the loving memory of his mother peeling a persimmon for him.]

—Casual thoughts—
Those were [Summer] days when the flowers had
disappeared and only leaves grew so thickly on the

wisteria trellis [in our garden]
[Both of the above are 5–7–5 syllable *haiku* poems.]

February 6, 1944 (Sunday)

It was December 9th when I entered the Naval Training Corps,* wearing the national flags on both my shoulders. It has already been two months since then. As I think back, it seems that those two months were so busy and so lacking in the slightest opportunity for any calmness of mind or self-reflection, that blood must have been rushing to my head the whole time. Now that I look back, those days seem far from being a time of fulfillment; rather, they were filled with something totally empty and lifeless. From the standpoint of sheer physical *arbeit* [i.e., work, in German], the continuous round of labor was something I had never experienced during the whole earlier part of my life; yet somehow my brain was occupied with a sort of empty and incoherent sense of void, or nothingness. If all the memories of my life in the Marine Corps were to be completely wiped from my brain I would not mind at all.

This sort of shading in my opinion may be due to the fact that, before I actually entered the barracks, my whole way of thinking and of exercising my imagination about the military life and/or mentality was an abstract, rather spiritual matter. When I finally did enter the military, the very first things I felt, frankly speaking, were the pains—physical and psychological ones—which attacked me alternately. More simply stated, the physical pains were those of being subjected to severe cold and the sheer bodily exhaustion that resulted from overworking; the psychological suffering arose from feelings of boredom and the non-existence of anything to read. Added to all this, and an inevitable part of each and every day, were the hunger and the thoughts about food that accompanied the hunger.

This is such a weak-spirited confession to make, but, honestly, there is no other way to describe it . ...

Even when I read a newspaper account of a fierce battle being fought somewhere, my current perspective, as a member of the military, is entirely different from the way I used to think when I was in the real world. When I was outside the military I used to view both the news about the war and the general harshness of the times with the feeling that I could stand up to the situation with a certain determination; in the military, however, there is no such room in my heart—and the freedom to stand up for what one thinks ought to be done is taken away.

The heart of military life has nothing to do with anything involving resolution or determination; instead, there is the day-long grind of much heavier and more coercive physical activity—a routine that ties me down from morning to night. I came to feel completely oppressed and restricted by that life. My morale as a military man tended to become negative and weak. I thought that, in the final analysis, the only solution to this problem would be to let time run its course. Just about when the end of the two-month training as a sailor in the Marine Corps was in sight, I felt that my psychologically painful condition was eased somewhat. I cannot truly say that the problem was solved: what I *can* say, and more accurately, is that my capability to tackle head on and think about the problem was gradually becoming numb.

Once having entered the military, I was in the end forced to come to terms with the delicacy both of my physical and of my psychological organization. Before I could discuss the nation and the military, I was first forced to ponder on just how both my body and soul might best become adjusted to this entirely new mode of existence.

My first wish was to start off, both psychologically and spiritually, absolutely fresh. I thought I needed to completely get rid of all my previous thinking about the world and my old attitude toward life. The military life can never be comprehended, regardless of when and where it is lived, by the application of any secular or worldly yardstick of the reality outside the military. I thought, then, that I had to find a way to deal with everything that had to do with the military by first dealing with my physical being.

February 16 (Wednesday)

.... For the first ten or twenty days after entering the barracks, any desire to do some reading was out of the question, and there was no time for it anyway. Once I gradually learned the basic elements of the life, however, and had some time—including that dead time on Sunday afternoons when, because I was a new recruit, permission to go out for a visit was denied—my nostalgia for books and reading started to bubble up again. So far as the composition of poems went, I could not even fashion twenty poems during that whole first month of my life in the Marine Corps, because I was trapped in that over-simple and uneventful environment from morning to night. In the reading department, I devoured whatever caught my eye, indeed whatever I could get hold of.

Concerning *Tan-I-shō* (a collection of the Buddhist Priest Shinran's works, compiled by Yuien): after having read it through three or four times, I saw that, for lack of background, I could not develop my thoughts further; so, I gave up and put it away inside my small box. As for newspapers, regardless of what paper it was or how old it might have been—even, e.g., if it was composed of tattered old sheets that my own muddy shoes had been wrapped in—I read them all thoroughly. When I got hold of a government pamphlet that was about half a year old and that someone had thrown under the silverware box, I spent nearly a whole week reading it over and over. Some new stage in the war between Germany and the Soviet Union, advice on the preservation of fuel, etc.—all news of this sort was rather old by the time it got to me, but I still read and digested the reports with much interest. I truly and keenly realized how serious an appetite one can develop for the written word when, while those in charge of the meal service were running around so busily, I sat on a hard wooden chair at the table and, in the few minutes before a meal was served, reread with utmost care a piece about the fine properties of Mentholatum!

February 18 (Friday)
                .... I am idly gazing out the window in front of me. Our student hall is standing midway up a little mountain, only a small distance from the Kurihama Beach [of Yokosuka city]. Moreover, because only the top row of the windows is of clear glass, and the rest is all frosted, the only scene within my view is the top half of another small mountain just in front of us, where the rough surfaces of the aqueous rocks are exposed because of the sports ground construction, and the sky that is framed in a triangle formed by that mountain and the window frames. You cannot see the ocean at all. It is such a narrow and simple field of vision, but, at that particular time in the morning, the sky and the light over this mountain scene keep changing just about every second. This phenomenon is due to the fact that the late winter sun rises from the mountain behind our student hall. In the beginning the mountain in front of us has a smokey, grey skin, but gradually it becomes pink, then turns to gold, and finally to a whitish yellow. In the sky, a large number of some type of waterfowl, which skim down along the two oceans' surface, come casually flying along as though they were involved in some type of group dance. Higher still, and reminding us of a very tough training program that had been in progress since early morning, the very latest model navy planes of the Flying Corps move off into the distance, stretching their smart-looking wings and trailing light engine sounds behind them. Occasionally, carried by the wind, the cheerful sound of the ship-builders' riveting comes over the mountains from the direction of Uraga Dock, even as far as this hall of ours. In this scenery, I somehow completely immersed my body and soul, which are confined in the self-study room, in the harmony of all of it. Even in the midst of my enjoyment of that sort of scenery, I kept dreaming a variety of daydreams—the memories of the time, about a year ago, when I was living as a student at home in Tokyo. There was the warm bed, the miso soup with steam rising from it, the parlor where the morning sun was shining in, the smell of the ink on a brand new morning newspaper that

had been placed on a rattan chair; there was myself, casually throwing a half-finished, filterless cigarette into a glass ashtray and then changing into a student uniform. The dress shoes are lined up in the vestibule, there is a leather briefcase, and the carp in the garden pond that I always went to see at least once whenever I left by the gate, and the cigarette shop located on the way to the station. . . . Circling very smoothly, those scenes go through my head just as though I were listening to a passage in a symphony. ....

March 26 (Sunday)
       .... With the arrival of spring, my heart becomes increasingly heavy. I first felt a little relieved through coming into contact with some warmth and brightness, but, after becoming accustomed to this weather, I am bound to get pushed into a dark and heavy mood.

Compared to the time when I first entered the school, the daily routine has gradually become more and more a matter of classroom studies [as opposed to the previous, more practical exercises]. The food problem has also become somewhat less of a problem. Even if I had the luxury of complaining though, a mental anguish seems to be squeezing me slowly but increasingly. Every day is a monotonous, stolid, and gloomy day. I feel relieved when, at the double, I go to the town of Uraga and see the street with a cigarette shop, a clothing store, a wine shop, and so on. On the March we crossed over the side of a mountain, and I saw a wheat field that had already grown quite tall. Suddenly the view in front of me became so bright. That shows how little my life nowadays has in the way of changes in surroundings. All day long and every day our Korean laborers are blasting away at the mountains. The muddy mountain and the rough beach of the reclaimed land that is linked by a railroad for cats—that dreary place is the sum of our existence for an entire week. And those weeks lead to other weeks, and on and on.

The dread of this suffocating life of confinement becomes increasingly keen. Whenever I go to sleep these days, I dream only of my home— and more than ever.

June 16 Friday Clear
The advance of the enemy's mobil units is so sudden.
Northern Kyushu was bombarded at two in the morning, and southern Korea at two in the afternoon.
On the 15th, there was a landing on the island of Saipan.
      ....

They tell us to "get rid of the attachment to self." But if the attachment to self is such an easy thing to get rid of, then it should already have been taken care of long ago, say after half a year of military life. I could not get rid of the self even if I tried. That image of myself which I believe to be the best is something I have to cultivate, and gloriously, until the very end.

And just how is this "self" of mine to survive—not just as a mere compromise or an outright falsehood, but in the genuine and true sense — the vicissitudes of a military career. This is the paramount issue for me. No one else can add anything to this or offer me any help. And it is not something for which I would seek others' help. I must deal with this issue sincerely and intelligently, and on my own.

I am a person who could very well die tomorrow. I, the self, am something that belongs to me, and yet not quite entirely.—Until now, I have been pressured by my everyday life and quite defeated by my surroundings. Moreover, I have been a vague witness to that defeat from a spot on the sidelines, in a world so simply sentimental that it seemed to belong to someone else. I thought of it then as a modest posture. *"Gushū no kokoro"* (the heart of an ignorant crowd)—I had made that sworn and heartfelt oath prior to entering the military life, and over the half a year since then I had done my best to keep the promise. I tried to achieve this by fighting down that dear internal desire of mine to stand high in my own estimation (and how I miss it!), a desire that urged me to throw the promises away and wanted to laugh at it.

The heart of an ignorant crowd—to immerse myself in the masses, however, does not necessarily mean that one must destroy oneself forever in the midst of the masses. Is now not the time to extend a hand in order to rescue the self, the image of the "I" which somehow floated out, gasping, from the waves of foul odor? This is the image that, amidst the ignorance and commonness of the masses, makes one breathless; this is the self that has endured to the end after having been cleansed of everything and having fought through every conceivable type of battle. Taken altogether, those were days filled with considerable ennui and lazy living, but it must have been my own *wallpurgisnacht*. Now is the time to think seriously about how one should go about living as a human being, as well as of the special problems posed by life in the sealed world of a naval officer.

To treasure and protect the self that had survived and would survive until the end—that I should say is the correct attitude which ought to be found acceptable even in the military life.

June 17 Saturday Rain
.... My once so powerful hunger for books has become considerably dulled lately. It would be better if such an almost biological

desire for those ordinary books, especially the extremely mild ones such as so-called cultural books, would soon disappear.—It would be also much easier emotionally. ....

July 21 Friday Rain
    With the coming of our first rain in several days, the heat is reduced a little.
    When living becomes a little easier and less eventful like this, the time available for self-reflection attacks me as though I were suddenly stumbling over something. ....
    "The love that is kept secretly in one's heart is a fine model. When a person loves someone so much that he or she would be willing to die for the object of that love, and not to make mention of that love all one's life because of consideration for the other, is indeed a truly profound accomplishment." (From *Hagakure*) [a book on Bushidō, the way of Samurai, based on an oral presentation by Tsunetomo Yamamoto of Saga Band].
    I thought that the constant perseverance through and the pains of everyday life were limited just to the habit and routine for the medieval sort of life.—

August 7 Tuesday Rain
    Weather conditions are not good, and long waves continue to roll in from the sea. A strong, pouring rain attacks many times throughout the day.
    In the evening, when I became thirsty and went to the dining room to have a cup of tea, I saw the *jūhei* sailors* [who are assigned to wait on an officer] standing in line on the dark beach. The scene made it evident that a lance corporal* had gathered those sailors and was administering their "psychological training" with an oak stick on his hip. At first he was saying something in a low voice, and then suddenly he was scolding the sailors in a much louder tone; shortly afterward he made each of them step forward and began hitting them around the hips with the oak stick as strongly as he could. Whenever the attitude of a particular sailor who stepped forward to get hit was not satisfactory, he would knock the man down by thrusting the stick even more forcefully, and then make him step forward again. Each one of the sailors who stepped forward to get hit had to stand up straight, with his hands up in the "holdup" position, to spread both legs wide, and to stand with his back turned before the lance corporal. The dull thud of the blows—"battarn," "battarn"—sounded as though they were grinding the men's hip bones to bits. I regretted the fact

that I had witnessed something so distasteful, but, far more than simply having seen something so outrageous, was the feeling that lingered inside after the sight.

One Sunday some time ago I saw another lance corporal who was standing around near the entrance to the soldiers' quarters, and he suddenly began to beat a *jūhei* soldier, accusing him of having returned late even though the soldier had returned to barracks ten minutes before the official deadline. That second lance corporal was a physically powerful man, almost hatefully so, with a big dark face. The man who was beaten up, on the other hand, was a lowly conscript with an obviously unhealthy, pale face, and with dark rims around his eyes. After he had undergone that sudden attack, the man groaned as though he were choking—something like "Uh . . . Uh"—and, like a dead body, fell flat on the gravel road. When some others of his own rank, in a flurry, hurriedly pulled him up to a standing position, he stood with his hands wide open, hips bent, and stood up in a weak, wobbly manner just like a drunk; instantly, however, he collapsed again onto the ground. From the back of his head, a ghastly and dark red stream of blood ran down inside his collar.

I was watching this scene from a smoking area, and with a cigarette in my mouth, but my heart could not help but to be greatly disturbed.

Servicemen such as those will soon be my subordinates. How should I interpret this?—But there is no need to worry too much. It definitely does not make sense to think about such things too seriously.

August 9 Wednesday Clear

After a round of inspections, everyone in the 3rd and 4th groups was standing in line and being subjected to "mental training" for a long time. As I lay listening in my bed, I could still hear Lieutenant Itozono's high-pitched voice.—It all began with their total lack of a positive attitude toward studying during the period allotted for self-study.

"Certain people are reading *Hagakure* during the self-study period. Although, at least technically, the reading of *Hagakure* is permitted during the self-study period, I do not expect you to have any leisure time for opening such a book now. You graduated from universities which cannot be considered true universities: you cannot accomplish anything if you are still attached to that sort of studying, as well as to those universities of the past which have long since vanished from the mainstream."

"You have not accumulated enough learning to earn the right to call yourselves intellectuals."

—About three days ago, I was reading the Iwanami Bunko edition of *Hagakure* in the self-study room. Sub-lieutenant Itozono walked in quietly, looked at what was on my desk, and said: "Oh, that's *Hagakure*?"

—"Yes, Sir; that is correct."—"If you have extra time, read it," he said. Then, without another word, he left the room.

    —Also, about a week ago, a document sent from the university was forwarded to me through my family back home. It was an application for receiving my graduation certificate. If I sent this form in, it would be the same as actually having graduated from the university. For my own part, I have no intention of going out into the world without further study, if and when I should be lucky enough to return home again from the battlefield. The idea is to remain in the university and continue studying until I feel satisfied, whether it will take four more years or even five. So I went to a divisional instructor's office, and it just so happened that Sub-lieutenant Itozono was there alone. I opened the document and asked his advice: "I still do not feel like getting out of the university without additional study. What should I do about this document?" The sub-lieutenant lost no time in responding to my question: "Stop thinking that way, stop it! In the middle of a war, you should not even be thinking about universities. To begin with, can you honestly say that, in today's universities, there are any great professors whom you can really and enthusiastically admire? Were the university so great that even Michelangelo would jump at a chance to become associated with it, then that would indeed be quite a different matter. . . . Now more than ever, the essence of the universities will continue to be twisted because of this war and of history itself. How could you say that there is any value to that sort of university and to that sort of learning? Now is the time, and as soon as possible, to get away from such attachments and to make yourself aware of what your genuine mission is. Since they are being so kind as to permit you to graduate, get out quickly —just get out." I felt that there was nothing I could add to that, and so I silently excused myself. Upon returning to my room, I completed the application, addressed it to the Dean of the Faculty of Letters, and casually left it on the desk while I went out for a smoke. Just because Sub-lieutenant Itozono's answer was so utterly simple and clear, for that very reason it made me feel somewhat unsettled and my head was full of disturbing feelings.

    (I wondered whether or not I was chasing the so-called dream of the culture of the past. Could it be possible that learning and the fine arts are nothing more than the fragile and faint thing I actually seem to be seeing now?)

August 15 Wednesday
....
    Every day in this life tends to be sluggish, i.e., there is no hope and there is no brightness in the future. All day long, we are so busy with

classwork, get so completely exhausted by gym and by swimming during a midsummer day, and then sleep just like pigs. Getting up in the morning, going to bed at night, eating three meals—all of these things are so mechanical, just as though we were human beings who had lost their central nervous systems. *Is it all right the way it is?* [author's emphasis]. But that shouting and questioning voice gradually grows appreciably weaker.

Each and every day many of those senior members [men who entered before me] and other wartime friends of mine are being scattered over the ocean as though they were garbage—and they just disappear from our sight. Each one of those lives, each of them precious and indispensable as an individual, disappeared into a maze of number and quantity and was dealt with accordingly.

It is simply a case of mental exhaustion—or, rather, the numbing of some essential faculty. Sufficient strength either to take a stand or to concentrate on a single issue is just lacking. The only refreshing medicines available to me are books (the books that I steal to read for a brief moment whenever I can).

Notes

* "*Kaihei-dan*" (Naval Training Corps): This was a basic training unit for those entering fleet duty in the navy as non-commissioned officers and sailors. Several new "*Kaihei-dan*" were established to accommodate those university students who were entering military service [because, otherwise, the only way one could become an officer in the navy traditionally was by graduating from the Naval Academy].

* "*Heichō*," and "*Suiheichō*": Lance corporal. In the army, "*heichō*" was the highest ranking among the soldiers. "*Jōtōhei*" was just below it, and "*Ittōhei*" and "*Nitōhei*" were the lowest levels.—In the navy, it was called "*Suiheichō*." "*Jōtō suihei*" was just below it, and then came "*Ittō suihei*" and "*Nitō suihei*."—("*Suihei*" is a general term for sailors, and "*hei*" means soldiers.) See the note under "*Naimu-han, Naimu*" on p. 117.

Kazuo Nagata

Born May 22, 1916. From Mie Prefecture. Through the Eighth Higher School, entered Kyoto Imperial University, Faculty of Agriculture, Department of Agricultural Economics, in April 1938. He led the Communist student group at the university, and was arrested in 1940. Released from the prison with four years of suspended sentence. Graduated from the university in September 1942. Entered the barracks, October 1, 1942. Died of diseases contracted while on the battlefield, in Imphal, India, July 4, 1944. Army corporal. He was twenty-eight years old.

[From notebooks kept while serving in the military]
February 23, 1943

Went to study about attacking a contemporary tochka [a very strong defensive position of the pillbox variety, with a thick concrete wall surrounding the gun]. As I studied the tochka and its enormously heavy structure, tall and deep on both sides, I wondered how it could ever be reduced by an attack. Could the military power mustered by a small platoon comprised of an attack squad, a demolition squad, a support squad, and an auxiliary squad seize it? I am supposing, of course, that there would also be support from heavy machine guns and infantry guns. At any rate, we can do it, and herein lies the essence of the Japanese military.

Over the skies of the training ground, formations of two-engined airplanes flew, either coming in for a landing or just having taken off, with their silver wings shining. I am reminded of what Superior Private Horiguchi said at the base of a public memorial tower: "My aging mother, when she sees an airplane flying in the sky . . ."

The sun is warm but there is a strong wind; clouds come and go, and I enjoy looking over the vast spread of our training ground. There is a faraway hill, and I remember that I used to look at such a hill long ago.

May 10

I was awakened by the vibrations from a train running along just below my window. The town of Otaru is cloudy again today. I wonder if it is always cloudy like this in Hokkaidō. These are gloomy days indeed. Hokkaidō gives me an impression of being really dark, because the houses around here are blackened by soot, and even the skies, with clouds hanging low, are dark and dull. ....

When I arrived here last evening, the canal was just packed with boats. Both waterway and boats—everything is covered with grease, and the people who live on top of all that! The bitter cold. It reinforces the general air of depression. I suppose that once upon a time numerous fishing ships and factory ships departed from this port of Otaru, heading for the northern sector of the Sea of Japan and the Sea of Okhotsk as their stages of activity. I imagine that there must have been some happy lives— and also some sad ones—lived there.

I am deep in thought in bed, in an inn in Otaru. There is no wake-up bugle here, so I can recover from the trip and rest my tired bones. I am leisurely letting the weariness of the trip wear away. Did I ever expect to experience a morning like this?

May 11

It has stopped raining, but the clouds are once again hanging low over the city of Otaru. I no longer feel uncomfortably cold. As I got up today everyone did gymnastics together; after that, we all talked about our last nights out.

On the evening of the 11th, I went out onto the rather quiet streets of Otaru. It had stopped raining as well. We will be saying good-bye to this friendly town tomorrow. I drank a beer at a noodle-shop. The amiable face of the young woman at an *oden-ya* [a modest eating house that serves Japanese hotchpotch with beer and other drinks] lingers more in my memory than the elderly woman's at this noodle-shop. Because she lived in Otaru all this time, ever since she graduated from grammar school, and has never been anywhere else, she said that she does not know much about worldly things. I should say that the town of Otaru is very nice indeed.

June 15

In the early evening, I went out behind the living quarters, and, quite spontaneously, I screamed aloud out of pure joy.

The shape of the roofs of the houses in my hometown, and the skies behind them, are set off by a mountain.

Happy memories suddenly bubbled out—and then just as quickly faded away—of the days when I was a child, in the middleschool and afterward.

It is time for me to report to the Sergeant Major for kitchen detail.

June 22

Sergeant Major Tani left in a hurry for the south.

June 16 – July 21

Invasion training.

July 27

There is a crisis on the island of Sicily.

Mussolini has resigned. I wonder what will happen to Italy.

And, right now, fierce battles are being fought without letup throughout the Solomon Islands.

August 1

Italy after that. . . . One gathers from the newspapers every day, even though the reportage is strictly of the surface variety, that a considerable change has taken place. I wonder what will become of Italy, and what will come out of the clash between the Fascist Party and its opponents.—But I shall not write about that.

August 17

This extremely harsh bayonet training goes on day after day. I am totally exhausted from morning to night, and even while I am asleep. As soon as we are awakened by a bugle in the morning, the full day of bayonet training begins immediately. Each and every day the wake-up call sounds long before my exhausted body has had a chance to recover. From the bottom of my heart, I yearn for a good rest—I daily and desperately crave one. All the joints in my body hurt. The places where I had injured myself once before repeatedly get reinjured. They tell me to put on Aka-chin (Red-tincture) [a popular name for mercurochrome used for an antiseptic tincture], and then more Aka-chin. In addition to all this, I am not getting any more skillful with the bayonet. My awareness of this fact, that my capability does not improve regardless of how hard I train, seems to double the exhaustion. When I stop to think about it, I realize that not even in my wildest imaginings could I have come up with a notion of this kind of existence.

....

In the evening, just about everybody went out to see a movie in front of the 2nd machine-storage warehouse. Superior Private Mukai has skipped out. Superior Private Ubugama says quietly, and sincerely, "Oh, how I wish I could have some *sake*" (Japanese wine). There are just four of us left in our squadron. Superior Private Sakuma is mumbling something about the problem of dividing snacks. In the quiet room, we can hear the loud buzzing of autumn insects. I suppose we can say that it is an early autumn already. Those freshman recruits who are in battalion training have gone off for night maneuvers.—I can hear the sound of the firing of light machine guns.

Suddenly I think of home.
I wonder how my mother is.
I wonder how my younger brothers are doing.
And I wonder what my friends are doing now.

Lance Corporal Deguchi returns from cooling off in front of the quarters and says: "What a lovely moon is out tonight. When I see the moon like that, tears wet my eyes." Lance Corporal Uraguchi returns from some official business, and says: "Oh, I am so darn tired."

August 22   Sunday

It is very hot again today. Cicadas keep on singing so loudly that they seem to agitate the late summer heat even more.

In the non-commissioned officers' meeting room, a visiting entertainment show is now going on for our benefit. Rather than watching such a show, what I really want right now is a good rest. The last few days have left no room for thinking, and I really believe that it is essential to have some leisurely time in which to think.

The same is true with regard to this bayonet business itself. Even while we are training like crazy, I would think that it is necessary for us really to reflect both upon ourselves and even about how one's bayonet moves. In our training we are now concentrating totally on the effective use of the bayonet. In the south, very fierce sea battles are being fought near Munda on New Georgia Island. The very essence of modern ocean warfare must be unfolding there. I think of how the nation's productivity is being put on exhibition via modern ocean warfare.

The Axis powers have finally withdrawn from the island of Sicily. And I wonder what the Sicilians must be thinking about now.

September 3

Various things occurred to me as I stepped down from being on duty for the week. . . .

What goes on in a soldier's head—activity which is primarily revealed though their performance of the jobs assigned to them. . . . It is a sad situation overall. I think people ought to be able to work much more happily, and to live more happily. I can feel the squad's deficiencies in these areas in our everyday living routine. There are those with poor mental attitudes. Whenever I happen to confront them, I can feel deep anger welling up from the bottom of my heart.—But then again, my anger turns round in the direction of my own heart when I look at the faces and into the eyes of those others whose hearts are so downcast.

September 5

It has been two days since I read in a newspaper that the Allied Forces had landed on the mainland of Italy. Many of the ancient capitals and cities of Italy are being bombarded. Bombing an ancient capital, I would think, means the destruction of the human race's artistic heritage and the fruits of its culture. Perhaps, however, and in these very same ancient capitals we speak of, there may lie sprawled under the black smoke some modern heavy industry. During wartime even the fine arts have to compromise and sacrifice themselves. I wonder whether the Leaning Tower of

Pisa is all shattered by this time, and about what has happened to all those architectural treasures of Italy which we came to know through the movies.

And how must the youth of Italy be at the present time! Now that the government has been overturned, all the young people who grew up in the Fascist mentality are now having to face its total refutation. They must be shaken up rather deeply right now as they face the rejection of their world-view by the new government, and at the same time as the country of their parents and grandparents is undergoing bombardment as well as being trampled down by enemy soldiers. Some of them must have been directly exposed to the bombing. And I wonder what is in their minds and what they are thinking of right now. They must defend the history of the Italian people. In the fulfillment of that responsibility, perhaps, they might find the meaningfulness of life, but at the same time they could just as well be feeling a sense of utter helplessness—that there is something inadequate about themselves. At least as I imagine the situation, the lives of these people today must be quite unbearable.

September 9

I heard the news of Italy's unconditional surrender. It had already been signed on September 3rd. I think seriously of a cross-sectional view of world history.—Italy has surrendered. The battles being fought between Germany and the Soviets are still of the most intense kind. Moreover, the war is played out over a vast territory. The enemy's offensive in the South Pacific is also extremely fierce.

Then there are the Balkans and Turkey.

The fundamental opposition between the combination of America and Great Britain vs. the Soviet Union.

Then, Africa, Western Asia, and South America.

Great Britain and America's hostile confrontation with Germany.

I wonder whether or not, given the impetus of Italy's surrender, a new shift will be given to this whole entangled situation. The fact of the matter is that the opposing forces' contentiousness is now altogether too keen to allow for any essential change.

September 17

In the midst of the heat of late summer, our bayonet training continues.

Italy was split into two parts.

The Republican Fascist Party (I wonder what "Republican Fascist" means?) and the Badoglio Administration.* "The battles of the Italian Peninsula" are once again steaming back and forth. One nation has to split into two parts and then have one part fight against the other.—What a shame!

October 12

I have not paid any attention to this diary in a long time and, for just as long a time, I have not written a single letter—even though I have received quite a bit of mail that I have to reply to.

Every day, as soon as we finished our swordsmanship training we went to Shimada Heights for firing practice. ....

The most painful part of living in the barracks is the food. Even though we have lived together every day in the same battalion, the same company, and the same platoon, once we came to the barracks a newly organized division was formed, and we have to eat according to each man's division. The divisional conflict at mealtimes is simply ridiculous. The place is filled with silent hostility, complaints, and general discontent even when not a single word is spoken.

The downpour has finally stopped and a moonlit night has arrived. From the windows, and beyond the dark roofs of the town, I can see blue Lake Biwa in the moonlight—the kind of blue that used to make me feel the drag of a journey. I went out to the back of the barracks and, in the cool breeze, stood gazing at that light with the innocent heart of a child.

October 14

The moonlight last night was very bright.—Somehow my mood was unsettled and I was unable to sleep.

November 3

From the end of last month until yesterday, I served as an Inner Shrine Guard [guard duty at the Imperial Great Shrine in Ise]. Luckily, I was able to meet my younger brother, who was about to leave for the front as a member of a tank company. He seemed well, but I thought I detected a slight sadness about him. There is a certain uneasiness connected with tank service, and I wonder whether or not his thoughts were on German tanks, Soviet tanks, and American tanks.

My youngest brother, Yōsuke, is very unlucky. He is now working as a substitute teacher at a *"kokumin gakkō"* (citizens' school)* [i.e., grade school]. And he ponders the future. That future will be entirely determined by family circumstances. He has the desire to improve himself, but the current family situation blocks it. His four older brothers had done pretty much as they pleased; now, by default, he has ended up as the one responsible for carrying all the burdens those older brothers left behind. Perhaps the love he feels for his parents makes those burdens even heavier. I pity this younger brother who is still so young and so ready to grow, and whose abilities have been restricted by those burdens he must bear.

I wonder what he is doing now. Is there any way I could help him to reach his fullest potential?

Today was supposed to be a day of rest, but I could not rest at all. I would certainly enjoy just one leisurely rest!

November 21

At last the day for crossing the ocean has come.

I went home to take care of the settlement of my affairs.

November 23

The day for leaving home.

Battles are being fought on a world-wide stage: the Germans in Russia; and in the Solomon Strait.

And their back stage. . . .

[A postcard addressed to Mr. Tsuneo Takeda, dated March 6, 1944]
[Dear Mr Takeda]:

I wonder whether or not this postcard will reach you at just about the time you will be competing at some athletic meet. It is still cold here in the barracks, and I am thinking hard about—and very much missing—that spring sun which used to shine over the firing range. The fact is that I have been here for quite some time now. This barracks is built on top of a red-soil base on the rim of a mountain. Its principal discomforts are the cold and the muddy red soil that is the result of poor drainage. I am earnestly looking forward to your arrival.

I did run into a friend from Osaka, but there is really nothing to write him about. I want to see you more than anyone else, even though I know that, at least for a while, this is a hope that will not be fulfilled. From the bottom of my heart, I am praying for your happiness and good health, and indeed that is the biggest thing I have to rely upon for life itself. Almost all of my friends have left for the front, but I have not received a single letter from any of them. The current war situation is expanding so rapidly that, right now, I wonder whose heart is beating fastest out of sheer excitement.

[A letter to Mr. Takeda mailed just before being sent off to
battlefields across the seas.]

[Dear Mr Takeda:]

The other night I dreamed of Watanabe and, the following morning, kept reminiscing about everybody over and over. I was thinking about what they might be doing now, etc., etc.—It has been several days since then.

Early evening two days ago, suddenly all the trucks in the barracks yard started up, and a bugle sounded assembly for those who had received their orders. That night—and all through the night—we packed everything in the office for shipping, and the next morning at 8 o'clock those five crates were shipped out as part of the company's equipment.

I shall be leaving you behind and will be one of the very last to cross the ocean. [All the co-defendants in the 1940 Incident, where numerous students were arrested and accused for their efforts to rebuild the Communist Party, have been sent to the front.]

Now I am sending you a tight handshake. Even under the harsh fire of combat, I shall be warming my heart by thinking of you.

P.S. Apparently we were originally supposed to be sent to what, for a garrison in the forward area, was a rather pastoral sort of place—the Malay Peninsula, or French Indochina. But I suppose the tactical situation since the 1st of this month has made a change of plans necessary. With absolute suddenness, we were ordered to embark immediately and to cross the ocean as quickly as possible.—The islands in the South Pacific naturally came to mind.

I am pondering the rule* to develop the self as powerfully as possible, and in the midst of a world war that is spreading so devastatingly. The Balkans, North Africa, the Mediterranean . . . It is in this area that I am becoming a front-line soldier.—I know that you understand very well what I am talking about.

After this last letter I shall have to cut off any communication for a while. I managed, over the very few brief moments I had to write both this letter and one to my mother. I pray for and trust in your good health. I am confident in my heart that I will be a quiet soldier.

[A letter to a friend, written just before departure]
I paid a visit home just before leaving for the front. My aging mother did not want me to see her tears, so she went out to attend a meeting of the women's society.* I devotedly said a heartfelt prayer as she walked away, and cried.

When you came to my house to make plans for our vacation time, that mother of mine wanted to welcome you so much that she put too much sugar in the lobster tempura and made all of us chuckle. . . . Remember?

The ship is heading south. The contrast between American productivity and that of Japan! ....

I pray for your good health.

Notes
* Badoglio Administration: Mussolini lost power on July 24, 1943, and Prime Minister Badoglio surrendered unconditionally to the Allies on September 8. In turn, the former Prime Minister Mussolini was subsequently rescued by German paratroopers and became the head of the pro-German Fascist Republican Government.

* *Kokumin Gakkō* (lit. citizens' school): In April 1941, and following Germany's lead, the Japanese grade school was reorganized as *"kokumin gakkō"* with the set goal of "basic training for the imperial citizens." After the war, it was returned to *"shō-gakkō"* (grade school).

* Concerning the censorship of letters: Censorship was extremely strict in the military. For example, in writing the opening sentence of a letter even the standard greetings [in the beginning of a letter] that had to do with the weather, such as "cold" or "hot," were forbidden. Needless to say, matters such as the battalion's destination were also prohibited. Of course such things were justified as precautions against enemy intelligence, but, nevertheless, censorship by a hancho (the chief) of "Naimu-han" was often based on his mood and on whether or not a specific item was to his liking. Therefore an expression such as the one indicated in the text, "I am pondering the rule to develop the self as powerfully as possible . . . in the midst of a world war," might be purposely vague, a sort of coded means whereby those who in the past had participated in some ideological movement could communicate with one another. Considering the military censorship situation, therefore, one could say that such writing was "a cold sweat" [i.e., flirting with danger].

* Women's societies: In 1942 three separate organizations—*Aikoku Fujin-kai* (Patriotic Women's Society), *Dai-Nippon Kokubō Fujin-kai* (Great-Japan Defense Women's Society), and *Dai-Nippon Fujin Rengō-kai* (Great-Japan Women's Federation) —were all combined into *Dai-Nippn Fujin Kai* (Great-Japan Women's Society).

Tatsu Udagawa

Born April 13, 1920. From Saitama Prefecture. Graduated from Waseda University, Faculty of Jurisprudence, September 1942. Entered the barracks of the Eastern 12th Unit, October 1, 1942. Killed in action, off Bōnotsu Misaki (Point), Kagoshima Prefecture, January 25, 1945. Army lieutenant. He was twenty-four years old.

[A letter to his wife, Kuniko, September 2, 1944]
Your letter arrived today, September 2nd, and I felt so very happy.

Twice, three times, and many times over and over—I read it repeatedly. Perhaps you and you alone would truly understand how I feel.

I am replying immediately, and I am filled with the desire to write several dozens of pages, but, when I first took up a pen, I cannot put anything down. It was already ten o'clock by the time I got to the second sheet, and then the lights were turned off throughout this entire city. It has just so happened that there is a full moon tonight, and I am writing this under the moonlight. What a feeling this is! There is a story told that Beethoven scribbled the *Moonlight Sonata* under the moonlight. And here I am writing you, Kuniko, this letter with the moonlight shining upon me. I wonder how your thoughts run as you read this.

I wish I could write much more fully and in depth, but I cannot do so because the Military Police are very strict here in Hiroshima, and every letter is subject to strict censorship at the post office. However, I do not wish to get killed in action [the original expression is: "for flower petals to fall"—*cf.* p. 2] without being able to say what I truly want to say.

It has been ten days since I arrived here, but somehow I do not feel settled just yet. I have such a strong desire to see your pictures, the more the better—several dozen, or even several hundred of them. I want to read your letters every day, even if the words are the same every day, and the only things that ease my lonely heart are those letters and pictures. As I look at the full moon like this, and sit here with your picture in front of me, the picture never fails to say "Keep up your spirit! Hold out, my Love!"

Ah, again, the night is growing late.

—The Devil's Bashi Channel—

The ocean between Taiwan's southernmost point, the Cape of Garanpin, and the northernmost point of the Philippines, Aparri, is called Bashi Channel. If one left Garanpin in the morning on a 17-knot ship, the ship would arrive at Aparri late in the afternoon, and it is this one small bit of ocean that is said to be the most dangerous spot in the entire Pacific.

The Great Asian War [*cf.* p. 63] had been presenting serious problems ever since it entered its third year or so, i.e., around the end of last year. Later, starting in July of this year, 1944, the situation suddenly accelerated most dangerously. So we members of the Akatsuki [Unit] have taken to calling the channel "the Devil's Bashi." The reason for this is that American submarines are constantly showing up in this relatively small sector of the ocean, and right now there seem to be more than eighty or so of them waiting to attack our transports. That number represents a combination of about forty of them that left from Australia at the end of

June and about another forty that came from Hawaii.—They have their base on the China coast.

Anyway, ever since July our transport ships have been quite fiercely attacked within this foreshortened basin. Since the beginning of August, and shortly after the 770th Convoy left Taiwan from the port of Takao, the *Ōshimayama-maru* [an oil tanker of about fifteen thousand tons] was hit by a torpedo, violently exploded, and sank—leaving a full two square kilometers of the sea a sheet of flames. Following this, the superbly built Ōsaka Shōsen's *Nichiran-maru* was also torpedoed and sunk. The next day, four more ships met the same fate.

After that 770th Convoy, the 771st Convoy left the [home] port, doomed to undergo an even more ghastly experience.

This latter fleet was composed of nineteen transports and more than a dozen ships guarding them—the screen included carriers, destroyers, and navy coastal defense vessels. They left port in an imposing fashion, and headed for Manila. All made it safely to Taiwan, and it was already dusk as they approached the Bashi Channel. Those on the ships were saying, "If we pass tonight safely, then, . . ."—suddenly, and quite typically of the South Pacific, a sudden squall arose. It was the rainy season in the Manila area around this time, and the moon almost never appeared for it was about the 25th-night moon [i.e., a very thin crescent moon].

When at last the squall with its accompanying cloudburst was just about to wear itself out, the very last vessel in line, a carrier, *Ōwashi*, suddenly lit up and then sank almost immediately, all the while burning furiously. Needless to say, it had been hit by a torpedo, and as a result all the other ships started to steam off as fast as they could in an attempt to escape,—"Here they come!" The weather just happened to be such that it was a jet-black night, and without a star in the sky. But, soon after [the fist attack], the sound of exploding torpedoes roared everywhere, and the remaining ships began to sink one after another. The fate of the *Tamatsu-maru*, which was carrying the Military flag [given by the Emperor for each regiment] and 5,500 men, is still unknown even today. The *Teia-maru* (20,000 tons), which had once been used for the U.S.–Japan exchange, sank from the impact of four torpedoes. Indeed, as many as twelve ships went down. Moreover, every one of them carried from three to five thousand of the very best men on active duty. And, in addition, also lost were those maximum loads of ammunition and arms that were absolutely essential for the defense of the Philippines.

Thirteen days later, the *Kashii-maru* rescued eight soldiers who were unconscious and floating on a raft in the straits. They were the only survivors of the *Tamatsu-maru*, the ship which carried the Military flag, and they had been floating without any food or water for thirteen days.

In the beginning of October, a transport convoy of seven ships, filled with airplanes as well as with soldiers, left Moji [an area now Kita-Kyūshū City, a major port in northern Kyūshū], also headed for Manila. We sent them off at Moji, but I heard later that five of them suffered the fate of their predecessors and that only two of them made it, and those just barely, to their destination.

Besides these, there must have been a great many other convoys we do not know of, but about which we may be certain that they ended up in the same way.

So one can easily see why the strait of Bashi, a mere spot on the map, is truly a Devil's Channel for convoys.

I cannot help but engage in silent prayer when I think of the fate of those scores of chartered ships and navy vessels, and those several hundred thousand soldiers, all sleeping deep on the bottom of this little strait. . . .

October 11, 2604th year[1] (1944) in Shanghai

P. S.—What I wrote here is absolutely confidential. So, please keep it only in your heart, my dear Kuniko, and never ever talk with anyone about all this.—

—A Record of the Disasters—

It was November 8th when we left Manila. Prior to departure, and because of the enemy's advantageous situation, we were delayed for more than two hours and then left port close to noon. On the ninth, around 3 o'clock, at the northern tip of Leyte Island, we were alerted that an enemy double-engine plane with two tail wings was above us. Just as we were approaching Ormoc Bay two hours later, we were suddenly attacked by a two-engine Lockheed fighter that came out of a pass between two mountains. The plane was firing both machine guns and small cannons, and it suddenly swooped down and made a bombing run. One bomb was dropped right alongside the *Kashii-maru* and caused all of its electrical functions to stop abruptly. On that day, I was the platoon's commanding officer, and on the second attack, the enemy pilot targeted the bridge where we all stood: the soldier, who was behind me and on my right, suffered a serious injury; Cadet Akiguchi, who was behind me and on my left, was also hit, but less mortally; Superior Private Kimura, who was manning a machine gun by the smokestack, was killed; two soldiers at a machine "cannon" [i.e., 20 mm. anti-aircraft cannon] were also killed; and

---

[1] 2604th is the Japanese imperial calendar's equivalent for 1944.

there were many others who were more or less seriously injured. From this second attack, we found forty-six bullet holes in the smokestack itself.

Four planes were in on the third attack—Lockheeds and North American B-25s—but this time the ship suffered no damage. During this battle, however, the bridge became a sea of blood, and the wounded were lying everywhere.

The sun had already gone down and of course it was dark. I was duty officer for the week on a ship that had no lights. I took Superior Private Kimura's belongings from his quarters, and also had our doctor cut off his left little finger and extract two teeth. These items would be sent to his family back home (the finger was to be cremated first), and his body would be buried at sea the next day in Ormoc Bay.

We had heard that the town on Ormoc Bay was now a dangerous place, so the ship anchored off a beach about a thousand meters south of the town, the plan being to transfer everything to shore in sampans. Unfortunately, however, all the small sampans had been washed ashore by the storm of the day before, and not even one could come for us. We knew that we were in trouble because the enemy was certain to attack us at first light. On the 10th, at about 3 o'clock in the morning, troops could only be brought to shore by Naval Coast Defense boats, and that operation was completed by 7 a.m. Only the weaponry remained to be taken care of, but it simply could not be landed except by sampan. We had no choice then except to return to Manila, and our ships started to move out about 10:40 a.m. When we reached the same spot where we had been attacked the day before, I saw one of our planes in a dogfight with a Lockheed in a bank of clouds right in front of us. Since it looked like a dangerous situation, we increased speed until, around 11 a.m., we noticed planes flying over a little island about two thousand meters to our left. When I looked through my binoculars, I spotted some thirty North American B-25s (the same type of plane as those that came to bomb Tokyo earlier in the war) headed straight for us. They formed up on our left, parallel with the convoy, then cut across in front of our ships and started to attack us from the right, two planes at a time.

On their first pass, two planes plunged into the sea in flames. However, and due to the impact of several near misses, our ship shook terribly. During the course of the second wave of the attack, they flew directly at our bridge and let loose with 13-millimeter automatic fire. Enemy bullets rained down furiously all around us. On their third pass, a pair of enemy planes came in extremely low, almost scraping the smokestack, and both of them dropped bombs. The fourth phase of the attack involved four of them, two coming in at the head and the other two at the tail of the ship. The first bomb scored a direct hit on the first squad, and the second one on the No. 1 hatch. The fourteen members of the first squad—squad leader Sergeant Kishimoto and everyone else—all ended up blown to bits. A huge fire burst from No. 1 hatch, where 180 drums of gasoline had been set off, resulting in a huge fire, and with respect to the tail of the ship, a huge hole was opened up at the No. 6 hatch—a gap large enough for a horse to walk through easily from outside. Another bomb hit the side of the middle trench mortar, which exploded and killed Lance Corporal Fujimoto [cf. p. 187]. Superior Private Minato died shortly after the explosion.

In the meantime, the fire had reached the ammunition stored on the ship, and the vessel itself started to split in half. Everyone was ready to evacuate the ship, but, since I am no good at swimming, I was almost ready to give up any hope in resignation. I stood on the deck wearing a life jacket, however, carrying a canteen, a map-and-chart bag, a toilet bag, and with a military sword slung over my back. The ship had become a whirl-pool of fire, and the enemy planes [Grumman fighters] chose this time to make strafing runs at us. I stood there on the deck where there was nothing I could do to protect myself from the whining bullets, and I lit a cigarette. And I kept shouting at the soldiers, who were running around in utter confusion, to throw anything that floats into the ocean. So they started to throw over wooden boards and tubs, etc.

The ship slowly started to sink. When the captain came to tell us to abandon ship, I told our soldiers to jump into the sea, and then I went over for one last time to where the gun had been. There I came across the bodies of Lance Corporal Fujimoto and Superior Private Minato, and I watched the soldiers jumping into the sea. Actually, it was the deck of the tail, the same section of the ship, where I had used to stand gazing at the stars and reminiscing about my hometown. My thought was that, even though as a sub-lieutenant I was the lowest-ranking officer, I was never-theless a commander until the very last moment: I had no wish to be a laughingstock, and so I intended to abandon ship only after everyone else had done so.

When a ship sinks, it always creates a large whirlpool. Those who are not good swimmers, therefore, would do best to hit the water as soon as possible and then to concentrate on getting as far away from the ship as possible. But I did not want all the others on the scene to be able to say that a commander jumped ship first. I also had the passing thought that you, my dear Kuniko, would smile for me were I to die with splendid dignity.

Once all our soldiers had abandoned ship and it became even more lopsided, I put on a pair of cotton work gloves that I had kept just in case, and slid along a rope to get down to the water. At that moment, I did not give a thought to the fact that I was not much of a swimmer. My only thought was that I had done everything I could have done. When I finally got into the water and looked up at the ship directly over my head, I saw the lettering of *Tokyo Kashii-maru* in Japanese and *KASHIIMARU* in English. As I started to swim the breaststroke, I heard a voice from behind me: "Please, Platoon Commander. . . . Help me!" It was Lance Corporal Sasagawa. I did not feel like asking what it was all about, so I simply said "O.K.," and started to swim again, but this time I was somehow unable to move forward. I thought that something was strange, and looked back. —Sasagawa was firmly hanging onto my sword with both hands! "Oh, no," I thought, and remarked that I was not much of swimmer either, but he said, "That is fine, Sir." Concluding that what had to be had to be, I shifted to the backstroke, and tried to put as much distance as possible between ourselves and the ship, or else we would be swallowed into the sea along with it. When we had made some progress, I noticed Lieutenant Shimokura nearby, holding on to a big board and calling out to us, "Come! Come this way!" It turned out to be that he was not a swimmer either. So the three of us together gave a signal to one another, holding on to the board, and started to swim in unison. It was at about that time that the heavy fuel oil which had leaked from the ship started to move over toward us, and very rapidly. After we had been swimming for about twenty minutes, the surface of the sea suddenly lit up: the fuel oil had ignited and came spreading our way even faster. If we did not do something we would, inevitably, be burned to death. So we started to swim toward the windward —but the speed of the fire continued to increase, and even my face got hot. I foresaw the end, and prepared myself for the worst. I thought that it would be all right to die there, if only because I wore photos of you and everyone tightly around my waist.

Apparently the ammunition in hatch No. 6 caught fire at that moment, and the ship shuddered under a tremendous explosion which sent enormous beams, steel boards, and other things flying high into the air. The fire on the waves was snuffed out by the sheer force of the explosion. We took advantage of the opportunity to begin swimming again as best we could. Another fire over the water was at a considerable distance, and we were therefore a little relieved. Around 2 p.m. we reached the bow of a Navy transport ship and were rescued at last by the crewmen, who threw us a rope and then towed us to the ship's stern. Night was just coming on. I was given a rice ball, and then I went to sleep in a corner of the ship. I had difficulty falling asleep not only because I was too exhausted to sleep, but also because my nerves were still tingling. I was really exhausted, to a point where I could not even think. In a while though, somehow, I did fall asleep still wearing my wet clothes.

Around six o'clock on the eleventh, we saw a coastal defense ship on the horizon, and we were transferred onto this vessel thirty minutes later. This ship was one of those that had been protecting us, or trying to, ever since we left Moji, and they really treated us most kindly.

They gave me three Hikari and two Sakura cigarettes, and there was a certain Engineer Lance Corporal Nakamura who came to visit me during breaks from his work. He brought me several personal items as well as accommodating me in general. This made me very happy and more appreciative than ever.

It was about 11:30 p.m. the night of the eleventh when we entered Manila Harbor.

I have never felt so grateful down deep in my heart—more than ever in my life—for the gracious protection of the Hikawa Shrine, all my ancestors, and everyone at home.

Nov. 15, 2604 [i.e., 1944]—at Santa Nosa
[*sic.*, probably Santa Rosa]

[From some poems of the tanka variety posthumously published in Hitō Sakuhin (Works in the Philippines)]

Having been rescued, I walk down a Manila street,
My military uniform still stained with oil

My poetry book that kept me company from Shanghai to Pusan
is now at the bottom of the sea off the island of Leyte

Looking at a photo of Kuniko, that survived with me
through the fiercest fire of battle, I think of her with love

In Manila, so far, far away from my fatherland
what a pleasure it is to hear Japanese radio

I held a cup of miso soup in my hand for the
first time in a very long time,
the aroma of Japan flowed out powerfully to my senses

After a ship sails for war so far away, pushing
through waves,
rough white-crested waves doing their dance.

Daizō Sakakibara

Born November 22, 1915. From Ibaragi Prefecture. Through Musashi Higher School, entered Tokyo Imperial University, Faculty of Medicine, in 1938: graduated in December 1941. January 1942, he was commissioned navy medical sub-lieutenant and entered the barracks. Killed in action, October 1, 1944, Peleliu Island of Palau Islands. Navy medical first lieutenant. He was twenty-eight years old.

—The night before leaving for the front—
My mother turned a light on:
　　　　　　　she wanted to mend a tear [in my clothes] for me
　　　who is leaving tomorrow for the war

What it must be like to vanish,
　　　　　　　to vanish without a trace—a huge carrier
　　　is burning furiously on the dark ocean

　　　—A poem sent to his wife, while he lay
　　　　　ill on the Island of Palau—
Being ill from dengue fever, my body is in so much pain
　　　I could not help but call your name
　　　　　　　—the wind whips the palm trees outside

Mitsutaka Baba

Born January 11, 1922. From the Tokyo Metropolis. In 1942, entered Tokyo Imperial University, Faculty of Jurisprudence, Department of Law. Entered Takeyama Naval Training Corps in Yokosuka, December 10, 1943. Killed in action off the shore of Nha Trang, Vietnam, March 21, 1945. Navy second sub-lieutenant. He was twenty-three years old.

　　　—At Takeyama Naval Training Corps—
Just a single postcard, nothing special,
　　　　　but I kept reading it over and over,
　　　because it was written by my mother's hand

　　　—At Fujisawa Navy Electric Surveying School—
At the bottom of this clear blue ocean

where seagulls play
there lurks the ghostly blue-black light of death

I suppose that people would die in the same way
        as these schools of dead fish floating—
    victims of a depth-charge*

* See note on p. 65

—When I returned home on leave—
As though the passage of one year did not exist,
    at *kotatsu*, mother and I sit facing each other and sip hot tea

Without knowing why, an uneasiness attacks me, and
    the books I used to read every day are just lined up [on a desk]

Even if there were no food or clothing,
    the only thing she wishes for

        would be for mother and her children, one day,
            to get together and talk. (Mother's wish)

—En route to my assignment in the South Pacific—
In the dark night, hidden and at anchor,
    the sound of waves is so quiet in a gorge of Yaso Island[1] in Shūzan

—In Taiwan—
When an evening is spent, the road where
        the buffalo walk is very long,
    and fog spreads over the red temples and red roof tiles

The rough bark of the trunk of a king-palm tree,
    a lone survivor standing by the fountain of an abandoned palace

Takashi Kimura

Born March 3, 1923. From Ibaragi Prefecture. In September 1943, graduated from Nihon University, College Division, majored in Fine Arts. Entered Eastern 37th Unit, March 20, 1944. Killed in action, Mt. Kangipot, Leyte Island, the Philippines, July 1, 1945. Army lance corporal. He was twenty-two years old.

---

[1] Translators' note: Yaso-shima could also mean many islands.

—In my hometown, just before leaving for the front—
A sodden relationship between loved ones is so sorrowful,
    even though Hitachi-no (Hitachi Field) is
      dressed with barnyard grass flowers

—From the front—
I am praying earnestly with hands held together,
    while I gaze out of dark eyes at the dark sea

Mannosuke Seta

Born August 23, 1923. From Mie Prefecture. April 1941, entered Tokyo
Foreign Language College, Chinese Language Foreign Trade Department.
Entered the barracks, December 1, 1943. March 7, 1945, died of battlefield-
related diseases, near Clark, Luzon Island, the Philippines. Army sub-
lieutenant. He was twenty-one years old.

[A letter to his parents]

My dear Father and Mother: March 5, 1945

I am going to entrust this letter to a colleague who is flying back to
mainland Japan tomorrow for liaison purposes. I picked up my pen in the
hope that this will reach you safely.

Currently, the battlefield is in a stand-down condition, but we cannot
be certain about just when a dramatic change in the situation might occur.
For that reason, there is something eerie in the air. Now that I am placed in
the position of wandering along the line between life and death, I regret that
I have been an atheist ever since student days. Right now, at this moment,
it is less a question of concern over what will happen after my death as of
how my heart is to deal with the loneliness I am experiencing for not having
any place for my heart to lean on (i.e., something to go by spiritually).
Against this back-ground, Father and Mother, I think I can understand why
you have always been so pious and so very devoted to your religion.

If you would be so kind as to send me a book on religion, I would be
most grateful, and it does not matter which sect. It all amounts to the same
thing in the end, I would think. If I could only get my heart's equilibrium
back, even just for the time being, that would be fine.

The language used in this area is Tagalog, and, for someone like
myself, who studied Chinese at the Foreign Language College, it is a dif-

ficult thing to tackle. I must say, though, that I have become familiar enough with the indigenous people's language to get along. When you can understand the other person's language the feeling of affinity comes more naturally. Even though the shade of one's skin may be different, we all share the same human emotions and, as you advised, Mother, I have strictly warned my men to avoid any indiscriminate killing.

The sunset in Manila Bay is absolutely splendid. When I gaze at the ocean as dusk gathers, and am as relaxed as I am just now, I feel the need to seriously question why people ever have to hate one another and to cross swords. Even if it turned out to be a fate that we could not possibly have avoided, I would still keep thinking and thinking about whether or not there had been something we could possibly have done to avoid the conflict and settle the difference another way.

Why do we have to spend the springtime of our lives in such misery as this, and all in vain? It is totally unbearable to see these talented young people being killed one after another.

Out of a clear blue sky, I have just thought back to and felt a desire for Nakamuraya's yōkan [Japanese sweet jelly].

I will be writing to you again. It would be so good if this letter reaches you safely. . . .

Please extend my very best wishes to my elder brother, elder sister, and little Wakako [a niece].

As ever,
Mannosuke Seta

Yoshio Ozaki

Born February 16, 1923. From Osaka Metropolitan Prefecture. Through Matsue Higher School, entered Kyoto Imperial University, Faculty of Economics, in April 1942. Entered the Navy, December 10, 1943. Killed in action, June 6, 1945, at Clark Field, the Philippines. Navy sub-lieutenant. He was twenty-two years old.

[A letter to his younger sister]

October 1944

To my dear Kazu:

The Osaka castle looked splendid in the autumn sky when I saw it on my way from Suzuka [Mie Prefecture] to Suikōsha [the navy officers' social club]. Have you been well since I last saw you? I suppose that by this time you must have become well accustomed to the military life, but, in a world like this, the most important thing by far is to have good health, when you are in a situation where you have to take full responsibility for taking care of your own body. Of course, you too know this perfectly well—right? This could become problematic, particularly when you are working day and night with military strategy duties; but I think it is imperative for you to pay attention to such things as recovering properly from exhaustion, especially because you have never been overly tough or even healthy to begin with.—At least with regard to your own health, you must pay attention to it most open-mindedly.

You are twenty. There is no doubt but that the rough waves of war will gently wear you down gradually, but I also realize that you have some psychological readiness of your own. The world, in any case, would not allow you to continue to be a mere child, and you will realize yourself that just reading a lot of fiction would not make you a grownup. I regret that I am not easily available now to be with you as your brother when you need me to talk to. Even though I may not be that much of an older brother, however, I know that you would think of me if and when anything important should come up. As I look back and reflect, I have been an absolutely lucky man. From Matsue [Higher School] to Kyoto [Imperial University], my one wish was to be able to study there to my heart's content, and I was indeed doing it when, right in the middle of everything, I had to give up my pen and was given a short sword instead. When I said that I really did not understand the goal of the war, our father was quite shocked and told me repeatedly never to come out with a statement like that in public. But just look at the world! If we young people would not fly airplanes, then who could fly them? So far as I am concerned, and simply because as long as my father and mother are healthy and doing well, there is nothing for me to worry about, I am the first man who can die light-heartedly at any time. In light of all this, I think you should give some thought to your own way of living.

As your big brother, the fact that you are too well liked is something that I do not feel badly about, because that fact is a combination of your own human nature and a few fortunate accidents of life, and none of these things are your fault. What I do think you have to do is to prepare yourself —through concentration and alertness—to solve each of your heart's concerns. You must also maintain your freedom, which is something you have a perfect right to. There is a distinction between being tense and never being off-guard. And it is necessary for you to be the sort of a person who is never off-guard. Also, anyone who has an empathetic heart would also pay close attention to everything—and then a sort of genuine quality would also project itself naturally. You must always be absolutely responsible in the matter of keeping your word, and, when you are talking with another person, the first thing is to be a very good listener. Even if you have to listen to a lot of things that do not seem important, you should refrain from talking about anything that only makes you feel good. As becomes quite evident from listening to other people's parts in conversation, it is usually carried on without much self-awareness—which is all the more reason both to pay attention to other people and to reflect carefully upon one's own contributions. Even though you are normally not guilty of this sort of behavior, I am writing this down because I think it is very important. In the military, there is a word, *"fukushō"* (repeating what the other said when one receives a command), which is actually quite a good custom, I think. It is best to repeat the other person's words before you respond to that person.

Because I have always been so close to you, I never noticed until recently what nice eyes you have. I can feel your gentle thoughtfulness and sincerity; and it seems that you have learned to discipline your own self as well. I think that your having to deal with different sorts of people is a good education in itself, and I also think that one's whole life ought to be filled with mind-training. Neither was it a bad idea that, in your case, you chose to shut out all selfishness. I do not particularly like the word "sacrifice," but I think it is something noble. Once I came to realize that you are the younger sister whom I can trust the most, all the worries about what might happen after my transfer totally disappeared, and that realization makes me quite pleased as I am now. Of course it is inevitable that the expanding war will reach you too in rough waves, and there are many family matters that have to be taken into serious consideration. Should I leave tomorrow, then I do not think we can ever expect to see each other again. Let me add, though, that I am neither disappointed nor in any way regretful. In fact, right now I am feeling completely natural and even exceedingly mellow.

There is a poem: "When my heart is feeling sad, I keep looking up at the great sky, as though it were a memento from the loved one." I have always liked this poem very much. Regardless of how painful it might be, it is easier to endure one's own pain than to inflict pain on someone else; in fact, enough endurance erases the pain altogether. "I do not want to lose at anything to anyone; so I would keep up with the opposition even if I had to stretch my own natural ability."—You wrote something like that to me once. Since you will not allow yourself to be overcome by extreme emotion, you will not only be able to console yourself but you can also be a help to others.

But I do have something that even you would not understand. At any rate, when my soul leaves my body, my soul will return to you regardless of where you may be. When I asked you whether or not you thought we were going to win the war, you put your finger over that little scar on your cheek—that scar you got from my scratching you when we were both little, remember? When I asked you whether I should scratch you, you said go ahead, and so I scratched your cheek—you very clearly answered, "Perhaps," and turned your face away. I remember that, when I used my hands to turn your face straight, your eyes were filled with tears. You said something so typical of yourself: "I am not crying, but I feel sad because tears fall." Do you remember all of this? I forgot, . . . but I will enjoy having the film of the pictures I took the other day of you in a military uniform and also those of other family members . . . developed in whatever place I get transferred to, and I will send them on to you. "Oh, my, she looks so darn good!" That was what I thought at that time.

No matter what, I would love to see you for even just one more time, but time keeps on slipping away; so I am going to send these greetings just in case, and until we finally find out when we shall have parted for the last time. You get the war news earlier than any others do, and you also have plenty of the current information that you will need in order to understand what is really going on. I have, then, one last request to make: please take care of everything for me once I am gone. I know that you are worthy of my full trust. To be passed the baton that I should still be holding may be a heavy and a heartfelt burden to one who is still so young at twenty, but since it cannot be helped, please try to maintain a positive attitude.—My one wish, and it is a keenly felt one, is that your transition out of adolescence will be a healthy time. I shall be praying for you most earnestly and at all times, wherever I happen to be. You do not have to worry about me on any count. Just concentrate on being your wonderful self at all times and in all places. The routine of my life in the navy is given in detail in my diary, and whatever else I wanted to say is written there as well—perhaps there is something in it that may be helpful to you. At any rate, I shall go off and try as hard as I can to polish up my manhood. Please be the source, in the emotional sense, for our father and mother. Death is certainly a sad affair, and therefore not something for you to dwell upon unnecessarily. It is something that seems to have become my destiny, but perhaps it will surprisingly be succeeded by some fine post waiting for me in heaven.

If it should turn out that we cannot see each other again, this will have to do as a good-bye. Please take really good care of yourself, and continue to keep on living with a high heart like a god. The fact that you happened to be my younger sister was more my good luck than yours. Please continue to live with strength and courage. If my friends should come again and ask you to function as something like an extension of myself, just act however you think you should, and that will be the best way. And please always be a good child to your father and mother. You as an individual are for everybody, and everybody is for you. And finally, if you do not hurry and fix up a place for me to return to, it just might be too late.

Yoshio

Shigenobu Matsubara

Born January 11, 1922. From Shiga Prefecture. Through the Preparatory Division, advanced to the Faculty of Economics, Dōshisha University, April 1944. Entered the barracks June 25, 1944. Died of a disease contracted at the war front, August 1, 1945, in Peking (Beiging), China. Army lance corporal. He was twenty-three years old.

—Diary—

This is my diary. Thinly and faintly, in order to survive the many years of solitude—or the eternal silence—I shall keep on writing as long as the sorrow keeps on.

July 4, 1944

Arrived Tientsin very early in the morning. Luckily I got some *yōkan* (sweets) and cigarettes. It occurred to me that I might be able to have someone take *yōkan* back to my father, so I am saving some for him. I wonder, though, whether or not my father will ever understand the nature of this loving feeling I have for him.—I enjoy just imagining my father's happy face as he eats this *yōkan*.

July 16

I reflect on the expression "to pick up bones." Sub-lieutenant Shōzō left it in writing for me that there may come a day when we will both pick up each other's bones.

I wonder who will be picking up my bones. The situation is such that there may or may not be anyone who could even pick up this writing, let alone my bones.

August 31 Rain

I heard that Paris has fallen.

A war is, after all, nothing but a go-between to escort us toward standing in front of the abyss of death.

When I slept, my heart was back home.

September 9

A diary cannot be kept openly in the military, and even if one does write things down he cannot take what he has written home with him; somehow, however, I intend to send this diary home. To anyone reading over what I have written, it may only seem to be a notebook filled with trivial matters, or perhaps just a fool's words set down foolishly. I was puzzled over what to do in my psychological state of not being certain as to whether or not I was really in love with a particular young lady, so what I did with a dream tale in an empty imaginary world was to play around with a single word, "sorrowful."

To say that one lives truthfully is an empty word if used for an insensitive life. One should never be so vainglorious over his or her intellectuality as to use it to explain away one's insensitivity.

There is no passion in me. With whom can I make a connection over this disquietude of mine, something which I cannot capture with all my words? On the other hand, the sheer abundance of words convinces me that there is someone out there. Just at present, though, there is no friend with whom I can discuss my first love.

If one wishes to ground his reasoning on something absolutely certain, it just might be that death itself is the best possible choice.

[A letter to his love, Sayuri]

January 31, 1945

My dearest Sayuri:

I feel much relieved after having read your letter, but I am especially concerned over this busy life you seem to be leading.

....

I immediately wrote a letter to my father, asking him for a favor. Since I believe that he is a very loving father, I think that he will do whatever he possibly can to help.

The fact is that I have a request to make of you too, concerning something I wrote to my mother about in late December. I am not certain whether or not she took me seriously, though.

Would you please take my mother to Zenkōji Temple [an old Buddhist temple in Nagano]? Since about three years ago when I was sick in bed she used to tell me at my bedside that she wanted to go there with me, just the two of us, but now of course I am sent off to the battlefield. I owe so much to my mother for everything for such a long time that I would like to see her indulge in something like that [i.e., a trip to Zenkōji] as a modest gift—from me to her—of "the Order of the Golden Kite" [the medal the Emperor gave to the soldiers deserving of the highest honor]. Since it seems she still has enough strength to ride on a train, please take her there once for me— provided, of course, that travel conditions in Japan are favorable. The trip would not be worthwhile if the both of you were tired or worried about one another, so why don't you make it in a leisurely way? The money I left should be enough to cover expenses, so please spend it—all of it. Although, of course, you have to consider your situation. . . .

If this is all right with you, would you please suggest this to her at your convenience?

I suppose you could not possibly make as big a fuss over her as I would (please excuse me!) on the train, but please arrange for her to sit in the forward direction. It would be better not to talk too much because she gets a headache quickly. Reading to her or playing the radio is not a good idea. She does not like to see anyone spending too much time on makeup —natural looks suit her just fine. Because she is strong-willed, getting on and off a train needs to be done smoothly. She suffers from neuralgia. As for green tea, she prefers it strong. As to clothing, she prefers something like a coat. She loves children, so on the train it is all right to sit near children. She does not care for wasteful luxury. So, please avoid perfumes and permanent waves. Conversation about kimono designs or about food would be fine.

I want to say something to you, who says she is lonely, but I have to put a brake on myself. I suppose that, when all is said and done, life has to be that way.—But perhaps you, who have such a clear object for your soft poetic emotions, might consider loneliness nothing but a foothold leading to the next level of experience. Don't you think so? ....

We have both a radio and a phonograph here, and right now the latter is playing "Life on a Back Street" [a popular song written in 1937]. It brings back dear memories of home.

Please tell my mother to take it easy.

I forgot to tell you about myself.—I am fine.

Thank you so much for the "mon-bukuro" (a package sent to cheer up the soldiers) I received the other day.

I pray for your good health.

Shigenobu

Takuji Mikuriya

Born June 3, 1923. From Saga Prefecture. In April 1942, entered Kagoshima College of Commerce. Entered Aiura Naval Training Corps in Sasebo, December 10, 1943. He was killed in action, June 5, 1945, as a member of the Shinpū [commonly known as Kamikaze] Special Attack Unit, in the mouth of Shibushi Bay, Kagoshima Prefecture. Navy second sub-lieutenant. He was twenty-two years old.

February 25, 1945

It is raining today. Apparently it had been quite a heavy downpour before daybreak, but, when I went out to attend a morning exercise, something was floating eastward that could not be classified as either rain or fog. After the morning exercise, I took a walk along the airport's drainage ditch.

Even though the winter has at last peaked out and it is nearly spring, the grass at the airport is still lifeless, soaking wet, and it seems to crouch on the ground and barely to hold on to whatever life remains. A drizzle is slowly creeping away and, one by one, dropping tiny white drops over this shaggy and withered turf. The turf is soaked, and there is a long stretch of black soil which has absorbed water plentifully. The clouds are low. It is not even possible to make out the horizon. A black nimbus with a tail of white fog is being sucked into the sea in the general direction of where the horizon should have been. As though they were afterthoughts, white waves puffed up here and there on the sea's grey surface.

From the shaggy turf under my feet, and also from the chunks of black soil and in everything that is spread over them, the warmth of the great earth and the fragrance of nature drift up thoroughly. This is the same smell as that of the soil at home. For all I know it may be the form of life itself, of everything.

This nameless turf, born out of the good earth, is now about to end its life. Embraced by the earth's motherly love, it is waiting for that "time" to come. It is by no means a negation of life—the turf kept up the fight in a fierce affirmation of life, and the end had simply come as it must. The turf, however, is filled with contentment, for in its warm chest it holds beautiful young sprouts that are full of hope and strength. Without the slightest concern or doubt, it is entrusting to these youthful successors the hope that the next generation might continue to live and be strong. The turf's own life had been a desperate struggle for sheer existence. Under a beautiful spring sunshine, but with no promise of joy to come—and simultaneously striving to grow and being stepped on—it kept on living with limitless perseverance and toughness. And what was behind all these efforts and such bitter struggles? At the very least, it was certainly not a matter of "one's own survival"; rather, it was for the bloodline that runs through the turf's body and also for the eternal growth and continuance of its kind. Its main priorities are "blood" and "eternal life," and in them this scrap of vegetation sees its true form. As the turf watches the way in which the young bloodlines fill out with hope, it is ready to return fully contented to its loving mother earth. In its way it is quietly praying for the growth of eternal life, and I thought that I had found in this one little clump of grass the image of the way a human being—a Japanese—should live.

No one thinks about "the death of the self" at the moment of striking a blow against the enemy. We simply strike the enemy target while praying for the growth of the eternal life of Japan—or rather, perhaps, just to kill the enemy. He [a Kamikaze pilot], for example, returns into the motherly love of his country in this way, i.e., by burning himself up in a confrontation with the most formidable foe he could find.—You might say that he died without completing his life's goals; what you would have to say, however, is that he died happy.

While I was walking along and thinking about this sort of thing, the farmhouse at the far end of the airport, which now happened to move into my field of vision, still stood quietly framed by the fog. Shrikes flew away noisily and then flew back again. The clouds are still low, but the western skies show some brightness. If this continues, we will be able to do some flying exercises this afternoon.

Ichizō Hayashi

Born February 6, 1922. From Fukuoka Prefecture. From Fukuoka Higher School, entered Kyoto Imperial University, Faculty of Economics, October 1942. Entered the Second Naval Training Corps in Sasebo, December 10, 1943. Killed in action as a member of the Second Shichishō (meaning "seven lives") Special Attack Unit, April 12, 1945, off Okinawa. Navy second sub-lieutenant. He was twenty-three years old.

[The last letter to his mother, from Wonsan, North Korea,
dated March 31, 1945]

My dear Mother:
　　The time has finally come for me to write a very sad letter.
　　How will the parents' loving hearts,
　　　　even exceeding the love of a child for its parents,
　　　　　　hear of the news of today?
　　　　　　[The last farewell poem of Shōin Yoshida, 1830–59]

　　I think of this poem because it touches my heart so very deeply.
　　I have been truly blessed with so much happiness. I sure did all sorts of self-centered things, didn't I?
　　But please forgive me and attribute all that selfish behavior to my baby-like over-dependence on you.
　　I am pleased to have the honor of having been chosen as a member of a Special Attack Force that is on its way into battle, but I cannot help crying when I think of you, Mom.
　　When I reflect on the hopes you had for my future, Mom, and how you brought me up as though it were a matter of life and death, I feel so sad that I am going to die without doing anything to bring you joys or to relieve your worries.
　　I may not be a great person, but I still cannot ever say to you: "Mom, please give me up," or "Please be happy that I died honorably."—But please do not let me say too much about this sort of thing; after all, you always know exactly what I am thinking anyway.
　　When I received the second letter about my engagement and some other things, I already knew [that I would be going off to the battlefield and death] but I could not bear to refuse. Actually, Mom, it was because I still wanted to be clinging on to you—just like a baby. Nothing has made me happier than your letters of those days. I really wanted to see you just one more time and have a heart-to-heart talk with you, though. I also wanted to go to sleep in your arms once again, but it seems that the time we spent together in Moji will turn out to have been our last time.
　　I am writing this letter in the knowledge that I am going to be part of an attack the day after tomorrow. I am hoping, though, that perhaps I might by chance be able to fly over the city of Hakata. In other words, even though you will not see me, I wish to quietly say good-bye.
　　I also seriously regret that I could not see my older sister Chiyoko, because I wanted to thank her. I affectionately remember so many things about our home in Miyazakicho, as well as the thoughtfulness of everyone in the family when I was taking the entrance exam for the Higher School.

Mom, I have finally reached the point where I stand now by going against your advice. I would like to think that I am happy because I did what I wanted to do, but now I feel rather that, at least perhaps, things would have been better had I done exactly what you told me to do.

Please be happy, however, that I have been chosen for my job because I so far exceeded the other competitors in our flying exercises. It is almost unheard of for someone with such limited flying experience as mine to be sent directly to the front. Moreover, even among those of us who were chosen, I was especially honored by being asked to take charge of another student like me.

Keep in mind the fact that, even when I pass on, you will still have Makio [brother-in-law?]. I know, Mom, that right now I might seem more important to you than he is, but, taking all in all—and with particular regard to his great potential—he is definitely not a person you want to relegate to a back seat.

Then there are my two older sisters, Chiyoko and Hiroko, and you also have a fine grandson you can count on. And I shall always be at your side, so spend your time joyfully. Your being happy means that I am happy too, and if you are sad I would also be sad.—So please go on living happily with all of them. ....

Occasionally, I get enticed by a selfish desire of wanting to come home in order to be near you, but this would not be a good thing. When I received the sacrament of baptism, was I not told to "die"? I was told to die "by the honorable hands of your Savior before you die from being struck by American bullets." I am remembering that, and I know that everything is in God's hands. For those who would truly place themselves under God's providence, the matter of life and death in this world would not matter, would it?

Jesus also prayerfully enjoined us to "Please do as Your heart desires." I have gotten into the habit of reading the Bible every day and, whenever I do, I feel as though I am very near you, Mother. On our next attack I am going to take the Bible and a book of hymns on board the plane with me. I will also take along the mission's badge that the schoolmaster gave me and your gift—the amulet for my protection.

On the subject of marriage, it might seem as though I pulled a joke on those people, but would you please ask them to excuse me and, circumstances being what they are, beg off in a nice way? Had time permitted I actually did intend to marry her—if for no other reason than to make you happy, Mother.

"Please forgive me" are the words I should say to you, but I know that I need not worry; you have always forgiven me about everything and anything I ever did. Am I right?

I know that you are a really great person, Mother. I always felt that I could never touch your true greatness, no matter what I did. You do everything, and you even undertake matters that cause you pain; that is something I could never imitate. Your only fault, Mother, is that you love and spoil your children too much, but is it not a bit more than unreasonable of me to call that a fault? I like it that way!

At least you, Mother, as well as my siblings and friends, know me very well, and so I can carry on free of having to worry about anything.

Because God always pays attention to your prayers, when I am zeroing in on a target I will be praying to you.

I am going to entrust Mr. Umeno with this letter to hand over to you, but please do not ever show it to anyone else—it is, after all, a little embarrassing. The realization that I shall be dying very soon feels like something that is happening to someone else. I mean that somehow I feel as though I can get to see you whenever I wish, probably because it is too sad to think that I will never see you again. ....

—The day before making a sortie.

Yutaka Sugimura

Born February 26, 1923. From the Tokyo Metropolis. From the Tokyo Higher School, entered Tokyo Imperial University, Faculty of Jurisprudence, Political Science Department, September 1942. Entered Takeyama Naval Training Corps in Yokosuka, December 9, 1943. Killed during special attack training at Chitose Air Base, Hokkaidō, on July 10, 1945. Navy sub-lieutenant. He was twenty-two years old.

May 21, 1944

I was told that having such senses as listening to the singing of birds or being attracted by wild flowers are definitely not soldierly pursuits. Perhaps this is true, but in my own opinion it is stretching things much too far. Frankly speaking, I even felt a sort of antipathy when I had to listen to talk like that. As it is, our senses have already become dry and unnurtured, and my own feeling is that our hearts are getting rough as well.

For the first time after a long separation, I met Mr. N the other day at visiting time. I somehow felt that there was a considerable psychological distance between the two of us. Of course this might be quite natural; after all, our environment has changed so much, and perhaps we did not have enough time for a real talk. I still felt a little sad about it.

I am completely alone even in the military. What an empty experience it is to feel like a stranger in the presence of a very good friend from school days. On the other hand, I really wish that I had a sweet-heart with whom, even when we were just sitting and facing each other, I could feel our hearts touching. ....

May 12, 1945

I received a letter from Ms. Sado the other day, and I was delighted to read it. In fact, my heart was very much consoled by the letter, full as it was of honest and innocent sentiments—sort of being coquettish. The occasion for writing had been her *mutter's*[1] return home from Tokyo after a while. It made me reflect seriously on the way today's Japanese women have to live.

We are constantly "corrected" [scolding with beating, etc.] by Sub-lieutenants Yoshie and Kagawa, and by others as well: they are very critical of everything about our class, the Fourteenth [the Fourteenth Class of students in the Naval Reserve], but I wonder what they really mean by *"Shaba-ke"* [the mood or style of life in the non-military world]. With respect to maintaining a military bearing: although I think that we should make every effort to be good military personnel, we should at the same time never forget to think about a broader variety of things. Becoming a fine military person should never come at the expense of being a fine "human being." I believe that the worst shortcoming among the men who come out of the Naval Academy is just this sort of immaturity as human beings. To stick close to matters at hand, for example, how could a man be a great leader of his subordinates if he lacks at least some background in the consideration of human psychology? I firmly believe that those who poison our contemporary navy—even though they would probably say it is the reserve officers—are indeed doing so because of their immature quality as human beings. In the final analysis, perhaps this situation can only be dealt with by tracing things all the way back to the traditional spirit of the navy. I wonder how many in the navy today—how many who truly care about the navy—are genuinely concerned about subordinates, and about sincerely training and educating them.

The American way—I refer to it in this vague manner—is certainly more *pleasant* [the author uses the English word] and comfortable [than

---

[1] In the original the German word for mother is used.

ours]. Such an idea of comfortable life catches and holds people's hearts, and the fact that this American way would be more likely to be welcome than our Japanese way—as in the Philippines, for example—poses quite a few problems that we ought to be seriously thinking about. I do not think that a successful conclusion of the Asian Co-prosperity Sphere (cf. p. 131) can be achieved so long as the Japanese do not do a lot of reflecting on how self-righteously they go about dealing with other people. This sort of treatment is too limited and ethnocentric, with too narrow a focus on Japan's ancient tradition.—There is no "spiritual strength" in America and I imagine that, even in America, people with true integrity are fully aware of that fact. Neither do I believe that I would have to take a back seat as far as placing a proper importance upon the Japanese "spirit" and "heart" is concerned. All I want to emphasize is the desirability of a way of looking at a human being that sees him in his totality. The fact should be more than obvious that, coincident with this broader view of "human beings," attention has to be paid to those very real problems of clothing, food, and shelter. What I wish to emphasize is that to make them more "comfortable" has a great significance—although it is so evident yet often neglected. Most certainly, any "ideal" nation—and I realize that I am using rather an old-fashioned word—would certainly take on the responsibility of making each citizen's life *comfortable* [once again, the author uses the English word]. I wonder whether or not those who governed nations in the past, perhaps out of their ignorance and/or in order to cover up the fact that they were so far from these ideals, were guilty of talking excessively about such things as spiritualism. At any rate, and without being hung up on mere prejudice, we ought to take a good look at the strong points of the American way—if we refuse to do so, it is my belief that our nation will not last much longer.

June 11, 1945

I read the late Sasaki [Hachirō Sasaki]'s posthumous writing, *Miyazawa Kenji: Ai to Ikusa to Shi ni Kanren-shite (Kenji Miyazawa: On Love, War, and Death)* [cf. p. 125], and I was very deeply touched. I really regret that I did not have the opportunity to carry on a serious conversation with him, and all my memories are about our arguments and quarrels over things quite trivial. Just as what I used to say that "those grown-ups who enjoy reading children's stories are great": he went to his death exactly like that, demonstrating the fact that he possessed a great soul. ....

June 30
....
On a train, and reflecting on my psychological state in connection with joining the Special Attack Force.—

My life's goal has been to live every day as the best human being I could possibly be. More specifically, I wanted to live as the best Japanese I could possibly be, and I always considered any effort expended to move myself closer to that ideal as just about the noblest thing I could do. I found a value in that effort itself. I simply wish to live as a truly first-rate Japanese. In the final analysis, that is all. You could say it is a shame that I spent twenty-three years in studies before entering the military. I am convinced, however, that studying is not an end in itself; the ultimate value is to be found rather in a process within which studying is only one element—and so I am content. As a matter of fact, I believe that, at least in the context of ultimates, my past studies were not a waste at all. I probably did not study enough!

I certainly cannot shut out the feeling that I would like to live a little longer, and there are probably a couple of reasons for this:

1. In the first place, the desire to live is implanted in the nature of any living being, no matter how hard or how painful that life might be.

2. A second reason would be the presentiment that, if I did manage to survive a bit longer, some good things just might be in the offing. Then of course there is the awareness of what an absurd irony it would be if, by some remote chance, I should turn out to be one of the last casualties in this war. Of course all of these things are left far behind when compared to what is required of us by our primary ideology.

Yasuo Ichishima

Born January 4, 1922. From Kanagawa Prefecture. Through the Second Higher School of Waseda University, advanced to its Faculty of Commerce in 1942. Entered Takeyama Naval Training Corps in Yokosuka, December 1943. On April 29, 1945, he was killed in action over the ocean southeast of Okinawa as a member of the Fifth Shōwa Special Attack Unit. Navy first lieutenant. He was twenty-three years old.

November 30, 1942 Monday Clear
When I woke up this morning the sun was burning up in a pure red ball, and it seemed to be encouraging me to spend a refreshing and meaningful day. I finished breakfast hurriedly and left for Yokohama.

It was 7:50 a.m., and there were only twelve minutes left before the train's departure. I could not find my friend Wakamiya. With great anxiety I was checking out the station from one end to the other: I ran up and down a platform packed with people seeing off those who were departing, and I finally found him. I could not say a word: I looked into his face and held onto his hands. He was very excited and he spoke in a rush of words: "Well, I am going now [i.e., good-bye]. Please take good care of what I am leaving behind." As he spoke these last words, my friend meaningfully moved his glance in his mother's direction. I said, "I was only surprised that your departure has come on so suddenly, and regret that all the fellows from Baku-kai [Waseda's horseback riding club] could not get together for a visit with you. Anyway, I will be following you soon enough, and I wish you all the best." I noticed out of the corner of my eye that Okabe and Morita and other members of the Baku-kai had just arrived, as well as Ōshima and some other fellow alumni. A train entered the station amidst a great uproar: the whish of waving flags, loud singing, and a general sort of pandemonium echoed throughout the station as though they all represented a combined explosion of the people's excitement. When I switched my gaze to a group of regular conscripts near my friend, I saw a pitifully poor-looking old woman who was holding her son's hands and clutching them tightly to her breast. She was voiceless, and seemed utterly lost, as the tears ran down her cheeks and her son stretched his neck out the train window. The son was also full of tears, and he was looking at his mother's face as though he wished to fill himself with it. This was by no means an unmanly situation for him to be in. It appeared to be a case of a mother and her only son. I was so deeply touched that I had to look away. The scene [I witnessed was that] of a mother who, humanly, could not give up her sorrow, could not do anything but cry when she was not supposed to cry! This was an almost unbearable picture of genuine human beings, and it may have been the very last time for those two together. Oh, that poor old woman. . . . I felt like telling her something without really speaking out loud: despite the tears that spring from your big, pure heart, please send your son off with a congratulatory and positive attitude toward his future.

I wish I could also tell her that the agony which Japan is currently undergoing is for the sake of making a grand ideal a reality. Without agony, the light cannot be attained, and her agony too is exactly that. . . . .

[A letter to Mr. Muneo Ichise, dated Oct. 25, 1943]
. . . . This past month has brought some harsh changes for us students, but, for me personally—and regretfully—the content of my brain

has shown no change—the same, slow movement as always has been. A habit is such a formidable thing that I find it difficult to break through, no matter how hard I try. As for building up my determination, though, I am doing quite well.

While I go about getting my things in order for entering the barracks, while I am thinking that everything is no longer necessary for me, I have such a difficult time deciding on exactly what to get rid of and what to keep that I am wondering about what kind of a brain I have.

Students leaving for war! This is certainly an occasion filled both with honor and a whole range of emotions. But, as you said, there seems to be far too much of a festival atmosphere about it. I can appreciate the various forms of generosity that are being shown us right now, yet, deep in my heart I feel something that I do not understand. .... I even feel a certain revulsion when I come across some students hanging around town and in train stations, as if wearing signboards hanging from their noses that they are heading for war. Just the other day a group of M University and T University students were making a great commotion, with Japanese flags over their shoulders. We should not be soliciting sympathy from the public. We are already being treated with too much special consideration. I really did want to attend the big send-off party sponsored by the Ministry of Education (cf. p. 165), wanted to soak in all the deep emotion and tears. Simple soul that I am, I know that I would most certainly have cried had I been there. But I could not go. But why should the students be the only ones to be especially pampered? Those young men of my age who did not attend colleges or universities have already gone off, and even those with wives and children are also going to the front in bunches. So why is there anything so special about our being called up now, and why are you saying that it is so tragic? If it is, then it is even more so for those with wives and children. Or is it rather a question of the great expectations people had of the students? If this is the case, then why, until just recently, did they exert such excessive pressure on us and look upon us so unsympathetically —only to turn around so suddenly now? This may be a cynical view, but I cannot let go of it. ....

The clear majority of students were well aware that they would eventually be going to war. Society in general has treated us in a very cruel manner at one time, and with a special kindness at another. I did not go to the send-off ceremony, but now I think that perhaps it would have been better if I had attended it. If I had thoroughly immersed myself in an atmosphere like that, I am certain that I would have undergone a very pure and a very deep emotional experience. Even here, I cannot shut off really deep feelings. But, finally, I do not know which would have been better —to have gone or not. Lately I feel I have been very fortunate. I think that I happened to come upon a very good time. Indeed [and from a more global stand-point], I feel that I am being greatly honored by the opportunity to stand front and center at a great moment in human history. The physical examination for the military is to be held on the 29th and 30th. I would really like to pass as Class A.—Please give my very best to everyone in your family.

[From the very last diary entry]

April 20, 1945

It was a day of emotional tranquillity. Although I did not get to see my family, I was able to talk things over with some other people whom I hold dear, and in general spent a very pleasant day.

I am in a predicament that I shall never see them again after today, but I did not find myself obsessed either with sorrow or sentimentality, and was able to part with them after we had talked and laughed together. How I ever managed to do so is something that even I wonder about.

As for me, I do not feel that I will be dead within a week—and neither do any exciting emotions or sentimental thoughts occur.

It is only when I think quietly of my very last moments that everything seems like a dream. I do not really know for a fact whether or not I could actually remain so tranquil right up to the moment of facing my death, but it seems as though it would be a surprisingly easy thing to do.

....

April 21

Test piloting in the morning.

My beloved plane (Ya-406)[1] out on the apron was readied so perfectly by the maintenance-crew personnel that I had tears in my eyes.

7:40 a.m.: I conducted my first and last test flight. The altitude was two thousand meters, and all cruising units performed well. I finally carried out my very last special training flight [a particular type of training requiring high flying skill] as a fighter pilot over the skies of Tsuchiura, and flew in all directions to my heart's content. Visibility was fairly good. It had been quite a while since the last time, but it was a very pleasant experience.—I said my last good-byes from the plane to those I love.

---

[1] *Ya* is the 46th syllable in the Japanese *kana* alphabet.

11:30 a.m.: A meeting.

13:00 (1:00 p.m.): I lined up in front of the command post. My classmates took care of everything for me, and decorated the plane with double cherry blossoms.

13:30 (1:30 p.m.): A parting *kanpai* (toast).

The engine is all charged up and booming away under the blue skies. As soon as we received the command to depart and had made the last salutation, I approached my dear plane in double time. A friend of mine gave me a headband with an inscription in blood. Swearing to myself that I shall never betray my friend's kindnesses, I tighten it around my head. Now I am I, and yet I am not I. Perhaps what I really am is a collection of one hundred million people's prayers. And I must be a man who deserves that. My muffler was fluttering in the wind, and there was a rather pleasant feeling in my heart.

13:50 (1:50 p.m.): The first plane prepared for takeoff, and my own swung along behind amid the harmonious sound of the quiet engines of eight planes, surging higher and then lower, and shaking the blue skies.

The faces of the friends with whom we have lived for a whole year—friends who are now waving banners and shouting things—are now passing away like phantoms.

13:55 (1:55 p.m.): The first plane left the ground, I followed, and then the other six planes took off behind us.

We flew in formation over our base.

Our second hometown, where we will never set foot again! Farewell!! —And the dear town of Tsuchiura was also dropping farther and farther back.

The engine was performing well, and I continued the trip in something like a state of ecstasy. I flew over my home in Kawasaki exactly on schedule.

About the time when we passed over Mt. Ashigara, I looked to my right and saw the utterly sublime Mt. Fuji. A lump came into my throat and tears fell—so emotional was the realization of how wonderful a thing it was to have been born in Japan. That view of Mt. Fuji which I saw from my plane was absolutely magnificent. It went beyond anything that could have been imagined.—After having offered a few cherry branches from the plane to Mt. Fuji, I continued flying due west.

15:30 (3:30 p.m.): We arrived at Suzuka.

April 23

.... The airport [Kanoya Airport in Kagoshima Prefecture, which served as a base for the Navy Special Attack Force planes to take off from] was full of bomb craters, and filled too with a front-line mood. While I was taxiing I was shocked to see six familiar faces: Second Sub-lieutenant Kaneko of the First Shōwa Squad, and Second Sub-lieutenant Marumo, Sub-lieutenants Sadakata, Kitahara, and Nemoto, and Flying Second Sergeant Yoshinaga of the Second Shōwa Squad. Because I was certain that Second Sub-lieutenant Kaneko and others had taken part in a strike against the enemy, I felt as though I was looking at phantoms. According to the details I heard later, they were still on the ground, lined up in preparation for takeoff, and were just about to take off when American Grummans mounted an attack from above. Second Sub-lieutenant Kitahara's #25 plane exploded under the enemy gunfire, and the explosion caused all the other planes to go up too. All of their planes had been wiped out within the blink of an eye. I heard that everyone except Nemoto and Yoshinaga would be returning to Yatabe the day after tomorrow. Kaneko and Nemoto are the only members of my class who are still around and, because Nemoto is to join us on tomorrow's mission, the only one finally left will be Kaneko. His emotional state must, to say the very least, be a complicated affair. The irony of Kaneko's fate involved his having been the first to arrive at Kanoya, and the fact that everyone from the First Shōwa Squad except himself has since perished. Then he sent a second set of friends off on another combat mission, and now he is doing the same for us. Whoever said that one never knows what is going to happen next was speaking the truth.

Our living quarters are in a grade school a little south of the airport. The building had a hole in the ceiling caused by bombardment, and there was nothing inside except some desks and a few bamboo beds. Someone had decorated a desk with a rose, oxalis, and a spray of Roger's bronze flowers, thereby lending a touch of loveliness to this inelegant place. The bones of Second Sub-lieutenants Shinozaki and Nishida rested in a corner. —The former met an untimely death by the enemy's gun, and Nishida was killed just as he was about to take off, the victim of a collision with an incoming plane.

....

Since we may be flying into combat tomorrow, I used some free time for a leisurely walk along a country road and then went in to take a bath [the author uses the English word].

My life of twenty-five [*sic*] years is approaching its end, but I do not feel like a person who is going to die tomorrow. I have already come to the southern end of Japan; tomorrow I shall dare fierce anti-aircraft fire and dive through enemy fighters into an enemy ship—but somehow I cannot feel that any of this is real.

While I wandered around on a footpath between rice fields, with a towel hanging from my hand, the surrounding area was filled with the sound of insects buzzing and frogs croaking, and memories from my childhood bubbled up. When relieved by moonlight, the flowers on Chinese milk vetch are truly beautiful, and it was all so similar to an early summer scene in Kawasaki. I remember with loving thought such things as taking walks with everyone in my family. When I returned to the room, they were burning oil in a pineapple can because there is no electric light. The flame reflected each person's swaying shadow. It is truly a quiet night.

With a mascot under my arm. . . .

April 24

Washed my face in a little creek nearby.

No enemy attack force has been spotted as yet. Been waiting for two hours, ever since eleven o'clock.

I entered my route on a flight chart, checked markings, etc., and prepared to be able to take off for the mission at any time.

My feeling is very lighthearted—just waiting for the order.

In the next room, someone is playing the song "Who would not think of his hometown?" [a hit song by Noboru Kirishima, 1940] on an organ. The whole atmosphere is that of the peaceful South. Since there was nothing else to do, I went outside to relax and to pick some Chinese milk vetch flowers, but now there is no one to present them to. I wrapped them up together with some pear flowers, and sank back into my memories. Then, just as dusk was gathering, I went off to my bath.

In the next room they are drinking and making happy noises, but that is fine too. I want to retain my heart's tranquillity until the time of my death. Until that time comes, human beings ought to continue to work very hard to improve themselves, and this is especially true for those of us who are members of the Special Attack Force which represents "Yamato-damashii" [that unique Japanese spirit, the special attributes of which are loyalty, courage, and uprightness]. Until I die, it is my firm intention to make my conduct correspond with that ideal. As for my life, I believe that I have walked one of the most beautiful paths that any human being could possibly walk. For the benefit of both body and soul, I lived beautifully through the way I received from my parents; I owe it all to the great love of God and the most beautiful love of those who surrounded me. I now feel great pride and pleasure over the dedication of my pure life to our most beautiful fatherland. ....

Akio Ōtsuka

Born March 23, 1922. From the Tokyo Metropolis. Graduated from Chūō University, College Division, 1943. Entered the Navy, December 9, 1943. Killed in action, as a member of the Special Attack Unit, off Kadena, Okinawa, April 28, 1945. Navy second sub-lieutenant cadet. He was twenty-three years old.

April 21, 1945

I am telling you, as clearly as I can, that I am not going to get killed because I want to. And neither am I going to die without any concern and worries in my heart. I am more worried about the nation's future. Even more than that, however, my concern is over what might happen in the future to my father, mother, and you. My anxiety about these things is such that I can scarcely stand it. If you are unable to regain peace of mind after you learn of my death, and should any one of you choose to take a wrong path, then what in the world would become of me?

If you could imagine what would be in my heart, and continue to live as cheerfully and as good to one another as always, then I will be perfectly happy.

All three of you are women, and so it is only natural that I should be apprehensive about the difficult lives that stretch ahead of you. I am sure, however, that each one of you—because you are all very intelligent—will choose her own path to follow as a human being that will be right for each one, and that you will all continue to walk on them.

I shall be living in your hearts.—When you wish to see me, just call my name.

April 25

I got up unusually early, 5:30 in the morning, and, naked above the waist, did some calisthenics. It really felt great. I heard that, nowadays, there is only a single piece of paper in the unpainted wooden box [the box designed to contain a dead soldier's bones—once a man fell, the military would send such a box to his family containing whatever remained of him], but I wonder if it is true. I thought I would give you my hair or fingernails, but unfortunately I went to a barber yesterday, and I had already clipped my fingernails. I realized my mistakes, but too late; after all, those things do not grow back overnight. Right?

Just one word of caution. Please remember that I do not want a tomb, or anything like that. All right? I would be ever so cramped and uncomfortable if I were squeezed into such a tight place. A vagabond [the author's word] like myself has no need for a tomb, so please somehow convey my wishes on this matter to our parents.

A human being can attain something like happiness just by the way he or she thinks. The fact that I am no longer around will not be a reason for you to feel completely downcast. If I were still living and someone else in the family should happen to die, in spite of it, I would try my hardest to do whatever I could for the family.

April 28

I got up today at 6 a.m. and inhaled the clean air of the mountaintop. —My last inhalation of morning air.

Everything I do today will be for the very last time in my life. All of the pilots are due to line up at 2 p.m., and departure is scheduled for shortly after 3 p.m.

I feel as though I still have a lot to write, yet I also feel as though I have nothing to write.—Strange!

I still do not feel as though I am going to die, but am rather as lighthearted as I would be on the verge of taking a short trip. Even when I look at my face in the mirror, there is no trace of the shadow of death— nowhere at all.

Dear Father, please take good care of yourself, because your neuralgia will get better if you do, and if you remember not to worry. I really wanted to exchange sake cups [i.e., drink together] with you once more, but unfortunately it was not to be.—Let us do it face to face at the *butsudan* [a family Buddhist cabinet containing tablets memorializing deceased members of the family].

Dear Mother, I hear that you weigh 13.8 kan (about 52 kg). That is splendid, even though it is a little less than I myself weigh. I could not bear the thought of you ever losing weight over anything that happened to me. Your good health has been a daily source of comfort to me ever since I entered the navy. Mother, I have always identified the health of our entire family with your own personal health.

I am a little worried because you cry so easily, Mother—Please do not cry. I am going to face death with a smile on my face.

Father has often said that "when one person smiles or laughs, another does too."—Because I will be smiling, please smile along with me.

Dear elder-sister, and [younger sisters] Atsuko and Tomoko too, I am very much concerned about your health. Please pay extremely close attention to your physical and emotional well-being. Yours is such an illness that any dark shadow in your heart has especially bad effects, so please pay especially close attention to that.

I imagine that by now cherry blossoms are about to start falling in Tokyo. Do you not think that it would be a pity were I to fall [as a petal of the cherry blossom falls—a traditional representation of a soldier dying for his country] while the cherry blossoms have not fallen yet?

Fall, cherry blossoms, fall! It is not fair that only you should blossom while I am about to fall.

11 o'clock in the morning:

It is now lunchtime, and afterward we head for the airport.

I shall have no more time to write because of maintenance duties there.

So I say farewell now.

I beg you to forgive me for my poor penmanship and for my usual poor writing.[1]

Let us all go off in high spirits.

Believing in the certainty of our victory in the Great East Asia War, praying for your happiness,

and apologizing for all the deeds I did contrary to filial piety,

I shall set off for the mission with a smile on my face.

Tonight there is a full moon. While viewing the moon over the shore of Okinawa's main island, we will search for the enemy, and will carefully strike once he is sighted.

I shall die very courageously and, you will see, thoughtfully too.

Respectfully,

Akio

Ryōji Uehara

Born September 27, 1922. From Nagano Prefecture. From the Preparatory Division, he advanced to Keio University, Faculty of Economics, in 1943.

---

[1] This is a standard epistolary closing line.

Entered the Matsumoto 50th Regiment, December 1, 1943. On May 11, 1945, killed in action as a member of the Army Special Attack Unit, by dashing into an American mechanized unit located in Kadena Bay, Okinawa. Army captain. He was twenty-two years old.

December 31, 1943 Friday

In the morning, I took a bath, did laundry, and also some classwork on grenade-throwers [small, tube-shaped firearms to be carried and used for firing grenades, smoke shells, flares, etc.]. In the afternoon I did more laundry, some self-study, and then went over to the Company with a superior private and five others to pick up jackets and pants. In the morning our former Hanchō (Squad Leader) Ikeuchi had paid us a visit. He is a very cheerful and vivacious character.

When I think of the fact that the eighteenth year of Shōwa (1943) ends today, I am overwhelmed with all sorts of emotions. This year has truly been a most memorable one. I entered the University in October, something which I had yearned for so eagerly for so long, and it was at just about that time that the nation-at-large's general mobilization efforts were enacted and that the extension for conscription was canceled. Following that, all sorts of most important events in my life, such as entering the barracks, followed one after another. Throughout that whole period I experienced a lot of things that clashed quite seriously with my own personal convictions, and I was very distressed over that. Time kept on ticking, however, and in fact it passed by very rapidly. I was involved in so many crises that I hardly had time to take a serious look at reality. I wonder what kind of final results will eventually come from those months that I spent only following government orders. It is a frightening thing to think about, but I shall not say anything about what cannot be undone. The only thing I can do is to hold on to my own convictions firmly. I shall be twenty-three years of age [Translators' note: the author means that he will be in his twenty-third year. This is the traditional way of counting age in Japan: everyone automatically becomes a year older each New Year].— More than ever, I must move on forward toward training my cognitive powers for problem-solving. I pray for good luck in my future.

There has been an air-raid exercise, and starting this evening I will begin dry-towel massage.

We had the evening meal with the Hanchō (Squad Leader); then, later, there was a combined talent show put on by the 4th, 5th, and 6th Infantry Companies. It was quite grand.

After a roll call, there was a fire drill.—I am now twenty-three!

March 10, 1944 Friday

This is my first Army Memorial Day since joining the military. It has been raining all day, and it is cold. This is the day of commemoration for a great victory in the Russo-Japanese War of long ago when Japanese troops entered the Castle of Mukden [southern Manchuria]. When we compare the situation that prevailed then to that of today, we see that the scale is quite different, but I think of the people's spiritual condition then and now as pretty much the same. Both cases involve a war against a major world power, and so something like a common mental stance must exist in both situations.—I would think that a certain tragic sense is what constitutes that common element. The differences between the comparative national strength of the two nations at war cannot of course be compensated for by any mental or spiritual power. In the world of materialistic civilization, such as today, there are probably not many people who would prefer the spiritual to the material; moreover, and even if there are such people, they are the fools who underestimate the power of civilization.

At the time of the Russo-Japanese War, and simply because the material side of civilization had not yet reached a point where it could overrun the spiritual, the relative weakness of the former could be rivaled by the spiritual. However, today the spiritual *cannot* win over the material. Although this is a fact that everyone recognizes at the present time, prior to the Great Asia War the Japanese people had simply expected too much from and relied too much on their spiritual powers. If the Japanese intelligentsia had only taken all this into account early enough to avoid the political mistakes that were made, then we would not now be over our heads in a war we cannot win—rather, we would currently be involved in a struggle that we could handle with at least some degree of control.

Comparing the Russo-Japanese and the Great Asia War, I see now that the spiritual power and the material power have reversed their positions with regard to primacy, i.e., with regard to the ascendancy of one over the other. Here again the history of the development of the human race is clearly demonstrated: those who respect culture flourish while those who ignore it perish. The power of culture is awesome. If we were to state our wish right now, it would be to conquer the United States, Great Britain and the Soviet Union as soon as possible, and then to spread a cultural life that would even exceed theirs. In time, as it was with the British Empire of the past, wherever one goes he would see the Japanese flag unfurled with dignity and power, and Japanese would be made the language of the world. ....

March 21   Tuesday

Someone committed a disingenuous act again last night. That was the second such occasion. That is, someone stole candies from a package. I do not know for sure whether or not the instructor found out about the theft, but what is certain is that the offender's attitude was even worse than his action—there was no evidence of self-reflection. Regarding food, it is imperative that student-officers hold themselves well above the gratification of their raw appetites.

It may be truly regrettable for an incident such as this to occur, but, if you cared to search for the cause, it would quite obviously be hunger. Is the food provided for us sufficient? Absolutely not. Any student-officer, however, if only out of pride, should be able to endure the scarcity.

Yamazaki struck an assistant instructor for the first-year class, and was struck back in return. Although we all felt keen pleasure over his having struck the instructor, it was too bad that Yamazaki had to suffer a blow himself. At any rate, Yamazaki's high spirits were made quite evident, and, because of that, he was assigned to be the student on duty for this whole week. It is truly a well-deserved assignment.

Today's first period was devoted to cleaning the motor we had been using as a teaching aid, and during the second there was a lecture by Instructor Nonoda. He said that we should refrain from criticizing the military because we had no qualifications for doing so. Close to lunch-time I heard that the Honorable Schoolmaster had arrived and we were instructed not to go out for laundry, if possible. This sort of hypocritical conduct does not seem appropriate for student-officers. We would be happy if the Honorable Schoolmaster could observe things the way they really are. I would think that he is already aware of this. Today we received a ration of the form for written apologies. It was the first time for us to have something like this.— Everything is done according to numbers, and I do not think that the use of these forms amounts to anything.

Even though we were told we were not qualified to criticize the Military, there are so many contradictions in the Military that I feel I should set at least some of them down here. Today it is true that the world in general is full of all sorts of contradictions, but the Military too has contradictions. The situation is such that I never would have imagined it before entering the barracks. If there is ever to be any improvement in the nation's Military it is imperative that these contradictions first be removed. Though some might say that this is idealistic and unrealistic, I believe in action rather than talk— and that we should look forward to the eradication of all contradictions.

During the last period I was temporarily assigned to work on motor maintenance. I went inside to study a twin-engine, advanced-level practice plane. It was comfortable and pleasant. It seems to be at once the end result and an amalgam of all the latest scientific achievement, and I said to myself that this is what a plane ought to be. When I climbed up to the pilot's seat it did not seem that it would be all that difficult to operate. I wonder whether or not this feeling was like that of a blind man who is not afraid of a snake.

July 11

There are no worries and everyone is content with their lot, filled with freedom, and we can live with abundant humanity; greedy desires exist always but are not overly strong; rather do we brim over with joyful, happy, and truly free human natures.—This is the type of era that is approaching, but it can only be attained by the triumph of liberalism.

Croce [Italian philosopher, 1866–1952] stated that there cannot be any special mission for a nation nowadays, and that anything that seemed to be such would be a myth. The ideology of "Hakkō Ichiu" ["Eight Corners of the World Under One Roof," i.e., universal harmony—a slogan used to rationalize the Great Asian War] contains within it some element of liberalism, simply because it advocates that each nation should strive to reach its full potential. On the other hand, it also includes the idea that all people are equal, which is a characteristic of Communism.—In the final analysis, the heart of the ideology probably falls somewhere between these two notions.

In liberal nations the spirit of competition thrives, and therefore progress does too. Freedom is a constitutive element of human nature, and it takes considerable self-cultivation for a human being to sacrifice himself for the good of the whole. A human being's concern over himself or her-self is a very fundamental thing, and so any demand for one's putting national ideology ahead of the welfare of the individual goes against nature. Further, it would seem that anything that goes against nature would not last very long. The pilots furnish good examples of this. Because they do what is contrary to the law of nature, they do not live very long, do they?

November 19

In the Japanese Military people are forced to discipline themselves so as to suppress that freedom which is a basic part of a human being's make-up. Once one's basic human yearning for freedom is placed under control, at least to a degree, the military establishment considers that the necessary self-discipline has been achieved and that their own mentality has become the recruit's. Then they go on to say that this transformed individual ought to feel proud. Of course there is nothing more foolish than such an argument. What a waste it would be for a person to put so much effort into suppressing that part of the self which is so fundamental to his very humanity! No matter how much a person thinks he has acquired the requisite self-discipline—even if he thinks that he has taken over the military mentality completely—the acquisition is no more than a surface phenomenon. There is no doubt but that, at the bottom of his heart, there lies a much stronger notion of freedom than he had originally.

Those fools who consider themselves embodiments of the military spirit demand from us the total elimination of our freedom and they consider physical pain as though it were its "supervising army" [i.e., the primary means for acceleration] to the end. The spirit of freedom will always resist, however, even in the face of severe flogging, and in the end that same spirit will always be the victor. Each and every time some of those morons try to steal our liberty and begin to recite "the spirit of the military man," which is a contradiction in itself, we are only renewed in our awareness of how great that liberty is which does not yield to anything. The great things are liberty and freedom!—You are forever and indestructible, the hope of all mankind and the true nature of humanity itself.

February 7, 1945

Suntzu [Chinese military strategist of the Chun-Chiu Period] said that, if you know your enemy as well as you know yourself, you could fight a hundred battles and not be in any crisis. In today's Japan, how many people really know the enemy, America? Anyone who wants to know anything about America, which is a free country, will first have to understand what liberalism is. Just what is liberty, after all? It is a fundamental feature of humanity itself and those who believe in it will always be powerful.

Japan has taken a wrong path ever since the 2.26 Incident.* That path had suddenly taken first a turnaround and then a steep dive—a movement to reject liberty (it appeared that way on the surface but turned out in the final analysis to be one of self-serving egoism) got started; those genuine patriots who stood in its path perished by way of cold steel. After their victory, those who believed in authoritarianism rode on to push Japan onto a path from which it can never ever be rescued. Instead of genuinely loving Japan, they pursued their own interests and forced the good people in a direction the latter only took unwillingly. Their next step was to lie to the ignorant masses by using twisted eloquence to convince them of how America should be dealt with. In this way they attempted to solidify their own position even more by getting the nation involved in a war, and the end result was of course the sacrifice of the populace itself.

So they were able to fool the ignorant masses temporarily, but, as time went on, heaven itself revealed the law of nature to us. The authoritarians tried to deceive the people through exploitation of the mass media, but the point has now been reached where they are about to be forced to bow to the power of nature.

They wanted and desperately tried to expand their own power, even by sacrificing the fatherland which we love more than anything. But now that
their efforts have proven futile, they are taking down with them not only Japan, which we so truly love, but also the good people as well. ....

—Having Become a Member of the Special Attack Unit (*Shinbu-Tai*)—

[Date unknown]
Everything has developed in just about the way I expected it to, and now I am happy to have an appropriate place for my death. I was chosen and received this honor as of today. And the serenity of my state of mind has not changed at all. Most certainly there is no change with regard to ideological conviction. Even if I lived I could not have done all that much for my homeland; this way I protect Japan with my own death.

I could not care less about living *"yūkyū no taigi"* (forever quietly under the law of justice), or things like that. [Translators' note: To live and die for the emperor was considered the eternally unchanging moral act.] I do truly love Japan. And I will fight for the independence and liberty of my fatherland.

There will be reunion in heaven—death is only a way to get there. My beloved Japan! And my dear Kyōko, the one I love!

—Will—[Date unknown]

To my dear Father and Mother:
I was so lucky ever since I was given my life some twenty years ago that I was brought up never deprived of anything. Under the love and affection of my loving parents, and with constant encouragement from my wonderful elder brothers and younger sister, I was so fortunate to spend such happy days. I say this in face of the fact that at times I had a tendency to act in a spoiled and selfish manner. Throughout, of all of us siblings, I was the one who caused you, Father and Mother, the most worry. It pains my heart that my time will come before I can return, or try to return, any of these favors I received. But in Japan, where loyalty to the Emperor and filial piety are considered one and the same thing, and total loyalty to the nation is a fulfillment of filial piety, I am confident of your forgiveness.

As a member of the flying staff, I spent each and every day with death as the premise. Every letter and each word I wrote constituted my last will and testament. In the sky so high above, death is never a focus of fear.

Will I in fact die when I hit the target? No, I cannot believe that I am going to die, and, there was even a time when I felt a sudden urge somehow to dive into a target. The fact of the matter is that I am never afraid of death, and, to the contrary, I even welcome it. The reason for this is my deep belief that, through death, I'll be able to get together again with my beloved older brother, Tatsu. To be reunited with him in heaven is what I desire the most. I did not have any specific attitude toward life and death.* My reasoning was that the cultivation of a specific attitude toward life and death would amount to an attempt to give a meaning and value to death, something that would have to stem from a person's utter fear of an uncertain death. My belief is that death is a passage leading to reunion with my loved ones in heaven. I am not afraid to die. Death is nothing to be afraid of when you look at it as just a stage in the process of ascending to heaven.

Succinctly speaking, I have always admired liberalism, mainly because I felt that this political philosophy was the only one to follow were Japan really to survive eternally. Perhaps this sort of thinking seems foolish' but it is only because Japan is currently drowned in totalitarianism. Nevertheless, and this state of affairs notwithstanding, it will be clear to any human being who sees clearly and is willing to reflect on the very nature of his or her humanity that liberalism is the most logical ideology.

It seems to me that a nation's probable success in the prosecution of a war would, on the very basis of that nation's ideology, be clearly evident even before the war was fought. It would in fact be so obvious that eventual victory would clearly be seen to belong to the nation that holds a natural ideology, i.e., an ideology which in its way is constitutive of human nature itself.

My hope of making Japan like the British Empire of the past has been utterly defeated. At this point, therefore, I gladly give up my life for Japan's liberty and independence.

While the rise and fall of one's nation is indeed a matter of immense importance for any human being, the same shift dwindles to relative insignificance when and if that same human being places it within the context of the universe as a whole. Exactly as the saying has it, "Pride goeth before a fall (or, those who savor victory will soon find themselves in the camp of the defeated)," and, even if America and Great Britain turn out to be victorious against us, they will eventually learn that the day of their own defeat is imminent. It pleases me to think that, even if they are not to be defeated in the near future, they may be turned to dust anyway through an explosion of the globe itself. Not only that, but the people who are getting the most fun out of life now are most certainly doomed to die in the end. The only difference is whether it comes sooner or later.

In the drawer, right side of my bookcase, in the annex of the house, you will find the book I am leaving behind.* If the drawer does not open, please open the left drawer and pull out a nail—then try the right drawer again.

Well, then,[1] I pray that you will take good care of yourselves.

My very best to my big brother [i.e., the older of the two elder brothers], sister Kiyoko, and to everyone.

Well, then, Good-bye. *Gokigen-yō* (Farewell). Good-bye forever.

From Ryōji

Notes

* 2.26 Incident (The Incident of February 26th): A *coup d'etat* that took place in 1936. It involved those young Army officers of Kōdō-ha, the "Imperial Way Clique," who, aiming at the reform of the nation and the destruction of Tōsei-ha, the "Control Clique," attacked the home of the Prime Minister and others.

* Attitude toward life and death: It refers to the view on these matters expressed in *Senjin-Kun (The Field Service Code)* which states "One must single-mindedly go straight on toward the completion of one's duty, transcending all considerations of life and death . . . and make it one's pleasure to live under the eternal justice."

* The book left behind: *Croce* by Gorō Hani (first edition, which was published by Kawade Shobō in 1939). Inside the book's back cover the author wrote another will, a different version. Also, circles were added to some letters (kana syllables) on the text, and it turned out to be a will he addressed to a young woman he was in love with.

(1) Photo: the book's front page. (page 239)

(2) Here and there some letters are circled.

(3) When you trace out and follow those circled letters (i.e., kana syllables), you come up with the will he left to the girl he was secretly in love with:

"My dear Kyōko-chan. Good-bye. I was in love with you, but you were already engaged to marry someone else—so my heart was really in agony. And yet, when I thought of your happiness, I gave up the idea of whispering the words of love to you. All the same, however, I will always love you."

---

[1] Translators' note: *"dewa"* is an opening word often used in the last statement, usually a statement of farewell. It literally means "then," or "well." The author's usage here, twice, may indicate his lingering attachment for his loved ones and his deep parting sorrow.

(1)

羽仁五郎著

クロォチェ

東京 河出書房

(2)

一 市民的哲學者

諸君。

パンを求めて、石を與へらる、こんな經驗に、諸君はめ⑩ているだろう。電氣の⑤な激烈な性質をもったものと、われわれが家庭において來た職場にないて、危險なく自由自在につかつて、高度の生活また生産さた交通をなす⑩とができるのは、ながいあいだの科學者だ⑫、その中にはあのシュタインメッツなどとゆう人も

(3)

きょうこちゃん さようなら
僕はきみがすきだった しかし
そのとき すでにきみは こん
やくの人であった わたしはく
るしんだ そして きみのこう
フクをかんがえたとき あいの
ことばをささやくことを だん
ネンした しかし わたしはい
つも きみを あいしている

(1) 上原良司の遺本(羽仁五郎著「クロォチェ」)の扉。

(2) 本文の文字のところどころに○印が付されている。

(3) それをたどっていくと、恋人への遺書が浮かび上がってくる。

Minoru Wada

Born January 13, 1922. From Ehime Prefecture. From the First Higher School, he entered Tokyo Imperial University, Faculty of Jurisprudence, October 1942. Entered Ōtake Naval Training Corps in Kure, December 1943. Died on duty, July 25, 1945, in an accident while training at the Hikari Base of the Kaiten Special Attack Unit in Yamaguchi Prefecture. Navy second sub-lieutenant. He was twenty-three years old.

November 18, 1944

Yesterday I heard the warning siren for an air raid along a river bank in Kawatana [a Special Attack Force training base, Nagasaki Prefecture], and today I happened to be at the scene of an accident in which a family of three, a mother and two children, were killed instantly by a plant engineering truck. I ended up running around everywhere with Kudō to try and help. ....

I wonder why, at the moment of death, that very same human being whom we believe to be so full of the spirit can turn into something we can only perceive as a sort of "thing."

February 1, 1945

I had my first ride in Kaiten.* The engine of #7 Kaiten did not fire at first because the rear-end starting valve was shut. I shut it down when I saw the S-flag [a semaphore system for ship-to-ship communication] of a shadowing boat, then opened the valve and started the engine up again. This time it was fine. .... We held a study group in the evening. ....

I read *Kokoro (Heart),* by Sōseki [Sōseki Natsume, 1867–1916], and also *Jinsei Gekijō (Life Theater),* by Shirō Ozaki [a popular novelist, 1898– 1964]. I have read both books before, but now that I am in this predicament and surrounded by an atmosphere of death, I find myself touched by them more than ever. I even had tears in my eyes! Works of literature and poetry in particular have lately come to appeal to me collectively—not so much as specific works but rather as literature and poetry in general. I realize that, on the face of it, this must seem way off the mark and even a little ridiculous, but how else am I to account for the fact that they—en masse, as it were—affect me so powerfully, even moving me to tears?

I no longer need anything. Consolation and encouragement— particularly if it is to be offered by way of a long-winded, militaristic harangue, or from a speaker who is playing to his audience—are nothing more to me than occasions for anger. What a cheap and trifling crowd they are! The things I want most right now are tears, the same tears I cried during my life in peacetime. I wonder whether or not my heart at the time, when I look at myself without benefit of a colored glass, was somehow lost. It is almost certain that I will give up my life for my fatherland before this spring is over, but that is no longer something I care about. Now I am simply trying my best to find a way to live this leisurely life that I have now for the first time. ....

March 26

Dear Father and Mother, your son, Minoru, is now in a place like this.

Do you remember the red velvet dress that Wakana [a sister] wore, all dressed up for a concert long ago?

Well, I remember how that dress was shining in the light, and the ocean is now shining glossily in the sunlight in just the same way.

It is a sleepy afternoon.

And I am in command of a four hundred-ton steel tugboat. I wear a pair of binoculars around my neck, and sport the green kikusui patch [a floating chrysanthemum crest] of our Special Attack Unit on my left arm.

Our course is S 56° W; left 4 points, Mizunoko Island; at right 3 points, Oki-muku Island, and Hoto Island.

We shall be arriving at Saiki [Ōita Prefecture] in an hour or so.

The elderly captain of the boat began to doze off. ....

Dear Father, a sub-lieutenant named Miyoshi has died. He failed to clear the bottom of a ship, and crashed. Water came in from the hatch above, and when he was dragged out after some two hours, he was dead—his body limp and his face all bloody. When we turned the Kaiten boat upside down, and drained the water from it, I first thought that the sea-water was a strange, rusty shade, but I suppose it must have been a mixture of seawater and Miyoshi's blood.—All of this went on in the rain.

On the following day, we had a ceremony of bidding farewell to him. ....

That evening, the commander and everyone below were drinking. Then a storm suddenly turned up and, around eleven o'clock, two torpedo boats ended up washed ashore.

That sobered up everybody and we dashed over there, but it was too late.

April 18

.... One more month left. I feel as though I were facing a semester's final exam. My only thoughts are how, in a month's time, I will be appearing before an enemy, and attack the enemy, not at all of my dying. We are fortunate in that we are under no necessity to make a big thing over discussing such matters as one's views on life and death. Or perhaps it is just possible that this itself is the best view on life and death. ....

I do not think that I would ever be able to spit words out with anything approaching Sub-lieutenant N's bombastic style. All his words and phrases are burning with a supreme patriotism. But my cold and dignified heart is prepared to submerge even that to the depth of my innermost feelings. This sort of reserve is of course certainly insignificant at this point in time, and perhaps should be considered unnecessary. For us, however, who at least once upon a time have learned how to think, I feel that all of this is an unavoidable and a heavy burden to carry but, at least in my case, it is only by carrying that burden upon our shoulders that we can close the book on my whole life.

"Cold is the people's heart; Okutsuki [a shinto graveyard] is my home"—Tatsuzō Ishikawa [a novelist, 1905–85] has a certain female protagonist write these words in *Tenraku no Shishū* (*Collection of Poems of Falling*).[1]

Now, at this point in my life, I reflected seriously on my own coldness of heart, and I deeply felt a penetrating sense of loneliness around it. Is it some cowardice on my part which brings on this sort of emotion after I have roused myself with what I thought was courageous excitement?

My fellow soldiers have been very kindly concerned over me the past few days, because I look tired. I came to realize that, even if I had to force myself to do it, I had been trying to make some kind of sense out of my impending death. I felt some comfort in coming to see that all things of that sort can be untangled, no matter how complicated they might seem, in the light of one particular emotion—an emotion which has truly and uniquely belonged to the Japanese people over the course of the past three thousand years. And, I have come to feel like gently stroking that coldness which is stuck in the underside of my heart, something that is perhaps unique to me.

I feverishly made an opposite angle chart so that I can successfully aim my body at an enemy target. I am now making considerably fewer errors in judging an angle of azimuth. ....

May 6
> Within this last month of my existence, am I about to come to a conclusion concerning this confusing life of mine?

---

[1] "Falling" in the sense of dropping lower and lower, either morally or else in terms of one's social or occupational status.

The hands of a sand-clock, which is not quite ready to give out, keep on ticking.

I know that precise time at which I am due to attack is the point when I cannot afford to maneuver; even then, though, I sometimes experience private fears.

Up until now, and just because I was so shallow, I managed to maintain a calm and expressionless front.

And now, for the very first time, I am truly at a loss over how to make sense of my past.

Impatiently I am struggling to find my true self, that is, without any pretense in my remaining life of just a month.

It already seems to me that I no longer really exist.

I also rode on a torpedo which, without ever floating up, prowled over the ocean floor, and rubbed briskly against it some thirty five meters below.

I operated another torpedo that stuck in the sand of the ocean floor, at a depth of thirty meters, inclination at 40°, looking under my shoes at my fellow rider's face.

There was another torpedo—when I opened the hatch a white smoke suddenly spread over the whole length of the tube because of the high internal pressure—and I felt as though someone had struck me in the face.

I have grown into manhood in this squad, and have come to be known as one of "amazing ability," recognized by others as well as by myself.

Others may even cry, wondering how I have ever survived this long—that is my life each and every day.

June 12

At 11:40 a.m., the order was given: "Kaiten, be on the alert!" It would seem that the target is an enemy carrier.

People who cannot put any confidence in human nature ought to be pitied.

When we first arrived here on assignment, we spent over a dozen easy days in total idleness. People might perhaps feel that we showed a lot of poise and grace in facing up to the death that was so soon to come, but I would have to say that it was all valueless, for it was just a natural, everyday habit assumed by people without any particular courage who are being forced to face death.

Now that I have regained my health, and have kept silence for several days, I have an onlooker's point of view. And now I can say without any hesitation that my spirit of true patriotism is unparalleled.

Our education at the First Higher School was so superb that nothing in the world can be compared to it. I felt such a sense of self-reliance, independence, and indeed peerlessness that I could stand resolutely, tall and alone. .... If I were to say in a single word, the spirit of the place was "the spirits of *shishi*" (a man of integrity, courage and loyalty). The *shishi*'s spirit is an aggressive one, and the atmosphere of those three years of Kōryō [the three years dormitory life of the First Higher School] made me—even as small-minded a person as I was—into a spiritual purist. It also made me able to stand up often to the more powerful people in this world.

Now that I am waiting for the enemy like this here in Ulithi [an atoll in the western Carolines], the highway for a supply route to Okinawa, I think of what I learned from those young and receptive patriots, and of the fighting spirit that was rooted in the place, and then I get a firm, quiet feeling in the lower abdomen. Others should not consider me arrogant; it is simply that I am very happy and content. ....

At night I walked up to the bridge and, off to my right, I spied the Great Dipper. The Southern Cross twinkled on the left, Corona was directly above, and the Milky Way looked like a white cloud.

June 20

On the evening of the 18th, the order finally came to give up the search and return to base. Just to make sure, I continued to search for the enemy yesterday and today, but there was none to be found. It was really disappointing and I could not help being upset. How could I show up at the Hikari Base [in Yamaguchi Prefecture] after a failed mission ?

Once one has thought through the questions surrounding life and death, the question themselves disappear. This must be a state of true mental readiness. To avoid thinking about life and death through the use of one's abilities to talk convincingly to false phantoms and, similarly, to face up to false, everyday illusions, might seem like something close to transcending these matters, but this is absolutely not the case. We can say that there is a spiritual awakening between life and death only when one is constant about doing his best at self-discipline.—Once reached, this accomplishment is not a fleeting thing.

My whole life has been one of vanity, and it has been also a life of obsequiousness. But for me, as I am, the days of quiet observation which this month provided me will turn out to be a period that provided punctuation to my life in every sense of that term. It has not borne fruit as yet, however. I recall how at one point, after I had read Shirō Ozaki's *Jinsei Gekijō (Life Theatre)*, I suddenly looked back and realized how full of the "theatrical" my whole life had been [in a sense parallel to that process through which the classical Greek word for a performer on the stage developed into our "hypocrite"].—Even those current views of mine on life and death that I am so proud of might only be another side of that same tendency. A renewed and increased effort in the direction of complete self-examination is in order.

[Editor's note: This diary was written in several notebooks. After the conclusion of the war, the very last portion of the diary was handed over to his family along with the rest of his belongings. The rest of it had already been secretly given to his parents during the course of their personal visits, by having each piece wrapped in oiled paper, placed in the bottom of a lunch box, and covered over with a layer of rice.]

Note

*   *Kaiten* (meaning "stupendous task," or "saving a nation on the verge of ruin"): a name given to a human torpedo. This special attack weapon was fashioned by taking a Model 93 torpedo apart and filling the nose portion with an explosive compound. It was operated by a single pilot and, when an enemy vessel was sighted, was launched from a submarine to smash against the target. It was designed in such a way that, once launched, there was no possibility of its returning.

Yōhei Aboshi

Born September 5, 1926. From Hyōgo Prefecture. Entered Ōsaka Foreign Affairs College, 1944. Entered the barracks July 7, 1945. Killed in action when The Rashin-maru was hit by an enemy torpedo and sunk in the Sea of Japan, August 8, 1945. Army first-class private. He was eighteen years old.

[From a diary, kept during the time the author was working as a
student under the Labor Mobilization Act]

May 8, 1945   Tuesday   Cloudy and cold

Our dream of advancing southward has fleetingly faded away, and we are in a state of anxiety about the enemy's landing. How can I explain how I feel over the fact that I gave up studying the Malay and English languages, and am now spending mundane days as a clerk and soldier in the making? I chose the infantry for my training as a Special Grade-A Military Cadet (*cf.* p. 52). Life is certainly dear to me. I am confident, however, that when the time comes for me to die, I can do so composedly and without getting unnecessarily excited. I can also resign myself to my fate. It seems to me a miracle that I have lived until now, and that I did so without ever having been made ashamed of myself. From the very beginning of the history of the human race—right up until now—that history has been filled with that of warfare. Even in matters of love, or even being in love, the struggles between men and women are ceaseless. The very fact of our having been born into this world only comes after what you might call a battle. It is man's fate that one is born by winning a struggle and dies after losing one. All men's efforts are directed toward winning wars, and sometimes I wish I could run away from all that and hide on some steep mountain or remote island. That would be too unbecoming for human beings, however. For the human beings of today, for whose benefit another great test like Noah's ought to be provided. At what would be that exceedingly ugly moment, I might get on a box-boat—just as a single human being—and escape to the top of the Alps or somewhere. But, if that should happen, what a painful experience something like that would turn out to be—or, alternatively, what a joyful one it might be! And, being unable to persevere after that, soon after I shall die. And that will be all right. I want to die after achieving a victory over the rest of the world. Because, after all, to live a long life is one of the greatest symbols of a victory. . . . My thoughts on these things run in all different directions; I know I can die, but I cannot die, etc.—There is nothing I can do except to wait until whatever is going to happen happens. You need to create your own fate, but at this point no good one seems to be in the picture.

I envy the people of Denmark, though I am sure they must have problems of their own. When I die, I want to become a tiny chickweed flower. I should like to go to my death quietly and joyfully, unknown to others, outside of the ugly struggles and wretched ends of powerful men and those in authority. All I ask is to receive the grace of God's very fullest blessing.

In Philippe's [French author Charles Louis Philippe, 1874–1909] *Letters from When I Was Young*, there are many sections that describe at length exactly how I feel right now. Having deserted the capital [Paris] in favor of the countryside, the author found himself hating all of mankind. Youth's pains of heart are the same all over, as are the worries of country-men. He even hated Paris, which is known as "the Capital of Flowers." I suppose there may not be any good place even in Paris. I am convinced that there is no place in any urban area where a man can really live.

Toshimasa Hayashi

Born November 18, 1919. From Ehime Prefecture. Through Matsuyama Commerce College, entered Keiō Gijuku University, Faculty of Economics, in 1941. Graduated in September 1943. Entered Mie Air Corps, October 4, 1943. Killed in action, August 9, 1945, over the ocean, east of Japan proper, as a member of the Shinpū Special Attack Unit. Navy sub-lieutenant. He was twenty-five years old.

April 13, 1945

First Lieutenant Kuniyasu was killed in action, as was Second Sub-lieutenant Takao Tanigawa. Everyone is dying away. The lives of plane pilots are short indeed. I just heard today that Second Sub-lieutenant Yatsunami also died the day before yesterday: he dove straight into the sea while participating in night-training, and I understand that his dead body was washed ashore yesterday onto the white beach of Kujūkuri-hama. Dear Yatsunami! I enjoyed getting together with him again here—the last time was in Mie. . . . Dressed in his nightclothes, he came to my room rather late on the evening before the day of the accident, and we drank beer together. I wonder whether or not it was some sort of premonition. He was very gentle and quiet. When I said, "What a splendid nightwear," he just chuckled and said that it had been made by his wife, whom he just married in January. His wife too suffered the misfortune on this earth of a typical pilot's wife. How is she going to spend the long life that stretches ahead of her?

Tanigawa has a fiancée too, in Kobe. Those who were left behind may be unlucky, but their sacrifice is an offering for Japan's ultimate victory. So I would ask to please continue to live with strength and pride, and in such a way so as not to bring shame to the brave men who courageously and willingly died for their country. ....

April 23

Nighttime flying began. After our flying operation we drank beer at a welcome party for Kamiōseko. I got a little high; and Second Sub-lieutenant Kamiōsako and I were enraged with indignation [about the current situation]. It was all about our position as reserve officers in the Imperial Navy. Now I declare! I will not fight, at least not for the Imperial Navy. I live and die for my fatherland, and, I would go so far as to say that it is for my own pride. I have nothing but a strong antipathy for the Imperial Navy —absolutely no positive feelings at all. From now on I can say in and to my heart: "I can die for my own pride, but I would not die—absolutely would not—for the Imperial Navy." How terribly we, the

13th class of pilots to come out of the "students mobilized for war" program, have been oppressed by them [the Imperial Navy]! Who exactly is fighting this war now anyway? A full half of my classmates of the 13th class who were bomber pilots on carriers, and my friends, are now already dead.

.... I make a solemn declaration that, from now on, I shall never ever compromise with a single one of them [i.e., graduates of the Naval Academy in the Imperial Navy].

I am going to shut myself up in a shell and protect my own "-ism." From this moment, I am going to dare to unfurl a *"fukan-ki,"* a flag with a motto of my own: "I cannot care."

The stand I have taken may only amount to a lonely and a very tiny resistance, but this is a bitter, bitter fruit that I have gained from my short life in the Navy. Just look at this pitiful fruit! It has even failed to grow normally, but as a navy person this was all I could manage. The shape may be small and ugly, but its bitter taste is not for me alone to sample. Once this and other little fruits are collected, they might soon become a poison that could kill the Imperial Navy. My heart is now trembling with something positively *dämonisch* [demoniacal, the author's usage in German].

I will live and die for my fatherland, my comrades of the 13th class, all those senior fighting men who are members of the "students mobilized for war" program, and, lastly, for my own pride. I shall do so cursing all the while the Imperial Navy, which to me merely means a certain group of officers who graduated from Etajima [the Naval Academy]. . . .

June 14

I received a letter from [Mr/Ms] Masuda [of a social club in Yonago, Tottori Prefecture, at Miho Navy Airbase (which is Yonago Airport today)]. It was a response to the letter I had Mr. Nishi mail for me the other day when he came to visit. If I should ever have a chance to go to Miho [Tottori Prefecture], I would love to visit [him/her] again.

People I knew in the past have all been so kind, and I miss them.

In the hills and mountains, Japanese buntins are singing incessantly.

There is a misty rain falling that looks like smoke.

In the room next to mine, someone is playing a record.

Its cheap sentimentalism runs beneath the level of my consciousness.

June 30

It was raining when I woke up this morning, and I was so glad I could sleep some more that I pulled a blanket over me again. I got up a little after seven, took a late breakfast, and at a barracks I went over some slides designed to help us recognize the different types of enemy ships. Now I have finished with the slides, I returned to my own room, and am writing this and playing a record. Next-door, on a blanket spread over the floor, Kamiōsako, Yamabe, Tejima, and Nasu are having fun playing bridge. No change outside—the steady rain continues.

I cannot begin to do anything about everything.

Simply because I shall have to leave this world in the very near future.

I should thank the Navy's traditional spirit, or rather their cliquishness, which drove Eguchi to say: "I want to go to the front soon—I want to die soon," and even drove me into that sort of psychological state. It even drove all the rest of us, university students transformed into pilots, into that same state of mind.

July 12

I have changed so much, but the pure flame of idealism still burns in the bottom of my heart. I can buy a woman, drink a lot, and even talk smut without being ashamed of any of it. Such trash occasionally makes me feel disgusted with myself.

But I still manage to keep intact the idealism that I built up during the springtime of my life. That self-confidence brings me great personal happiness, and I only wish I could convey it to my older brother, Yukimasa. I would want to tell him, "Older brother Yukimasa, please believe me when I tell you that I have lived my whole life through as an idealist, and now that I have at last been able to keep that promise I made to you then, I am happy to fall like a cherry blossom petal [i.e., to be killed in action for the Fatherland].

The western sky has cleared up a little, and the wind that streams through the window feels very pleasant. I am writing this at dusk, at my window.

July 31

Today is a sortie day. It is the day for the eight planes of our Ryūsei (Falling Star) Squad to carry out a special attack. The fog was extremely thick when I got up. It turned into water that dripped from the leaves and treetops on the mountain.

When I arrived at the airport, the items that were to be carried onto our planes were neatly set out in rows.

Last night, I completely changed everything that I was wearing. I also wound tightly around my waist the thousand-stitch cloth [cf. p. 129] my mother sent me. Then there was the brand-new white muffler my aunt in Yudate gave me.—In other words, I put on the very best things I had.

I am all alone and, expecting the sortie command to come along at any moment, I am writing this in an air-raid shelter.

Farewell dear Father, Mother, Brothers and Sisters, and other relatives and friends.

Please continue to live on enjoying very good health.

This time I am going right into Hans Christian Andersen's fairyland, and I will become its prince.

And I shall be chatting with little birds, flowers, and trees.

I pray for the eternal prosperity of the great Japanese Empire.

August 9   A clear day

Once again the enemy's mechanized divisions are approaching the home islands.

In one hour and a half I shall leave here for the sortie, as a member of the special attack force [*cf.* p. 9]. The skies are a breathtakingly deep blue, and there is a sharp touch of autumn.

August 9th!

Today, I shall fly one of the very latest in war planes, a Ryūsei, and will slam it into an enemy carrier.

Good-bye, my dear parents, and everyone.

Thank you, all my comrades.

Note

*   A note on student cadets and the active-duty officers: The student cadets were those regular university graduates (later supplemented by the students mobilized for war) who were accepted into the service to become the first level of reserve officers that would back up the regular officers who were all graduates of the Naval Academy in Etajima. Within the service, a severe antagonism existed between the Etajima products and the reserves who came out of the student cadets. The voices—such as Toshimasa Hayashi's—that were raised against the tyranny which was inflicted by the regulars upon the students were many and loud.—On this see Hiroyuki Agawa's *Kumo no Bohyō (Grave-posts of Clouds)*. Incidentally, among the 4,726 student cadets of the 13th class of the Navy Specialized Flying Corps who entered the Military in September 1943, as many as one-third of them became casualties—1,605 killed in action. Their tragedy occasioned the publication of *Kumo Nagaruru Hate ni (At the End of the Skies Where a Cloud Floats)*, compiled by Hakuō Izoku Kai (the White Gull Surviving Family Members' Society).

Kuninosuke Misaki

Born March 8, 1921. From the Tokyo Metropolis. Through the Tokyo Higher School, he entered Tokyo Imperial University, Faculty of Letters, Japanese Literature Department, in 1940, and graduated in September 1942. Entered the barracks in July 1944. He died in an infirmary north of Taishet while

detained in Siberia [by the Soviet Union after the end of World War II],
March 31, 1946. He was twenty-four years old.

[From a letter to Mr. Rokurō Hidaka, #1]
   Sorry about not having written you for so long. How are you? I am
well too and am working in good health. Each day I can clearly see how
the winter is deepening, and I am amazed by the evidence of the forces of
nature which are headed toward us. Even when I stand on the very same
patch of ground I stood on a day earlier, and look around, it is almost
shocking how much the winter has done in just one night. The feeling of
the flaky red-brownish pebbles which crunch under my boots—whether
you wish to call them rocks or just hard chunks of soil—is surely different,
and colder, compared to yesterday. It is something like the feeling one
gets, back home in Japan, when the soles of the feet come into contact
with hard, frozen little columns of frost.
   Hereabouts, there is nothing in sight that we would call a tree, but
even those things which might be said to remotely resemble trees have lost
all their leaves and stand there in semi-nakedness with no flair. The same
is true with a small shrub that is shorter than a man's height. There are no
real shrubs here, i.e., none that compare with those commonly found in
Japan, such as azaleas. Here, in the middle of a place where everything
green has disappeared, one only catches sight of two or three branches
growing from a thin stem so pitifully.
   I thought, how will these sad-looking things manage to grow sprouts
when spring comes round again? But when I took a close look at them I
saw some buds; moreover, only the branches with buds grow out into the
shape of arches that are tilted toward the sun, much like fishing rods that
are at once supple and tight. Perhaps they are silently showing their desire
to be as near the sun as is possible. Compared to the leaves, all dried up
and dangling downward in brown shade, those branches, even without a
single leaf, that are tenaciously standing up toward the skies with at least
some life in them, appear so much more strong and reassuring. I reflect
that our present situation should also be more like those branches.—I
thought too that those leaves, dead and yet hanging on, were like dead
souls.

[From a letter to Mr. Rokurō Hidaka, #2]
   .... When spring arrives at last on a western wind, the
beautiful thing is the color of the soil's surface. The orderly ridges of
fields are truly beautiful too: not yet tilled or even green, but they remind

us that people have worked on them until last autumn. Such orderly lines are delightful to eyes that have only been accustomed to looking at vast, dry stretches of dead fields. Field fires burn almost every night throughout the surrounding mountains, and, at their fiercest, we could see a thin red line spreading out here and there, even in daylight. When we look up at them in the evening, they do not have the horror of homes on fire, but rather they look really gentle (though I am certain that if you went near it, it would be seen to be burning intensely enough). They give me the same feeling as those red charcoal fires that have burnt themselves out and become dead silent. Once I happened across such a burnt field and there was nothing left but scorched, dead weeds—nothing interesting. But when multitudes of dandelions and other flowers suddenly shoot out all over the charred black mountain surfaces and surround us, and when new, fresh green sprouts begin to come out, everything turns green within three days.

This eye-opening change of colors, from black to green, is something that I could never have experienced back home in Japan. There is only one thing that I do not yet understand, even though it is often discussed, and that is the emotion with which people in this snow country greet the arrival of spring. My puzzlement stems from a conviction that it would be more accurate to consider this a land where there are only winters and summers.

At about the same time the mountain surface turns green and is clouded over by warm rain; the river flows so abundantly, and the tilling of fields begins on a huge bar in the middle of the river. Ferry boats also begin to pick up their activities. Along the river, I can see a Korean woman beating her laundry with a stick and rinsing it with the river water. The first vegetables to appear are green onions, striped with contrasting white and green layers that penetrate our eyes. Elder women put them in baskets and go into town to sell them, and I have never experienced a pleasure that rivals that of the fresh and harsh smell of those green onions.
....

[From a letter to Mr. Rokurō Hidaka, #3]

Sorry I have not written you for so long. There are no changes here. Is everything all right in Kamakura? Since there is no talk about it, I have no idea as to what is going on at the university, but, I suppose several of the buildings have been destroyed. Well, at any rate, Germany too has fallen at last. For those of us who happened to have the opportunity to know the great Germany of the past, the Germany that always rose up after sinking down to rock bottom many times, it is difficult to imagine them giving up without a struggle—as an enervated people who cannot accomplish anything.

I can say the same thing about France. Or, rather, what I should say is that Europe is not quite yet composed of peoples and nations which have become so antiquated that they are ready to be stored away behind the glass windows of museums. The truly immense problem of a brand-new world looms before us, a world where a new Europe, a new Asia, and a new rest of the world will all be linked together. I am so certain that a second-rate kind of study will prove woefully inadequate for dealing with a challenge of this magnitude, that I know we will be left behind in this whole new development if we allow ourselves to be utterly consumed by the problems that face us right now.

The end of hostilities will most certainly provide a great opportunity for change, but somehow I cannot feel that the close of the war is coming any time soon. It is most likely, moreover, that war—as the father of all things—will not simply disappear at the cessation of actual combat. I would not know whether or not it would affect the current fighting, but I think there has to be an absolutely essential kind of study made that would put human beings more in line with their own humanity. We might call this sort of thing *"werden"*[1]—And it is also the sort of thing that we constantly—day and night—ought to be making improvements on, despite the difficulties involved.

Please continue your studies in the best of health.

Kiyoshi Sekiguchi

Born February 7, 1919. From Gunma Prefecture. Through the Preparatory Division, he advanced to and graduated from the Tokyo Fine Arts Academy, Oil Painting Department, September 1943. Entered the barracks, November 10, 1943. He died on August 19, 1945, from diseases contracted while on the battlefield, at the Fourth Field Hospital, the 28th Division, in Miyako Island, Okinawa. Army sergeant major. He was twenty-six years old.

[From a note found among his belongings]

Once when I was a young boy, I brought home six shrike chicks [also known as butcher-birds]; I fed them and watched them grow little by little every day, and soon I found myself waiting for them to be able to fly away. But the six of them did not all open their mouths to be fed in the same way. One of them had a ferocious appetite and desperately wanted to be fed, and there was another that just kept on sleeping and showed almost

---

[1] The German original for "development" or "growth".

no interest at all in eating. As the days went by, those chicks which ate well kept on growing, but the one that did not want to eat remained rather weak and stayed almost the same every day. It made me wonder when it would ever be able to fly, and it made me worry a lot too. And when a few more days passed, those that had grown well were almost ready to fly away. Their wings fluttered and their screeching sounded as sharp as that of their parent birds, and they showed by their spirit that they were ready to take off. I remember waiting as anxiously from one moment to the next for the healthiest and strongest one to take flight.

Ironically enough, among those baby shrikes which were not growing well was one who did more than his share of eating. Perhaps he had been hit or suffered some sort of accident and, pitifully, the lower stomach was protruding sharply—his flying future did not look promising. When the oldest brother bird was able to fly a distance of nearly one meter, just about all the others at last began to eat better, and they began to screech like their parents. For whatever reason, however, from about that time on, the smallest one ate less and less and almost stopped eating altogether. The shrike always stayed on its perch, practically never moving; in the end, it completely stopped showing any interest at all in food—did not even look at it. It was a baby bird that in appearance had lost all its baby-like qualities, and had almost acquired the dignity of an aquatic fowl. The only things he seemed to be interested in were the occasional chirping sounds made by small birds outside—sounds he seemed to listen to intently.

This silent baby bird gradually became weaker and weaker. The following morning, I found him stiff and dead under a perch. I still remember vividly how helplessly dumbfounded I felt at that moment.

Next day, I decided to release the rest of the baby birds to the open sky, and took them outside, but they were not quite ready to fly. So, I had them perch on a round tree branch in the garden, and I fed them there. Now and then, and more or less in a group, they would leave the branch and come to the kitchen door, chirping in unison as if to say "Please let us come in." But the pitiful bird with the big tummy could not join the rest of them in anything they did, and fell off the branch even when I tried to assist it. And even when the rest of them could fly more than a meter or so, this deformed one barely scraped along with its swollen middle chafing the ground. One day my older brother gave me an air rifle and told me to shoot that crippled little chick. I thought it over and, mostly because it was just too pitiful to watch the poor bird's endless suffering, decided to go along with his idea. I reflected on the future misery of a bird that would never be able to fly. Perhaps it would be better for him to be finished right off with one shot. I stood about four or five meters away and took aim. The little bird opened its mouth wide and kept on chirping, wanting more food. Not moving a muscle, I took dead aim at that big opened mouth, but I just could not pull the trigger. I lowered the air gun, feeling that, one way or another, this pitiful little bird would somehow survive.

Just because my brother asked me what the problem was, I aimed the gun at the bird once again, at its head, and fired. The little thing jerked a couple of times and died. Afterward, I buried the dead bird under a tree and placed a small stone there to mark its resting place.

When that was done, I kept on waiting every day for the remaining four birds to fly off. One morning I was puzzled by the fact that none of the four were in sight, and I looked for them all over the garden.—I later found out that every single one of them had been taken by a cat.

I could not sleep at all that night, thinking about how those little lives were destroyed without any fuss at all.

After that, I vowed never to rob a bird's nest—and I prayed for those pitiful creatures.

□ Mr. Ideology speaks to Mr. Senses. "You are now going over the sea, and heading south for the front. And we are going to fight, and will probably be killed. Or, even before you ever arrive on a battlefield, you might be killed on a troop transport. It is all just a matter of time."—But Mr. Senses would not reply. He, Mr. Senses, has fallen into a deep sleep, and he is off chasing dreams in a world of wonderment.

[From a diary kept in a sickbed]
July 1, 1945
□ At dawn today an enemy plane appeared.
The weather is clear and it felt fine all day.
□ The past is what I have enjoyed the most, and the present time has turned out to be the most painful.—There are both hell and heaven on this earth.

Therefore, I cannot die. I believe that the most righteous thing to do is to live.

I still have much work yet to do after having seen that both heaven and hell are on this earth.

□ At 3:30 p.m. A Private First Class named Yasuda passed away. All three, Kurosawa, Tsubaki, and Sakota, were killed in action.

July 2
□ Enemy planes flew over once this morning.
In bed all day. I went to the Sunagawa's house just before dinner.

July 3

Enemy planes flew over once in the morning.

July 4   At 1 p.m. enemy planes flew over once.

☐ As a human being, I have had so many precious experiences. They will become invaluable treasures of the whole of mankind. I do not wish to bury this priceless "gym" of sweat, oil, and tears that has seeped out of my body—just to become part of the soil of Miyako-jima Island.

The more and more painful it gets, so much the more do I want to live. As my adverse fortune turns worse and worse, my desire to cling on to life only gets stronger.

I am impressed over what good luck it is to have been born at a time when, more than ever, it makes a real difference to be alive. I want to see the end of this war and of the human race and, more than either, the end of everything. I must stay alive. In order to leave this precious treasure of mine to future generations, I must fight against the sickness, exhaustion, hunger, and the unbearable summer heat. Fortunately, I am young and full of tenacity, and my life is filled with enough pride to carry a heavy burden.

Just like a plant bulb—one that shields its life from harsh conditions and waits for springtime—gets as big and fat as possible [i.e., stores up for the future as much reserve strength as possible] in preparation, I shall calmly wait for my own time to sprout out!!

I am firmly convinced that that time will definitely come.

☐ Around 1 p.m. I went to a neighboring family's house. I was insulted there by a drunken local civilian (*cf.* p. 98).

July 5

☐ Enemy planes came once in the morning.

And it was in the morning that my diarrhea came on, probably because I exposed myself to too much direct sunlight yesterday.

July 6

☐ The probability of an enemy landing is very high.

Some thirty enemy planes flew over around 10 a.m.

Suffering a little from diarrhea.

July 11

My physical condition is good. Starting today, I am taking regular meals [i.e., not just a dietician's special preparations for the sick]. Our planes came over early this morning, and none of the enemy's.

Army nurse Tsunoda gave me a pickled plum.

Completed reading Nobuko Yoshiya's *Hana (Flowers)*, a book I found very interesting. Sergeant Kai came to see me in the evening. Compared to my emaciated frame, what a healthy-looking, golden-red body he has. I promised myself that I would get well and be as healthy as he is.

The outline of his face was tight and most beautiful.

"At the field hospital in Miyako-jima Island.

July 14.

At present. I do not think it is possible to get any thinner than this." These are drawings that Mr. Sekiguchi, the author, drew in Miyako-jima Island just prior to his death by starvation

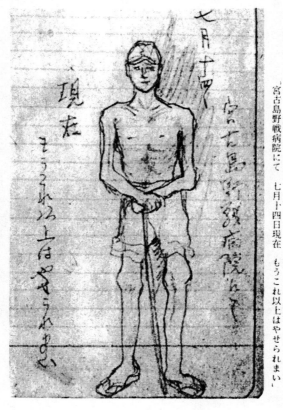

関口清氏が，宮古島において，餓
死直前に描いた絵（以下同じ）．

"August 9th"

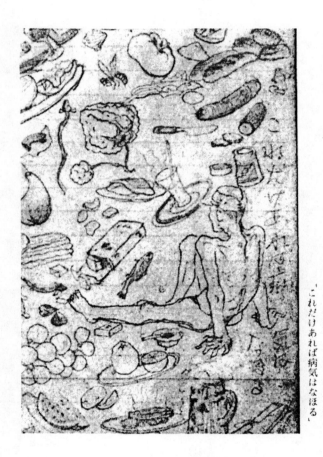

"If I could have all these, I can recover from my illness."

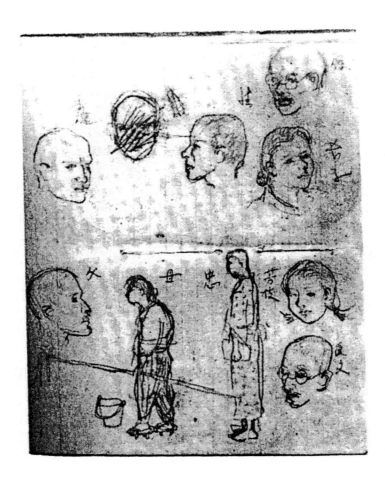

[Each face has a name on it: e.g., the lower section, from left corner] —"father," "mother," "Tadashi," "Yoshie," etc.

Hiroshi Hachiya

Born March 18, 1922. From Okayama Prefecture. From the Sixth Higher School, entered Tokyo Imperial University, Faculty of Letters, Japanese Literature Department, October 1942. Entered the barracks in December 1943. Killed in action on Iwō-jima, December 24, 1944. Army lance corporal. He was twenty-two years old.

[From his *Iwō-jima Oboegaki* (Memo on the Battle of Iwō-jima),
December 1944]
[The following poems are *tanka*]
Iwō-jima is so tranquil in the smokey-gray rain;
    The cannonade of yesterday
        must have been a dream.

I am writing a poem in a bomb-shelter and listening
    to the sound of the bombs;
        how pitiful it is that the springtime of my life
            is now about to end.

Struggling through the loneliness of this southern land,
    I am alive in a bomb-shelter filled with others' breath.

So pitiful is a man who has to live so alone,
    in a bomb-shelter that is becoming
        even more foul from the comrades' breath!

We watch a darkening cloud over Iwō-jima:
    The sun has gone down as we wait for a plane
        that has not yet returned.

Hisashi Inoue

Born May 1, 1922. From Aichi Prefecture. From Shizuoka Higher School, entered Tokyo Imperial University, Faculty of Jurisprudence, Political Science Department, April 1942. Entered Ōtake Naval Training Corps in Kure, December 10, 1943. Killed in action, on board The *Ōyodo* [light cruiser], near Eta-jima, July 24, 1945. Navy sub-lieutenant. He was twenty-three years old.

—"Reflection on *Kojima no Haru (Spring on a Small Island)*
[which housed a leper colony, by Masako Ogawa, a work that
was later the inspiration for a film," published in *Ryōhō
(Dormitory News)*, No. 115, Nov. 26, 1940]. [The following poems
are *tanka*.]—

A mother reads poems about leprosy
    to her blind, stricken daughter
        —will the maiden ever know what is in her mother's heart?

In the shadow cast by fear of this hideous disease,
    even the word "love," spoken by a friend,
        seems so solemn.

Despite suffering from such a sorrowful fate in this world,
    a maiden maintains peace of heart
        as she composes poems.

—[From two collections of poems: *Gekkō (Moon-light)* and
Tachi no Uta (Songs of a Sword)—poems the author composed
from late July through late September of 1944, while he was
recuperating from an illness]—

—Song of a Hawk—
A hawk makes sorrowful cries in the great autumn skies,
    making circles and floating away.

—Purple Smoke—
Because life is so short,
    the dance of purple smoke is so sorrowful.

—A Nun—
A sasanqua flower that single-mindedly and quietly
    survives by seeping the cold water of a jar.

A sasanqua flower does not even talk openly of
    the quiet loneliness of autumn skies and earth.

—A Student Mobilized to Go to War—
At this moment, our only thoughts are to serve the country;
    we go about our business
        without talking impertinently.

It is a leaden morning of snow that comes from
   all directions, as I leave home to fight
     a war for the emperor.

—Miscellaneous Poems—
Knowing so very well that there will be many things
   that go against our will this year—
     my twenty-third year—I dropped a fishing line.

I read a letter from my mother, to whom my life of
   twenty-three years cannot be substituted for
     by anything in this world.

Stepping over the shuddering shadow of death,
   I think of the life that simply wants
     to live itself out quietly.

—[From a diary kept while the author was in the
Ōtake Naval Training Corps]—

December 31, 1943

My mother's letter arrived this morning. I had already received two
letters from my father, but this was the first one from mother. I suppose it
is because [she] is so busy around the house at the end of the year.[1]

But now that I, and of my own volition, am training like this to hurl
myself into the war, her mental preparedness as a mother must be great,
and I am very pleased to hear that she is carrying on so full-spiritedly.

Although this world we live in is so vast, perhaps my parents are the
only ones who truly care and who worry from the bottom of their hearts
about my going to war. Now that I think of it, yesterday the squad leader
told us about a telegram that read: "Your father is critically ill: Be strong-
minded and do your best"—the story brought tears to my eyes. Every day
here of late, and deep in my heart, I keep thinking both about my love for
my parents and my appreciation for everything they did for me. It seems
that, at least for us soldiers, our love for blood relations is one of the most
serious problems that we have to become clear about in our minds.

As I think back, I can see now that the problem has never left my
mind since I first ran into that recruiting officer in early November. It was
at the place for the physical examination of conscripts in Okazaki [Aichi

---

[1]This line could also be interpreted as: "I suppose it is because [he] is so busy around
the house at the end of the year that she wrote this letter for him."

Prefecture]. The officer very cruelly reminded us that we must "switch our brains" (i.e., change our thinking) completely, and cut off any love or attachment that we might have for our blood relations. Although there are a variety of ways in which that command, cutting our attachment, could be complied with, the only way the weak ones among us would choose would be, in a muddle of self-deception, simply to close their eyes, cover their ears, and dull their senses in order to be able to forget their parents. That is absolutely not the way I would choose. Rather, I would seize this last opportunity to show some courage and to feel my parents' love for me more deeply than ever. Then, and with a calm heart, I would cut off that very same love which I had just been feeling so intimately.—Here lies the end result of twenty-some years of my self-cultivation, and also the measure of the stature of a human being who had pursued learning so avidly.

At this point I remember some phrases by Shōin Yoshida [a great patriot at the end of the Tokugawa Period, executed during the mass execution of the Ansei Era, 1830–59] to the effect that "due to the shallowness of my studying in everyday life . . . how would my parents' loving hearts, even exceeding the love of a child for its parents, hear of the news of today" [his farewell poem]. Shōin sent this letter of farewell in a calm mood, and while feeling deeply his parents' unwavering love for him. The biggest problem concerning what we all have to learn lies right here. I hope that I too will never forget about my mother's tender love until that final moment when I perish in some southern sea. Until the very end, then, led on by my parents' love, I shall not forget what is in the heart of a true samurai.

In the waistband I wear there is my mother's writing: "Hisashi. Ganbare!" ("Hold out, My son Hisashi!") No matter how tough and painful things may yet get, I am glad to feel a renewed strength whenever I think of this.—Dear Mother. Please wait. The time that will make you rejoice is coming soon. Or, rather, I shall bring you such a time myself.
....

Konokichi Sumiyoshi

Born February 15, 1921. From the Tokyo Metropolis. From Shizuoka Higher School, entered Tokyo Imperial University, Second Faculty of Engineering, Electric Engineering Department, in October 1942. Under the Student Mobilization Act, worked at the Institute of Aeronautics Research, beginning at the end of 1944. Killed in an air raid, May 24, 1945, together with his entire family of six at home in Meguro, Tokyo. He was twenty-four years old.

❀ ❀ ❀

December 1, 1943 Wednesday Clear

Having left his hair and will behind as personal effects, a friend of mine has just left for the war front.

Because the morning lecture was canceled, I took my time leaving the house. As someone who has been left behind, [i.e., still here while my friends have already been conscripted and have gone off to fight on the front lines], I have feelings that are all but unbearable. Each and every day of my life I see myself pointed directly at death. Death is certainly a very important matter to me. But death does not solve the problem. And, there remains life, which is much more powerful than death. I do not see the need, at this point in time, to write out a proper will.—This diary is my will. What with my birthday coming up next year, the extension of my deferment from conscription will be ending. Also I have heard that our training period in the barracks, i.e., prior to being sent on to the front, is going to be greatly shortened. In a way I even feel like I want to be called up and go to the front, but at the same time I do get choked up when I think of a certain—and beautiful—someone. Even though my heart is being torn into a thousand pieces, I must somehow discipline it and, steadily and firmly, continue to do what I have to do.

March 5, 1945 Cloudy

It has been a gloomy day, and I kept thinking deep thoughts about all sorts of things. I sat in front of a heater all day, and then came home early. Why do we have to say good-bye to those whom we love? I think too of the miserable condition of human lives these days, and of the tragedy involved in abusing nature's gifts to kill one another. However, one must be strong and tough. Regardless of how unpleasant things may become, an ultimate solution can only be reached through all-out efforts—and at every moment—on the part of every individual. I am confident that, out of love for my fatherland, I can face death in a serene frame of mind, but I cannot deny that I do have some questions about what is going on in this country.

The nation as a whole is not the problem, and indeed there is much about current Japan which may well be the answer. No one is more appreciative than I am of my good fortune in having been born in this beautiful land. But this same heart of mine that prays for our nation to become even more beautiful and sublime also aches over a lack of conviction about too many things in today's Japan.

I want to do my best. I want to do whatever I really have to do with every ounce of my being. It would solve everything if I can do all this cheerfully and in high spirits.

March 7th
....

I must endure a good deal of pain. Because there is no way to find a solution except by enduring and suffering through and through. A true heart as well as hope will only begin to shine out through suffering and pain; and, therefore, I shall accept my current predicament. I must be duly thankful for whatever gifts I am already blessed with, and at the same time have to come up with even more fighting spirit. This is such a life as would destroy even my willingness to be a dead stone, but that is only because I myself am still not strong enough. Even in _xx_ ko's case [reference to a girl the author had become friendly with while he was at the Aeronautics Institute]—and even in today's situation with its dark, unknown future—the two of us must share our true hearts and trust each other; we will have to go through sweat and tears to make this love of ours even deeper and truer. Yes we will indeed make our love the truest and deepest possible; and that is why, dear_xx_ko, I must ask you to endure today's suffering. I know how you must be suffering, but please put up with the pain for my sake. You must know how to pray, so please pray for us. And, with your tears, please purify our love even more. I shall labor even more mightily than before. As we watch our love develop into a truly great one, let us move on to the next stage in its creation—marriage.

What is certain is that, at this point, self-reflection should never be drowned in a foolish mood. Reality is too harsh. My body is being held to the fire [i.e., my life is in imminent danger]. Notwithstanding all ideals and idealism, no matter how great, everything will be completely destroyed unless this fire is extinguished. Regardless of how uneventful and dry life might be, I should—if I relied on that ethical code on living which I have acquired over the past years—be able to live joyfully and with a sense of hope. Just now, however, that code does not seem quite good enough. The nation's tragic plight projects itself into part of the great, throbbing pain in my own heart. Correspondingly, I also feel that the ethics of life I have learned may not be quite adequate to the situation. I would also think, however, that—even while suffering through this tragic passage in both our national and personal histories—the individual should be permitted to make his own best use of himself for the good of the nation, and to maintain his hope of feeling fulfilled in this life.

The two things that one must work at persistently are happiness and good health; from these spring cheerfulness and self-reliance.

April 2

There are a hundred or perhaps two hundred days left in my life. I asked my father to please send my mother out of Tokyo, as well as other people who are important to us.—It is time for self-reflection. Do I have any real conviction? Whatever the case, I must truly treasure the short time that is left of my life. Now I am alone quietly. I am thinking about many things.

Convictions are so important. And I must have a determination to make the moment of my death as glorious as possible. I can feel simultaneously calm and very powerfully about that. All the pain I went through in the past was not in vain. I do not fear death, but can only anticipate a beautiful end and my dying with a smile on my face. The reason is that I can devote myself totally both to the fatherland and to those I love. But I will not throw my life away. There will not be many more times when I shall be able to walk up the stairs in this beloved two-story house or to look at the scenes which surrounded it. I must reflect more upon myself to check on whether or not I am living with the appropriate appreciation for each and every moment that remains to me. I shall devote myself to doing so.

My feeling now is that I can accept Buddha's teaching on this situation that "one must not meet those whom he or she loves." Dear xx ko! I do miss her terribly and—without even the trace of a falsehood. I want to admit that I do. I want to see her. But even if I could it would be meaningless in the end. Life is certainly painful, and so fleeting. Having gone through it, at least to a certain extent, and reached the point of resignation, my emotion is calm simply because it is empty.—It is very calm indeed.

April 13

Pulling a rear-car (a bicycle-drawn trailer), I went to the Aeronautics Institute. On my way there, I passed the front of the military barracks and became depressed—what a drab life military men lead! But I cannot be defeated by that sort of thing; I must be stronger.—And another premonition of mine came true: a letter arrived from xx ko. A second letter came from Tsuchida [a classmate at Shizuoka Higher School]. There are at least some things that turn hope into belief.

April 14

We suffered through a massive air-raid last night, so I went to work this morning somewhat later than usual. I did some unloading in the afternoon and then came home a little early. It was a spring day, and I feel rather sad. The cherry blossom season has already passed its peak. I watched a cadet* training soldiers, shouting at them. All they are doing now is going through the motions, wasting time that is empty in the first place. It is impossible to find anything meaningful in meaninglessness. Eating, sleeping, giving false evidence of high spirits, and having to lie—that is the military.

April 15

Compulsory memorization of the Imperial Instruction for Soldiers (*cf.* p. 51) has been imposed, and it is so foolish. This reaction reminds me that my feelings nowadays are gradually becoming more and more cosmopolitan. I find myself almost automatically locking into almost anything that falls outside Japan's traditional framework. I must build my own path more solidly, make the effort required and show the dauntless courage that I need in order to move toward that path.

April 26

A letter came from _xx_ ko. I feel uncomfortable about my own inability and my weak will. _xx_ ko is moving forward a step at a time. At this moment I feel that I have not quite come up to the mark, but at least I have the desire to be absolutely positive and *sunao* (gentle, honest, and open, i.e., the opposite of manipulative, rebellious, or pretentious). Moreover, and as I wrote in my "green notebook" [the small notebook that the author always carried with him], I am trying to be more appreciative, love people more, and make a real effort to practice that love assiduously. I am not quite up to that state of mind as yet, but I do believe that there is this path to take.

To die fighting in a war that we were winning would be easy. But, even given a situation wherein, in a losing effort, I were to be killed by enemy gunfire, I must still strive my very hardest to do my duty toward what I believe in and dream of.

April 30

I am totally discontented. I came home in silence, and with a depressed feeling so deep that I could not shake it off no matter how hard I tried. The skies were the clearest of blue. Such blue skies. From very early in the morning we were subjected to a large-scale raid. I went outside to sit on the lawn and [compose some poetry]:

> It is so sad to have this helpless
>   feeling of pricking up one's ears for the
>   bombers' buzzing sound.

> I simply feel sorrow over
>> this bleak spring,
>> and think of someone far away.
> The springtime is passing way helplessly;
>> the sky is filled with light
>> and the wind is mild—
> Already full of the green leaves
>> that peak in this season.

This depression about not being able to fulfill [my life], not only involves myself—inside and out—but other people as well, and indeed everything about the present situation. In short, everything is absolutely unpleasant. The tragic position that Japan finds herself in these days is the reason for all this, and there is no light at the end of the tunnel.—And I must part from my loved ones for that reason.

May 4

I keep writing over and over again, but never enough, about how simultaneously serene, tragic, and harsh this life is—and also about how I must become much stronger, more righteous, and more in command of the situation. My honest feeling about Japan is that I like it—rather, I love it. But instead of just talking about Japan's *kokutai* (national polity),* and so on, I should think that the Japanese people ought to be thinking more broadly about the fate of all humankind. Mt. Fuji is so beautiful and serene, and if in fact love for the fatherland is the same thing as the love for one's hometown and his own people, then I feel that I have no less of it than anyone else. What I cannot understand or accept is the idea of fighting just for the past history and for the national polity. The emperor can do nothing to alleviate humankind's miserable and tragic condition; unless every individual makes him- or herself better in order to accomplish that. Human beings must become much more broad-minded, and big-hearted too, and must know more about the sweat and tears of others. If this does not happen, then the fate of the human race will forever remain a tragic one. Truly, in order to rescue humanity from such a tragedy, we must all of us be most diligent both about choosing the best path to follow in our current situation, and about sticking to it after the choice is made.

May 6

We must create a new Japan from the ashes of the old. Because of those who speak so loudly of national policy, Japan has essentially penned itself up within a limited sphere and remained fearful of the outside world. Let us make the new Japan a place that is bright and full of hope. It should be vibrant with life and full of energy—like new green leaves when they sprout out. We cannot deny that we had high hopes for the old Japan. Of course, I do not intend to discuss such things as the longevity of the single imperial bloodline and so on, but the fact is that the Military totally ignored reality, as did those antiquated and stubborn so-called patriots, who trampled on the very nature of human beings and prevented our society from being developed in the way it should have been developed —and they did all this in the name of *kokutai*, the Imperial Line, and the existence of the Imperial Prescripts. The simple fact in recent years was that these people controlled Japan and kept the Imperial glory from shining out. My wish would be to wipe out these feudal customs—such as separating members of the Imperial family from all commoners—that ignore basic human nature. What I would like to see is a society in which neighbors love one another and help one another, caring for the whole family of man and being genuinely grateful for all the good things in life.

May 16

Morning. I intended to spend the whole day reading. Yesterday we were assigned to do manual labor, and today I am spending a day this way. One thing, though: I felt an almost uncontainable joy in life welling up inside me. I devoted every spare moment to reading the second volume of *Yoake-mae (Before the Dawn)* [by Tōson Shimazaki]. My thoughts immediately spring to a comparison between our national strength today and that of the past—and a quiet little hope also emerges. I really think I must make my own convictions much more firm. I also want to do my very best at cultivating myself in the directions of a broader vision with my utmost positive self-confidence.

I am in pain with longing for _xx_ ko. She is someone I can trust. I really believe that; still, I am quite anxious for a letter from her simply because there has not been a word for such a long time. As for thoughts about my parents and brothers and sisters—even as I was just walking down the street, my heart was simply hurting with my longing for them.

May 17

I carried Ms. Uno's luggage from Jōmei-in Temple to Umishima Temple with Ms. Hirono, Mr. Yamada, and Mr. Yamanaka. The skies are eternally clear and high. Just as beautiful are those gigantic columns of clouds which keep rising up, and even the surface of the mountain can be picked out with great precision.

Everyone is in agony. I was very touched by *Doitsu Senbotsu Gakusei no Tegami (The Letters of the Fallen German Students)* [Japanese translation of selections from *Kriegsbiefe gefallener Studenten*, compiled by Philipp Witkop] (*cf.* p. 149) as I read it for the second time. What a gap there is between idealism and the reality! And how painful is the suffering of those young men who give up their lives in war. My life too will last for just half of another year: there is no way to prevent that. I would be fooling myself were I to pretend that there could be space left in my heart for any little peaceful hope of salvation. Still, and although I am suffering and in pain, I want to continue to do my very best as long as I can. I continue to read *Yoake-mae (Before the Dawn)* [by Tōson Shimazaki] and *Kumo to Kusahara (Clouds and a Grass Field)* [by Kihachi Ozaki]. It is a very quiet evening. I had some rice cookies that Hajime [a friend who had also been mobilized] offered me, and then I went outside. The light of the bow-shaped moon slanted down and shone faintly over the graveyard, and the starlit sky did not hold a single cloud. Singing the dormitory song—"Oh, Youth, skies, and life—this is the only life!"—I stepped on my own shadow that had been made by the moonlight.

For this last half a year, and for as long as they flow out like they are now, I shall never get bored writing about my deep feelings. Especially since those feelings are entirely free of pretense, I want to continue to write about them honestly—and I also wish to enter into an emotional state correspondent with them. Praising nature, enjoying life, and enduring the pain—my wish is that, each and every day, will afford me something to write down in this diary which I am planning to leave behind. Of course it is probable that the fires of war will consume the diary too. Regardless, I shall keep on writing anyway.

Notes

* *Minarai-shikan* (student cadet, lit., officer trainee): The official title bestowed on *shikan kōhosei* (officer on probation, lit., officer candidate) and *kanbu kōhosei* (student cadet) in the army, just prior to their appointments as sub-lieutenants.

* *Kokutai* (national polity): Japanese Imperial system. According to an official statement made in 1937 in *Kokutai no Hongi (The Essence of "Kokutai")*, it is set down that "the Great Japanese Imperial Nation is governed forever by an unbroken line of Emperors through ages eternal under the divine prescript of the Imperial ancestor. This is our eternally immutable *kokutai* (national polity)."

Haruo Unagami

Born March 27, 1921. From Shanghai. From Shizuoka Higher School, entered Tokyo Imperial University, Faculty of Economics, in October 1942. Entered the barracks December 1, 1943. Killed in action, January 9, 1945, in Lingayen Bay, the Philippines, as a member of the Maritime Advanced Fighting Unit. Army shipping cadet. He was twenty-three years old.

—My Will—

Death is truly life's deepest abyss, and it must always be kept in any person's heart. I would think, however, that it is imperative—when one is actually facing it—for this focus to be renewed and reinforced.

As I look back over the twenty-some years since I was first given life on this earth, I see that I have been showered with the very greatest and most loving favors that heaven and earth had to offer, but also that I have not done anything in particular in return for all that.

For the sake of everything that existed only for me, I do not wish to die in vain. I shall walk deliberately and single-mindedly along the path of requiting all the kindnesses and favors I have received.

November 1943   Haruo Unagami

[The author's last writing, jotted down in pencil on a "memo" just before
        he left on a sortie, January 1945, Luzon Island]
To my dear Father and Mother:

In high spirits and good health, I am heading out to my assigned position. [In spite of everything,] Haruo is and has been truly a student after all—in every sense of the term.

Haruo

PART
III

—Losing the War—

On August 15, 1945, Japan's war of aggression ended in defeat, leaving scars among the peoples of the affected countries that would not easily be healed. Additionally, both Japanese servicemen and civilians were made to suffer intense pain and such hardships as the atomic bombs, detainment, and a variety of other things. It was only a short period after Japan embraced —with the Preface and Article 9 of the New Constitution—the hope for a lasting peace that the Korean Crisis arose, and it was in this situation that the people's determination never again to take part in any wars gave birth to *Kike Wadatsumi no Koe*. Through reading and under-standing the causes and results of the tragedy of "Wadatsumi," i.e., the tragedy of those fallen students, we wish to face and accept "the entire Japanese people's at least remote responsibility" for permitting that war of aggression.

Minoru Suzuki

Born October 19, 1924. From Aichi Prefecture. From the Eighth Higher School, entered Tokyo Imperial University, Faculty of Jurisprudence, October 1944. On October 10, 1944, he entered the Toyohashi First Army Reserve Officer's Cadet School. He suffered injury from the Hiroshima Atomic Bomb, on August 6, 1945, and died at Ōno Army Hospital, August 25, 1945. Army sub-lieutenant. He was twenty years old.

—Will—

Dear Father and Mother: Please forgive me for having failed to fully live up to the duties of filial piety. Just when I was at last ready to be a good son to both of you and live up to my filial duties from now on, I have to fall short. I have always been most appreciative and grateful to you for your generosity in allowing me, despite our poor financial situation, to go on to the Eighth Higher School and from there to Tokyo Imperial University. I have caused you a lot of worry since my school days, and I am truly sorry and deeply regret that just now I have suffered such a serious injury—at that very point in my life when I was about ready to begin to make some returns on your kindness and all you have done for me.

Both my older sister and younger sisters were considerate enough to put aside the idea of getting married, and instead they are helping you out and teaching grade-school children at the same time. I cannot find any words that would adequately express my gratitude to them.

Father and Mother, you have always toiled so endlessly, getting up so very early in the morning with the moon still in the sky, and working away so steadily and hard until the stars twinkled at night—all in order to send me as far as the university. No appropriate apology is possible now. I am so sad that I am dying without returning all the kindness and everything else you did for me, while all I did was to cause so much hardship for you. However, my dear Father and Mother, I am thinking that, even though my body dies, my spirit will always be in front of the *butsudan* (family Buddhist altar)—and it will be protecting you all, my beloved parents and sisters. When I become transformed into a spirit, I fully intend to serve all of you in filial piety, so please do not cry. As a spirit, I shall always be with you, will work together with you, eat together with you, and share laughter and sorrow together with all of you. Soon another autumn will arrive and you will hear hundreds of insects singing, and even when winter comes and the leaves are gone and the forest looks lonely—even then please do not cry. Regardless of whatever kind of situation you may be called upon to face, please take really good care of yourselves, deal with matters firmly and with conviction, and live on and on in good health.

Dear Father and Mother, the atomic bomb that was dropped the other day, on the 6th, was an extremely powerful one, and I suffered extremely severe burns on my face, back, and left arm. But I have received the kindest care possible under the hands of the attending army doctors, nurses, and friends, and I feel very fortunate to die while being attended by the utmost care.

Minoru Suzuki

August 25, 1945. Nine o'clock in the evening
   To my Mother and Father

Tsutomu Takagi

Born January 7, 1922. Hometown unknown. Graduated from the College Division of the Tokyo University of Commerce (Hitotsubashi University), September 1943. Entered the army, December 1943, and sent to the war front in Northern China. He met the defeat of the war in Hamhung, North Korea, en route south from Peking, 1945. Died on February 25, 1946, in Yenchi Pingcheng Hospital, Chilin Province, Northern China. Army sergeant major. He was twenty-four years old.

August 17, 1945

Worked on the last part of winding up the committee's [postwar] unfinished business, [i.e., cleaning up after Japan's surrender]. I heard the voice of independence surging throughout the Korean Peninsula. Public feeling is in turmoil everywhere. Local people are to be found loitering in groups, and usually talking very stridently. Itō has returned from Hungnam (in North Korea). Going out alone on official business is now prohibited. The food allotment is to be two and a half meals, standard portion. One rumor had it that the Soviet troops were on the way. I also heard another rumor about a Soviet destroyer entering the port of Hungham. At the government office, we burnt all the important documents and others as well. The history of the military has now come to an end.

A shower of sparks, and then more sparks are sucked up into the blue-black skies. A mix of half-burnt documents, some new and unopened accounting books, and assorted other new office supplies were smoldering in a dug-out pit. I stirred them up with a long pole, and more sparks flew up. Smoke and flames also shot up from other pits that had been dug around the garden.—It all made for an extremely ghastly *finale*, and a grief too deep for tears.

August □□ [The date is indecipherable.]

Soviet troops have arrived, and the Korean people received them with great cheer. In Yamato-cho I saw two officers passing by in a sedan. A Soviet flag flew alongside the Korean independence flag atop the public hall. (I burned all my personal possessions into a heap of ashes—my diary, and all the letters from my mother and from my younger brother and sister. My past is now dead.)

September 21

....

Our agreement is just for the moment: we will never waste time by worrying over either the past or the future. Solutions will come only if we can manage to maintain a kind of guarded optimism.—That is one of the basic requirement for happiness. In the sort of situation in which we find ourselves false rumors are flying around constantly; perhaps as many as ninety percent of them are ghosts of optimistic views. The next step is to build a castle of faint hope on that *grund* [foundation, in German, in his original]—a foundation usually made up of rumors so false that they do not even have a single ounce of validity. And, again, this castle too will be destroyed from the foundation up by more false and this time the pessimistic rumors from a questionable source.

After a while, another and an equally meaningless and ineffective construction will begin to arise, put together with pieces picked up amid the ruins of that destroyed castle. This might well be the side-effect of a psychological stance that people in our predicament cannot help but assume. Whatever the case, it would be difficult to imagine a more foolish waste of energy. We do not believe rumors. And we distinguish microcephalic activities, such as imagination, supposition, and judgment. We simply accept those facts which are confirmed, and we accept the resultant situation whether we like it or not. Whatever is going to happen will happen. The only invariable is any order that has been issued. What we have to do is to act in accordance with that order, and then wait for the next one. It is not necessary to do anything or to think about anything else, simply because we have essentially been deprived of all personal power. What we have to master thoroughly is to take on the hearts of sheep as our own. Just eat grass until you are chased out to the next pasture. This is an obvious attitude [for us to adapt for survival]. Until recently the three of us—Itō, Tanzawa, and myself—accepted this idea as our own, and since then we have also joined forces with Satō and Matsutani. I concentrated on instilling this sheep mentality into them. I am not certain about how effective I was, but at least we were able to maintain reasonable poise and emotional tranquillity, and fortunately everything went well. One might go so far as to say that things went just as well as we expected them to, insofar as we have gotten into the habit of always believing that "whatever circumstances we happened to be in were the best possible."

What good would it do if one were constantly to be looking back over the path he has taken, or regretting one or another of the actions he has taken in the past? Or what good would it do either to envy other units or other individuals' circumstances or actions, or to survey one's surroundings with pessimistic eyes and a discontented spirit? Given his limited powers, it is impossible for a human being to return once again to his starting point and to plot out an altogether different course of action.

We have a rule among ourselves that, if anyone ever says something foolish like "I should have done such and such," he receives a severe penalty from one of us other two. We also prohibit remarks such as "Oh, how I wish I could go home soon." We do this because our return home is a virtual certainty and is only a matter of time, and also because it has become known that the actual order instructing us to leave is expected quite soon. In light of all this, careless words such as those mentioned above would not serve a constructive purpose, but would instead make our homesickness worse; and it would not do anything but throw us into a depressed atmosphere, and waste precious time as well. Whenever we feel homesickness sprouting, it has to be squashed before it advances any further. It is absolutely necessary for the sake of our happiness (as in Alan's words) to prevent anyone—and especially when it is just a matter of childish impatience—from disturbing other team members' emotional stability.

A human being is an animal that does a lot of regurgitation or rumination. When there is nothing else to do—and our current life is typical of that—our heads somehow begin to ruminate and ponder over things. Any ruminating about homesickness is the worst thing you can possibly do. Remembering and imagining things connected with one's beautiful hometown is different from rumination, however. But, this can produce depressive rumination when it focuses on that part of the reality which cannot immediately be attained.

This is the reason that being in the condition of not having anything to do is not good. So we have to come up with a project of our own. It would be the best if we could find books, but there are no books here. So we busy ourselves with mending such things as pants, shirts, and backpacks. We make vests. We make waistbands. We make haversacks. And make chopsticks and spoons. We roll cigarettes and write notes. By keeping ourselves as busy as possible in these various ways, we more or less manage to forget almost everything else.—These are very good ways to avoid that endless and terrible brooding.

The three of us have all made playing cards, and we wear them hung on our hips wherever we go. Whenever we become bored we play cards. The playing of games, and particularly of games that arouse the competitive urge, is the best medicine against all that brooding and pondering. I am keeping the cards as a kind of amulet for happiness, and I am planning to take them home as a reminder of what life was like here.

October 24 Clear very strong wind and severely cold

An enormously powerful wind was blowing when I woke up, and the trees both in the back mountain and the schoolyard were screaming in pain. The sky is still roaring. The school building is squeaking as though it were terror-stricken.

"Darn it! In a gale like this the ocean would be too rough for a ship to be able to sail."

"It is brutally cold, and more of the same type of weather is gradually coming on. Hey, if we were left here until the New Year, we would all be dead, I am sure."

The people who woke up in the next *han* (squad) started talking quietly. Their voices, mixed with the sound of the wind, carried a strangely ominous tone of despair. All of a sudden I became unsure of what the future would hold and began to feel rather irritated. And at that very moment, I imagined myself placed in this temporary hospital in the middle of a winter.—There is no heat; it is a large and empty room; and the wind is coming through any and every opening. The severe cold comes right through the plain plank floor regardless of how many blankets I cover myself with. Moreover, there is nothing to eat, and no calorie intake. So my body turned thoroughly cold inside and out, and I could barely stand the penetrating stomach pains. All day long I keep going to the toilet, more than a dozen times, and the condition of my illness becomes truly desperate. There is no medicine, no one pays any attention, and I am left alone. Nobody even comes even when I call for help. The only person around is a Soviet soldier with a machine gun, intent only on stealing our private possessions.

In such ways ill-omened imaginings rise up one after another and run wildly through my head. I tell myself: "Oh, no! Idiot! That cannot be. Is there any dark evidence anywhere indicating that we will be held here until next year? We doubtless will be leaving soon regardless. Stop imagining. . . . No matter what, I must somehow be included on the next ship's boarding list. All right, it does not matter what my physical condition may be, I am going to use some excuse to get on that ship. So long as I can count on reaching Japan proper, I will survive. But what if I should fail to get on the next ship, what then? Then this imagination will become reality." When I at least partially convinced myself by telling myself that, my emotions came a little more under control.—Once again the wind is blowing and howling along.

October 28 Clear and cold

It seems I have caught a cold. I had better pay attention to it.

For three days—October 25, 26, and 27—life was like running the same scene from a film over and over. There is no indication whatever of us doing any moving. Even Hanchō (squad leader) Satō is beginning to say: "I really wish I could go home!"

During these periods when there is nothing to do, the conversations are all about who wants to eat this and who wants to eat that. People say such things as: "When I get home, I am going to eat *daifuku* (rice-cakes stuffed with sweet bean jam)!" Imagining ourselves biting off a big chunk of *daifuku* or *ankoro* (rice-cakes covered with sweet bean jam) when we get there, we say again: "Oh how I want to go home!"

So I came up with an idea, i.e., to make a cookbook out of everything we want to eat; afterward, when we get home, we can take this book out and cook whatever we feel like eating. I began to work on a "how-to-cook" piece myself, the idea gained an instant popularity, and the whole thing started to take on the feel of a seminar. Each of us took turns pretending to be either a chef, cook, or apprentice, and we played out the roles all day long as though we were actually cooking. As if he had the real thing right in front of him, each speaker very enthusiastically explained what he was doing; likewise, and as if they were eating the real thing—eyes shining and jaws working—the audience did their parts as well. Just imagine that scene! The irony was that the whole idea of homesickness had been at least temporarily banished. But, somehow I, the very person who had come up with the cooking scheme in the first place, began to get tired of it. From morning to night—and backed up by his experience of being a street vendor in Tokyo—Mr. Y comes round to sell us whatever imaginary food we want. He does this without letup, and seems to be self-intoxicated over the business. Thanks to his carryings-on, my brain suffers from an acid indigestion.

(Some news just came that we wanted to hear, news according to which that certain female Russian doctor came and asked our own doctor how many of us were healthy enough to travel. A spontaneous cheer went

up, and the whole situation is like that of a drowning man grabbing at anything, even a straw.) I wonder about and am afraid of what is going to happen if and when everybody gets tired of this cookbook business.
....

Mitsuo Inagaki

Born March 12, 1924. From the Tokyo Metropolis. From Tokyo Higher School, entered Tokyo Imperial University, Faculty of Jurisprudence, October 1943. Entered the Navy Accounting School, October 1944. Died at National Numazu Hospital, June 22, 1947. Navy first lieutenant. He was twenty-three years old.

[Translators' note: The following poems are all haiku, 5–7–5 syllables, but the first two do not contain any word indicating a season which is a requirement of a genuine haiku, and yet are too serious in subject to be a senryū which requires no word of a season.]

—Coming Home—
A repatriated son, carrying a thought that
    has not been spoken—even to his late mother

At the tomb of my dear mother—her child has a doubt.
    So, his return has only been reported.

In a dream dreamt in the chill of dawn, the longing for
    my departed mother was in vain.

—Autumn Night—
In the capital city, with a lone white star,
    my baby sister lives

I eat a chestnut, and my home thoughts
    grow even stronger

—A Twenty-Third—and Lonely—Autumn—
In bed on a very cold night,
    pulling the spread over my head, I shed tears
It is so cold, an arm and an arm,
    each embraces the other.

The "X" of Gaffky[1] is sorrowful, in the darkness
   by the young leaves [growing outside the window]

Feeling so lonely, I let the raindrops
   put out my cigarette

January 13, 1947 Monday Clear
   10 o'clock in the evening.
   Mr. Nishijima's condition has worsened and he can no longer talk,
but his mind is quite clear. He is a man marked for death soon; indeed its
shadow has already enveloped him.
   The shadow of death too ought to be a happy one.
   We should all share our happiness with one another, but that is so
difficult to grasp.
   Everyone has died away.
   These are the only things I think about. Is it because I am superficial,
or . . . ?

May 17 Saturday Clear, and later gradually cloudy
   The chief physician stopped by this morning to tell me that there is a
cavity in the apex of my right lung. To say the very least, this is an
extremely important matter. I was even able to face that terrible shock
with relative calm (despite the fact that those two full years of medical
treatment turned out to have been undergone completely in vain. Worse,
those years turned out in fact to have been of a negative value.) Since I
could not sleep last night, I kept thinking all these things over until deep
into the night. At just about the time I was on the verge of falling asleep,
I was thinking that I would not marry all my life, that I must resolve not to
think of my own pain, and that I wanted to continue to live on for the sake
of those who are even worse off than I am. Maybe it was that type of
thinking that helped me to handle today's shocking news so surprisingly
well. Anyway, my hope had been to return to the university, but that too
has now become impossible.—In the morning, for a little while, I simply
covered my cheeks in the white pillow and endured the sorrow.

June 19
   Surgery tomorrow.—Thoughts about my attachment to life and the
immense amount of work that still awaits me.

---

[1] Gaffky indicates the degree of advancement in a tubercular condition, and "x"
underlines the extreme seriousness of such a condition.

I must conquer my illness and regain an active life.

In this present state of confusion, I must find some order and put a certain rhythm into my life.

Once upon a time I felt such great pleasure in taking on the entrance examinations [for the higher school and the university] simply because I was so confident of passing them successfully.

Energy. Affirmation. Creation. I welcome pains [if only I could have them].

Hisao Kimura

Born April 9, 1918. From Ōsaka Metropolitan Prefecture. From the Kōchi Higher School, entered the Kyoto Imperial University, Faculty of Economics, April 1942. Entered the barracks, October 1, 1942. Executed as a war criminal at Changi Prison, Singapore, on May 23, 1946. Army superior private. He was twenty-eight years old.

I obtained this book quite accidentally only a few days before my death, so I wanted to read it just once more before the end [Translators' note: The reference is to *Tetsugaku Tsūron (Introduction to Philosophy)* by Hajime Tanabe.—Everything that follows was written along the margins of this book.] I remember when I read the book for the first time. It was some four or five years ago, in my study; now I am reading it under the shadow of death and on a "concrete bed," thinking of my home so far away and going over my past in general. Even though I shall perish on the scaffold within a few days, it is nice to reflect once more on how my passion has always been for the pursuit of learning and truth.

When I am reading this book like this, there is a genuine pleasure that springs out from somewhere. Even though I may die on the scaffold tomorrow, I am attracted to the book with an insatiable interest. This will be my third time through it.—April 22, 1946.

Yes, I am able to understand this work quite well. Especially since it is known for being an extremely difficult book to grasp, and in spite of the fact that I have already been away from the world of academia for four years, I feel grateful that my mind is still able to handle it without much difficulty. Whenever I look back, as I do now, on my past life of studies and see how earnestly I went about cultivating myself, I feel very pleased that my life as a student was so enjoyable and meaningful an experience.

I shall be transcribing, in fragments, my thoughts on facing death. Since now I am not allowed to write anything down on paper, there is no other way except to write on this book.

I was given a death sentence, and who would ever have expected it? Who could ever have foretold my fate, that I would have to leave this world in the midst of my studies, not yet thirty years of age? My life has been filled with plenty of turbulence, but this time the turbulence is so violent it seems I shall perish in it. I even feel in my own mind that I am reading fiction. Once I realized, however, that even this was something dictated by my fate, the final sense of resignation came flowing out. When I realized further that there had been countless numbers of people, people just like me, who were sacrificed behind the scenes at every important turning point in history, my sense was that even my death, which appears to be utterly meaningless, may be the dictate of a greater world history.

Japan was defeated. Sitting squarely in the middle of the entire world's outrage and condemnation, Japan lost the war. When the numerous unreasonable deeds and injustices perpetrated by Japan in the past come to mind, the world's anger seems perfectly natural. Now, therefore, I am going to die as one source of emotional relief for all of humanity. If my death could make the whole human race feel a little calmer, then that would be fine with me, because it would mean that I am leaving behind a seed for the happiness of the Japan of the future.

I have never done any deed so evil as to warrant execution. There were indeed others who committed evil deeds. In my particular situation, however, any thought of exoneration is out of the question. My case involves something more like "taking revenge in Nagasaki for a wrong done in Edo," [i.e., taking one's revenge in a manner entirely unrelated to the original crime, or to the original offender]. At any rate, and at least from the world-at-large's point of view, the guilty ones and I are both—and equally—Japanese. For me to die by assuming responsibility for what they did certainly seems totally irrational, but, since such irrationality is precisely what the Japanese have in the past too often forced upon others, I would not be so bold as to complain about that now. There is no place to which I can take my grievance; all I can do is to consider myself unfortunate for having been picked out as an example. I could not die peacefully if I considered my death as a sacrifice for the deeds of Japan's Military, but I would not be so upset if I thought that I—my single self—was shouldering alone all the sins committed by the

Japanese people as a whole, as well as all the criticism that has been leveled against them.—Then I could die with a smile on my face.

With regard to this case also, there were many career army officers who conducted themselves in the most despicable manner possible. By comparison, the behavior of naval officers was much more respectable by far.

At my trial, and even after the verdict was handed down, I always did my very best to prove my innocence, but I ended up having to accept the condemnation even though I was totally innocent. It was all just because I had worked much too hard for Japan. The same applies to those *gunshin* (military gods, i.e., war heroes)* who gave their lives in Hawaii and now are nothing but war criminals and violators of international law. My offense was the discovery of an enemy spy in the Nicobar Island Garrison, a discovery which I was showered with the whole army's appreciation for making, including compliments from superior officers. There was even talk at the time of my receiving a special award from the regional military unit,* but because of Japan's surrender only one month later things suddenly turned around. What had originally been viewed as a great and meritorious deed performed on my country's behalf has latterly turned out to be my ruin, simply because the standards of judgment have changed so dramatically. Japan's surrender was something that was necessary for all of its people, however, and so the sacrifice of an individual like myself just has to be endured. The sole target of any complaint I might make would be the military that started this war, knowing very well that there was no way it could be won. But once again if we consider matters further, we must recognize the fact that there is a remote possibility that a certain share must be owned up to by the entire Japanese people. It was the Japanese people, after all, who tolerated the military and who allowed them to conduct themselves so outrageously following the Manchurian Incident.

I imagine that our people are currently going through a period of great self-reflection. This process, taken in conjunction with today's generally adverse state of affairs, will eventually be seen to have played a significant role in preparing for a brighter Japan in the future. I regret that I have to die without witnessing all this, but there is nothing I can do about it. From every conceivable aspect—socially, historically, politically, ideologically, and humanistically—Japan was hopelessly unequipped to deal with the situations it was thrust into. Our leaders made us believe that we were so superior to all others in everything—but the ultimate responsibility lies in the collective brain of the people who permitted those leaders to exist.

What a problematic attitude had been developed over the course of the past has now become clearly evident, as has what it led to. Anything that did not suit our convenience or our liking was all bad, and therefore it had to be eliminated—and through the power of the Military. Now is the time for all Military power and merely physical strength to be discarded, and it is imperative that we recognize everything correctly, examine everything closely, and make wise evaluations and judgments. This will be the way to bring about our nation's real development.

There is more than ample room for Japan's redevelopment if we re-examine everything from the bottom up. Even though, from just about any standpoint you choose, Japan will inevitably fall into chaos, that will still be all right. From now on Japan will be fortunate where and whenever all kinds of dogmatic ideologies fall to the earth. The day will come when, whether it be Marxism or Liberalism, every system will be thoroughly studied and more or less finally resolved at the level of its fundamental theory. I believe that Japan's true growth will begin from there. I am sad over the fact that all this fabulous development will take place after I am no longer around to see it, but there will be someone—someone who is a better man and more brilliant—to replace me who will see it and will lead the Japanese people. Whatever happens, Japan has to change from its foundations up and must be restructured. I only hope and pray that the young students will play important roles.

Please allow Kōko to marry soon. What I am most afraid of is that, because of my death, my parents and younger sister could become so extremely despondent that the whole family might decline and fall. Dear Father, Mother, and Sister, please do not let this be your reaction. My hope for you all is that you will live cheerfully and in peace.

Our guards are Dutch soldiers who were once prisoners of war under the Japanese. Their treatment of us is quite severe and is actually a form of revenge, since, as they say, they were treated so terribly by our own soldiers. Beating us up or kicking us are a few of the milder forms of their harassment, but I cannot complain once I reflect on the fact that Japanese soldiers probably did the same to them, if not worse. Army officers comprise the majority of the chronic grumblers and whiners among us. Such an attitude involves setting aside the unacceptability of their own past conduct, and even the rest of us, their fellow Japanese and fellow prisoners, cannot stand such hypocrisy. It is really regrettable that I, who have never on any occasion either been in charge of or mistreated a single prisoner, should in this kind of a place be handled in the same way as the guilty ones. So far as my captors are concerned, however, I am just another Japanese, and perhaps asking them to distinguish between us might not be altogether reasonable. Taking everything into consideration, the most fortunate thing is that I personally have never been beaten or kicked. I am in fact quite well liked by everyone. We get two meals a day: a rice powder paste in the morning and rice gruel in the evening. We are very hungry all day long and we have barely enough energy to drag ourselves along. Perhaps because they like me, however, my guards are kind enough to secretly bring me things such as a piece of bread, a biscuit, or a cigarette at night. Last night one of them even brought me a bottle of cider. I was so touched that I had tears in my eyes—not because of the things they give me, but for the kindness behind the giving. One of the guards told me that he might be going to Japan as a member of the Allied Occupation Forces, so I gave him a letter today with my home address in it. The guards in general are very sympathetic and treat me kindly. They look upon me as an innocent man who is being brought up on false charges. As a group, of course, they are extremely anti-Japanese, but, on the level of individual interaction against that background, there are some who show me real kindness.—I think the bottom line is that we are all human beings.

This soldier in particular who had a been prisoner under the Japanese told me about all sorts of atrocities that he had witnessed, and suffered, during that time—things like getting beaten, kicked, and even burned. He said that he was simply unable to fathom just how his captors could do what they did in cold blood. It seems that he was also puzzled by the comparatively low status of Japanese women.

I inhale a breath, I exhale, I eat a spoonful of rice-gruel—each one of these things, in my predicament now, puts me in touch with the reality of this world. One man yesterday, and two today, were sent out to perish on the gallows. Soon, in a few days, a call will come for me too. These are my senses' last experiences, the last time I can really feel this world. These are things I never paid any attention to in the past, but now I am truly amazed that, the more things I taste, the more keen a taste each of them has. Each spoonful of rice that I put into my mouth gives an indescribable stimulus to my tongue, and I feel it going down from my throat as though it were melting away—all the way down to my stomach. I experience this feeling so firmly and full that, with my eyes closed, I feel as if all the innumerable, complex contents of this world are contained in this one sense. Sometimes I feel like crying. But right now there is no psychological placidity to shed tears. Once a human being is pushed to the last extremity, there is no anger left, no disappointment, no tears. The only thing he can do is to be appreciative of every moment he has left, and to take things as they come. Whenever I give any thought to the moment of my death, I most definitely sink deep into a fearful and unpleasant mood, but I am determined not to think more about it until the moment itself arrives. And I counsel myself—and console myself—by thinking that death might perhaps come rather easily if, once the moment does arrive, I consider myself already dead.

I accidentally and quite unexpectedly got hold of this book a few days ago, and wanted to read it just one more time before I died. Several years go, when I was a young student with a keen interest in searching out the fundamental principles of social science, I found that this masterpiece of Mr. Tanabe's was a great help. I remember that, since the book was well known as an extremely difficult work to tackle, I was determined to persevere in reading it through despite the tremendous effort and labor it took. At the time I was working in a study-parlor in Rakuhoku Shirakawa (northern Kyoto), but presently I am in Singapore, so far away from home—and do my reading nowadays on a cold concrete bed in a prison. To be able to read this book once again just what seems moments before closing out the chapter of my life is something that has given me a great last pleasure, an emotional respite, and, not least of all, a renewed passion. My latest reading of this book has only taken place after a few full years of a non-scholarly life, and, whether correctly or not, I felt as though in its every line I had rediscovered the old image of myself—a young man burning with ambition—and I was shaken by the strong emotion that accompanied truly affectionate memories. A real masterpiece is something that simultaneously implants a burning passion and peace of mind in the reader, regardless of where the reader might happen to be at any particular time, and equally regardless of any predicament in which he might find himself. You might say that I read the book in a single breath, putting aside any personal, goal-oriented desires. Then I read it over once again. It was so utterly refreshing that no words could describe that sensation. It gave me a feeling comparable to the one generated by the Buddhist Sutra-chanting before death. It was not like that joy of long ago which was mixed with such an ambitious and burning passion for pursuing the truth. Rather, the feeling it gave me this time was something beyond any and all adjectives, a truly reviving feeling that is outside the realm of words. I am leaving this book after my death as a kind of unwritten will and as the most suitable remembrance of me—as something that would in a way symbolize me. I am not saying that I totally understand all the philosophy and meta-physics in this work; it may even be that what I do understand may be quite far from its real content. What I really want to say is that the mood Mr. Tanabe must have been in when he picked up a pen to write this book coincides exactly with the mood or feeling that I have been searching for all my life.—That is the reason I wish to leave this book behind as something that best symbolizes me.

Perhaps many of my professors and classmates will grieve for me and think kind thoughts when they hear the news of my death. They will be sad and say in loving thought that "he could certainly have become such a great scholar," and so on. But even if I could live for a long time—if that life were to have been spent as just an ordinary person, then perhaps dying now is the happier alternative. To end my life now, while still maintaining the purity of a young scholar and without being completely soiled by worldly desires and greed, may be the more beautiful and honorable thing. Naturally, of course, I would like to continue my long journey in pursuit of the truth, but, from the standpoint of the gods, perhaps it would be better for me to die now, as my fate commands. Even if, in the final analysis, all my studying amounts to nothing more than just piling up so much reading, this pure passion that I feel today might turn out to be the highest achievement of my entire life.

I did everything I possibly could in order to stay alive, and also to prove my innocence. My superior officers strictly forbade me against making any true statement before the court, and, as a result, those same men, who ordered me, ended up being sentenced to imprisonment at hard labor while I, who had to follow their commands, was given the death penalty. This is clearly unreasonable, and I reflected on the fact that my life would represent, many times over, a greater contribution to Japan's future than the lives of those officers who issued orders. Judging from the facts surrounding just this one case, it is quite obvious that the blame ought to have been placed upon the officers; they absolutely forbade me to reveal the facts, because they were fully aware of what the consequences of such a revelation would be. I thought that staying alive would be my natural right and would also be the right thing to do for the sake of Japan as a nation; moreover, I looked at it as a last act of filial piety. So even though the verdict had already been rendered, I appealed to the authorities by writing out an account of the whole incident, in English. Because the verdict had already been rendered, and also because there is no appeal after this type of trial, I had no idea whether or not my exposé on what exactly had happened would be taken seriously. Neither did I know whether or not the investigation would be taken any further—I just had to try, had to make one last, best effort. In the beginning, I reluctantly obeyed my superiors' order to present false testimony, simply because I thought I had no choice and also because I hoped my obedience might help all the Japanese people. The end result, however, turned out to be quite contrary to my expectation: aside from bringing harm to all of us who followed the orders, nothing was accomplished. For that reason, and even though it was probably too late to do any good, I had to reveal the facts in their entirety. If what I had to say was taken seriously, perhaps several colonels, lieutenant colonels, and majors, as well as several officers of "*i*" rank (captains, lieutenants, and sub-lieutenants), would be subject to death sentences, but that is the way it ought to be, and, based on the facts, that is precisely what they deserve. And, also, were my life to be exchanged for their deaths, I firmly believe that from the national point of view it would be many times more beneficial for Japan. While they may have used beautiful phrases and high-sounding words that lacked substance—their version of so-called "spiritual" language—those military men were essentially nothing but embodiments of vanity, material desires, and lust for fame. Supposing that in the future they will continue with the same lifestyle they have pursued in the past, I am convinced that it is more than obvious that they will never do anything that would benefit the country. Maybe there were some great men among Japan's career military class, but there were not many among those whom I personally observed. To sum up, even among the generals there was no one whose personal character could match up with that of any individual professor at my higher school. There are quite a few generals and colonels among the prison population with whom I have lived together. Once stripped of their fancy uniforms, however, as of course in prison they had to be, their conduct—whether one was listening to them or just watching them—was utterly disgusting and unbearable. It made me think that, with these sorts of men as generals and leaders, Japan could never have won the war even if it had unlimited scientific and material resources. Our career military men, particularly after the Manchurian Incident (*cf.* p. 10), and even more so after Japanese occupation of the southern territories, reached lower and lower levels of mean disposition, even lower than that on which those merchants operated whose single daily task was chasing after profits. Where did those former ones stow away that "loyalty to the nation" and "spirit of sacrifice" they shouted about so much? When the war was over and their outer plumage had been removed, the true color of their own skins was revealed and was so absolutely disgusting that no one could stand looking at it.

But the Japanese people must accept the fact that not only did they tolerate these military men before criticism of the military became popular—they actually and actively supported them. The ultimate responsibility, in the long run, rests upon the shallowness of the Japanese people's collective intelligence. And of course this shallowness of intelligence translates into the shallowness of Japanese history. We can say that Japan has some 2600 years of recorded history, but we cannot afford to brag about that history from the standpoint of length alone—if quality of content is poor in a nation's history. If someone said that Japan was lacking both in training and experience as a modern nation today, he would not be punished by the military as a traitor any more as in the past.

My life as a student, which may have appeared to be rather rebellious, was nothing more than a refusal to follow the militaristic trend blindly.

In my experience with the military, the usual thing was for the officers to talk big and to talk loud. Whenever I challenged their thinking, even in the most indirect and gentle manner possible, they would immediately reject the challenge by calling me a "radical liberal." The sins and crimes that I observed in the world of the military were so numerous that, were I to begin listing them here, there would be no end to it. I intend to forget all about them, however, just because even the criminals are, after all, Japanese. But I must say one last thing: They, the military leaders, must apologize in front of the whole nation, just as though they intended to commit *seppuku*, and must exclusively commit what remains of their lives to the service of society.

I must add that those who were most excessive in abusing the Emperor's name, and in using it in vain, were these same military men.

My parents will be so sad about my misfortune; now the war is over at last and I have to die on the gallows. What I am most worried about is that my parents may be so bewildered that they will become despondent. When I think about it, though, I have been very lucky indeed in fighting through this war. I was in the forefront of the fighting on the Indian Ocean, when the enemy's opposition was most fierce, and many times I resigned myself to the fact that I was going to die. Despite all this, until now I have lived through it all without receiving even the slightest injury. I am most grateful to the gods for having protected me so well up until now, and instead of crying over my bad luck I want to face death showing my gratitude to them for their protection.—Dear Father and Mother, please do not cry either. Just consider that I have been fortunate to live as long as I have. That is what I too wish to believe and how I want to face death.

Unexpectedly, I have just picked up some petty gossip. They say that there will be a reduction in the number of those items that are used to designate men as war criminals, and also that a considerable reduction in penalties is expected for those of us who have already been sentenced. Several days ago I heard from a guard that a change has been made in the rules, to the effect that soldiers who can be proven to have acted upon what they were ordered to will not be penalized. With this in mind, I started to have a faint hope, but I have a gut feeling that, looking at things from an end-result standpoint, such developments just amount to small waves washing over a process that eventually leads to death. I am writing about this particularly because I wanted to get on record the fact that, until he reaches his last moment, a human being has to go through a whole range of emotional discord. Even when human beings accept and are resigned to the fact of death, the attachment to life is still very difficult to break off.

A Payment Inspector (or, Accounting Major) named Minoru Uchida, who was the navy's Chief Paymaster in the Andamans [an island group in the Bay of Bengal] was truly a great man. Before he was even thirty years of age he had been a brilliant graduate of the Tokyo University of Commerce [currently Hitotsubashi University]. What an irony it was that, so far as human character is concerned, the vast majority of our high-ranking officers were so far inferior to this comparatively humble accounting officer, a graduate of a commerce university! I have to wonder whether or not the whole nation might be in a somewhat similar situation [i.e., a situation wherein inferior types are set over finer grades of people]. All this made me keenly aware, in this matter of personal character, of the huge difference there is between those who have come through the processes of reading, thinking—and so much deep, personal reflection—and those who have not.

The image of my grandmother in Hitotsuya, who did so much for me in spite of all the troubles I caused her, has always been carved deep in my heart, even when I was a little child. An important prayer and hope that I always kept deep in my heart was that I might one day be able to repay her for her kindness.—It was the first thing I wanted to do when I grew up. But now I must leave this world before that dear grandmother of mine. To be unable to fulfill my most important promise to myself is one of the biggest regrets I leave behind. My hope is that, by one way or another, my younger sister Kōko will somehow realize this desire of mine for me. I have never mentioned this before, but, now that I am facing death, I would particularly like to get it out in the open.

With regard to things such as my funeral, please make it simple. Simply burying my remains will do. Doing it in a grandiose manner would be contrary to my wish. I would like my tombstone to stand up like my late grandmother's. As a child, I wondered whose tomb would be the next to be placed alongside her brand-new tombstone. I never expected it to be mine, though. Do you remember how far we could see from there—Suita Broadcasting Building [Suita City, Osaka Metropolitan Prefecture], a switch-yard, and the whole panorama? I also remember how, when I visited there in the evening during the *Bon* [the Buddhist Lantern Festival] season, we would watch from a distance the fireworks that were set off in a remote flower garden. When I return home [coming back to the Bon Festival after death], I will sit in front of the tombstone and eat persimmon fruit to my heart's content. Instead of the traditional graveyard flowers, please place some colorful Western flowers—dahlias and tulips, for instance—both before our *butsudan* [family Buddhist altar to pray at home] and in front of my tombstone. The reason for this is because those colorful Western flowers symbolize what is in my heart and, especially after my death, I wish to continue to go on ever more happily and cheerfully. Finally, please also place a lot of delicious French pastries there. The *butsudan* as I remember is just too quiet: I want mine to be more cheerful and bright. Perhaps this will be seen as contrary to the conventional Buddhist way, but since I am the one who is becoming a Buddha it should be all right for me to make such a request, do you not agree?

As for my other personal wishes, would you please celebrate my birthday—April 9—in front of the *butsudan* instead of the day of my death? I want to forget all about the day I die. I only hope and pray that the only day which will stay in our memory is my birthday.

Of all my life, the time to be most commemorated is August of 1939. It was then that, for the first time, I opened a social science book in the valley of Omogo in Shikoku: It was also the occasion for my first feeling just how the dignity and serenity of *gakumon*—pursuit of the truth—could be. And it was then I restarted life as a human being possessed of a full awareness of his humanity.—Any deep emotional life that I have been fortunate enough to experience dates from that point in time.

The person whom I am trusting to bring this book home to my parents is Colonel Ueda. He was the head of the civil government of Car Nicobar [an island in the Nicobar Islands, southeast Bay of Bengal], and is a man who has been extremely kind to me over the past two years. All the other officers treated soldiers just like slaves and never paid any real attention to them, but Mr. Ueda was more than just kind to me; he even treated me with full respect for my personal character. I have never received a scolding from him, and he treated me more as a college student than as a soldier. Had I not been lucky enough to have met him, my life in the Nicobars would have been even more miserable than it was. Just like other soldiers who were forced to do hard labor on a daily basis, I probably would have sickened and died. It was only thanks to him that, in the Nicobars, I was treated even more courteously than the officers were. I truly owe it all to Mr. Ueda, and nobody else. Father and Mother, you should be grateful to him as well.—To top everything else off, his conduct at the war criminal trial was really remarkable.

I am sending you this book as one of my personal effects, which are to be left behind after my death. I have finished reading it over here at the Changi Prison in Singapore.

Although it only arrived just before my death, this book both gave me the kind of pleasure which words cannot describe and fed my quiet passion for the truth. Somehow, and transcending all emotions, this book was something that shook me and once again woke up my true nature. This is the very last book for me in this world, and having come across it so near the end gave me peace of mind as well as some added meaning to my dry and tasteless existence.—Please do not cry, dear Mother, and neither will I.

It has finally been decided that my sentence should be carried out. Now that the war is over, it seems more than a shame that a life which survived combat must be destroyed now. But at least I am going to die for my country at a time when the path of world history is taking a great turning.—Father and Mother, please resign yourselves to fate by imagining that I was struck by enemy bullets and met a glorious death in action.

As for the details of the incident for which I have been sentenced, please wait to hear them from Captain Eizō Fukunaka. I would really rather refrain from discussing it all here.

Are you well, dear Father and Mother? And are you in good health, [dear little sister] Kōko? Dear Kōko, you are already twenty-two years old, right? I bet that you must already have grown into a lovely young lady. I am truly sorry that I cannot take a look at you now. Please get married soon, and succeed the family line in my place. After all, once I am gone you will be the only one who can carry out the duties of filial piety.

I was brought up with such love and care even though I caused a lot of trouble as a child. Then, and just when I was on the threshold of being able to return all those favors and kindnesses, things fell out the way they have. This is fate on the grand scale, something that individuals such as myself cannot do anything about, and there is absolutely no alternative to resigning myself to it. There are many things I could say if I chose to complain, but it would all be in vain. So I shall not do that. It is the same thing as disappearing without a trace after having been hit by a huge bomb.

When I wait here for my death in this quiet way, scenes from my beloved hometown keep coming back one after another. Even now I can remember so vividly that view of Saidera village I used to have as a child, looking down from the branch family home's peach orchard. Mr. Tani used to fish in the pond below, and, as though it were yesterday, I can still see a certain very lively crucian carp coming up fighting on his fishing line.

What I remember next is of course the city of Kōchi. Since it was where I lived through the most turbulent period in my life—both so far as personal surroundings are concerned as well as ideology—here too my memory is endless. The house in Shin-yashiki, Kōnomori forest, the Kōchi Higher School, the town of Sakai, Ino-no (Ino field), and so on; the memories are running through my mind like a revolving lantern [or: kaleidoscope].

I wonder how the three professors are—Professors Shiojiri [Kimiaki Shiojiri, an ethics scholar, 1901–69], Tokuda, and Yatsunami. I know that they will shed tears for me when they find out what has happened. They were so kind and did so much for me. Had I been able to go on living, there would have been no end to my thinking about them, and what I most regret is having to die in a remote, foreign land without being able to return any of their kindness. I really wish that I could at least live until I develop into a better human being. As I stipulated when I left for the war, I want you to please give all my books to the [Kōchi] Higher School through Prof. Shiojiri, and also to convey my very best wishes to him. Even after my death, I shall always remember and carry with me his teaching and kindnesses. I truly and deeply regret that I was unable to read his book, *Tenbun to Aijō no Mondai (The Issue of Talent and Love)*, not even once, because we are so far off the beaten track here that the book was not accessible.

The emotional state of a human being who has lost all hope is truly strange, and it cannot be described by any one of or every one of the words in this world. That state is a thing that has already passed one step beyond the real world. I can no longer feel any fear of death.

I imagine that, since the surrender, Japan must have changed quite a bit. Ideologically as well as from the standpoint of its politico-economic structure, I suppose the nation will undergo many trials and a whole host of changes, and each area will bear close watching. I regret of course that I will not be personally present in that time and space, but what is happening to the history of the world is far greater. It completely dwarfs such an insignificant existence such as I. No one would even spare a glance at the existence of someone like myself, and what happened to me would be seen as nothing more than the fate of an ant that was crushed in a great mountain-slide. There are many cases just like mine. Those *gunshin* (military gods) who were killed in the war are such, as also are those who perished by the atomic bombs. When I think of situations like this that exist throughout the world, then I can more easily accept my own death. And when I think of all those who have already passed on, then I think that it would be pretentious and that I would owe them apologies for spending any time over considerations of my desire to live. If I did continue to live, perhaps I could become a full-fledged person who would be able to accomplish some good work. Then again, it is possible that I could end up being just an ordinary person. To die as a bud, and without even showing a petal, i.e., blossoming out as a flower does, may itself be a form of existence. Finally, the only thing left for me to do is to die as the gods command.

Death, at long last, has recently become something that is not to be feared so very much. Honestly, it is not a matter of my refusal to face defeat; I think that even people who die of illness would probably, just before death, feel the same way as I do. Only occasionally, and then just for a few seconds or so, my attachment to this world pokes its head in—but soon it disappears. If things keep on this way, I feel certain I can face my death without behaving embarrassingly. When all is said and done, there is no test greater than this [i.e., facing imminent death] during the course of a human being's life.

Now I have no picture of my father, mother, or younger sister, so I greet them every morning and every evening by closing my eyes and remembering their faces from the past.—Would you please close your eyes too and return my greetings in the same way?

I trust that my comrades-in-war, who will soon be being repatriated one after another, will tell you about what happened to me. Whenever you hear from them—and even though it may involve a long trip—please visit those comrades of mine and listen to what they have to say about me. I know that I have not done anything disgraceful, and I also know that, when I die, I shall do so gloriously. Even though I was by no means a paragon of the Japanese Military, I know I have conducted myself well and have never done anything to disgrace myself as a Japanese equipped with the added benefit of a higher education. Yet the fact is that I was given the notoriety—and so unexpectedly—of a war criminal. And I am very much concerned that all this may cause some problem for Kōko's future marriage, or even for the future of the family. Everyone who was stationed in Car Nicobar until the end of the war would know that I am innocent, and all of them would so testify.—Please believe me, and ease your minds.

If, as people say, there should indeed be "that other world," then it is there that I will be able to see my grandparents again, as well as those classmates of mine who were killed in action. I will go there, and will look forward to be talking with them about this world. Again, if what people say is in fact possible, I shall always—even though from behind the scenes—be watching over my father and mother from there, and my younger sister and her family too. Please remember me now and then, even though I may perhaps be a constant reminder of some sad things.—But above and despite all, try to transform your thoughts of me into supplies of courage and strength for getting you through your everyday lives.

My death is set for May 23, 1946.

There is nothing more for me to write. I am leaving for death at last. Please stay well, everyone. Good-bye. Good-bye.

1. I hope for the Japanese Empire's new prosperity.

2. Please stay well, everyone, and thank you so much for everything you did for me during my lifetime.

3. Please give me some water to moisten my lips at death.

4. There will be no remains (i.e., bones) to be shipped home. I will leave my fingernails and hair instead.

[The following poems are *tanka*]:

My heart is sad as I sip the morning rice-gruel,
    Because my life is soon to disappear
            —like southern dew.
As I sip the morning rice-gruel I think of father
        and mother at home;

Do not be grieved, Father,
        and please forgive me, Mother.

Even more than the loneliness attached to dying in a
        foreign land
    is the thought of grieving parents.

While listening to the Buddhist chant for a friend
        who is leaving

    I am counting off with my fingers the days left
            between now and gallows-time.

Biting my finger and in tears I pray to my father
        and mother so far away
    —Good-bye, good-bye!

Closing my eyes, I think of my mother,
            the loving image of her from my childhood
    never disappears—even for a moment.

Even though it left me without a sound,
            I wrote the word down and
    thought about the meaning of "tomorrow."

It was sorrowful when a slight breeze came my way:
    It blew some dust off my sunken heart.

I am holding onto life and ignoring the word "tomorrow"
    —but my heart has not lost the desire to read.

The following two poems were written during the night before the
execution:
    There is neither fear nor sadness; I shall go to the gallows
        with my mother's smiling face in my heart.

The wind has died down and it has stopped raining—
    Tomorrow will come refreshingly
        with the morning sun shining over [me, I] shall go [to the
        gallows.]

                —Written half an hour before the execution.

                        Hisao Kimura

NOTES

* *Gunshin* (military gods) who perished in Hawaii: The members of the special attack force against the American Naval Base at Pearl Harbor. Those who manned special submarines on that first day of the war were given this honorific title.

* A general outline of the structure of the Japanese Army: *Shidan* and *Hōmen-gun:* A *Shidan* (with specific reference to infantry) is an entire Army corps, consisting of five separate sub-elements in the following hierarchical order: *Ryodan - Rentai - Daitai - Chūtai* - and *Shōtai*. [That is, a *Shidan* was composed of *Ryodan*, which was composed of *Rentai*. A *Rentai* was a regiment contained within a division, or *Ryodan*; a *Daitai* was a battalion within a regiment; a *Chūtai* was a company within a battalion; a *Shōtai* was a platoon within a company.] The smallest unit involved in strategic planning was a *Shidan*, and the smallest unit for the actual combat tactics was a *Daitai*. For infantry purposes, the size of a *Shidan* was normally based, as a kind of axis, on the combined strength of two *Ryodan* (consisting of four *Rentai*). In peacetime a *Shidan* might include some 10,000 soldiers, but once war broke out, and by combining a variety of other units such as the artillery, cavalry, the engineering corps, transportation corps, and field hospitals, it would expand to become a huge unit of some twenty to thirty thousand soldiers. After our plunge into the total war between Japan and China in July 1937, a newly formed structure of three-unit *Shidan*, each with three *Rentai* of infantry as the core, became common. A multiple of *Shidan* was *Gun*, and a multiple *Gun* formed a *Hōmen-gun*. Just before the final defeat, a multiple *Hōmen-gun* was, as an emergency measure, organized into a *Sōgun*. The force projected for defending against any enemy landing on the home islands—which it was assumed would take place in the fall of 1945—was to be the First *Sōgun* in the east and the Second *Sōgun* in the west, a total of eighty units of *Shidan* and 3,100,000 men.

POSTSCRIPTS TO THE EARLIER EDITIONS

Postscript to the First Edition
Published in 1949 by the University of Tokyo
Consumer Co-op Publication Department

Nihon Senbotsu Gakusei Shuki Henshū Iinkai
(Committee for the Compilation of the Fallen
Japanese Students' Writings and Notes)

Published in December 1947, *Harukanaru Sanga ni (In Far Away Mountains and Rivers)* was put together by the Tōdai Senbotsu Gakusei Shuki Henshū Iinkai (Committee for the Compilation of the Fallen University of Tokyo Students' Writings and Notes)—itself an organization within the Student Government of the University of Tokyo and was published by the Publication Department of the University of Tokyo Consumer Co-op. It caused all sorts of responses. Falling as its publication did within certain constraints both of time and finance, the work did have one rather significant shortcoming: the material it contained had been produced by the students of only a single university. From the very outset, however, both compilers and publisher had viewed their project as only the foundation for a future and much broader-based compilation, one that would include the letters and notes of fallen students of colleges and universities all over the country.

Since then we have received both critiques and strong encouragement from people everywhere, and it is in the light of these developments that we have a separate committee within the Publication Department—Nihon Senbotsu Gakusei Shuki Henshū Iinkai (Committee for the Compilation of Writings and Notes of the Japanese Students Killed in War) in the Spring of 1948. We have asked Mr. Kazuo Watanabe, Mr. Shin-ichi Mashita, Mr. Hideo Odagiri, and Mr. Tsuneji Sakurai to oversee the collection of material. Helped enormously by the goodwill of a number of organizations, we used the media, both newspapers and radio, to effect a broad solicitation of the posthumous writings produced by fallen students from all the colleges and universities. The result of all this is what you see before you: over three hundred pages that represent the work of seventy-five authors—all selected out of an enormous amount of writing produced by three hundred nine people. Naturally enough, the *Harukanaru Sanga ni* which the whole project grew out of is now out of print, and we have included a few pieces of material from it within the present volume. What we now have is the end product of the total of four years' concentrated effort.

Generally speaking, the contents are arranged in chronological order. We paid special attention to allowing the reader to see how the students' thinking reflected changing conditions during the course of the war; needless to say, we took care to ensure against the addition to that thinking of any post-factum fakery. We divided the entire work into three general sections: (I) the pre-Pacific War; (II) the Pacific War; and (III) the post-defeat period. As a help to the reader, we also added a rather simple chronological table at the end.

Brief biographies of each one of the posthumous authors, some more detailed than others, serve as headnotes to specific selections. An overview containing and connecting more detailed information follows the body of the book, and this same overview does double duty as a table of contents. Following Western tradition, the authors' ages are counted in full years [i.e., in contrast to the traditional Japanese way of counting, whereby everyone becomes a year older each New Year's]. Out of respect for these original writings, the text, so long as it did not cause serious confusions of meaning, is left exactly the way it was written. This procedure was followed even in the cases of the erroneous usage either of Chinese characters or of *kana* syllables so long as it did not confuse meanings.

The title was chosen from a widely publicized contest which received some two thousand entries. The committee chose a submission from Mr. Takio Fujitani of Kyoto, and the poem on the closing leaf is what, along with the title, he sent in at that time. The drawing on the inside cover is a copy of one by Mr. Kiyoshi Sekiguchi, one of the authors in this book, just before he starved to death on Miyako Island.

We were seriously concerned over the possibility that, contrary to what was intended, some contemporary warmongers might misuse the desperate voices that fill this entire book, the voices of those very finest of young men, whose eyes were shielded from the sight of the truth, who were abused, tyrannized, and killed. So we asked Mr. Kazuo Watanabe and Mr. Hideo Odagiri to write a "how-to-read" section for this book. (*cf.* pp. 301f., or 301–8). The reason behind our request for this explanatory addition was a change of trends within Japanese society over the past four years, the very period during which we were working up this volume.

One of the fallen students, Shigenobu Matsubara, left the following words behind: "Should we survive, perhaps there may eventually come a day when we can say that 'Those were very, very long nights, the nights in which it was almost impossible to see a star.'" Our sincere hope and motivation in putting this book together was to help this "day" to become a reality for all the survivors, and as soon as possible.

September 1949

For the New Reader of This Book
(For the edition published by Kōbun-sha Kappa-books, 1959)

Hideo Odagiri

This book was first published exactly ten years ago by the Publication Department of the University of Tokyo [Consumers] Co-op. During the course of this decade Japan has undergone a very real transformation. Today's younger generation has experienced particularly marked changes over that period of time. Those young students who were the readers of ten years ago were people whose memories of the war were still very vividly carved in their hearts and indeed under their skins. Had the war continued just a little longer, they could well have been the ones who would themselves have written the same sorts of notes and letters as those included in this book. But currently, the present younger generation, which grows larger every year, remembers the war only in fragments, or just has faint recollections from childhood. We find ourselves coming into contact with increasingly large numbers of young people who do not have either realistic images of the war or any real feel for the pain and cruel destruction it caused. Neither is there any sense of the sheer human breakdown brought about by the war. From one standpoint, of course, all of this is something to be happy about, i.e., that for the fourteen years since the end of the war we have not had another one. By very reason of the fact that the dark and monstrous arm of war did not directly reach into the lives of these susceptible young people, we can say that they are almost incredibly fortunate—at least when their lot is compared to that of those who grew up right in the middle of the conflict.

There is, however, a second standpoint, one from which not only does the threat of still another war seem to be rising, but this time the war which is threatened would be, by far, an even more massive and destructive one. So it is absolutely imperative that today's younger generation acquire an adequate knowledge of war, and especially of the war that is still relatively recent history. It would be impossible to prevent an encore of that tragedy without a thorough knowledge of and serious thought given to the inordinate amount of bloodshed it caused, as well as considering the societal structure that led to its coming about in the first place. But there are more and more among today's younger generation who oppose any open discussion of the war experience. There are those who say such things as "Why are you so taken up with a war that is ancient history? Why do you not simply stop worrying about it?" These young people have no desire whatsoever to learn about either the war itself or those wartime conditions they are ignorant of. Although there may be a number of reasons for their opposition and lack of concern, one of them is most definitely the following.

Older people who lived through the war often talk about it in a sentimental way, either to reminisce or just for pure entertainment, and by so doing they trivialize it. None of the wisdom that is so needed today will come out of that sort of thing; a better way of proceeding would be to think in some depth while searching for the significance and relevance of one's personal war experience.

However, the war experience was simply too costly to the whole Japanese race in every respect—individually, socially, and ideologically —to waste it, which is what anyone would be doing who rejects that experience or puts it down as insignificant out of a knee-jerk reaction to some of the lighter and shallower talk on the part of a few older people. Any such wasteful decision would make it extremely difficult for their generation to gain anything resembling a concrete grasp of both the structure and trends of the contemporary world situation. In addition to the very real threat of a new war, this situation I refer to includes the uniqueness of Japan within its own historical process. So long as the possibility of war exists, we ought not to miss the opportunity to learn as much as we possibly can from such bitter past experiences. And the danger of a nuclear war does indeed exist! One proof of this is the very existence of the large-scale anti-nuclear conference that is held every summer. Were there no threat of war, who would attend such a meeting?

No thorough analysis of the late war has as yet been completed, and there is no evidence that anyone has a really meaningful grasp on its relevance. Rather than merely dealing with each individual's personal memories, what is so badly needed today is an effort to put to use the whole nation's general experience of the war by really getting to the bottom of it. If we follow through on that effort the experience can be made to transcend any so-called generation gap and will become something truly societal. Precisely because they have no personal wartime experience, today's younger generation is uniquely presented with an opportunity to raise all this past experience to the level of an ideology—is indeed under the stern necessity of doing so. The job at hand is to take a good look at a number of individuals' past experiences without being overwhelmed by them. Under the attractive title of "equalization of the status of the U.S. and Japan," our nation's present government is preparing the Security Pact revision. Thereby, that is unless the activities of various opposition groups are successful, Japan will become entangled in a dangerous military alliance with America. This involvement would carry with it an expanded military defense system, including nuclear weapons, and of course it would also mean an increase in the government's plundering. Other corollaries would be a negative revision of the Constitution, the introduction of a conscription system, and the choking off of democratic rights by a secrecy protection law and a new Security Police Administration Law, and other [undesirable policies] will descend upon us one after another. And all these trends will only increase international tension and provoke the threat of war even more. So far as the members of the younger generation are concerned, all of these possible developments are things that will soon come to weigh heaviest on their shoulders. It would seem obvious then that these are the very issues which they ought to be most seriously concerned with. A war might just possibly be set up and somehow actually begun without their being aware of it—while they are only too preoccupied with the short-sighted self-centered matters of their everyday lives. Once started, it would be exceedingly difficult if not impossible to stop, and they would in turn probably be swallowed up in it and lose their lives in vain. This whole process has already been made evident, and with quite literally painful clarity, by the students of the time of "Kike Wadatsumi no Koe." Those students have already provided a whole variety of precious experiences that could be made useful nowadays through that ideologizing process already mentioned. Their book, for example, contains in abundance wartime experience earned the hard way—earned at the cost of immeasurable, and bloody, sacrifice. We should like to encourage readers to conduct either individual or group research into the wealth of material offered in this volume.

I must go on to mention a few other things you ought to keep in mind as you read this book. The first is the fact that the notes and letters included in it were not written under normal circumstances. You have to remember not only that these documents were wartime productions, but that the Japanese military's total control over every individual even extended to such things as personal letters and diaries. *Everything* was placed under the strictest censorship and, as a result, free expression was simply impossible. Rather than to protect military secrets, this way of doing things was, in general, designed to control people—not only physically but also in what you might call matters of conscience. Often even the farewell letters those young men sent to their families just before their last missions were written in the standard militaristic style; any genuine and really heartfelt ways of expressing themselves were forbidden. In some cases things were written secretly and mailed when the senders had an opportunity to get away from the barracks, or else they were smuggled out with friends who had come to visit them. Both of these procedures were true exceptions, and the messages relayed through them were kept to themselves both by friends and family members. Among the letters and notes included in this book there are at least some that seem to be written with a certain degree of freedom, but they are equally exceptional. Incidentally, the restrictions may occasionally have been eased back a bit when one became a cadet or an officer, but control over the rest of the soldiers remained most severe and extreme. The truth of this is borne out in the following excerpt: "If a second-year private [i.e., senior private], or anyone else, ever finds out that I wrote this sort of a letter, it is a certainty that I would be killed."

The point is that the sheer humaneness of the reactions to their experiences—even in those inadequate forms of expression which were the only ones the restrictions made available to them—somehow survived, despite the strict censorship, in some of the letters that reached the hands of the students' families. Even though virtually all the writings included in this volume were produced under the sternest possible constraints, yet those tremendous human qualities still shone through—and how eternally rich and keen they still are!

In the cases of the student soldiers, however, they were at least a little better off than the majority of their comrades, in the sense that they were both intellectually and psychologically better equipped to express the deep *umeki* (a groan) and *kawaki* (dryness and thirst) that the war evoked. In their hearts all servicemen—whether they were students or just ordinary soldiers—shared the same natural human emotions. The only exceptions consisted of those who, in a twisted sort of way, accepted their roles as professional soldiers, as well as those who had deliberately chosen that path. The contents of this book are limited strictly to those written by college and university students, but they could and do at the same time serve to represent the voices of those innumerable other men who fell in battle. These selections serve to represent those young soldiers who died and left only the standard words—the formulas of farewell, as it were— simply because they lacked either the opportunity or the know-how to express their inner feelings.

This book is indeed a collection of the writings of those fallen student soldiers, but it should also be kept in mind that, under the peculiar conditions which existed during the war, there was only the slightest shading of a difference between the chance of being killed in action and the chance of returning home alive. There was case after case in which someone came home alive just because he managed to catch an earlier train, or another man was killed by a bullet because he was standing just one meter to the left, etc. What all this means, of course, is that, with only the tiniest shift of fate, the situations of the fallen student soldiers and of those who returned home to live into the post-war years could have been exactly reversed. So, to a greater or lesser extent, the writings of those student soldiers who fell have not only so clearly pried open and furnished insight into their own wartime experience; they have done the same for those fortunate ones—and oh how precious that good fortune was!—who survived and are now living their own peacetime lives. This book's importance lies then in its being something of a dual record: it leads both to yesterday and into the lives of those who are still with us.

Moreover, this volume includes many selections which not only expressed their authors' doubts, mistrust, and criticisms concerning the war, but also their deep sense of despair. In this latter sense the work stands as somewhat different from the actual picture of many students of those days, who, from grade school to the university, had literally been brought up by the military regime which mobilized everything— newspapers, magazines, the radio, the family, and even neighborhood associations. And those young men, who were thus educated and molded in the harsh light of those militaristic ideas, came to believe with a holy fervor that the war was a sacred one. Among other things, all that I have just said means that what we have collected here are the records of those who, at least to a certain extent, had the courage to look into themselves and the predicament they faced. They also had the extra courage that it took to analyze that predicament, as well as to utilize their opportunities for intellectual follow-up. Even though many students may inwardly have begun to feel doubtful and distrustful, etc., as a result of the forceful molding of their personalities by the military, they never knew how to carry their investigations further. For the same reason even their internal efforts toward questioning were constantly being blocked. Even when they were able to take stock of things, their situations were such that they had no opportunity to leave behind anything like this sort of writing.

At any rate, the fact that there are so few selections in this book that represent anything close to a strong militaristic view is the result of those circumstances that Mr. Kazuo Watanabe outlined in the Preface to the first edition. He wrote:

In the beginning, I had leaned quite far in the direction of all-inclusiveness and insisted that it would be much more fair and just to include even rather fanatical Nipponism, or even a few short essays shading towards the glorification of war, but the members of the Publication Department did not show any sign of agreement with my position. The primary reason for their opposition was that the publication of this book must not at all affect negatively the current social conditions, and so on. I finally came to consider their position reasonable. Moreover, I thought, seeking for "fairness and justice" in a merely formal manner might in fact result in the contrary, i.e., a decided lack of "fairness and justice." In addition, I thought about the fact that the very cruel condition that made a few of those fallen young university student-soldiers, even momentarily, to write something that sounds like an outburst of ultra-nationalism, or even close to glorifying war, was that dark and extremely hideous national structure, the military, and its principal members. Therefore, such occasional *pitiful and painful* writings must actually be viewed as the voices, recorded in print, of the tormented spirits of young people who were driven to the utmost limits of sanity itself, and might be read more realistically as cries for help. Certainly we had to consider possible ill effects of publishing those writings, and also that their public exposition would be painful—more than we could bear. I, therefore, agreed with the position of the Publication Department. . . .

Around that time I was in general agreement with Mr. Watanabe, but now I think that, in the matter of choosing the selections, his original "fairness" policy would have been a better way to go. Of course, if we had chosen some of those pieces that came close to praising the war, it would be difficult today to avoid feelings of revulsion—but even so I think it would have been better to include them. The fact is that there was quite a bit of this warmongering material, and, since we wanted to examine our national experience in its entirety, it should have been found necessary to include such writings. The panoramic view that would have resulted might well have shed considerable light on the relationship between war and human beings, and about the total effect on young people of a militaristic education. It is doubtless true that a broader view of the war—with all its inhumanity, wretchedness, and coarse brutality—would bring clarification to other matters as well. At that time the humanistic energies of our young Japanese students, their sense of responsibility for society and our people, and finally their very perseverance and sense of ethics were subjected to inhuman pressures. Those militaristic writings which are largely missing from this volume just might have helped us see both how those pressures affected the students' inner selves and how their power to see through and evaluate them was totally taken away.—The irony is that the inclusion of those very same military-oriented writings would have given greater point and clarity to the selections we do have. Somewhat surprisingly, even in this collection as we have it, there is virtually no expression of any severe or even serious self-criticism. Most of the contributors, for example, feel perfectly comfortable with their positions as specially privileged military officers. There is also a very small minority who demonstrate a rather strange psychological condition, i.e., they show no natural human emotions—and offer no criticism—in connection with the horrible incidents they have described in their writings. There are more than a few other cases in which we can see how those young students' sensitivity and inner thoughts were ruthlessly forced into a certain "frame." With all of this in mind, therefore, we have to be truly touched by and feel deeply for these youngsters even while we cannot avoid feeling a certain bitterness and sadness about those cases. This sort of "side view" is something we need to evaluate critically when going through this volume.

Shortly after its publication in the autumn of 1949, this book rather unexpectedly became a best-seller. Something like a quarter of a million copies were sold, which is very unusual for such an unpretentious book as this. Indeed, at the time a great many people expressed their opinions of it and wrote us about how deeply touched they were; some of them appeared in a book published by the Tokyo University Press: *Wadat-sumi no Koe ni Kotaeru (Responding to Kike Wadatsumi no Koe)*. Differing from the general run of those forgettable best-sellers that shoot up to be ultra-fashionable for a short period of time, this book has been deeply carved into the hearts of students and of countless others who were hurt by the war.—To this day it still maintains its life as a book, and will almost certainly continue to do so. In the middle of the Korean War and the desperate mood it engendered, there was an organization formed by the intelligentsia, including college students. Started in 1950, the Nihon Senbotsu Gakusei Kinen-Kai (Japan Memorial Society for the Fallen Students)—Its short name was "Wadatsumi-Kai" (Wadatsumi Society)— had a clearly stated goal: "The blood that was shed because of the war cannot be compensated for unless we can make sure that it will never ever be shed again." Many helpers joined Mr. Katsurō Nakamura, the central figure in the compilation of this book, and started to work toward the goal with total dedication. This was an important part of an overall social movement protesting war and promoting ideas for a permanent peace. The movement spread all over Japan for the following eight years. Right after the first edition was published, incidentally, a heightened social consciousness—pushing peace and excoriating war—was born. There was a film *Kike Wadatsumi no Koe*, a sculpture by Arata Hongō, and many stage plays as well as a lot of *sprechchor* at quite a few universities. From these sources the movement spread and was expressed in many organized activities in colleges and high schools throughout Japan. Meetings were held in many Japanese universities around December 1st, and "the students' oath against engaging in war" was another response to Mr. Takeshi Yasuda's suggestion in an Asahi newspaper. All this was primarily organized by the chapters of Nihon Senbotsu Gakusei Kinen-Kai all over Japan.

The students' component of this organization, which was its main group, dissolved in 1958, and other members left as well. Shortly after that, however, a new movement for reconstructing the society began, and, as of this year, a preparatory meeting was held and those meetings consisted of three separate sub-groups: professors, those who were students during the Second World War, and current students. In order to promote the idea of never repeating the "tragedy of Wadatsumi" ever again, we decided to define ourselves as a society that will expand our mental and psychological connections throughout the nation, and that the formal reinauguration of the society would take place immediately following the publication of this volume. So long as a single threat of war fails to disappear, Nihon Senbotsu Gakusei Kinen-Kai will not disappear—and, just like the phoenix, it will always be ready to rise to life again. This book too will always and continuously be read as strong evidence of the Japanese people's most sincere hope for peace and opposition to war.

As one who has been deeply involved in this project, I should once again like to express my deepest gratitude both to those who worked directly on this book and to those who engaged in other activities related to it. I also want to extend my appreciation to those outsiders who loaned us their support and protection, as well as to those who are currently working on and helping out with the publication of this edition of the book.

October 1959

Postscript to the Earlier Iwanami Bunko Edition
Published by Iwanami Shoten, 1982

Katsurō Nakamura

Until now I have not made any statement as a person who participated in the compilation of this book.

The reason was that I thought that the words of our deceased heroes would say what had to be said on these matters far more eloquently than I ever could. It seemed to me that, as a mere editor, the very least public posturing possible would be by far the best course to follow. However, now that I have far surpassed the ages of our mentors in that earlier time, and I am now steadily walking up to the last hill of my life a step by a step, perhaps a postscript is in order. So I decided to write down the following matters as a postscript. This book is not only the charnel-house honoring the spirits of those fallen student-soldiers, but it is also a memorial tower for what we were able to accomplish in our youth.

This book's precursor, the collection of writings of the Tokyo University students killed in the war, *Harukanaru Sanga ni (In the Far Away Mountains and Rivers)*, was released by the University of Tokyo Co-op Publication Department two years after the end of the war, in the winter of 1947. To commemorate this event a gathering was held at Sanjō Conference Center of the University of Tokyo and was attended by a distinguished roster of guests: President of the University Shigeru Nambara; Professor Tarō Tsujimura of the Geography Department, Faculty of Science; Mr. Tokutarō Yamane (Mr. Akira Yamane's father); Mr. Yoshimoto Nakamura (Mr. Tokurō Nakamura's father); and over a dozen others. Mr. Tatsuo Besshi, Mr. Kurazō Inagaki, Mr. Shōzō Ōtsuka, and Mr. Yukio Chō of the University of Tokyo Co-op Publishing Department were also present, as were Mr. Kikuo Nomoto and myself, who were compilers. Suggested by Mr. Hiroshi Shimizu, responsible for the book's format, Messrs. Inagaki, Ōtsuka, Nomoto, Nakamura, and Shimizu sang the hymn, "Is There a Finer Friend Than Mother?" [the title given to an old Japanese version for "What a Friend We Have in Jesus"]: its music score was printed on the back cover. I remember very well that the winter sun was shining upon the unheated room in Sanjō Conference Center. I remember very well too the tears that filled the eyes of every single person there who stood facing the table.

Harukanaru Sanga ni was so immediately popular and its first printing snapped up in such a short time that it was almost as though the reading public thought they foresaw an imminent rise in the price of paper. The book's appeal continued, and subsequent reprintings were only interrupted when we turned to the new task of compiling this volume. Due largely to strong urging on several fronts by, for example, Messrs. Hideo Odagiri, Hajime Noguchi, Tametomo Mitsui, Tsuneji Sa-kurai, and Shin-ichi Mashita, to the general effect that to contain only those of the University of Tokyo would be too limiting and that the published material should be chosen from a broader base, we decided that we would publish a more inclusive, all-Japan edition. So, in the spring of 1948, *Harukanaru Sanga ni* was discontinued for publication at the point where about 200,000 copies had already been sold.

It had also been true with *Harukanaru Sanga ni* that opinion was considerably divided over which editorial policy would have been the best to follow. One position was that, for example, "it would be much more fair and just to include even rather fanatical Nipponism or even a few short essays resembling glorification of war" (Kazuo Watanabe). Another position was that, "[This book] represents something different from the actual picture of many students of those days, who, from grade schools to the university, had literally been brought up by a military regime which mobilized everything—newspapers, magazines, the radio, the family, and even neighborhood associations. Those young men were thus educated and molded in the harsh light of those militaristic ideas, and came to believe with a holy fervor that the war was a sacred one" (Hideo Odagiri). There was also some very strong criticism such as:

The collection [*Harukanaru Sanga ni*] is for the most part devoted to those more dramatic and impassioned accounts of the pain and sadness, etc., of those who were being shipped off to die. This emphasis is understandable, but occasionally it seems to have been placed at least partially at the expense of those other young men, far from a few, who went to face their quite certain deaths more stoically—even lightheartedly. "Tragedies" are not solely confined to those cases wherein the protagonists are loudest about lamenting their fate—the "tragedy" is even more applicable to those who are more silent, by their own effort cutting off their ability to think, to the point of no longer feeling the pain, in facing up to their own. Perhaps a somewhat less than fully rounded-out editorial policy paid less attention than was due to the less vocal of the fallen students, and as a result may even have fallen a bit short of revealing everything, or actually distorted things a bit, and thus the full depth of the tragedy was not clearly presented (Yoshirō Hoshino).

In my opinion the criticisms quoted above are overly harsh, even cruel. Far from "those voices are hardly represented," the matter of the fact is that, if one reads carefully, their voices are found in the book everywhere.

In the case of *Harukanaru Sanga ni* in particular, the absence of certain militaristic terms and slogans popular at the time, that Prof. Watanabe talks about—such terms as *"hakkō ichiu"* (the eight corners of the world under one roof), *"bansei ikkei"* (an imperial line unbroken over time immemorial), *"tenjō mukyū"* (eternal sky and earth), *"shichishō hōkoku"* (live seven lives to serve the country), *"Shōsho hikkin"* (unquestioning compliance with the emperor's wishes), *"Tennō-heika ban zai"* (Emperor, 10,000 years), or *"Kudan no shatō de aō-yo,"* (Let's meet at the entrance of the Yasukuni Shrine), was due to the fact that there was strict censorship by CIE (of General Headquarters, GHQ, of the Allied Forces during the Occupation after Japan's defeat, located in NHK (Japana Broadcasting System [building]), Uchisaiwai-cho, Tokyo. When Mr. Tatsuo Besshi and I brought the manuscripts of *Harukanaru Sanga ni* to CIE for inspections, each of those words were ordered to be deleted.[1] Therefore, those words could not be printed. This fact must be noted.

Having received approval of the Central Committee of the University of Tokyo Student Government, we decided to make *Harukanaru Sasnga ni*

---

[1] These expressions seem sufficiently harmless and innocent today, even picturesque and edifying, and others such as "Emperor, Banzai" are familiar even to Western readers and do not sound particularly ominous or threatening to people possessed of sense and education. For non-Japanese audiences, certain other and less quasi-poetic slogans, e.g., "We shall meet at the entrance of the Yasukuni Shrine," might call for some brief explication. The shrine referred to, in Tokyo, is a memorial to Japan's war dead, and during the Second World War soldiers who were going into combat against heavy odds often used the slogan (or a shortened version: "See you at Yasukuni") in shouting encouragement to one another. During the post-war period, support for Yasukuni and its seeming glorification of emperor-inspired martyrdom has occasionally become a matter for some discussion and even protest, but, regardless of politics and public sentiment alike, rallying cries such as the one last quoted have constituted vital segments of the world's recorded military traditions since the very dimmest origins of human warfare. Unfortunately, at least in the case of the matter under discussion, to establish the point I was attempting to make at the conclusion of the preceding paragraph is simultaneously to miss the point of the discussion itself; and, with all due respect of course, I fear that we must count Prof. Watanabe among the missing. It is his view that the omission of the militaristic and super-patriotic material dealt with above either detracts from or even makes any truly panoramic portrait of the late conflict impossible. The irony is that, ideally speaking, he is undoubtedly correct. The problem is that in matters as practical as the publication business one can most definitely strive for the ideal—but we must also rest assured that business *practica* will of their very nature forever prevent the attainment of that ideal. (JQ)

a compilation by the Committee for the Compilation of the Notes and Writing of Fallen Students, in the University of Tokyo Student Government. But as for compiling this book, a new group, "Nihon Senbotsu Gakusei Shuki Henshū Iinkai" (Committee for the Compilation of Notes and Writings of the Fallen Japanese Students) was established in the University of Tokyo Co-op Press in the spring of 1948, with Messrs. Nomoto and Nakamura in charge, and Tatsuo Besshi, Kurazō Inagaki, Masaki Akashi, and Akihiko Yoshioka representing the publisher. Armed with the letters of introduction from Mr. Besshi and Mr. Tsuneji Sakurai of the University of Tokyo Newspaper, we visited such newspapers as Asahi, Mainichi, Yomiuri, Kyōdō Tsūshin, NHK, and others. We asked them to advertise for manuscripts that would fit the frame of our project and also, during the first meeting of the Zengakuren (National Federation of Student Self-Government Associations) at the Sanjō Conference Center, we offered a public explanation of the ideas behind the call for manuscripts.

Posthumous material was submitted from 309 sources, and from all this we chose the seventy-five "finalists" presented in this volume. The arrangement of these selections is for the most part chronological, carefully compiled in such a way as to make it easy for the reader to gauge the moods and thinking of the students throughout the vagaries of the war situation. Having divided the whole of our selected material into three main sections (I. Before the Pacific War; II. During the Pacific War; and III; After the Defeat), we were able to deliver *Kike Wdatsumi no Koe*'s first printing to book dealers on October 20, 1949. It would actually be more accurate to say that, even before delivery, the project's popularity had many book dealers coming to the binding plant of Ōkura Printing Company, frequently and impatiently, to make inquiries. People in the book business at that time referred to the work as *Kike Wada*, largely because *wadatsumi*, the term to which appropriate lexicographical attention has since been paid, was a rather obscure term. The title was chosen from some 2,000 submissions entered in a public contest. Mr. Takio Fujitani of Kyoto had suggested *"Hateshinaki Wadatsumi"* (Eternal Sea) as the title, and in the margin of his entry included a *tanka* [a poem of 5–7–5 7–7 syllables] of his own: *"Nagekeru-ka, ikareru-ka, hata modaseru-ka, kike hateshinaki wadatsumi no koe,"* (Are these voices grief-filled or angry? But can they be silenced or ignored?—Listen to the eternal voices of the boundless sea). Mr. Fujitani underlined the *"hateshinaki wadatsumi"* in it. At first, this title was one of those rejected. Personally I had favored the title, *"Mite ite goran. Ima ni Watakushi-tachi no Jidai ga Kuru"* (Keep on watching. Soon our time will come). My feeling was that a long title was not necessarily bad because, at just about that time, a book with a rather interminable title, *Aijō-wa Furu Hoshi no Gotoku (Love Is Like Falling Stars)* by Hotsumi Ozaki, had proven to be a smash hit; but this feeling of mine was overridden on the grounds that it was still too long—period. It was in this atmosphere of indecision that Mr. Fujitani's postcard again caught my eye. It was a fatal moment, [what Joyceans would call an "epiphany"] and I shouted out: "I've got it! Let's go with *Kike Wadatsumi no Koe*!" So, the title which later became so widely known, *Wadatsumi*, was chosen.

In February of 1952 this book was published by the University of Tokyo Press, formerly the University of Tokyo Co-op Publication Department, as a Tōdai Shinsho (University of Tokyo New Book Series); and also, in October 1959, it was published again as one of the Kōbunsha's "Kappa-Books" ("Kappa" Paperbacks), and reprinting has continued ever since.

During the course of several of the many visits I paid Professor Kazuo Watanabe, both at the French Literature Research Institute and his home in Hongō-Masago-cho, he kept urging me to read Erasmus' *Heiwa no Uttae (An Appeal for Peace)*. Despite the deep interest which I was prepared to take in this work, I knew full well that Erasmus had written in Latin and that there was no way I could take the professor up on his offer. One day he said: "Mr. Nakamura, I was able to get hold of a German translation of *Appeal*.—You can read it, right?" No way I could reject this, so I borrowed the book and eagerly took it home to devour. Because the volume was quite valuable and, moreover, was not my own property, I was unable to annotate the text itself; so I copied out several excerpts from it in my notebook. Although I had a variety of motives for organizing Nihon Senbotsu Gakusei Kinen-kai (Japan Memorial Society for the Students Killed in the War)—Wadatsumi Kai (Wadatsumi Society), which came to be considered the first Japanese peace organization, this book by Erasmus, loaned to me by Professor Watanabe, was the beginning. *An Appeal for Peace* has since been translated into Japanese by Mr. Saburō Minowa and published by Iwanami, and is now readily accessible to the general reader. I hereby pass along the enthusiastic recommendation which the professor made to myself. Whenever anyone asks me to name, if possible, the great book in my life, I always say that, (aside from *Kike Wadatsumii no Koe*) Erasmus' *Appeal* would have to be the answer.

The afterword with which Mr. Hideo Odagiri concluded the University of Tokyo Co-op Publication Department's edition of *Kike Wadatsumi no Koe* is an absolute masterpiece. Even half a lifetime later (i.e., thirty-three years) nothing substantial could by way of improvement be added to what he wrote. Therefore, allow me to quote, with respect, from a few passages in the closing portion.

.... I could talk forever about this book, talk of any single one of the broken lives and spirits, contained in this book, wounded by the pain and hurt, which they could not put away, of those young men who were thrust into the "house of death" by the Japanese military and its war of aggression. Strong personalities were too often transformed into desperate ones, and their firmly awakened rationality and intellectual honesty make them declare: "I cannot accept anything, or even understand anything, in its totality," (Tokurō Nakamura), but for many others that pain too often disintegrated into the very sorriest forms of resignation —something that they had to force themselves to somehow solve by themselves. Of course pain and suffering were not the only things that existed, and there was another side to the story. Even though we get no more than a glimpse of it in this book, there were some who were only too happy to put on older officer's attitudes along with their uniforms, and some common soldiers were treated badly. Still and all, and even including that side, now more than ever and without any reservations, we must push our protests as forcefully as possible against those who so systematically and structurally perverted those young spirits of Japan to such a condition as is indicated in this book; and we must press hard for our demand for humanity and for rationality. We cannot afford to ignore the fact that, for decade after decade, the social structure of the nation itself had not only allowed but even depended upon the existence and growth of the very same military authorities who later mobilized Japan for war. Neither can we avoid facing such facts merely because similar authority has not only survived into our own day, but, with something like a supreme irony, seems once again to be gaining ground. . . . We must face these facts courageously. Actually, even during the war, painful cries (and groans) like "peace!" and "world peace is the first priority" have been heard, (Tadashi Kawashima) but from this day forward we must move beyond the simple wish for peace, however heartfelt, towards making concrete efforts to secure that peace which is now and forever will be threatened. We cannot atone for the blood already shed in any way other than to make sure that it will never, ever, be shed again.

From the very beginning of recorded history have we ever had a single significant example of peace having been maintained, whether between individuals or nations, by either violence or by weapons? In the final, the irrefutably true analysis, cancer and the military mentality bear a striking, indeed an identical resemblance: cancer consumes an individual human organism; the military destroys an entire race. This is the truth. Any one man's distrust is the seed of another's; violence begets violence; hate causes more hate. The progressively sophisticated development of weaponry, including the nuclear variety, has the single intent of intimidating one another: and neither side would stop. One thinks of *"Hitachi-gokko"* (the Japanese-minks game, i.e., the rat game) and finger-wrestling.

Distrust and hate must be eliminated. Any and all armaments must be eliminated. Unless that is done, the spirits of those whose deaths were "as squeezed" rather than deaths "as dripping" (Osamu Takei) can never rest in peace. Would it not be the obvious, rather, more than obvious, duty for those of us who survived? Human beings will never be redeemed through the simple reformation of social and political systems and structures. The most important thing is for every individual human being never to renege on his or her solemn pledge—deeply engraved, as it were, on their hearts—to reject war and the instruments of war once and for all. Because this is the truth, we must not give up hope even though the road towards achievement of this state of affairs seems, and is, a long one. There is an expression "ideologization of war experience": it was with all this in mind that I talked with friends and made preparations that led to the founding of the Nihon Senbotsu Gakusei Kinen Kai (Japan Memorial Society for the Students Killed in the War), Wadatsumi Society, on April 22, 1950. Since then, though not overwhelming in numbers, it has continued to struggle along. It has been a long road and one held together, as it were, by varying lengths of string.

In the past thirty-two years The Wadatsumi Society has naturally gone through many changes: the first phase was under the leadership of the Chairman of the Board of Directors, Mr. Kenjūrō Yanagida (father of one of the authors in this book, Mr. Yōichi Yanagida), and Mr. Takanobu Matsue, the Secretary General, with Mr. Sōkichi Tomimoto, Mr. Kōzō Hasegawa, and others in the executive office. The second phase, the so-called reconstructed Wadatsumi Society was under Mr. Tomoji Abe, Chairman of the Board of Directors; Secretary General Hajime Yamashita; with Mr. Yōzō Furuyama, Ms. Aki Izumi, and Mr. Takeshi Yasuda in the executive office. The current Wadatsumi Society is under the third Chairman, Katsurō Nakamura; and Secretary General Kiyoshi Watanabe; supported by Messrs. Hiroyuki Hirai, Shigeru Kume, Hitoshi Suzuki, Yasusaburō Hoshino, Takei Ikeda, and Ms. Fusako Watanabe and Ms. Wakana Nishihara (the younger sister of Mr. Minoru Wada, one of the authors in this book), Ms. Keiko Mori, and Mr. Isao Nagahama. Most certainly the activities of those above mentioned are not limited to any specific phase, and also I think of the fact that there are a great number of other involved people all over Japan, but that will have to be told as a separate history.

I should like to extend my deepest appreciation to both The University of Tokyo Press and Kōbunsha for their graciously having permitted this book to be republished, this time as an Iwanami Bunko Book. This Iwanami Library edition's text is based on the first edition by the University of Tokyo Co-op Publication Department, and Professor Watanabe's remarks, as well as the chronology at the end of the book derived from the same source. The cover art (inside the cover) on that first edition was a copy of a sketch which one of the contributors to this volume, Mr. Kiyoshi Sekiguchi, drew in his notebook just before he died of starvation on Miyakojima Island. For the current volume we used photographs of the sketch taken in connection with Mr. Sekiguchi's work and kindly made available to us by Nihon Hōsō Kyōkai (Japanese Broadcasting System) Publication Department as it published *Inori no Gashū (Collection of Drawings for Prayers)*, and inserted the material into the text. The authors of every selection included in this book died untimely and most tragic deaths, but over the years this printed, living legacy of theirs, has reached over one and one-half million copies after many reprintings. And now it is ready to be published as an Iwanami Library book with the over-whelming support of those whom I mentioned above. As a member of one of the surviving families, I cannot help but express my most heartfelt gratitude to readers as well as to those on the production end of the enterprise.

To mark the occasion of this new edition I polled surviving members of all the fallen students' families for information such as changes of address, etc., whereby we might update the brief listings offered in the concluding section. As was of course to have been expected, several deaths as well as other ravages of time have made some omissions inevitable; and we would naturally welcome any additional information from whatever source. I received many kind words from surviving family members. One wrote: "To be published in the Iwanami Library he enjoyed reading. . . ." Another wrote: "I know the deceased would be most pleased to see his writing published in the Iwanami Library which he loved reading." One family wrote: "I wish to express my deepest gratitude, on behalf of the deceased, for your efforts leading toward the publication of his writing in Iwanami Bunko; for which I am very, very grateful. Soon I shall be visiting Muroto Misaki (Muroto Point, or Cape Muroto), and I'll tell *kuroshio* (the black current, or the Japan current) about this." I particularly wished to mention this.

February 27, 1982

On the Occasion of the Publication
of the New [1995] Edition

Nihon Senbotsu Gakusei Kinen-kai (Wadatsumi-Kai)
(Japan Memorial Society for the Students
Killed in the War—the Wadatsumi Society)

Kike Wadatsumi no Koe was compiled by the Nihon Senbotsu Gakusei Shuki Henshū Iinkai (Committee for the Compilation of the Writings of Fallen Students of Japan), out of all the contributions from all over Japan, and published first by the University of Tokyo Consumers Co-op Publication Department in 1949. Since then, there has been a variety of editions published by different publishers, and the work has been continuously read by a great many readers transcending generational differences. In the ups and downs of post-war Japan, many bestsellers came and disappeared, but this book was read by all those who pray for peace, and it has gained the reputation of being a modern classic.

For this new edition, we made basic revisions on the very first edition, which all the editions in the past used as a basis. By so doing we restored as closely as possible the original posthumous writings. We are publishing this new edition with the hope that perhaps the new reader may read it with an unexpected new reading, and that the older reader will discover something new. There have been many proposals as to translating the work into English and German: this new edition would be the version for all future translations into any foreign language.

The first of the New Edition's characteristics is the validation of the original posthumous writings. We conducted so-called "text critique" very strictly. For that, we depended on (a) the original writings or a photocopy of them; (b) the copied manuscript of the original writing; (c) the mimeographed manuscripts used in the first edition; (d) collections of individual writings, including a private family edition, which were published either during or after the war;[1] (e) among other sources, such

---

[1] For example, Eiko Ōi, *Ai to Shinkō no Tegami (Letters of Love and Faith)*, 1943; Yōichi Yanagida, *Gakudō-ki (A Record of Scholarly Life)*, 1943; Hachirō Sasaki, *Seishun no Isho (A Will at the Springtime of Life)*, 1981; *Yutakeki Mune no-Inoue Hisashi Ikōshū (Of Splendid Heart—A Collection of the Posthumous Writings of Hisashi Inoue)*, 1984; Ryōji Uehara, *Ah, Sokoku-yo, Koibito-yo (Oh, My Fatherland, Oh, My Sweetheart)*, 1985; *Iwagaya Jiroku Nikki (Diary of Jiroku Iwagaya)*, 1990; Ichizō Hayashi, *Hi nari, Tate nari (It's the Sun, It's a Shield)*, 1995; and others.

items as were certified to be accurate as a copy of the original writing; and (f) those publications we consider to be authentic and loyal to the original writing among those books which contained the posthumous writings that we included in our book. Such works are *Haruka naru Sanga ni* (*In the Far Away Mountains and Rivers*) (by Tōdai Senbotsu Gakusei Shuki Henshū Iinkai [Tokyo University Committee for the Compilation of Fallen Students' Writings], 1947), *Chi no Sazamegoto* (*Utterance of the Earth*) by Kyūsei Shizuoka Kōtō Gakkō Senbotsu-sha Ikō-shū Hensan Iinkai (the Old System Shizuoka Higher School, Compilation Committee for Fallen Students' Posthumous Writings, 1966), *Inori no Gashū* (*Collection of Drawings and Prayer*) (by Akiharu Nomiyama, Sakon Sō, and Takeshi Yasuda, 1981), and *Bessatsu Ichioku-nin no Shōwa-shi: Gakuto Shut-sujin* (*A Hundred Million People's History of the Shōwa Period: Students' Departure for War Front*. Separate Volumes) (Mainichi Shinbun-Sha, 1981). Needless to say, we confirmed and checked with every possible source that we could get hold of, including the earlier editions, the published materials by surviving family members and those who were connected with them, and also their friends' memories of them.[2] The process of validating the materials itself yielded a considerable amount of material, and we were able to make the New Edition with more solid content.

The second characteristic is the fact that, for our revisions, we paid the closest attention to portraying a complete image of each of the authors, irrespective of any preconceptions of our own. Concretely speaking, as much as possible, we included an entire text of the writing of the same day or the same theme. As we were working on the compilation of the New Edition, once again we vividly saw the image of the fallen students who were convulsed in the contradictions that could not be solved, as they were shaken and moved in different directions, while thinking and worrying about family members and close friends, and, at the same time, thinking and longing over how much they wanted to study freely, and to live in a peaceful world, etc.—especially the image of them as they were torn between their own emotion and that extreme situation of facing their

---

[2] Though some of them may duplicate the materials cited in the above category [i.e., in note #1], the following titles cannot be omitted: Kimiaki Shiojiri, *Aru Isho ni Tsuite (On a Certain Will)*, 1951; Toshihiro Tanabe, *Yoru no Shunrai (Spring Thunder in the Night)*, 1968; Tokurō Nakamura, *Tennō Heika no Tame no Tame Nari (It Is For the Emperor)*, 1988; Minoru Wada, *Wadatsumi no Koe Kieru Koto Naku (Keeping the Voice of Wadatsumi from Fading Away)*, 1995; and others.

imminent death. We are confident that we were able to come up with a New Edition which would enable the reader to trace and feel the path, by more than anything else, our editing, in the way most true to the originals.

A variety of raging stages and scenes of Japan's war of aggression which pushed and surrounded each of the fallen students is deeply engraved in the texts of their writings. The New Edition followed the old one's tripartite division, but named Part I as the period of The Japan–China War, II as the Asia–Pacific War period, and III as the defeat in the war: and we rearranged the manuscript guided by each person's most characteristic writing where the author's thoughts seem to be most crystallized. As a result, we think special characteristics and problematic qualities of each of the period are made clear: the first period, when China was the primary battlefield, and the picture of "the enemy" could be seen together with their expressions; the second period, where most [authors] ended their lives as "special attack" force members without having any time even to have a glimpse of the human image of any individual in the enemy; and the third period, the reader can see the many problems the end of war left behind after the curtain of the war was closed with the Japanese Empire's unconditional surrender on August 15, 1945. This variety is the third characteristic of this new edition.

In the older editions, Ryōji Uehara's "Will" was placed in the beginning of the main text containing those posthumous writings, and Haruo Unagami's "Last Writing" was placed at the end. In this new edition, Uehara's "Will" is placed in the main text following its time of writing, and his note entitled "Thought," is used as Prologue. This latter was written the night before his day of "special attack," but after his demise it somehow accidentally escaped the military censorship, and, therefore, it so succinctly expresses the essence of the thoughts of the millions of the young student-soldiers who had to die while watching Japan's defeat play itself out before their eyes. Thus, although unintended it has become a testimony of the tragic fate of that generation. On the other hand, we chose the writing by Mr. Hisao Kimura as Epilogue, not only for the reason that the time of his death was the very last among them, but also because so shortly after the war, and in only that very brief time which was granted him to contemplate—during the course of the Allied Forces' B- and C-class War Criminal Tribunals—he even got around to discussing "the Japanese people's remote responsibility" and also to bring up our contemporary issues.

Incidentally, there were seventy-five fallen students included in the previous editions, but there are seventy-four in the New Edition. This is because very recently we confirmed that one of the authors, Mr. Kaoru

Okamoto, is alive and well. A certain friend of his assumed that he was killed in action, because he was not repatriated until long after the end of the war, and [assuming that he was killed in action], the friend sent in the author's writing in response to the call for manuscripts by Nihon Senbotsu Gakusei Shuki Henshū Iin-kai. It was so much later, after having been repatriated long after the end of the war, that Mr. Okamoto himself realized that his "posthumous writing" was published. Most probably, while he was somewhat embarrassed to come forward since he was alive, and therefore was hesitant to do so, also at the same time, he seemed to feel that his present living self was an entirely different personage from that soldier—now dead—who had served in the Japanese Army. Though we are not getting into discussing the details of what happened [we would say that] this case too may be one of the testimonies of the fact that, though it has been fifty years since the war ended in defeat, the scars of the war are still lingering on both objectively and subjectively. We should like to apologize sincerely to the readers of any of the older editions at this time as we recompiled this new edition.

Of all the fallen students included in this book, the youngest is eighteen years of age and the oldest was thirty-three years of age when killed in action. The average age at the time of death was twenty-four years. Those who were twenty-four years of age at the time of the defeat of war would be seventy-four years of age this year if they were still living. That is, those fallen students ended their lives at the age of the grand-children of those who survived and are still living. Here too, the tragedy and the cold-hearted nature of war are apparent. We should like to keep in mind that those who are dead always remain young.

It was not a war which they had either begun or even consented to; those students were quite literally rounded up to take part in that war of aggression. Even while they were staring death directly in the face, they still maintained their love, indeed their passion, for studying and searching for the truth and intellectual pursuits. They left the later generations their keen hopes for peace and liberty. The reader can find that everywhere in this book. The supreme irony is that these fallen students are enshrined in Yasukuni Shrine as "military gods" and "the souls of the fallen heroes," and they are being used to shore up "Yasukuni worship"—a stout pillar supporting the Tennō (Emperor) system. Some time ago, Mr. Hideo Odagiri lamented over how sorrowful and pitiful a circumstance it was to see the fallen students being hanged, so to speak, in midair, and all in aid of what might be called the "mistaken history of modern Japan." Even today when the cold war between East and West has ended, the deplorable situation is even worse than before. In the situation where the issues of war responsibility and post-war indemnity are problematic, how do we hear "the voice from the sea" and how should we receive those fallen students' wishes?

The fundamental structures of the contradictions of the Japan in which we live today and those of the contradictions that those fallen students felt when they were alive and lingering on even today, if we subject them to deep historical analysis, are the same. Everyone hopes for peace: yet, why can't we prevent wars? This is a most pertinent and urgent issue today, not only for Japanese but for the entire human race, but when we restrict ourselves to thinking about it in national terms, we once again have to inquire into the lives and deaths of those deceased "wadatsumi" student-soldiers. The compilation and publication of the new edition of this memorial to them—happening as it did to coincide with the fiftieth anniversary of Japan's defeat—is an attempt to supply a response to such an urgent historical demand.

In the postscript of the Dai-ni-shū (Second Collection) *Kike Wadatsumi no Koe* (Iwanami Bunko, 1988), Mr. Hiroyuki Hirai states that all three books, *Harukanaru Sanga ni, Kike Wadatsumi no Koe*, and *Dai-ni-shū Kike Wadatsumi no Koe*, are collections of posthumous writings which came from the same womb. That means all these three books are in the same flow with regard to the motive and purpose behind them. In addition to a certain continuity following from the primary compilation, and the commonality of the writings contributed, these are three books that those who were able to survive World War II compiled and published with the strong determination of "no more war," based on the self-reflection never to repeat the tragedy of war again. Not only were they truly from the same womb, but the three books together or each individually played an important role as an ideological and ethical source of post-war Japan's peace movement. However [we cannot ignore the fact that] there was a gap between their times of birth, and, in particular, there were considerable differences among the postures of those who effected the compilations.

As we look back throughout this period of time, we notice that *Harukanaru Sanga ni* was published in 1947 when the U.S. Army was there as the Occupation Forces, and it included only the University of Tokyo fallen students. Therefore, naturally, it was a collection of posthumous writings with a very strong sentiment of mourning seeping through [all the pages], and [the editors] focused the light upon the humanity, which the fallen students never lost even until the very end. It was a publication under the restriction of the Allied Occupation

Headquarters and it was published when even the paper to print it on was very difficult to come by.

In the case of *Kike Wadatsumi no Koe*, the target population for the collection was expanded to include all the institutions of higher learning throughout the entire nation. It had only been two years since the publication of *Harukanaru Sanga ni*, but because the first edition of this book was published in October 1949 when the crisis of the Korean War was just around the corner, the emphasis for compilation was shifted from the past emphasis on "humanity" to a new one—"peace." Both the social conditions which prevailed at the time and their relationship with the posture of the compilation and the basic policy are exactly as discussed by Mr. Kazuo Watanabe's preface to that first edition, entitled "Opinion." The selectors of the texts to be included never intended "to make even the slightest bit of a negative impact on societal conditions, etc." It was for that reason, that it became a book which contributed so greatly toward the formation of the peace and anti-war ideology and elevating anti-war movement.

At the same time, on the other hand, because those writings which did not suit the selectors' intentions were omitted, we cannot deny, however regretfully, that this first edition wound up with a serious shortcoming. The book made it more difficult for readers of subsequent generations, particularly those who had no direct experience of the war, to see the fallen students' image clearly and in its entirety. Also obscured was the whole process of how they became entangled in that war of aggression. In that sense, then, it cannot be denied the fact, regrettably, that the first edition ended up somewhat short of supplying any really concrete and realistic knowledge of the war, as well as of how it affected other Asian peoples—of effecting, i.e., a broader grasp of the war's meaning through the discovery of just who was responsible for it. Having said that, however, we do not wish to push the whole burden of blame onto Nihon Senbotsu Gakusei Shuki Henshū Iinkai. Book publishing, after all, tends to cater to readers' expectations and to their way of thinking. Then too, and perhaps more than any other single factor, it conformed to the norm of the peace movement which existed for a while in the post-war period. For the old edition's limitation, which was burdened by the restrictions of that period, to become evident, the passage of time and the maturing of the peace movement were necessary.

The first collection of posthumous writings that the Wadatsumi Society compiled, *Senbotsu Gakusei no Isho ni Miru Jūgonen-Sensō (Fifteen-year War Through the Fallen Students' Wills)* was planned during a time when the numbers of young people with any experience of the war were giving way to succeeding generations who knew nothing about it. It was published in February 1963 (by Kōbun-sha "Kappa Books") when the Vietnam War with American intervention was about to intensify. Simply put, the compilation policy that time was to correct and supplement what was lacking in [the original edition of] *Kike Wadatsumi no Koe.* The title of this book was later changed to *Dai-ni-shū* (second collection) *Kike Wadatsumi no Koe* in 1966.

Since 1970, the Wadatsumi Society has been paying serious and continuous attention to the issues of the Tennō (Emperor) System and the Yasukuni Shrine—all from the society's special standpoint on reexamining responsibility for the war. In preparation for a later date if and when China, Korea, and other Asian nations should voice harsh criticism of what they consider Japan's distortion of history, the society has gradually but steadily been building toward a position that is sufficiently independent for the framing of a sincere response.

It was after only having gone through this sort of process that the Wadatsumi Society made an inevitable and natural decision to bring out a new edition, while maintaining the strong points of the two earlier titles. In this way *Harukanaru Sanga ni*'s emphasis on the students' humanity and the aspirations for peace stressed in *Kike Wadatsumi no Koe,* are so presented that readers can face and grip the cold harsh reality of how the students of that time were made to carry a war of aggression upon their shoulders.

Though they are all based on the same original text, as mentioned earlier, each of the older editions made its own best response to what you might call the historical trends which were prevalent at the time of their publication. With this in mind, we chose three postscripts here reprinted to help readers understand how our predecessors' thought and how that thinking worked itself out in what they produced.

Incidentally, we should like to mention that, even during the time when we were waiting for the opportunity to ripen for a revised edition, the society continued its serious effort for revisions, as much as possible within the framework of the first (1949) edition. The fruit of all this labor, which indeed we should like to add as a page in the history of this collection, is on display in the thirty-sixth through the forty-second printings of the Iwanami Bunko old edition, and also in "the Great Books" Reprint Edition of Kappa Books (1995).

Now that the long-labored-over publication of this new edition is a fact, we are by no means persuaded that our job is complete. The effects of student mobilization were not limited to Japanese college students. Though they were nominally "volunteers," both Korean and Taiwanese students, colonials within the Great Japanese Empire of that time, were in fact conscripted and then thrown into the swirls of the same war, perhaps under even more brutal conditions and in more emotionally stressful ways than had been the case with the Japanese. There is not a single piece of their writing in this book. In order to reflect about colonialism and to contribute toward making peace in Asia an unshakable reality, to fill these missing pages is our big assignment for the future.

As you, the reader, go on through the rest of this book, we pray that you will give your minds and imagination free play over the fate of that countless number of people killed in the war, not only Japanese but people from many other countries of Asia, and also those of the Allied Forces. Of course we would like you to think of those, even among the Japanese military, farmer-soldiers, and other ordinary Japanese, and also about those who were killed even though they were non-combatant civilians. It would also be interesting to figure out just how our self-consciousness about having caused so much harm to other Asian peoples—so strong today and apparently so weak back then—evolved as it did. It would also be interesting to learn why the "posture against wars," as seen in The German *Shiroi Bara wa Chirazu (A White Rose Refuses to Fall)* [Japanese translation of *Die Weisse Rose,* by Inge Aicher-Scholl, 1953] weakens with the passage of time. We hope that you will think about these questions, and others as well.

We owe most of all to the surviving family members who offered us both the original writings and other valuable source materials, thereby enabling us to make this edition a truly new edition. Respectfully we wish to express our deepest gratitude. We also wish to thank all our seniors who, directly and indirectly, and ever since the first edition, have extended helping hands for the purposes of compiling, publishing, and/or advertising this collection.

Lastly, we should like to express our deepest appreciation to certain people in Iwanami Publishers: President Ryōsuke Yasue, and Minoru Suzuki, Chikao Shiojiri, Noriko Ishikawa, and other members of the Editorial Department of Iwanami Bunko (Iwanami Library), who accepted our frequently unreasonable requests, allowed us to make a vast revision, and also helped generously in the tedious work involved in that revision. We are very grateful.

December 1, 1995

This translation is based on the 1995 edition, 8th printing, published by Iwanami Shoten. As for the posthumous manuscripts of Tokurō Nakamura (pp. 143–158) and Minoru Wada (pp. 239–244), the originals were made available after the publication of the new edition [of 1995]. Therefore, following the intent of the publication of this new edition, some revisions were made for those two authors' writings.

(September 1999)

CHRONOLOGICAL
TABLE

	WHAT WAS HAPPENING IN JAPAN	WHAT WAS HAPPENING IN THE WORLD	EDUCATION — STUDENTS
1924-1930	September 1924: Formation of Gakusei Shakai Kagaku Rengōkai (Student Federation of Social Sciences) of the universities, higher schools and colleges in all Japan. April 1925: Enactment of the Law for the Maintenance of the Public Peace; the Law for Assigning Active Army Officers to Schools. January 1926: The Kyoto University Students Federation Incident (students belonging to social science study groups are arrested). May 1926: Minister of Education gives notification of the prohibition of all social scientific researches. March 1927: Financial depression begins. May 1927: The first dispatch of troops to Shantung [Peninsula, China]. March 1928: The 3.15 Incident (Oppression of Japan Communist Party). April 1928: Issuance of the Order to disband the Tokyo University Newman's Club and all social science study groups of all universities. Professors Hajime Kawakami, Yoshitarō Ōmori, and Itsurō Sakisaka are purged from the universities. June 1928: The retrogressive revision of the Law for Maintenance of the Public Peace. October 1928: Ministry of Education orders universities to establish Student Affairs Department as the measure to control students' thoughts/ideologies. April 1929: The 4.16 Incident (Oppression of the Communist Party). 1929: University graduates have a difficult time getting employment. Movie, "Though I graduated from a university." February 1930: Wholesale arrests of Communist Party members. May 1930: Professors Moritarō Yamada, Yoshitarō Hirano, Kiyoshi Miki, and others are arrested. February 1930: Prime Minister Hamaguchi is shot by gunman. 1930. Showa Depression as World Great Depression spreads to Japan.		
1931	9/18 Japanese Kuantung Army causes the Liut'iao-hu Incident, and begins invading the northeastern area of China (Manchurian Incident).	9/21 China brings the Liut'iao-hu Incident to the League of Nations.	7/7 Ministry of Education establishes Committee for Investigating the student ideology problems. Severe oppression against the student ideology movement begins.
1932	1/28 Shanghai Incident 3/1 Proclamation of the founding of the false "Manchukuo." 5/15 The 5.15 Incident. 6/29 [The status of] Tokubetsu Kōtō-Keisasatsu-ka (Special Higher Police Section) [known as Tokkō] of the Keishichō (the Metropolitan Police Bureau) is elevated from *Ka* (Section) to *Bu* (Department). 9/15 Japan and Manchukuo exchange "a protocol." Colonial control over Manchu strengthens.	10/1 Litton Investigating Team's report denies Japan's claim that the Manchu Incident is an action of self-defense.	5/20 Beginning of the publication of the series, "History of the Development of Capitalism in Japan." 8/23 Establishment of Kokumin Seishin Bunka Kenkyūjp (the Research Institute of National Spiritual Culture). 10/23 The Research Institute on Materialism is founded.

Year			
1933	2/20 Takiji Kobayashi dies from Tokkō Police torture. 3/27 Japan withdraws from the League of Nations. Apr. - Jul. Takigawa Incident at the University of Kyoto.	1/30 Hitler becomes Chancellor of Germany. 10/14 Germany withdraws from the League of Nations.	Jan. - Mar. Kinnosuke Otsuka and Hajime Kawakami are arrested. 2/4 The "Incident of Teachers Turning Red" happens. 7/1 Volunteers among students from colleges and universities all over Japan organize the "Federation of Universities for the Protection of Freedom" and protest the Takigawa Incident.
1934	3/1 The beginning of the Imperial Rule of Manchukuo, with Administrator Pu-Yi as the emperor, backed by the Kuantung Army and the Japanese government. 10/1 The Ministry of the Army [issues] "The Principles of National Defenses and Proposals for Strengthening It." Attacks against individualism and liberalism. 12/29 Japan denounces Washington Military Deduction Treaty.	8/2 Hitler becomes the Führer, head of state, and strengthens the structure for dictatorship. 10/5 Chinese Red Army begins the Long March.	6/1 The Ministry of Education establishes Shisō-kyoku (Bureau of Ideologies). 6/6 Professor Izutarō Suehiro of the University of Tokyo is indicted for violating the Law for the Maintenance of the Public Peace.
1935	2/18 Tatsukichi Minobe's "emperor-as-an-organ" theory becomes a political issue.	10/3 Italy begins invading Ethiopia.	4/1 Promulgation of the Youth School Act. 4/10 Taking the opportunity of the emperor-as-an-organ theory controversy, the Ministry of Education issues an official instruction on "Clarification of the National Foundation."
1936	2/26 The 2.26 Incident. 5/18 Restoration of the system requiring an active general and/or admiral as the Minister of the Military.	7/17 Spanish Civil War starts. 12/12 Hsian Incident in China.	5/17 The Ministry of Education provision for the establishment of "The Lectures on the Study of the National Polity" at the University of Tokyo and the University of Kyoto.

Year			
1937	11/25 Japan and Germany sign an anti-Comintern Mutual Defense Pact.		5/29 Promulgation of the Law on the Protective Observation of the Ideological Offenders.
	6/4 The Konoe Cabinet is formed.	Apr. International conference against war and for the protection of peace, is held in Paris.	7/22 The Ministry of Education requires all colleges and universities to establish "The Lectures on Japanese Culture" and to carry on ideological education.
	7/7 Lukouchiao Incident. The Japan-China conflict becomes a general war.	11/6 Japan–Germany–Italy Anti-Comintern Pact is signed.	5/31 "Kokutai no Hongi" (The Basic Principle of the National Polity), compiled by the Ministry of Education, is distributed.
	10/12 Formation of the Central League for the General Mobilization of National Spirit.		Sept. Members of the Communist group inside the University of Tokyo Settlement are arrested.
	12/13 Occupation of Nangching. A large-scale massacre.		12/24 The "Lectures on the History of Japanese Spirit" is established at the University of Kyoto. In the following month, "Lectures on the History of Ideologies in Japan" is established at the University of Tokyo.
1938	4/1 Promulgation of the National General Mobilization Law.	9/29 Great Britain, France, Germany, and Italy sign the Munich Agreement.	2/1 The Laborers' and Peasants' Faction group arrested.
	7/11 Chang Kü-fêng Incident at the Soviet–Manchuria border.		Feb. The Metropolitan Police Bureau conducts the rounding up of college students cutting classes.
	10/27 Occupation of the three Wohan cities.		6/9 The Ministry of Education sent notification on the collective labor work movement.
			8/24 Law for Restricting the Use of School Graduates.

Year			
1939	1/4 Resignation of Konoe Cabinet. 7/8 The Personal Service Drafting Law is promulgated. 9/15 Nomonhan Cease-fire Agreement is reached. During this year the government policy to censor books becomes more strict.	9/1 German Army invades Poland. 9/3 Great Britain and France declare war against Germany.	Jan. Professors Kawai and Hijikata of the University of Tokyo are suspended (known as the Hiraga Purge of the University [of Tokyo]). 3/30 The Ministry of Education imposes military training in all colleges and universities as a requirement. 5/22 The Emperor reviews college and higher school student troops from all over Japan to commemorate the policy of placing active military officers to schools; "the Imperial rescript to youth and students" is granted. May 107 Members of the student Communist group are arrested. Suppression of all [students'] autonomous activities takes place.
1940	10/12 Opening ceremony of Taisei Yokusan Kai (the Imperial Rule Assistance Association). 11/10 Celebration of the 2,600th year of the Imperial Reign. 11/23 Founding of the Great Japan Industrial Serve-the-Nation Society.	6/14 German Army enters Paris. 9/27 Japan, Germany, and Italy sign a Tripartite pact.	Apr. The Tokyo Student Consumer Union is dissolved. 8/30 Ministry of Education issues "notification regarding university, college, and higher school students for self-control." Summer. Suppression of the movement to reconstruct the Communist Party. A great many college and university students are implicated.
1941	1/8 The Minister of the Army, Tōjō, issues instruction Senjin-kun (the Field Service Code).	June. Germany and Italy declare war against the Soviet Union. 12/8 U.S. and Great Britain declare war against Japan.	4/1 Elementary schools are reformed and reorganized as "kokumin gakkō" (national elementary schools, [lit, national citizen's schools]).

3/10 Promulgation of the Revised Law for the Maintenance of the Public Peace.	12/11 Germany and Italy declare war on Great Britain and the U.S.	8/8 The Ministry of Education issues a directive for organizing "*gakkō hōkoku-tai*" (school serve-the-nation troops).
4/13 Signing of the Soviet–Japan Neutrality Pact.		8/30 Active military officers are assigned for the military training at universities.
July. Japanese Army advances to Indo-China.		10/16 Promulgation of "On the matters relating to shortening the required time for completing study at universities, colleges, and vocational schools."
10/18 Formation of Tōjō Cabinet.		
12/8 Surprise attack on the Malay Peninsula and Pearl Harbor. Declaration of war is issued against the U.S. and Great Britain.		Dec. Moving up the university graduation for the first time (by three months).
12/19 Promulgation of the law to Control Speech, Publication, Assembly, and Organizations.		
1942		
2/15 Occupation of Singapore.	1/1 In Washington, 26 allied nations issue a joint declaration.	8/21 The principle for shortening school years for middle and higher schools is decided upon (effective the following year).
3/2 Occupation of Batavia.	1/18 Japan, Germany, and Italy sign a military alliance.	
5/20 Formation of the Imperial Rule Assistance Political Association.	6/5 The Allied Forces turn to the offensive in the battle of the Pacific.	11/24 The length of study [at universities and colleges] to be shortened also for the academic year of 1943 (six months to three months). Effective also for the following year.
6/5 Battle of Midway (the turning point of the Pacific War).		
8/8 The first round of the Solomon sea battle.		
8/24 The second round of the Solomon sea battle.		
11/14 The third round of the Solomon sea battle.		

Year			
1943	Feb. The Japanese Army announces its "change of the course of battle" to Buna [New Guinea] and Guadalcanal. 5/29 The Japanese garrison on Attu Island was annihilated. 8/1 A draft system is adopted in Korea. 9/23 A draft system is adopted in Taiwan. 11/6 Announcement of the Great Asia Joint Proclamation. 11/21 Allied Forces begin landing on Makin and Tarawa [Gilbert Islands]. 12/15 The Allied Forces begin landing on the island of New Britain [New Guinea].	2/2 German army in Stalingrad surrenders. 7/25 Mussolini resigns and Badoglio becomes Italian Prime Minister. Nov. Roosevelt, Churchill, and Chiang Kai-shek meet at the Cairo Conference.	Feb. - Mar. A student movement at Waseda University and others to give up the privilege of extension for military conscription. Mar. Osaka Commerce University Incident: about 100 students are arrested. 6/25 Outline for the establishment of the war-time student mobilization structure/system is decided upon. 10/2 Promulgation of "The temporary special exception on extension of conscription for the college and university students" (ending the deferment from conscription). 10/21 Great Send-off Party for those university students who are to depart for the war is held at the Meiji Shrine Outer Garden sports field. 12/1 The first group of university students conscripted, because of the end of the conscription deferment, enter the military barracks. 12/24 The age for military conscription is lowered by one year.
1944	2/1 The Allied Forces land on Marshall Islands. 2/25 Cabinet meeting makes a decision on outlines of emergency regarding the decisive battle/war.	7/21 A new government is formed in Poland. 8/25 German army occupying Paris surrenders; and Paris is liberated.	1/18 Outline of the policy for the emergency mobilization of students for work is decided upon. 2/4 Announcement of the policy/measures for strengthening the military education of the students.

6/15 The Allied Forces begin landing on Saipan Island.	9/29 Great Britain, the U.S., and China hold Dumbarton Oaks Conference.	3/7 Cabinet conference makes a decision on the students' work mobilization to be effective throughout the year.
7/18 Tōjō Cabinet resigns en bloc.		3/18 Strengthening of the measures on women volunteer corps is published.
7/21 American Forces land on Guam.		
8/3 Japanese Army withdraws from northern Burma.		6/30 Cabinet meeting decides upon grade-school children for collective evacuation [out of big cities].
9/20 Japanese forces in Burma and Chinese border area are totally annihilated.		10/18 A decision is made to include all seventeen-year-old [males] for military service.
10/12 Air battle offshore Taiwan.		
10/20 American Forces land on Leyte Island, the Philippines.		
10/24 Battle offshore Leyte.		
10/25 First attack by the Shinpū Special Attack Force.		
10/– Special Attack Force operation/ campaign becomes vehement.		
11/24 The first air bombing of Tokyo by B29's.		

1945

2/16 American Mechanized Unit attacks Japanese mainland.	2/4 Yalta Conference of Roosevelt, Churchill, and Stalin.	3/18 Cabinet decision: following the "Outline for the educational measures for the final stage of war," all classroom education at every school, except the elementary division [first to sixth grades] of national elementary schools, is to cease.
3/9 A massive air raid over Tokyo by American Air Force.	4/5 Soviet notification regarding non-extension of Japan–Soviet Neutrality Pact.	
3/17 Japanese army on Iwō-jima Island is totally annihilated.	5/2 Berlin falls.	

3/23 A decision is made to organize a people's volunteer army.

4/1 Allied Forces begin landing on the main island of Okinawa.

4/5 Koiso Cabinet resigns en bloc.

5/2 English and Indian Combined Army occupies Rangoon.

June. The very last stage of fighting on Okinawa.

8/6 Atomic bomb is dropped on Hiroshima.

8/9 Atomic bomb is dropped on Nagasaki.

8/14 Acceptance of the Potsdam Declaration.

8/15 The war ends in Japan's defeat.

9/2 Japan's unconditional surrender is signed on board [battleship *Missouri*] in Tokyo Bay.

5/7 Germany signs unconditional surrender in Reims.

6/25 The United Nations Charter is signed in San Francisco.

7/26 Potsdam Declaration (Declaration by the U.S., Great Britain, China, and the Soviet Union against Japan) is published.

8/8 The Soviet Union declares war on Japan: (actual fighting begins on 9th).

日中戰争期の「日本の版図」

（『新選大地圖 日本篇』一九三八年、帝國書院發行より）

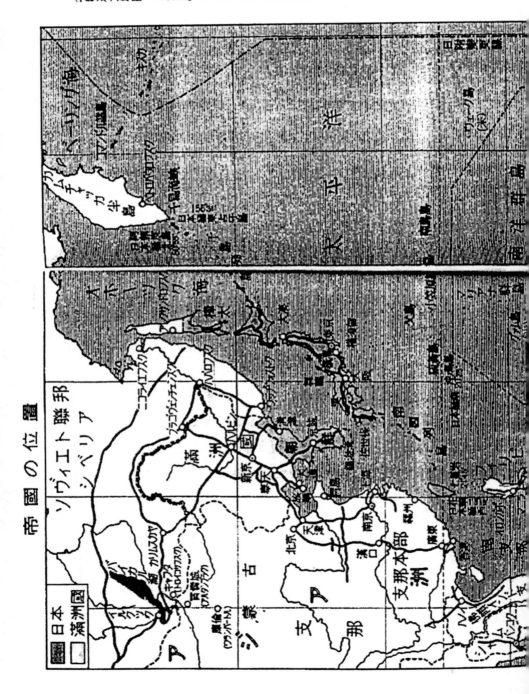

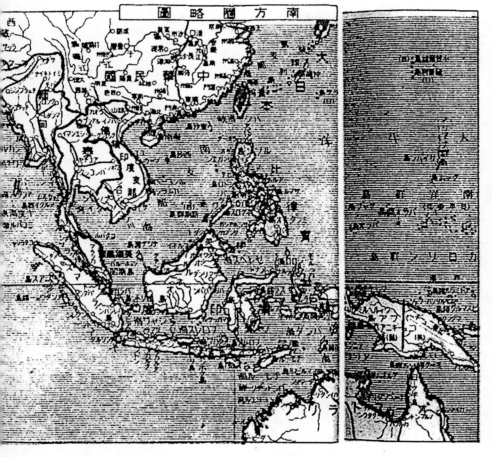

南方圏略図

アジア・太平洋戦争期に日本が戦火を拡大した「南方図」

（上村元太が所持していた「聖戦日記」に既製の手帳）所載の地図）

SELECTIVE GLOSSARY
(For the reader of the English edition):

(In order to avoid clattering the text, we are listing explanations that might be helpful to the English language reader here. Other terms which were footnoted and explained already in the Japanese text, therefore we did not include here, please check the index to locate such explanations.)

Haiku: (See under *Tanka.)*

Higher School (of the old system): *Kōtō-gakkō.*
In the old system of the Japanese educational system, the compulsive education covered eight years, combining the first six years after which most students advanced by passing an examination, the academic track of *Chūgakkō* ("middle schools," for five years) for boys and *Kōtō-jogakkō* ("girls' high school," for five years) for girls. Then, by examinations, good students could advance to the next level, professional/ college level (known as *Kōtō/Senmon-gakkō*) for three years. This used to be the highest level for girls, except a very rare exceptions of those women who advanced to the next level, and also for professional training for both gender. This level also contained eight numbered national higher schools and few others serving as a preparatory school for the highest level (*daigaku* – universities) for the most chosen young men, concentrating on studying philosophy and one of either German, English or French (for humanities and social sciences). This level also included the preparatory division called *Yoka* of the private *daigaku,* universities, where the students could advance without having to take another entrance examination. *Daigaku* was for three years. The highest ranking in prestige was the Tokyo Imperial University, followed by Kyoto, there were a few other imperial universities including one in Seoul, Korea, and one in Taipei, Taiwan. Because of the number of acceptance was extremely limited, the entrance examinations for *kōtōgakkō* were extremely competitive, particularly for the First and the Third, because of the advantage they may have for entering the best universities, which, in turn, lead to successfully passing the entrance examination for *daigaku*, for getting into the best one virtually guaranteed them a

339

successful career especially in the government. So students studied extremely hard to get into the school of their choice, and, therefore, known as *Semaki mon* (the narrow gate).

Those who chose professional colleges, they completed at the college level, including medical school to be physicians (but needed the next level to become an M.D.), engineering school, etc., while more fortunate ones would continue to study those disciplines at the university level.

After the education reform under the Occupation, pattern after American system, in 1948, all the *Kōtō-gakkō* and most of *Senmon-gakkō* became *shin-sei daigaku* (colleges/universities under the new system), with a very small number of exceptions which chose to be *tanki daigaku* (junior college). That means the new system college/university expanded in number because the former two levels ended up as the same level. For that reason, the old system *daigaku* graduates are normally accorded as equivalent of having a graduate degree of the new system.

Tanka:

The traditional form of Japanese poem, which features a strict syllabic arrangement according to the following configuration: 5–7–5, 7–7. Developed from the earliest form of the Japanese poems, *Waka* (lit. 'Japanese poetry'), developed in the mid-sixth century, which contained a long version, *chōka* ("long poem") and *tanka* ('short-poem). By the late eighth century, the term *waka* was used synonymously with *tanka,* a type of verse consisting five lines in 31 syllables, in the pattern of above mentioned 5–7–5 7–7, and is still composed today. *Haiku* contains the first half, 5–7–5 syllabic arrangement, thus known as 17 syllable poems: it requires a word that represents a specific season, however. *Haiku* without any reference to a season is a more contemporary poem known as *Haikai,* less serious and usually joking/ humor in nature.

AUTHORS INDEX

INDEX OF MAJOR TERMS

Historical Terminologies:

Terms for the reader of the English edition:

Haiku poems

Higher schools (old system *Kōtō-gakkō.* College level)

Yoka (Preparatory Divisions for the old system universities. College level)

Tanka poems/Waka poems

School system during that time (known as *kyūsei,* the old system)